The Princeton Sourcebook in Comparative Literature

TRANSLATION | TRANSNATION

SERIES EDITOR **EMILY APTER**

Edited by

DAVID DAMROSCH

NATALIE MELAS

MBONGISENI BUTHELEZI

The Princeton Sourcebook in Comparative Literature

From the European Enlightenment
to the Global Present

PRINCETON UNIVERSITY PRESS

PRINCETON AND OXFORD

Published by Princeton University Press, 41 William Street, Princeton, New Jersey 08540

In the United Kingdom: Princeton University Press, 6 Oxford Street, Woodstock, Oxfordshire OX20 1TW

Library of Congress Cataloging-in-Publication Data

The Princeton sourcebook in comparative literature : from the European enlightenment to the global present / edited by David Damrosch, Natalie Melas, Mbongiseni Buthelezi.
    p.   cm. — (Translation/transnation)
  Includes bibliographical references and index.
  ISBN 978-0-691-13284-6 (hardcover : alk. paper) — ISBN 978-0-691-13285-3 (pbk. : alk. paper) 1. Literature, Comparative.   2. Literature, Comparative—Methodology.
3. Literature, Comparative—Theory, etc. I. Damrosch, David. II. Melas, Natalie.
III. Buthelezi, Mbongiseni, 1980–
  PN865.P74   2009
  809—dc22   2009006521

British Library Cataloging-in-Publication Data is available

This book has been composed in Minion with Gill Sans Display

Printed on acid-free paper. ∞

press.princeton.edu

Printed in the United States of America

10 9 8 7 6 5 4 3

CONTENTS

PART FOUR
CONTEMPORARY EXPLORATIONS

Comparative literature is a quixotic discipline. Its practitioners press against institutional constraints and the limitations of human capacity as they try to grasp the infinite variety of the world's literary production. And why stop with literature? Comparatists venture into art history, musicology, and film studies, while interdisciplinary work draws on insights from anthropology to history and from psychology to evolutionary biology. As they have wrestled with their many options, comparatists have regularly engaged in processes of self-scrutiny and redefinition, issuing proposals, manifestos, counterblasts, and rebuttals at every opportunity. This volume brings together thirty-two essays illustrating the variety of ways in which the discipline has been conceived and practiced over the past two centuries. Collectively, these materials can help us to explore the long history of current debates and chart our course going forward.

An entire anthology could be composed purely of essays complaining about the term "Comparative Literature" itself. Institutional as well as intellectual concerns have fueled the debate over the label and the relative merits and nuances of a host of alternatives, from *Vergleichende Literaturgeschichte* to "Literary and Cultural Studies" to "World Literature" to, simply, "Literature." Ambiguously situated in relation to national literature departments, Comparative Literature programs take many forms and show a protean tendency to shift over time even in a single setting, shaped and reshaped by changing faculty availability and the sometimes uneasy dynamics of relations with the departments around them. Intellectually, comparatists rejoice in their freedom to cross national and disciplinary boundaries, and today there is great interest in an emergent global perspective on literary studies. Yet this growing range confronts comparatists with important conceptual challenges and breeds profound uncertainties about how to maintain cultural and literary-historical depth in our work. Comparatists have often been leaders in the development and promulgation of literary theory, but theory itself needs to be freshly theorized in light of the far greater range of cultural difference it can now be asked to take into account.

Comparatists around the world have been exploring new approaches to these concerns, and the creative ferment of comparative literature today finds expression in the almost annual appearance of major statements on the shape and direction of the discipline, including Charles Bernheimer's influential committee report for the American Comparative Literature Association, published with responses as *Comparative Literature in the Age of Multiculturalism* (1995), Pascale Casanova's *La République mondiale des lettres* (1999), Gayatri Spivak's *Death of a Discipline* (2003), and Haun Saussy's 2006 ACLA report, *Comparative Literature in an Age of Globalization*. As engrossing as these current debates are, it is equally important for comparatists to attend to the discipline's longer history. A prime goal of this collection is to enable readers to encounter various configurations of the discipline over the past two centuries and to counterpoint old and new statements on issues of recurring concern. Édouard Glissant's vision of Caribbean discourse recalls Herder's argument for the intimate relation between nation and language, even as Glissant's claim about the double function of postcolonial literature bears affinities with Georg Lukács's distinction between epic and novel. Franco Moretti's evolutionary model for the global spread of the novel represents a sophisticated return to the Darwinian/Spencerian framework already employed by Hutcheson Macaulay Posnett in 1886. Pascale Casanova's concern with the imbalance of cultural power in the global literary system is foreshadowed in Hugo Meltzl's 1877 essay "Present Tasks of Comparative Literature," which describes less-spoken languages and their literatures as endangered species that must not fall victim to literary great-power politics.

We have envisioned this collection more as a provisional genealogy than a definitive history, selecting essays from earlier periods that seem to us to speak with particular pertinence to comparatists today. In this respect, this volume differs from Hans-Joachim Schultz and Phillip H. Rhein's 1973 collection *Comparative Literature: The Early Years*, still valuable for readers wishing to go further into the discipline's nineteenth-century roots, which includes various items of more historical than current interest. Comparatists often seem to suppose that today's issues have sprung full-blown from the mind of some theorist just discovered in a Parisian café or an Italian prison. For a discipline that has moved beyond formalism to a close engagement with cultural history, it is fundamentally important to give direct attention to the discipline's history as well. As a way into this history, there is no substitute for the testimony of its participants, and these essays show them working out questions that remain central today, often suggesting avenues of approach that are well worth exploring afresh.

The opening part, "Origins," gives foundational statements from the turn of the nineteenth century up through the start of the twentieth. The initial four selections represent the first stirrings of organized reflection on the problems and possibilities of comparative literary study, not yet enshrined in any academic disciplinary setting. Johann Gottfried Herder—philosopher, pastor, poet, and essayist of humble origins and immense ambition—and Anne Louise Germaine de Staël-Holstein, aristocratic traveler and woman of letters, each look at modern literature in comparison to the classics, their views interestingly inflected by their national situation, class position, and gender. In Goethe's conversations with his young disciple Eckermann, we see a major writer reflecting on Germany's place—and his own—in an increasingly international literary world. These writers' counterpointings of classicism and modernity find explosive echoes in the selections from Nietzsche's *Birth of Tragedy from the Spirit of Music*, written as he was about to abandon academic life as a classicist. All four writers accept the nation-state as the dominant social form in which literature is written and read, yet each uses comparative study to press back against nationalism and to address fundamental concerns in contemporary culture at large.

The next four essays, by Meltzl, Posnett, Brandes, and Gayley, give programmatic statements by pivotal figures in the first generation of academic comparative study, exemplifying the work of the creative scholars who established the first programs and journals of comparative literature in the third quarter of the nineteenth century. If comparative literature began largely as a Franco-German enterprise, this group of writers displays a much more varied outlook. Professors in, respectively, Transylvania, Ireland/New Zealand, Denmark/Germany, and the United States, they were fully alive to the tensions between "major" and "minor" literatures, and they took full advantage of the possibilities opened up by the transnationalism of their day.

Principal founder of the first journal of comparative literature, Meltzl assembled an editorial board from around the world and listed ten official languages for his journal, insisting on "the principle of polyglottism" as crucial for any meaningful comparative work. Hutcheson Macaulay Posnett, by contrast, worked as readily with translations as with original texts, a choice that enabled him to give substantial space to Chinese, Sanskrit, and Arabic literatures in addition to works written in the several languages he could read. The Danish critic Georg Brandes and the American

Charles Mills Gayley used studies of the European literary "great powers" as means to challenge the provincialism of their local cultures. Similar in some respects, these four differed greatly in their methods. Brandes devoted himself to analyzing the literatures of a few European countries, while Posnett read an astonishingly wide range of material as he wrote his book before moving from Dublin to take up a professorship in Auckland. Meltzl and Gayley, on the other hand, emphasized the need for collaborative work as the only responsible way for comparatists to combine the needed depth and breadth of study—a call that remains too little heeded to this day.

Part 2, "The Years of Crisis," looks at the reshaping of the discipline during the period from the First World War through World War II and its aftermath in the 1950s. These essays are profoundly marked by the global upheavals associated with the two world wars and the acceleration of economic and cultural exchanges during these decades. Georg Lukács formulated his immensely influential *Theory of the Novel* (1916) amid the tensions of wartime Germany, a period of crisis that led him to reassess the relations of modern literature to its ancient antecedents; Kobayashi Hideo's "Chaos in the Literary World" discusses the challenges facing post–Meiji era writers and critics as they strove to relate to foreign models without abandoning their classical traditions outright. Writing in internal exile in Stalin's Soviet Union, Mikhail Bakhtin reworked Lukács's analysis of epic and novel to celebrate the novel as the quintessential modern—and anti-authoritarian—genre.

The selections that follow Bakhtin show ways in which World War II raised the stakes of comparative study. Ernst Robert Curtius writes that he began his career as a comparatist in the aftermath of World War I, working on modern literature in the hope of promoting greater cultural understanding between the recently combatant nations. With the rise of the Nazis and the approach of the Second World War, Curtius determined to go farther back in time, and he spent the war years studying medieval Latin literature in order to recover a viable European heritage. Erich Auerbach, meanwhile, spent the war in exile in Istanbul; there he wrote his masterwork *Mimesis*. After the war he emigrated to the United States, where he wrote the essay included here, on the problem of world literature in an age of growing cultural consolidation in the postwar years.

Further meditations on literature and politics are provided by the next two authors. While Auerbach was writing *Mimesis* in Istanbul, the philosopher and cultural critic Theodor Adorno was living in exile in southern California, a venue in some ways more foreign to him than Istanbul was to Auerbach. In *Minima Moralia* Adorno used literature, philosophy, and music to probe the complex engagement of art with modern capitalist society. Octavio Paz's "Poetry, Society, State" argues for the critical freedom of artists from state control even as they necessarily address political and social concerns. Writing from a perspective that is at once Mexican and global, Paz discusses the stimulating challenge provided for Mexican writers by the double foreignness of the inherited traditions of Europe and of the Aztecs.

The section concludes with a pair of essays that outline a key methodological debate of the postwar period: the conflict between the "French school" of comparatists (represented here by Jean-Marie Carré) and the new "American school" dominated by émigrés such as Auerbach, Leo Spitzer, and René Wellek. In "The Crisis of Comparative Literature," Wellek denounces what he sees as the French school's narrow positivism. His aim is ethical as much as methodological: he calls at his essay's close for an expansive vision of the unity of humanity expressed in the transnational and transhistorical patterns of art.

Part 3, "The Theory Years," focuses on the period when comparatists played a key role in the elaboration and circulation of literary theory. Theory had long figured in comparative study, as writers such as Lukács, Bakhtin, and Wellek sought general principles on which to understand and analyze works from differing countries and periods. Literary theory grew in prominence during the 1960s, and many comparative literature programs became known as meeting-places for students and scholars of literary theory. Lukács and Bakhtin themselves were rediscovered by comparatists during the 1970s and 1980s and constantly discussed during this period; after a lifetime of censorship and exile, Bakhtin first achieved international recognition only during these years. Even to sample the full range of literary theory—from Russian formalism to Frankfurt School Marxism to Lacanian psychoanalysis to feminist film theory and much more—would require a large volume of its own. Presented here are eight notable examples of work from this period, tracing certain lines of theoretical and disciplinary inquiry that had major effects on the evolving shape of comparative literature as a discipline.

Of particular importance for theory as practiced in comparative literature from the late 1960s through the 1980s were the approaches broadly known as structuralism, poststructuralism, and deconstruction, represented here by programmatic essays by four leading practitioners: Roland Barthes and Julia Kristeva in France, and Paul de Man and Barbara Johnson in the United States. Among the most often cited of all twentieth-century critics and theorists, Roland Barthes was not formally a comparatist or even

a professor of literature; he ranged widely over many modes of cultural production, from advertisements and wrestling matches to history, philosophy, photography, and literature. Trained in linguistics, Barthes found in
semiotics an organizing discourse that could serve as the basis for broad-
based cultural critique.

Having worked both with Barthes and with Jacques Lacan, the
Bulgarian/French theorist Julia Kristeva combined linguistics and psychoanalysis to investigate the revolutionary potential of language. Her essay
"Women's Time" explores "women" and "the nation" as socially constructed
categories, in a poststructuralist challenge at once to authoritarian politics,
to essentialist feminism, and to masculinist psychoanalysis. Equally concerned with language though far less sure of its revolutionary potential,
Paul de Man turned structuralism on its head in his essay "Semiology
and Rhetoric," arguing that language always undermines the very claims
it appears to underwrite. For de Man, literature achieves a privileged place
as the one discourse that fully admits its deconstructive force—a view that
can be interestingly compared to Adorno's more directly political framing
of art as "magic delivered from the lie of being truth."

The insights of structuralism and deconstruction were often developed in the United States in less political and more formalist terms than
in France, but in the 1980s American theory increasingly began to turn
outward from the text, often drawing on the work of Kristeva and Michel
Foucault in France and Adorno and other members of the Frankfurt School
in Germany. A notable index of this shift in the United States is the career
of Barbara Johnson, who began as a de Manian rhetorician but then started
exploring socially as well as linguistically constructed rhetorics of difference, focusing especially on African American studies and women's studies. Included here is her retrospective essay "Writing," which looks back at
the rhetorical criticism of the 1970s and carries forward to discuss French
feminism and then African American writing.

During the 1980s, poststructuralist theory became a resource for
many comparatists deeply concerned with issues of cultural difference in
a world of unequal power relations. Writing in small, "peripheral" countries, the Israeli Itamar Even-Zohar and the Martinican Édouard Glissant
explored issues of language and of translation in a global, post- or neo-
imperial world. Even as Paul de Man was arguing for close rhetorical study
of literary works free from direct social referent, Even-Zohar and Glissant
were demonstrating the importance of understanding any poetics in its cultural framing; both attend closely to relations between major powers and
smaller countries in the formation of any national literature. In the United

States, the Palestinian émigré Edward Said helped inaugurate a major shift of attention in his pathbreaking *Orientalism* and in the essays collected in *The World, the Text, and the Critic*, whose title essay is included here.

Meanwhile, writing out of quite different colonial and postcolonial experiences, Ngũgĩ wa Thiong'o was thinking institutionally as well as ideologically about literary studies, wrestling with issues of multilingualism at home and the complex influence of British literature in the educational systems set up in the colonial era. In the section given here from his book *Decolonising the Mind*, Ngũgĩ brings postcolonial insights to bear on issues of disciplinary formation and pedagogy, discussing the struggle that he and other Kenyan faculty waged to gain a place for African literatures within their English-dominated curriculum.

Part 4, "Contemporary Explorations," concludes the volume by taking up the tension between the global and the local in the context of contemporary globalization. In "Comparative Cosmopolitanism," Bruce Robbins explores modes of interrelation that can foster a cosmopolitan perspective that does not simply project hegemonic Western values around the world. In terms that relate interestingly to Adorno and Paz, Pascale Casanova argues for a qualified autonomy of "the world republic of letters," which she sees as a system that stands outside state power while creating its own means by which writers from peripheral regions negotiate the unequal power relations between their national traditions and powerful metropolitan centers such as Paris. Zhou Xiaoyi and Q. S. Tong discuss the explosive growth of Comparative Literature in China as a response to the advent of global modernity; they argue for the need to move beyond mere assimilation to Western norms on the one hand and a defensive localism on the other.

Global border crossings concern all of the remaining writers in the book. The translation theorist Lawrence Venuti considers ways in which translation mediates between cultures, often with problematic effects but ultimately in the utopian hope of creating a community alive to cultural difference. Gayatri Spivak's "Crossing Borders" extends the discussion of literary border-crossing to the space of academic institutions and human rights intervention, proposing a fruitful interrelation of comparative literature and area studies while arguing for the importance of imagination in cross-cultural engagement. Like Pascale Casanova, Franco Moretti sees contemporary literature in terms of a world system that is "one, but unequal." Revisiting Goethe's concept of *Weltliteratur* in light of world systems theory, Moretti renews Charles Mills Gayley's call for a scientific study of literature, looking at the interplay of literary form and social networks of creation, distribution, and reception. Finally, Emily Apter's manifesto "A New Comparative Literature" combines themes seen in Glissant, Said, Venuti, Moretti, and Spivak to argue for a comparatism based in ideas of creolization and differential translation.

For each essay, an introduction situates the selection within the writer's life and work. Endnotes identify key literary and historical references. In the interest of keeping the notes (and the volume's size) within reasonable bounds, we have not annotated every scholar or work mentioned in passing in an essay, but we have tried to identify any name or source that is directly discussed or for which information is needed for an understanding of the argument. Those who wish to go further into an essayist's work and the issues it raises will find guidance in the bibliographies at the end of the volume; the listings provide a sampling of important works by our authors and the most interesting discussions of them.

In making our selections, we have benefited from recommendations by the several readers for Princeton University Press who read our initial proposal or the first draft of the full volume. From the beginning, we were aided by consultations with the membership of the American Comparative Literature Association. Several of our selections come from these collegial exchanges, and we would like to express our gratitude to the ACLA's board of advisers and to the ACLA's presidents during the period of the book's development, Margaret Higonnet, Kathleen Komar, and Sandra Bermann. Special thanks go to Ellen Peel, who proposed the selection from Madame de Staël and very kindly provided the sparkling headnote as well; to Haun Saussy, who gave us his elegant translation of Brandes; to Jan Kueveler, for his lucid translation of Herder; and to Olivia Loksing Moy, for her assistance in assembling the bibliographies. We are grateful too for the strong support of our editor at Princeton University Press, Hanne Winarsky, who has displayed an admirable blend of enthusiasm and stoic patience throughout the process of this book's creation.

We hope that this collection will inspire its readers to go much farther into comparative literature's past history and present possibilities. We would also be pleased if this volume can evolve along with the discipline. New inspirations, new methods, and new quarrels are percolating even as this book goes to press and will merit inclusion in a future edition. The collection's global range is likely to grow in future as well. We warmly invite our comparatist colleagues, both in the United States and elsewhere, to propose new selections that can further extend the multifaceted dialogue already under way in these pages.

PART ONE

Origins

Results of a Comparison of Different Peoples' Poetry in Ancient and Modern Times[1] (1797)

Johann Gottfried Herder

The German philosopher, poet, and literary critic Johann Gottfried
Herder (1744–1803) was a key figure in the articulation of the idea of
national language and culture, without which the study of national literatures and therefore of comparative literature would be inconceivable.
Born in a poor household in eastern Prussia, Herder educated himself
largely from his father's Bible and songbook. He managed to get a college
education, studying philosophy while preparing for the ministry, before
embarking on a career as a teacher and wide-ranging thinker; his later
years were spent in Weimar, where his friend Goethe had secured him
a government post. Deeply concerned with the philosophy of language
and of history, Herder positioned himself in his literary work against the
cultural predominance of models from classical antiquity on the one hand
and the influence of French letters on the other. He argued for an organic
connection between a people and a language and exhorted the Germans
to return to the spontaneous utterance of the folk. Living in a Germany
still divided into small principalities, Herder elaborated an idea of the
nation founded not on the state but on the organic unity of a people,
a unity expressed in a *Volksgeist*, or national spirit. Literature holds a
privileged place in his thought as the most direct reflection and cultivation
of national character.

In Herder's view, the greatness of any given literary expression
is not to be judged according to a single universal standard; rather, each

language develops its own particular genius in its own particular context. As part of his advocacy for the return to common speech and popular language in poetry, he avidly collected folk expression, particularly song. Arguing against the divine provenance of language in his treatise *On the Origin of Language* (1772), Herder laid the grounds for the study of comparative philology. His most famous work, *Reflections on the Philosophy of the History of Mankind* (1784–91), was widely read at the time, particularly in Eastern Europe, where it inspired many national literary movements in places lacking the distinct political form of the nation-state. During the nineteenth century his ideas reverberated powerfully in the Americas and elsewhere, and his work became fundamental for the philosophy of Hegel and Nietzsche, among many others. In the 1797 essay given here, Herder mounts an argument for understanding German literature as an integral expression of German culture, to be valued on its own terms as highly as the productions of France, Italy, or ancient Greece and Rome. Poetry, he famously argues, is protean and must fully take on the form of each national spirit it expresses.

Poetry is a Proteus among the peoples; it changes form according to the peoples' language, customs, habits, according to their temperament, the climate, even according to their accent.

As nations migrate, as languages mingle und change, as new matters stir men, as their inclinations take another direction and their endeavours another aim, as new models influence their composition of images and concepts, even as the tongue, this little limb, moves differently and the ear gets used to different sounds: thus the art of poetry changes not only among different nations, but also within one people. Among the Greeks poetry was a different thing at Homer's time than at the time of Longinus,[2] even with respect to its very conception. The associations accompanying poetry were utterly different to the Romans and to the monk, to the Arab and the crusader, to the scholar recovering times long past, and to the poet and the people in different ages of different nations. Even the term itself is an abstract, ambiguous concept, which, unless it is clearly supported by distinct cases, vanishes like a phantom in the clouds. Thus the quarrel between the ancients and the moderns was very empty, as people hardly had anything specific in mind.[3]

It became the emptier because a mistaken standard of comparison —or none at all—was applied: for on what principles should the ranking be decided? The art of poetry considered as an *object*? How many minute diagnoses would be needed to ascertain the epitome of perfection—in each form and genre, considering space and time, ends and means—and to apply them unbiasedly to everything being compared! Or should the poet's art be considered with respect to the producer: to what extent one surpassed another in appropriating the fortunate gifts of nature or a more propitious situation of circumstances, in more diligently making use of what had been there before him and what was lying around him, in having a nobler goal, and in employing his powers more wisely in order to attain this goal? What another ocean of comparison! The more standards have been posited for the poets of one nation or of several peoples, the more vain effort has been expended. Everybody assesses and ranks poets according to his favorite notions, according to the fashion in which he got to know them, according to the impression that one or another has made on him. Along with their own ideal of perfection, educated people possess their individual standard of how to attain it, which they prefer not to swap with someone else's.

Thus we must not blame any nation for preferring their poets to all others and for not wanting to relinquish them in exchange for foreign ones; after all, they are *its* poets. They have thought in *its* language, have exercised their imaginations in *its* context; they have felt the needs of the nation within which they were raised and have answered them in turn. Why then should the nation not feel *with them*, too, since a bond of language, of thoughts, needs, and feelings firmly ties them together?

The Italians, the French, and the English, being biased, think highly of their poets while tending unjustly to deplore other peoples' poets; only the German has let himself be seduced into excessively exaggerating the merit of foreign peoples, particularly that of the English and the French, thereby losing sight of himself. Certainly, to Young (for nothing is said here about Shakespeare, Milton, Thomson, Fielding, Goldsmith, Sterne) I do not begrudge his perhaps overblown adoration among us after he was introduced through Ebert's translation;[4] a translation that does not merely possess all the qualities of an original, but that—by creating a musical prose and through the rich moral annotations from other nations—at once corrects and softens the exaggerations of the English original. But yet the Germans will always have to meet the reproach of an indecisive lukewarmness toward the purest poets of their own language, who are generally forgotten and ignored to a degree unheard of in any neighboring nation. How shall our taste, our way of writing be formed? How shall our language be determined and regulated, if not through the best writers of our nation? How shall we acquire patriotism and love of our fatherland, if not through its language, through the most excellent thoughts and sensations, expressed in it like a stored-up treasure? Assuredly, we would not still be erring, after a thousand years of constant writing in our language, through many a dubious linguistic construction, if we only knew, from youth onwards, our best writers and elected them as guides.

On the other hand, no love of our nation should prevent us from recognizing *everywhere* the good that could only be increasingly produced *in the great progression of times and peoples*. That sultan of old[5] rejoiced over the many religions that were worshipping God in his kingdom, every one of them in their specific manner; it seemed to him like a pretty, colorful meadow, in which all sorts of flowers blossomed. The same holds for the poetry of peoples and eras on our globe; in every era it has been the embodiment of a given nation's faults and perfections, a mirror of its dispositions, the expression of its highest ideal (*oratio sensitiva anima perfecta*).[6] Juxtaposing these pictures (ideals more and less accomplished, true and false) yields an informative pleasure. In this gallery of various ways of thinking, inclinations, and wishes we are sure to get to know eras and nations more deeply than we would by treading the deceiving, desolate path of their political and military history. In the latter we rarely learn more of a people than how it was governed and destroyed; in the former we learn about its way of thinking, what it wished and what it wanted, how it rejoiced and how it was guided by its teachers or inclinations. Admittedly, we still lack many resources for achieving this overview into the souls of the peoples. Aside from the Greeks and Romans, dark clouds are still hanging above the Middle Ages, from which everything sprang for us Europeans. Meinhard's weak *Essay on the Italian Poets* does not even get as far as Tasso,[7] let alone that anything similar could have been accomplished for other nations. An *Essay on the Spanish Poets* has died along with the erudite connoisseur of this literature, Dieze, editor of Velázquez.[8]

There are three paths by which one can achieve an outlook over this flowery and fructiferous field of human thought, and all of them have been trodden.

In accordance with his theory, Eschenburg's popular collection of examples[9] takes the path of *genres and forms*; an instructive pathway for young students, if they are guided by an adroit teacher: for they can be led astray by a term that is applied to widely different things. The works of Homer,

Virgil, Ariosto, Milton and Klopstock all go by the name of epic, and yet they are very distinct productions according to their inherent conceptions of art, to say nothing of the spirit that animates them. As writers of trage-dies, Sophocles, Corneille and Shakespeare have nothing in common but the term; the genius of their artistry is utterly different. The same is true for all genres of literature, all the way down to the epigram.

Others have classified the poets according to *sentiments*, on which Schiller in particular has expressed himself very subtly and admirably.[10] If only the sentiments did not tend to blur together so much! What poet stays true to one kind of sentiment, so that it could define his character, espe-cially in different works? Often, he strikes a chord composed of many or even all notes, which enhance each other through dissonance. The world of sensations is a realm of ghosts, often of atoms; only the hand of the crea-tor may shape forms from it.

What I would call the third natural method is to leave every flower in place and to scrutinize it there just as it is, according to era and form, from the root to the crown. The most humble genius hates ranking and comparison, and would rather rank first in the village than second behind Caesar. Lichen, moss, fern and the richest spice plant: each flourishes in its own position in the divine order.

Poetry has been classified *subjectively* and *objectively*, according to the objects it describes and according to the sentiments with which it por-trays objects; a true and useful viewpoint that seems justified for the char-acterization of specific poets, such as Homer and Ossian, Thomson and Kleist et al.[11] For Homer tells the stories of a prehistoric world without pal-pable personal involvement on his part; Ossian sings them from his wounded heart, from his bittersweet memories; Thomson describes the seasons as nature gives them; Kleist sings his spring as a rhapsody of views inspired by sentiment, often branching out into thoughts about himself and his friends. And even this distinction is but a weak measure of the poets and eras of poetry: for Homer, too, does take an interest in his objects, as a Greek, as a narrator, like the balladeers and writers of fabliaux in the Middle Ages, and like Ariosto, Spenser, Cervantes and Wieland in more recent times. To have done more would have been outside his calling and would have disrupted his narrative. And yet as far as the arrangement and depiction of his characters is concerned, Homer too sings most humanly; where it ap-pears to be otherwise, the difference lies in the ways of thinking of different times and is easily explained. I am confident that I could discover among the Greeks every single human attitude and disposition, perhaps in the most beautiful degree and expression—only everything in relation to its time and place. Aristotle's *Poetics* unsurpassably categorizes plot, characters, passions and attitudes.

Man has been the same at all times; yet he has always expressed himself according to the conditions wherein he lived. Greek and Roman poetry is so varied in its wishes and laments, in its descriptions filled with joy and delight! The same holds for the poetry of the monks, of the Arabs, of the moderns. No new category caused the great difference that has arisen between the Orient and the Occident, between the Greeks and us, but rather the mingling of peoples, of religions and languages, eventually the progress of customs, of innovations, of knowledge and experience—a difference hard to subsume beneath one word. When I used the expression "poet of reflection" for some moderns, this was imperfect as well: for a poet of *mere reflection* is actually no poet.

Imagination and *temperament*, the *realm of the soul*, are poetry's ground and soil. By using words and characters poetry evokes an ideal of bliss, of beauty and dignity, slumbering in your heart; it is the most perfect expression of language, senses, and the temperament. No poet can escape the inherent law of poetry; it shows what he does and what he does not possess.

Nor can one separate the eye and the ear. Poetry is no mere painting or sculpture, which might objectively present pictures as they are; poetry is *speech* and has *purpose*. It affects the inner sense, not the artist's eye; and with anybody who is educated or being educated this inner sense comprises *temperament* and *moral nature*, and hence among poets a *reasonable* and *humane* purpose. Speech has something *infinite* to it; it makes deep impressions, which are in turn enhanced by the harmonic art of poetry. Thus a poet could never want to be merely a painter. He is an artist by virtue of impressive speech that paints the depicted object onto a *spiritual*, *moral*, that is *infinite* ground, into the *personality*, into the *soul*.

Should not some kind of *progress* be inevitable here as well, just as with all successions of the developing effects of nature? I do not doubt this at all (progress being understood properly). In language and customs we will never become Greeks and Romans; we do not want to become them, either. Does not the spirit of poetry, through all the oscillations and eccentricities in which it has so far bestirred itself among nations and times, increasingly strive to abandon all false ornament, all rudeness of sensation, and to look for the center of all human endeavour, namely the *true, whole, moral nature of humanity*, the *philosophy of life*? The comparison of eras makes this very plausible to me. Even in ages of the greatest crudity of taste we may hold fast to the great rule of nature: *tendimus in Arcadiam, tendimus!*[12] Our path leads toward the land of innocence, truth and morality.

Notes

1. From Herder's *Briefe zu Beförderung der Humanität* (Letters for the Advancement of Humanity, 1797). In his *Sämmtliche Werke*, ed. Bernhard Suphan (Berlin: Weibmannsche Buchhandlung, 1883), 18:134–40. Translated by Jan Kueveler.

2. Dionysius Longinus was the supposed author of the important first-century Greek treatise *On the Sublime*.

3. The "Querelle des Anciens et des Modernes" was a literary and cultural dispute that arose in late-seventeenth-century France between classicists who argued for the unsurpassable greatness of Greek and Roman writers versus proponents of Enlightenment values and new modes of expression.

4. Edward Young's poem *Night Thoughts on Life, Death, and Immortality* (1742–45) was translated into German by J. A. Ebert in 1751 and was extremely popular in Germany, though Young was a minor figure in comparison to writers like Shakespeare and Milton.

5. Referring to the sixteenth-century Ottoman sultan Suleiman the Magnificent.

6. "Speech that is sensitive to the soul's perfections."

7. Herder is referring to Johann Nicolaus Meinhard's book *Versuche über den Charakter und die Werke der besten italienischen Dichter* (1763–64). Torquato Tasso had lived two centuries before Meinhard's time.

8. J. A. Dieze published an extensively annotated German translation of Luis José Velázquez de Velasco's *Origenes de la poesía castellana* in 1769.

9. Johann Joachim Eschenburg had compiled a massive collection entitled *Beispielsammlung zur Theorie und Literatur der Schönen Wissenschaften* (Collection of examples of the theory and literature of the aesthetic sciences; 8 vols., 1788–95).

10. Schiller's influential aesthetic treatise *On Naïve and Sentimental Poetry* (1794–95) contrasted the "naïve," instinctive artistry of poets like Homer and Goethe with the "sentimental," reflective writing of poets such as Ariosto and himself.

11. James Thomson's *The Seasons* (1726–30) depicted a balanced, harmonious nature; Ewald Christian von Kleist (1715–59) was known for his poem "Der Frühling," a passionate celebration of spring.

12. "Let us make our way to Arcadia"—the home of pastoral simplicity in ancient Greece.

2

Of the General Spirit of Modern Literature[1] (1800)

Germaine de Staël

Nearly a century ago, Irving Babbitt claimed that Germaine de Staël "has perhaps done more than anyone else to help forward the comparative study of literature as we now understand it."[2] There is renewed interest today in many aspects of the work of Anne Louise Germaine Necker, Baronne de Staël-Holstein (1766–1817), who wrote fiction, drama, memoirs, sociology, and political reflections in addition to literary history and cultural analysis. Her comparatist activities were nourished by her studies in five languages, her extensive travels, and her interaction with the most prominent European intellectuals of her day. No doubt her development as a comparatist was helped by her dual status as both an insider and an outsider. She was born in Paris, but her parents were Swiss Protestants, and her husband was Swedish. Wealth and privilege helped make her an insider, but as a female she found herself excluded from wielding the influence she desired. Even so, she was sufficiently outspoken that Napoleon exiled her for a decade.

Deeply patriotic, de Staël nonetheless deplored chauvinism, which she satirized in her most famous novel, *Corinne ou l'Italie* (1807). She celebrated the values of a neighboring culture in *Corinne* and in her study *De l'Allemagne* (1810, 1813), which is often credited with introducing German Romanticism to France. "The General Spirit of Modern Literature," given here, is the ninth chapter of her book *De la Littérature, considérée dans ses rapports avec les institutions sociales* (On literature, considered in its relations to social institutions, 1800). Here de Staël compares ancient and modern writers in terms of eloquence and morality, making the proto-feminist argument that the novel could not develop until modern times, when an increase in respect for women made possible the attention to the private sphere that is the subject of so many novels. Her chapter closes with an anguished account of the difficulties of writing dispassionate analysis amid swirling memories of the violence of the French Revolution—an early expression of the fact that critics as well as poets reflect the stresses as well as the opportunities of their times.

———

It was not the imagination but the power of thought that built up new artistic treasures during the Middle Ages. As I have already remarked, the principle of the fine arts, imitation, does not admit of unlimited perfection; the moderns, in this respect, can never do more than follow the path traced out by the ancients. All the same, if the poetry of imagery and of description always remains nearly the same, more eloquence is added to the passions by a new development of sensibility and a deepened knowledge of character, which give our literary masterpieces a charm that cannot be attributed solely to poetic imagination.

The ancients esteemed men as their friends, while they considered women merely as slaves brought up for that unhappy state. Indeed, most women almost deserved that appellation; their minds were not furnished with a single idea, nor were they enlightened by one generous sentiment. This circumstance was no doubt the cause why the ancient poets rarely represented anything more than mere sensations in love. The ancients had no basis to praise women other than for their beauty, a quality shared by many women. Only the moderns, acknowledging other talents and other ties, have been able to express that sense of predilection that can incline a lifelong destiny toward the sentiments of love.

Novels, those varied productions of the modern spirit, were a genre almost entirely unknown to the ancients. They did compose a few pastorals in the form of novels, at a time when the Greeks endeavored to find means of relaxation amid servitude. But before women had created an interest in private life, matters of love had little ability to excite the curiosity of men, whose time was almost entirely occupied by political pursuits.

Women discovered in the human character a myriad of nuances that the need to dominate, or the fear of being dominated, led them to perceive; they supplied dramatic talents with new and moving secrets. Every sentiment to which they were permitted to devote themselves—the fear of death, the regrets of life, unlimited devotion, resentment without end—enriched literature with new expressions. As women, so to speak, were not at all responsible for themselves, they went as far in their words as the impulses of their spirit led them. A solid understanding, with a scrutinizing discernment, may clearly perceive these developments of the human heart when it appears without restraint. It is for this reason that the modern moralists have, in general, so much more finesse and sagacity in the knowledge of mankind than did the moralists of antiquity.

Among the ancients, those who could not acquire fame had no motive for self-development; but once people paired up in domestic life, the communications of the mind and the exercise of morals always took place, at least in a limited circle. Children became dearer to their parents from the reciprocal tenderness that forms the conjugal tie; and all the affections bore the imprint of that divine alliance of friendship and of love, of attraction and esteem, of a merited confidence and an involuntary seduction.

The aridity of old age—which might be crowned with glory and virtue but which could no longer be animated by feelings of the heart—was consoled with a pensive melancholy which allowed individuals to remember, to regret, and still to love what they had always loved. When moral reflections have been united to the violent passions of youth, they may be prolonged in noble traces to the final end of existence, and present the same outlines beneath the funereal draperies of time.

A profound and dreamlike sensibility is one of the greatest beauties of some of our modern writings; and it is women who, knowing nothing of life but the capacity to love, transmitted the softness of their impressions to the style of certain authors. Reading books composed since the Renaissance, we may see on each page those ideas that were not to be found until women had been accorded a kind of civil equality.

In some respects, generosity, courage, and humanity have taken on a different meaning. All the virtues of the ancients were founded on the love of their country; women exercise their qualities in a different manner. A pity for weakness, a sympathy for misfortune, an elevation of soul without any other aim than the enjoyment of that elevation itself, is much more in their nature than political virtues. Influenced by women, the moderns easily gave way to the bond of philanthropy, and the mind acquired a more philosophical liberty when it was less under the sway of exclusive associations.

The only advantage that the writers of recent centuries have over the ancients in their imaginative works is the ability to express a more delicate sensibility, and to give greater variety to situations and characters, from a knowledge of the human heart. But far superior are the philosophers of the present era in the sciences, in method and in analysis, in generalizing ideas, and linking their results! They possess the thread that they can unroll further every day, without ever losing their way.[3]

Mathematical reasoning resembles the two great ideas of metaphysics, space and eternity. You can add up millions of leagues and multiply centuries; each calculation is correct, and can extend indefinitely. The greatest step ever taken by the human understanding has been to renounce all ungrounded systems and adopt a method subject to proof, for there has been no achievement for the general good other than truths demonstrated by evidence.

As for modern eloquence, though doubtless it may be deficient in the emulation of a free people, nevertheless philosophy and a melancholy imagination have given it a new character, whose effect is very powerful. I do not think that a single ancient book or orator could equal Bossuet, or Rousseau, or the English in some of their poetry, or the Germans in some of their phrases, in the sublime art of affecting the heart. It is to the spirituality of the Christian ideas, and to the somber truth of philosophy, that we must attribute the art of introducing, even into private affairs, general and affecting reflections which touch every heart, awaken memories, and induce man to consider the interest of his fellow creatures.

The ancients knew how to enliven the arguments needed for every occasion; but in our time the succession of centuries has left people so indifferent to the concerns of individuals—and perhaps even to those of nations—that writers find it necessary to achieve new heights of eloquence in order to awaken the feelings which are common to everyone. Without doubt, it is necessary to strike the imagination with a lively and detailed picture of the object intended to move the reader; but the appeal to pity only becomes irresistible when melancholy gives general effect to what the imagination has portrayed.

The moderns have had to supplement a purely persuasive eloquence with an eloquence of thought, for which antiquity presents no model but Tacitus. Montesquieu, Pascal, and Machiavelli can achieve eloquence by a single expression, by a striking epithet, or in a rapidly sketched image, whose purpose is the elucidation of an idea but which enlarges still further what it explains. The impression given by this peculiar style may be compared to the effect produced by the disclosure of an important secret: it seems to you likewise as if many thoughts had preceded what has just been explained to you, and each separate idea appears connected with the most profound meditations; a single word can suddenly allow you to extend your ideas into immense regions that have been traversed by the efforts of genius.

The ancient philosophers having served, so to speak, as the educators of mankind, always had universal teachings as their goal. They discovered the fundamentals, they plumbed the bases of things, leaving nothing undone; they had no need to protect themselves from that mass of commonplace ideas which it is necessary to point out along the way without succumbing to the fatigue of retracing them. No ancient writer could have had the least rapport with Montesquieu, and none would need to be compared with him, had the centuries not melted away, had the generations not succeeded one another in vain, or had the human race gathered any fruits from the long history of the world.

The knowledge of morals necessarily advanced with the progress of human reason; it is to morality above all that philosophical demonstration is applicable in the intellectual realm. We must not compare modern virtues with those of the ancients in their public life; it is only in free countries that there can exist that constant duty and that generous relation between the citizens and their country. It is true that, under a despotic government, custom or prejudice may still inspire some brilliant acts of military courage; but the continued and painful attention given to civil affairs and legislative virtues, the disinterested sacrifice of one's whole life to the public sphere, can only exist where there is a real passion for liberty. It is therefore in private qualities, in philanthropic sentiments, and in a few superior writings, that we should examine moral progress.

The principles of modern philosophy are much more conducive to personal happiness than were those of the ancients. The duties imposed by our moralists are courtesy, sympathy, pity, and affection. Filial piety knew no limits among the ancients, whereas parental attachment is livelier among the moderns; and without doubt, in the connection between father and son, it is best that the one who should be the benefactor should also be he whose tenderness is the strongest.

The ancients were unsurpassed in their love of justice, but they never considered benevolence as a duty. Justice can be enforced by the laws, but it is only general opinion that makes beneficence a criterion and that can exclude from esteem anyone who is insensible to human misery.

The ancients only required of others to refrain from harming them; they simply desired them not to *stand in their sunshine*,[4] so as to be left to themselves and to Nature. Gentler sentiments inspire the moderns to seek assistance, support, and that interest which their situation inspires. They have made a virtue of everything that can serve mutual happiness and the comforting connections of individuals with one another. Domestic ties are cemented by a rational liberty, and man no longer possesses an arbitrary legal power over his fellow man.

With the ancient people of the North, lessons of prudence and competence, the maxims which commanded a supernatural empire over their afflictions, were placed among the precepts of virtue. The importance of duties is much better classed by the moderns: reciprocal obligations among people hold the first rank, and what concerns ourselves must be considered above all in relation to the influence which we may possess over the destiny of others. What each individual can do for his own happiness is a counsel and not an order; morality does not consider as a crime the sufferings which a man is unable to do more than sense and share, but those that he himself has caused.

In sum, what the Gospels and philosophy alike inculcate is the doctrine of humanity. We have learned to deeply respect the gift of life; the existence of man is now considered as sacred to man, and is not viewed with that political indifference which some of the ancients believed compatible with the true principles of virtue. Our blood now boils at the sight of blood; and the warrior who calmly braves his own personal danger does himself credit when he shudders at killing another. If circumstances suggest that a condemnation has been unjust, that an innocent person has perished by the sword of justice, entire nations will listen with horror to the lamentations raised against an irreparable misfortune. The terror caused by an unmerited death persists from one generation to another; children are told the tale of so great a grievance. When the eloquent Lally, twenty years after the death of his father, demanded the rehabilitation of his spirit,[5] all the young men of the day—who could not have seen or known the victim for whom he entreated—were deeply moved and shed tears in abundance, as if that terrible day when blood flowed unjustly had never ceased to be present in every heart.

Thus the century has progressed toward the conquest of liberty; for virtue is always its herald. Alas! How shall we banish the painful contrast that so forcibly strikes the imagination? One crime was recollected during a long succession of years; but we have since witnessed numberless cruelties committed and forgotten almost at the same moment! And it was under the shadow of the Republic, the noblest, the most glorious, and the proudest institution of the human mind, that those execrable crimes have been committed! Ah! How difficult do we find it to repel those melancholy ideas; every time we reflect upon the destiny of man, the revolution appears before us! In vain do we transport our spirit back over times long past, in vain do we desire to comprehend recent events and lasting works within the eternal connection of abstract patterns: if in the regions of metaphysics a single word awakens certain memories, the emotions of the soul resume their full sway. Reflection no longer has the strength to sustain us; we have to fall back into life.

Nevertheless, let us not yield to this despondency. Let us return to general observations, to literary ideas, to anything that can distract us from personal sentiments; they are too strong and too painful to pursue. Talents may be animated by a certain degree of emotion, but long and heavy affliction stifles the genius of expression; and when suffering has become the mind's habitual state, the imagination loses even the wish to express what it feels.

Notes

1. Chapter 9 of *De la Littérature, considérée dans ses rapports avec les institutions sociales* (1800), ed. Paul Van Tieghem (Geneva: Droz, 1959). Translated by David Damrosch, with some period phrasings adopted from the first English edition, *The Influence of Literature upon Society* (Boston: Wells and Wait, 1813).

2. Irving Babbitt, *Masters of Modern French Criticism* (Boston: Houghton Mifflin, 1912), p. 20.

3. De Staël here compares the modern scientist to the ancient hero Theseus, guided through the Minotaur's labyrinth by the thread provided by the princess Ariadne.

4. Referring to a story about the ancient philosopher Diogenes. When Alexander the Great came to visit and asked if he could do anything for him, Diogenes replied, "Stand out of my sunshine!"

5. Following a crushing defeat by the English in India, the Irish-born French general Thomas Lally was condemned to death by the French Parliament; he was publicly beheaded in 1766. His son Trophime grew up to become one of France's leading orators, and successfully pressed for a posthumous reversal of the sentence against his father.

3

Conversations on World Literature[1] (1827)

J. W. von Goethe and J. P. Eckermann

A major figure in world literature, Johann Wolfgang von Goethe (1749–1832) was also the first person to formulate the concept itself. While older contemporaries such as Herder and de Staël had pioneered the study of aspects of world literature, it was Goethe who developed the term *Weltliteratur*. He came to the idea from his perspective as a writer of multifarious interests and talents. A voracious reader as well as a prolific writer, Goethe wrote an early series of erotic poems based on Roman models (*Römische Elegien*, 1798) and a later series imitating the Persian poet Hafiz (*West-östlicher Divan*, 1819). He read widely in several languages and more widely still in translation, and he was fascinated with the international circulation of literature. Writing in a Germany that was divided into small principalities (he served for a number of years as a minister in the government of the duchy of Saxe-Weimar), Goethe was keenly aware that Germany lacked the unified culture and political force of its major rivals, France and England. By circulating abroad, works such as his own novel *The Sorrows of Young Werther* or his drama *Faust* could reach a far wider audience than they could enjoy at home. Conversely, reading foreign works could give a writer important stimuli for new modes of writing—especially valuable, Goethe felt, when the writer was active in a region such as Germany that lacked a long and distinguished national literary tradition of its own.

Goethe never devoted an extended essay to the concept of *Weltliteratur*, but he alluded to it in a variety of contexts in his later years.

Most significantly, he expounded upon the idea to his young secretary and disciple Johann Peter Eckermann, who published an extensive portrait of Goethe under the title *Gespräche mit Goethe in den letzten Jahren seines Lebens* (Conversations with Goethe in the final years of his life, 1837). Translated into many languages in the ensuing decades, Eckermann's *Conversations* became a work of world literature in its own right, and brought the concept of *Weltliteratur* to the world's attention. In the following selections from the *Conversations*, we see Goethe reflecting on the worldly circulation of literature, including his own works as well as poetry from Rome, France, Persia, and Serbia, and classical Chinese novels—an exceptional range of reference that foreshadows the global scale of world literature today.

Thursday, January 25, 1827.

At seven o'clock I went with the manuscript of the novel and a copy of Béranger[2] to Goethe. I found M. Soret in conversation with him upon modern French literature. I listened with interest, and it was observed that the modern writers had learned a great deal from De Lille, as far as good versification was concerned. Since M. Soret, a native of Geneva, did not speak German fluently, while Goethe talks French tolerably well, the conversation was carried on in French, and only became German when I put in a word. I took my Béranger out of my pocket, and gave it to Goethe, who wished to read his admirable songs again. M. Soret thought the portrait prefixed to the poems was not a good likeness. Goethe was much pleased to have this beautiful copy in his hands.

"These songs," said he, "may be looked upon as perfect, the best things in their kind—especially when you observe the refrain; without which they would be almost too earnest, too pointed, and too epigrammatic for songs. Béranger reminds me ever of Horace and Hafiz; who stood in the same way above their times, satirically and playfully setting forth the corruption of manners. Béranger has the same relation to his contemporaries; but, as he belongs to the lower class, the licentious and vulgar are not very hateful to him, and he treats them with a sort of partiality."

Many similar remarks were made upon Béranger and other modern French writers; till M. Soret went to court, and I remained alone with Goethe.

A sealed packet lay upon the table. Goethe laid his hand upon it. "This," said he, "is *Helena*,[3] which is going to Cotta to be printed."

I felt the importance of the moment. For, as it is with a newly-built vessel on its first going to sea, whose destiny is hid from us, so is it with the intellectual creation of a great master, going forth into the world.

"I have till now," said Goethe, "been always finding little things to add or to touch up; but I must finish, and I am glad it is going to the post, so that I can turn to something else. Let it meet its fate. My comfort is, the general culture of Germany stands at an incredibly high point; so I need not fear such a production will long remain misunderstood and without effect."

"There is a whole antiquity in it," said I.

"Yes," said Goethe, "the philologists will find work."

"I have no fear," said I, "about the antique part; for there we have the most minute detail, the most thorough development of individuals, and each personage says just what he should. But the modern romantic part is very difficult, for half the history of the world lies behind it; the material is so rich that it can only be lightly indicated, and heavy demands are made upon the reader."

"Yet," said Goethe, "it all appeals to the senses, and on the stage would satisfy the eye: more I did not intend. Let the crowd of spectators take pleasure in the spectacle; the higher import will not escape the initiated— as with the *Magic Flute* and other things."

"It will produce a most unusual effect on the stage," said I, "that a piece should begin as a tragedy and end as an opera. But something is required to represent the grandeur of these persons, and to speak the sublime language and verse."

"The first part," said Goethe, "requires the leading tragic artists; and the operatic part must be sustained by the leading vocalists, male and female. That of Helena ought to be played, not by one, but by two great female artists; for we seldom find that a fine vocalist has sufficient talent as a tragic actress."

"The whole," said I, "will furnish an occasion for great splendour of scenery and costume. I look forward to its representation. If we could only get a good composer."

"It should be one," said Goethe, "who, like Meyerbeer, has lived long in Italy, so that he combines his German nature with the Italian style and manner. However, that will be found somehow or other; I only rejoice that I am rid of it. Of the notion that the chorus does not descend into the lower world, but rather disperses itself among the elements on the cheerful surface of the earth, I am not a little proud."

"It is a new sort of immortality," said I.

"Now," continued Goethe, "how do you go on with the novel?"

"I have brought it with me," said I. "After reading it again, I find that your excellency must not make the intended alteration. It produces a good effect that the people first appear by the slain tiger as completely new beings, with their outlandish costume and manners, and announce themselves as the owners of the beasts. If you made them first appear in the introduction, this effect would be completely weakened, if not destroyed."

"You are right," said Goethe; "I must leave it as it is. It must have been my design, when first I planned the tale, not to bring the people in sooner. The intended alteration was a request on the part of the understanding, which would certainly have led me into a fault. This is a remarkable case in aesthetics, that a rule must be departed from if faults are to be avoided."

We talked over the naming of the novel. Many titles were proposed; some suited the beginning, others the end—but none seemed exactly suitable to the whole.

"I'll tell you what," said Goethe, "we will call it *The Novel* (Die Novelle); for what is a novel but a peculiar and as yet unheard-of event? This is the proper meaning of this name; and many a thing that in Germany passes as a novel is no novel at all, but a mere narrative or whatever else you like to call it. In that original sense of an unheard-of event, even the *Wahlverwandtschaften*[4] may be called a 'novel.'"

"A poem," said I, "has always originated without a title, and is that which it is without a title; so the title is not really essential to the matter."

"It is not," said Goethe; "the ancient poems had no titles; but this is a custom of the moderns, from whom also the poems of the ancients obtained titles at a later period. This custom is the result of a necessity to name things and to distinguish them from each other, when a literature becomes extensive. Here you have something new;—read it."

He handed to me a translation by Herr Gerhard of a Serbian poem. It was very beautiful, and the translation so simple and clear that there was no disturbance in the contemplation of the object. It was entitled *The Prison-Key*. I say nothing of the course of the action, except that the conclusion seemed to me abrupt and rather unsatisfactory.

"That," said Goethe, "is the beauty of it; for it thus leaves a sting in the heart, and the imagination of the reader is excited to devise every possible case that can follow. The conclusion leaves untold the material for a whole tragedy, but of a kind that has often been done already. On the contrary, that which is set forth in the poem is really new and beautiful; and the poet acted very wisely in delineating this alone and leaving the rest to the reader. I would willingly insert the poem in *Kunst und Alterthum*,[5] but it is too long: on the other hand, I have asked Herr Gerhard to give me these three in rhyme, which I shall print in the next number. What do you say to this? Only listen."

Goethe read first the song of the old man who loves a young maiden, then the women's drinking song, and finally that animated one beginning "Dance for us, Theodore." He read them admirably, each in a different tone and manner.

We praised Herr Gerhard for having in each instance chosen the most appropriate versification and refrain, and for having executed all in such an easy and perfect manner. "There you see," said Goethe, "what technical practice does for such a talent as Gerhard's; and it is fortunate for him that he has no actual literary profession, but one that daily takes him into practical life. He has, moreover, travelled much in England and other countries; and thus, with his sense for the actual, he has many advantages over our learned young poets.

"If he confines himself to making good translations, he is not likely to produce anything bad; but original inventions demand a great deal, and are difficult matters."

Some reflections were here made upon the productions of our newest young poets, and it was remarked that scarce one of them had come out with good prose. "That is very easily explained," said Goethe: "to write prose, one must have something to say; but he who has nothing to say can still make verses and rhymes, where one word suggests the other, and at last something comes out which in fact is nothing but looks as if it were something."

Wednesday, January 31, 1827.

Dined with Goethe. "Within the last few days, since I saw you," said he, "I have read many things; especially a Chinese novel, which occupies me still and seems to me very remarkable."

"Chinese novel!" said I; "that must look strange enough."

"Not so much as you might think," said Goethe; "the Chinese think, act, and feel almost exactly like us; and we soon find that we are perfectly like them, except that all they do is more clear, pure, and decorous, than with us.

"With them all is orderly, citizen-like, without great passion or poetic flight; and there is a strong resemblance to my *Hermann and Dorothea*, as well as to the English novels of Richardson. They likewise differ from us in that with them external nature is always associated with the human figures. You always hear the goldfish splashing in the pond, the birds are always singing on the bough; the day is always serene and sunny, the night is always clear. There is much talk about the moon; but it does not alter the landscape, its light is conceived to be as bright as day itself; and the interior of the houses is as neat and elegant as their pictures. For instance, "I heard the lovely girls laughing, and when I got sight of them they were sitting on cane chairs." There you have, at once, the prettiest situation; for cane chairs are necessarily associated with the greatest lightness and elegance. Then there is an infinite number of legends which are constantly introduced into the narrative and are applied almost like proverbs: as, for instance, one of a girl who was so light and graceful in the feet that she could balance herself on a flower without breaking it; and then another, of a young man so virtuous and brave that in his thirtieth year he had the honour to talk with the Emperor; then there is another of two lovers who showed such great purity during a long acquaintance that, when they were on one occasion obliged to pass the night in the same chamber, they occupied the time with conversation and did not approach one another.

"There are innumerable other legends, all turning upon what is moral and proper. It is by this severe moderation in everything that the Chinese Empire has sustained itself for thousands of years, and will endure hereafter.

"I find a highly remarkable contrast to this Chinese novel in the *Chansons de Béranger*, which have, almost every one, some immoral licentious subject for their foundation, and which would be extremely odious to me if managed by a genius inferior to Béranger; he, however, has made them not only tolerable, but pleasing. Tell me yourself, is it not remarkable that the subjects of the Chinese poet should be so thoroughly moral, and those of the first French poet of the present day be exactly the contrary?"

"Such a talent as Béranger's," said I, "would find no field in moral subjects."

"You are right," said Goethe: "the very perversions of his time have revealed and developed his better nature."

"But," said I, "is this Chinese romance one of their best?"

"By no means," said Goethe; "the Chinese have thousands of them, and had when our forefathers were still living in the woods.

"I am more and more convinced," he continued, "that poetry is the universal possession of mankind, revealing itself everywhere and at all times in hundreds and hundreds of men. One makes it a little better than another, and swims on the surface a little longer than another—that is all. Herr von Matthisson[6] must not think he is the man, nor must I think that I am the man; but each must say to himself that the gift of poetry is by no means so very rare, and that nobody need think very much of himself because he has written a good poem.

"But, really, we Germans are very likely to fall too easily into this pedantic conceit, when we do not look beyond the narrow circle that surrounds us. I therefore like to look about me in foreign nations, and advise everyone to do the same. National literature is now rather an unmeaning term; the epoch of world literature is at hand, and everyone must strive to hasten its approach. But, while we thus value what is foreign, we must not bind ourselves to some particular thing, and regard it as a model. We must not give this value to the Chinese, or the Serbian, or Calderon, or the *Nibelungen*; but, if we really want a pattern, we must always return to the ancient Greeks, in whose works the beauty of mankind is constantly represented. All the rest we must look at only historically, appropriating to ourselves what is good, so far as it goes."

The bells of passing sleighs allured us to the window, as we expected that the long procession which went out to Belvidere this morning would return about this time.

We talked of Alexander Manzoni;[7] and Goethe told me that Count Reinhard not long since saw Manzoni at Paris—where, as a young author of celebrity, he had been well received in society—and that he was now living happily on his estate in the neighbourhood of Milan, with a young family and his mother.

"Manzoni," continued he, "lacks nothing except to know what a good poet he is, and what rights belong to him as such. He has too much respect for history, and on this account is always adding notes to his pieces, in which he shows how faithful he has been to detail. Now, though his facts may be historical, his characters are not so—any more than my Thais and Iphigenia. No poet has ever known the historical characters he has painted; if he had, he could scarcely have made use of them. The poet must know what effects he wishes to produce, and regulate the nature of his characters accordingly. If I had tried to make Egmont[8] as history represents him, the father of a dozen children, his light-minded proceedings would have appeared very absurd. I needed an Egmont more in harmony with his own actions and my poetic views; and this is, as Clara says, *my* Egmont.

"What would be the use of poets, if they only repeated the record of the historian? The poet must go further, and give us if possible something higher and better. All the characters of Sophocles bear something of that great poet's lofty soul; and it is the same with the characters of Shakespeare. This is as it ought to be. Nay, Shakespeare goes further, and makes his Romans Englishmen; and there too he is right; for otherwise his nation would not have understood him.

"Here, again," continued Goethe, "the Greeks were so great that they regarded fidelity to historic facts less than the treatment of them by the poet. We have fortunately a fine example in Philoctetes; which subject has been treated by all three of the great tragedians, and lastly and best by Sophocles. This poet's excellent play has luckily come down to us entire; while of the *Philoctetes* of Aeschylus and Euripides only fragments have been found, although sufficient to show how they have managed the subject. If time permitted, I would restore these pieces, as I did the *Phaethon* of Euripides; it would be to me no unpleasant or useless task.

"In this subject the problem was very simple: namely, to bring Philoctetes with his bow from the island of Lemnos. But the manner of doing this was the business of the poet; and here each could show the power of his invention, and one could excel another. Ulysses must fetch him; but shall he be known by Philoctetes or not? And if not, how shall he be disguised? Shall Ulysses go alone, or shall he have companions, and who shall they be? In Aeschylus, there is no companion; in Euripides, it is Diomedes; in Sophocles, the son of Achilles. Then, in what situation is Philoctetes to be found? Shall the island be inhabited or not? And if inhabited, shall any sympathetic soul have taken compassion on him or not? And so with a hundred other things; which are all at the discretion of the poet, and in the selection and omission of which one may show his superiority to another in wisdom. Here is the grand point, and our present poets should do like the ancients. They should not be always asking whether a subject has been used before, and look to south and north for unheard-of adventures; which are often barbarous enough, and merely make an impression as incidents. To make something of a simple subject by a masterly treatment requires intellect and great talent, and these we do not find."

Some passing sleighs again allured us to the window; but it was not the expected train from Belvidere. We laughed and talked about trivial matters, and then I asked Goethe how the novel was going on.

"I have not touched it of late," said he; "but one incident more must take place in the introduction. The lion must roar as the princess passes the booth; upon which some good remarks may be made on the formidable nature of this mighty beast."

"That is a very happy thought," said I; "for thus you gain an introduction that is not only good and essential in its place but also gives a greater effect to all that follows. Hitherto the lion has appeared almost too gentle, shown no trace of ferocity; but by roaring he at least makes us suspect how formidable he is, and the effect when he gently follows the boy's flute is heightened."

"This mode of altering and improving," said Goethe, "where by continued invention the imperfect is heightened to the perfect, is the right one. But the remaking and carrying further what is already complete—as, for instance, Walter Scott has done with my 'Mignon,' whom, in addition to her other qualities, he makes deaf and dumb—this mode of altering I cannot commend."

Notes

1. From Johann Peter Eckermann, *Gespräche mit Goethe in den letzten Jahren seines Lebens* (Brockhaus, 1837). Translated by John Oxenford as Johann Wolfgang von Goethe, *Conversations with Eckermann* (1850); reprinted with some alterations.

2. Pierre-Jean de Béranger (1780–1857) was the author of popular poems in the form of songs, many set in bars and brothels, often carrying a progressive political message.

3. An experimental drama that Goethe had just completed, which begins as a classical tragedy and ends as a modern opera.

4. Goethe's epistolary novel *Elective Affinities* (1809).

5. *Art and Antiquity*, a journal that Goethe established and then edited from 1816 to 1832.

6. Friedrich von Matthisson, a popular poet whose collected works were published in eight volumes in 1825–29.

7. The poet, dramatist, and novelist Alessandro Manzoni had just published his masterpiece, the historical novel *I promessi sposi* (*The Betrothed*, 1827).

8. Hero of Goethe's historical drama *Egmont* (1788), set in the sixteenth century.

4

From *The Birth of Tragedy*[1] (1872)

Friedrich Nietzsche

Explosive German philosopher, occasional poet and composer, Nietzsche was born in 1844 into a Lutheran family but turned away from religion and devoted his university studies to philology and the Greek and Roman classics. He took up a professorship in Classical Philology at the University of Basel at the precocious age of twenty-five. He was soon to move from philology toward philosophy, and went on to write many books of unparalleled originality, despite the declining health that led him to retire from his professorship in 1879 and write in increasing solitude while convalescing in clement climes. He suffered a serious mental breakdown in 1889 and lived out his remaining years in a reduced mental state until his death in 1900. Even during his decade as a professor, Nietzsche rapidly found himself at odds with the careful, cautious research of his colleagues; he later spoke sarcastically of the "dwarves" he found around him in academia. Along with Karl Marx and Sigmund Freud, Nietzsche had a decisive, formative influence on European culture and philosophy in the twentieth century.

Nietzsche's philosophy does not offer a system; instead, he takes many different avenues and approaches as he pursues with unflinching rigor the consequences for thought and culture of the absence of transcendental authority. He is perhaps best known for the declaration in *The Gay Science* (1882) that "God is dead. And we have killed him. How shall we comfort ourselves, the murderers of all murderers?" In books such as *Beyond Good and Evil* (1886), *The Genealogy of Morals* (1887), *Twilight of the Idols* (1889) and *The Antichrist* (1895), he fiercely criticized the Judeo-

Christian tradition and explored the social, psychological, cultural and philosophical consequences of relativism, advocating what he calls "the transvaluation of all values."

In keeping with its refutation of systematic thought, Nietzsche's philosophical writing often takes literary form, particularly the form of the aphorism and the fable; his works are admired for their style and considered among the most accomplished in the German language. His significance for literary criticism and theory, particularly in the post–World War II period, however, also derives from the importance of interpretation in his philosophy. If, as he writes in *Beyond Good and Evil*, "there are no moral phenomena at all, only moral interpretations of phenomena," then criticism's central task, the act of interpretation, gains new magnitude.

His first book, *The Birth of Tragedy from the Spirit of Music* (1872), reflects the turn from philology to philosophy, building on his classical studies to develop a philosophy of culture through a searching critique of classical ideals of order and harmony. It is a fundamentally comparative work, for Nietzsche is intent upon offering an account of ancient Greek tragedy not for its own sake but in order to gain insight into the problems of art and existence in the present. Ancient Greece is counterpointed against modern Europe (Germany in particular), and classical tragedy sets the stage for a discussion of modern opera. *The Birth of Tragedy* bears the mark of the two great influences over Nietzsche's early work, the philosopher Arthur Schopenhauer and the composer Richard Wagner. Nietzsche identifies two tendencies in Greek tragedy: the Apollonian, associated with dream and the individuating, form-making capacity of art; and the Dionysian, associated with intoxication and with art's irrational, immersive and deindividuating powers, exemplified in music. The rich and conflicting interconnection between them animates human symbolic faculties but it is crushed, in Nietzsche's account, by Socratic reason and Hellenistic academicism. In the final sections of his book Nietzsche argues that the work of his contemporary Richard Wagner heralds the rebirth of tragedy in German culture. *The Birth of Tragedy* is a major early example of comparative study as a mode of oppositional cultural criticism, blending linguistic, literary, and philosophical analysis to pose a stark challenge to the moral norms, and the intellectual protocols, of his day.

———————

1: We shall gain much for the science of aesthetics when we perceive not only by logical inference but by the immediate certainty of intuition that the continuous development of art is bound up with the duality of the *Apollonian* and the *Dionysian*: just as procreation is dependent on the duality of the sexes, involving perpetual conflict with only occasional periods of reconciliation. These terms we borrow from the Greeks, who disclose to the intelligent observer the profound mysteries of their view of art, not in concepts but in the impressively clear figures of their divinities. Through Apollo and Dionysus, the Greeks' two artistic deities, we learn that there existed in the Greek world a deep opposition, in both origin and aims, between the Apollonian art of the sculptor and the non-plastic art of music, that of Dionysus. These so disparate tendencies run parallel to each other, for the most part openly at variance and continually inciting each other to new and more powerful births, perpetuating in them the strife of this opposition, which is only superficially bridged over by the common term of "Art"; until at last, by a metaphysical miracle of the Hellenic will, they appear coupled with each other, and through this coupling finally give birth to an artwork at once Dionysian and Apollonian: Attic tragedy.

In order to grasp these two tendencies, let us think of them first of all as the separate art-worlds of *dream* and *drunkenness*; between these physiological phenomena there exists a contrast similar to that between the Apollonian and the Dionysian. In dreams, according to Lucretius, the glorious divine figures first appeared to the souls of men, in dreams the great sculptor beheld the charming bodily forms of superhuman beings, and the Hellenic poet, if questioned about the mysteries of poetic inspiration, would likewise have suggested dreams and would have offered an explanation resembling that of Hans Sachs in *Die Meistersinger*:—

> Mein Freund, das grad' ist Dichters Werk,
> dass er sein Träumen deut' und merk'.
> Glaubt mir, des Menschen wahrster Wahn
> wird ihm im Traume aufgethan:
> all' Dichtkunst und Poeterei
> ist nichts als Wahrtraum-Deuterei.[2]

> [My friend, that is exactly the poet's task, to ponder and note his dreams. Believe me, man's most profound illusions are revealed to him in dreams; and all poetic art and verse-making are nothing but true dream interpretation.]

The beautiful appearance of the dream-worlds, in whose creation everyone is a perfect artist, is the presupposition of all plastic art, and also, as we shall see, of an important half of poetry. We take delight in the direct perception of form; all forms speak to us; there is nothing indifferent, nothing super-fluous. But together with the highest life of this dream-reality we also have, glimmering through it, the sensation that it is only an appearance: such at least is my experience, of which I could adduce many proofs—including the sayings of the poets—of its frequency, even its normality. Indeed, a philosophic man has a foreboding that underneath this reality, in which we live and have our being, there lies concealed another and altogether different reality, and that therefore it is also an appearance. Schopenhauer in fact designates the gift of occasionally regarding men and things as mere phantoms and dream-pictures as the hallmark of philosophical abil-ity.[3] Accordingly, the man susceptible to art stands in the same relation to the reality of dreams as does the philosopher to the reality of existence; he is a close and willing observer, for from these pictures he reads the mean-ing of life, and by these processes he trains himself for life. And it is perhaps not only the agreeable and friendly pictures that he experiences with such perfect understanding: what is earnest as well, the troubled, the dreary, the gloomy, the sudden reversals and tricks of fortune, the uneasy presentiments, in short, the whole "Divine Comedy" of life—including the Inferno—passes before him, not merely like pictures on the wall (for he too lives and suffers in these scenes), and yet not without that fleeting sensation of mere appear-ance. And perhaps many will recall, as I do, having sometimes called out cheeringly and not without success amid the dangers and terrors of dream-life: "It is a dream! I will dream on!" I have likewise been told of people who could continue the thread of one and the same dream for three and even more nights in a row: all of which facts clearly testify that our inner-most being, the common substratum of us all, experiences our dreams with deep pleasure and joyful need.

This joyful need for the dream-experience has also been embodied by the Greeks in their Apollo: for Apollo, as the god of all shaping energies, is also the god of prophecy. He, who (as the etymology of the name indi-cates) is "the shining one," the deity of light, also rules over the fair appear-ance of the inner world of the imagination. The higher truth, the perfection of these states in contrast to the only partially intelligible everyday world, the deep consciousness of nature, healing and helping in sleep and dream, is at the same time the symbolic analogue of the prophetic ability and of the arts in general, which make life possible and worth living. But our pic-ture of Apollo must also include that delicate line which the dream-picture must not overstep, lest it act pathologically (in which case appearance, being reality pure and simple, would deceive us): that measured limitation, that freedom from the wilder emotions, that philosophical calmness of the sculptor-god. His eye must be "sunlike," in accordance with his origin; even when it is angry and looks displeased, the sacredness of his beautiful appearance is still there. And so we might apply to Apollo, in an eccentric sense, what Schopenhauer says of the man wrapt in the veil of Maya (*World as Will and Representation*, I. p. 416): "Just as a sailor sits in a boat and trusts in his frail vessel in a stormy sea, unbounded in every direction, rising and falling with howling mountainous waves; so in the midst of a world of sorrows the individual sits quietly, trusting in his *principium individuationis*."[4] Indeed, we might say of Apollo that he embodies the sublimest expression of the unshaken faith in this *principium* and the quiet sitting of the man wrapped up in it; and we might even designate Apollo as the glorious divine image of the *principium individuationis*, through whose gestures and looks all the joy and wisdom and beauty of "appearance" speak to us.

In the same book Schopenhauer has described to us the stupendous *awe* which seizes upon man, when he is suddenly at a loss to account for the cognitive forms of a phenomenon, when the principle of reason in one of its forms seems to admit of an exception. Add to this awe the blissful ecstasy which rises from the innermost depths of man, and indeed of nature, at this same collapse of the *principium individuationis*, and we shall gain an insight into the essence of the *Dionysian*, which we can perhaps best grasp by the analogy of *drunkenness*. Either under the influence of the narcotic drink celebrated in the hymns of all primitive men and peoples, or through the powerful approach of spring penetrating all nature with joy, those Dionysian emotions awake, and as they grow the subjective vanishes to complete self-forgetfulness. So also in medieval Germany singing and dancing crowds, ever increasing in number, were swept from place to place under this same Dionysian power. In these St. John's and St. Vitus's dancers we once again see the Bacchic choruses of the Greeks, with their previous history in Asia Minor going as far back as Babylon and the orgiastic Sacaea.[5] There are some who, from stupidity or lack of experience, will turn away from such phenomena as "folk-diseases" with a smile of contempt or pity prompted by the consciousness of their own health: of course, the poor wretches do not divine what a cadaverous and ghastly appearance this very "health" of theirs presents when the glowing life of the Dionysian revellers rushes past them.

Under the spell of the Dionysian not only is the covenant between man and man again established, but estranged, hostile or subjugated nature once again celebrates her reconciliation with her prodigal son, man. Of her own accord earth proffers her gifts, and peacefully the beasts of prey approach from the desert and the rocks. The chariot of Dionysus is bedecked with flowers and garlands: panthers and tigers pass beneath his yoke. Change Beethoven's "Ode to Joy" into a painting, and, if your imagination can rise to the occasion when the awestruck millions sink into the dust,[6] you will then be able to approach the Dionysian. Now the slave is a free man, now are broken down all the stubborn, hostile barriers which necessity, caprice, or "shameless fashion" have set up between man and man. Now, with the gospel of cosmic harmony, each one feels himself not only united, reconciled, blended with his neighbor, but as fully one with him as if the veil of Maya[7] had been torn and were now merely fluttering in tatters before the mysterious Primordial Unity. In song and in dance man displays himself as a member of a higher community: he has forgotten how to walk and speak, and is on the point of taking a dancing flight into the air. His gestures express enchantment. Just as the animals now talk, and as the earth yields milk and honey, so too something supernatural sounds forth from him: he feels himself a god, he himself now walks about as enchanted and elated as the gods he saw walking about in his dreams. Man is no longer an artist, he has become a work of art: the artistic power of all nature here reveals itself in the tremors of drunkenness to the highest gratification of the Primordial Unity. The noblest clay, the most precious marble, man, is here kneaded and cut, and the chisel strokes of the Dionysian world-artist are accompanied with the cry of the Eleusinian mysteries:[8] "Do you bow down here, you multitudes? World, do you perceive your maker?"

2: In the Dionysian dithyramb man is incited to the highest exaltation of all his symbolic faculties; something never before experienced struggles for utterance—the annihilation of the veil of Maya, unity as the spirit of the species and even of nature. The essence of nature is now to be expressed in symbols; a new world of symbols is required, indeed the entire symbolism of the body, not just the symbolism of the lips, face, and speech, but the whole pantomime of dancing which sets all the limbs into rhythmic motion. Then the other symbolic powers, those of music in rhythm, dynamics, and harmony, suddenly become impetuous. To comprehend this collective release of all the symbolic powers, a man must have already attained that height of self-abnegation which seeks to express itself symbolically through these powers: thus the dithyrambic devotee of Dionysus is understood only by those like himself. With what astonishment must the Apollonian Greek have beheld him! With an astonishment that was all the greater as it was mingled with the shuddering suspicion that all this was really not so very foreign to him, indeed that his Apollonian consciousness like a veil only hid this Dionysian world from his view.

3: In order to understand this, we must dismantle the artistic structure of the *Apollonian culture* stone by stone, so to speak, until we behold the foundations on which it rests. First we see here, mounted on this structure's gables, the glorious figures of the Olympian gods whose deeds, represented in far-shining reliefs, adorn its friezes. Though Apollo stands among them as an individual deity, side by side with others and without claim to priority of rank, we must not allow this to mislead us. The same impulse which embodied itself in Apollo has given birth to this whole Olympian world, and in this sense we may regard Apollo as its father. What was the enormous need that brought forth such an illustrious group of Olympian beings?

Whoever approaches these Olympians with another religion in his heart, seeking moral elevation, even holiness, bodiless spirituality, sympathetic looks of love, will soon be obliged to turn his back on them, discouraged and disappointed. Here nothing suggests asceticism, spirituality, or duty: here only an exuberant, even triumphant life speaks to us, in which everything that exists is deified, whether good or bad. And so the spectator may stand quite bewildered before this fantastic exuberance of life, asking himself what magic potion these merry madmen could have taken for enjoying life so that, wherever they turned their eyes, Helen—the ideal image of their own existence "floating in sweet sensuality"—smiled upon them. But to this spectator, already turning away, we must call out: Do not depart, but first hear what Greek folk-wisdom says of this same life, which spreads out before you with such inexplicable cheerfulness. There is an ancient story that king Midas hunted in the forest a long time for the wise Silenus, the companion of Dionysus, without capturing him. When at last Silenus fell into his hands, the king asked what was best of all things and most desirable for man. Fixed and immovable, the demon remained silent; till at last, forced by the king, he broke out with shrill laughter into these words: "Oh, wretched race of a day, children of chance and misery, why do you compel me to tell you what it would be better for you not to hear? The best thing of all is forever beyond your reach: not to be born, not to be at all, to be *nothing*. The second best thing for you, though, is—to die soon."

How is the Olympian world of deities related to this folk-wisdom? As the rapturous vision of the tortured martyr is to his sufferings.

Now the Olympian magic mountain opens, as it were, to our view and shows us its roots. The Greek knew and felt the terrors and horrors of existence: to be able to live at all, he had to set the shining dream-birth of the Olympian world between himself and them. The excessive distrust of the Titanic powers of nature, the Moira ruling inexorably over all knowledge, the vulture of the great philanthropist Prometheus, the terrible fate of the wise Oedipus, the family curse of the Atridae which drove Orestes to matricide;[9] in short, that entire philosophy of the forest god, with its mythical examples, which wrought the ruin of the melancholy Etruscans—was again and again surmounted anew by the Greeks through the artistic *middle world* of the Olympians, or at least was veiled and withdrawn from sight. To be able to live, from direct necessity the Greeks had to create these gods. We might picture the process in this manner: that out of the original Titan theocracy of terror the Olympian theocracy of joy evolved by slow transitions through the Apollonian impulse to beauty, just as roses break forth from thorny bushes. How else could such a sensitive people, so vehement in its desires, so singularly qualified for *suffering*, have endured existence, if it had not been shown to them in their gods, surrounded with a higher glory? The same impulse which calls art into being as the complement and consummation of existence, seducing the living to go on living, brought forth the Olympian world, in which the Hellenic "will" held up a transfiguring mirror before itself. Thus do the gods justify the life of man, by living it themselves – the only satisfactory Theodicy![10] Existence under the bright sunshine of such gods is regarded as desirable in itself, and the real grief of the Homeric men refers to parting from it, especially to early parting: so that we might now say of them, reversing the wisdom of Silenus, that "to die early is worst of all for them, the second worst is—to die at all." Once the lamentation is heard, it will ring out again: for the short-lived Achilles, for the transience of the human race like leaves blown in the wind, for the decay of the heroic age. It is not unworthy of the greatest hero to long to live on, even as a day-laborer.[11] So vehemently does the Apollonian "will" long for this existence, so completely at one does the Homeric man feel himself with it, that the lament itself becomes its song of praise.

Here we must observe that this harmony which is so eagerly contemplated by modern man, this unity of man with nature, for which Schiller introduced the technical term "naïve,"[12] is by no means such a simple, natural and so to speak inevitable condition, which must be found at the gate of every culture leading to a human paradise: this could be believed only by an age which sought to imagine Rousseau's Émile as an artist, and supposed it had found such an artistic Émile in Homer, reared at Nature's bosom.[13] Wherever we meet with the "naïve" in art, we should recognize the highest effect of Apollonian culture, which always has to begin by overthrowing some Titanic empire and slaying monsters, and which must have employed powerfully dazzling representations and pleasurable illusions in order to triumph over a terrible depth of world-contemplation and a most keen capacity for suffering. But how seldom is the naïve—that complete absorption in the beauty of appearance—actually achieved! And thus how inexpressibly sublime is Homer, who as an individual bears the same relation to this Apollonian folk-culture as the single dream-artist does to the dream-capacity of the people and of Nature in general. Homeric "naiveté" should be understood only as the complete triumph of the Apollonian illusion: it is the same kind of illusion as Nature so frequently employs to achieve her ends. The true goal is veiled by a phantasm: we stretch out our hands for it, while Nature attains her goal by this deception. In the Greeks the "will" desired to contemplate itself in the transfiguration of the genius and the world of art; in order to glorify themselves, its creatures had to feel themselves worthy of glory; they had to see themselves again in a higher sphere, without this perfect world of contemplation acting as an imperative or a reproach. Such is the sphere of beauty, in which they saw mirrored their images, the Olympians. With this mirroring of beauty the Hellenic will combated its artistically related talent for suffering and for the wisdom of suffering: and, as a monument of its victory, there stands before us Homer, the naïve artist.

16: By this developed historical example we have endeavored to show that just as surely as tragedy perishes with the evanescence of the spirit of music, so too it can be reborn only from this spirit. In order to mitigate the strangeness of this assertion, and to disclose the source of this insight of ours, we must now confront with clear vision the analogous phenomena of the present; we must enter into the midst of the struggles which, as I have said, are being carried on in the highest spheres of our current world between the insatiably optimistic perception and the tragic need for art. In so doing I shall leave out of consideration all the other antagonistic tendencies which always oppose art and especially tragedy, and which at present once again extend their sway so triumphantly that, of the theatrical arts, for instance, only the farce and the ballet put forth luxuriant blossoms, which perhaps not everyone finds so fragrant. I will speak only of the *most illustrious opponent* to the tragic conception of things—and by this I mean science, optimistic to the core, with its ancestor Socrates at the head of it. And then I will name the forces which seem to me to guarantee *a rebirth of tragedy*— and who knows what other blessed hopes for the German genius!

Before we plunge into the midst of these struggles, let us array ourselves in the armour of the knowledge we have acquired so far. In contrast to all those who insist on deriving the arts from one exclusive principle as the necessary source of life for every work of art, I keep my eyes fixed on the two artistic deities of the Greeks, Apollo and Dionysus, recognizing in them the outstanding living representatives of *two* worlds of art which differ in their intrinsic essence and in their highest aims. Apollo stands before me as the transfiguring genius of the *principium individuationis* through which alone true redemption in appearance is to be attained, while by the mystical cry of Dionysus the spell of individuation is broken, and the way lies open to the Mothers of Being,[14] to the innermost heart of things. This extraordinary antithesis, which opens up yawningly between the Apollonian plastic arts and the Dionysian art of music, has become manifest to only one of the great thinkers, to such an extent that even without this key to the symbolism of the Hellenic divinities he assigned music a different character and prior origin in advance of all the other arts. He saw that unlike them music is not a copy of the phenomenon, but a direct copy of the will itself, and therefore represents *the metaphysical of everything physical in the world*, the thing-in-itself of every phenomenon (Schopenhauer, *The World as Will and Representation*, I). To this most important perception of aesthetics (with which the serious study of aesthetics properly begins), Richard Wagner affixed his seal of approval, confirming its eternal truth when he asserted in his *Beethoven* that music must be judged according to aesthetic principles quite different from those which apply to the plastic arts, and not according to the general category of beauty: although an erroneous aesthetics, inspired by a misguided and degenerate art, has been induced by the concept of beauty prevailing in the visual arts to demand from music an effect like that of works of plastic art, namely the arousing of *delight in beautiful forms*. Upon perceiving this extraordinary antithesis, I felt impelled to approach the essence of Greek tragedy, and by means of it the profoundest revelation of Hellenic genius: for I at last thought myself to be in possession of a charm to enable me—far beyond the phraseology of our usual aesthetics—to represent vividly to my mind the primitive problem of tragedy, and thereby I was granted such an astounding insight into the Hellenic essence that it necessarily seemed as if our classical-Hellenic scholarship that carries itself with such pride had until now managed to subsist almost exclusively on phantasmagoria and externalities.

18: It is an eternal phenomenon: the insatiable will can always spread an illusion over things, so as detain its creatures in life and compel them to live on. One person is chained by the Socratic love of knowledge and the vain hope of using it to heal the eternal wound of existence; another is ensnared by art's seductive veil of beauty fluttering before his eyes; still another by the metaphysical comfort that eternal life flows on indestructibly beneath the whirl of phenomena—to say nothing of the more ordinary and almost more powerful illusions which the will always has at hand. These three kinds of illusion are on the whole designed only for the more nobly endowed natures, who in general feel profoundly the weight and burden of existence, and who must be deluded into forgetting their displeasure by exquisite stimulants. All that we call culture is made up of these stimulants; and, according to the proportion of the ingredients, we have either a specially *Socratic* or *artistic* or *tragic* culture: or, if historical examples are wanted, there is either an Alexandrian or a Hellenic or a Buddhistic culture.[15]

Our whole modern world is entangled in the meshes of Alexandrian culture, and recognises as its ideal the *theorist* equipped with the most potent means of knowledge, laboring in the service of science, of whom Socrates is the archetype and progenitor. All our educational methods have originally held this ideal: every other form of existence must struggle onwards wearisomely beside it, as something tolerated but not intended. In an almost alarming manner the cultured man has been found here for a long time only in the form of the scholar: even our poetical arts have been forced to evolve from learned imitations, and in the main effect of rhyme we still recognise the origin of our poetic forms in artistic experiments with a non-native and thoroughly scholarly language. How unintelligible must Faust—the modern cultured man, who is intelligible in himself—have appeared to a true Greek: Faust, storming discontentedly through all the academic disciplines, devoting himself to magic and the devil out of a desire for knowledge, whom we have only to place alongside Socrates for comparison in order to see that modern man begins to perceive the limits of the Socratic love of perception, and amid the wide waste of the ocean of knowledge longs for shore. When Goethe once said to Eckermann with reference to Napoleon: "Yes, my good friend, there is also a productiveness of deeds," he reminded us in a charmingly naïve manner that the non-theorist is something incredible and astounding to modern man; so that the wisdom of Goethe is needed once more in order to discover that such a surprising form of existence is comprehensible, even pardonable.

And now we must not hide from ourselves what is concealed at the heart of this Socratic culture: Optimism, which supposes itself limitless! Well, we must not be alarmed if the fruits of this optimism ripen—if society, leavened to the very lowest strata by this kind of culture, gradually begins to tremble through wanton agitations and desires, if the belief in the earthly happiness of all, if the belief in the possibility of such a general intellectual culture is gradually transformed into the threatening demand for such an Alexandrian earthly happiness, into the conjuring of a Euripidean *deus ex machina*.[16] Let us note this well: Alexandrian culture requires a slave class in order to be able to exist permanently: but in its optimistic view of life, it denies the necessity of such a class, and consequently, when the effect of its beautifully seductive and tranquillizing utterances about the "dignity of man" and the "dignity of labor" is spent, it gradually drifts towards a dreadful destruction. There is nothing more terrible than a barbaric class of slaves who have learned to regard their existence as an injustice and now prepare to take vengeance, not only for themselves but for all generations to come. In the face of such threatening storms, who dares to appeal with confident spirit to our pale and exhausted religions, whose very foundations have degenerated into scholars' religions? As a result, myth—the necessary prerequisite of every religion—is already paralysed everywhere; even this domain has yielded to the mastery of the optimistic spirit, which we have just designated as the annihilating germ of society.

While the evil slumbering in the heart of theoretical culture gradually begins to disquiet modern man, and makes him anxiously ransack the stores of his experience for some means to avert the danger, though not believing very much in these means; while he begins to divine the consequences his position involves, great and universally gifted natures have managed, with an incredible amount of thought, to make use of the apparatus of science itself to point out the limits and the relativity of knowledge in general. Thus they have firmly denied the claim of science to universal validity and universal goals, thereby exposing the illusory quality of the notion that pretends to use causality to fathom the innermost essence of things. The extraordinary courage and wisdom of Kant and Schopenhauer have succeeded in gaining the most difficult victory, the victory over the optimism hidden in the essence of logic, the optimism which in turn is the basis of our culture. While this optimism, resting on apparently unobjectionable *aeternae veritates*,[17] believed that all the world's riddles can be understood and solved, and treated space, time, and causality as totally unconditioned laws of the most universal validity, Kant showed instead that these served in reality only to elevate the mere phenomenon, the work of Maya, to the sole and highest reality, putting it in place of the innermost and true essence of things, thus making the actual knowledge of this essence impossible—that is, as Schopenhauer puts it, to lull the dreamer still more soundly asleep (*World as Will and Representation*, I). With this knowledge a culture is inaugurated which I venture to designate as a tragic culture; whose most important characteristic is that wisdom takes the place of science, turning a clear-eyed and comprehensive gaze on the world, seeking to take the eternal suffering found there as its own with sympathetic feelings of love. Let us imagine a rising generation with this undaunted vision, with this heroic desire for the prodigious, let us imagine the bold stride of these dragon-slayers, the proud and daring spirit with which they turn their backs on all the effeminate doctrines of optimism in order "to live resolutely" in wholeness and fullness: would it not be necessary for the tragic man of this culture, with his self-discipline to earnestness and terror, to desire a new art, the art of metaphysical consolation—tragedy—as his true Helen, and to declare with Faust:

> And should I not, most longing power,
> bring this most singular form to life?[18]

But now that the Socratic culture has been shaken on both sides, and is only able to hold the scepter of its infallibility with hands that tremble— first through the fear of its own conclusions which it finally begins to surmise, and secondly because it is no longer convinced with its former naïve trust of the eternal validity of its foundations—it is a sad spectacle to behold how the dance of its thought always rushes longingly toward new forms, embracing them but then, shuddering, suddenly letting them go, as Mephistopheles does the seductive Lamiae.[19] It is certainly the symptom of the "break" which people speak of as the primordial suffering of modern culture that the theoretical man, alarmed and dissatisfied at his own conclusions, no longer dares to entrust himself to the terrible icy torrent of existence: he runs timidly up and down the river's bank. He no longer wants to have anything entire, with all the natural cruelty of things, so thoroughly has he been spoiled by his optimistic views. Besides, he feels that a culture built up on the principles of science must perish when it begins to grow *illogical*, that is, to avoid its own conclusions. Our art reveals this universal trouble: in vain does one seek help by imitating all the great productive periods and natures, in vain does one accumulate the whole of "world literature" to surround modern man for his comfort, in vain does one place oneself in the midst of the styles and artists of all ages, so that one may name them as Adam did the beasts: one still remains eternally hungry, the "critic" without joy or energy, the Alexandrian man, little more than a librarian and proofreader, a pitiable wretch who goes blind from book dust and printers' errors.

21: If our analysis has shown that the Apollonian element in tragedy has used its illusion to gain a complete victory over the primordial Dionysian element of music and has made music itself subservient to its goal, namely, the highest and clearest elucidation of the drama, it would certainly be necessary to add a very important qualification: that at the most essential point this Apollonian illusion is shattered and annihilated. Aided by music, drama spreads out before us with such radiant clarity in all its movements and figures—so that we imagine we see the fabric unfolding on the loom as the shuttle flies to and fro—that it attains an overall effect that *transcends all Apollonian artistic effects*. In the collective effect of tragedy, the Dionysian gets the upper hand once more; tragedy ends with a sound which could never emanate from the realm of Apollonian art. And the Apollonian illusion is thereby found to be what it is, the careful veiling during the tragedy's performance of the intrinsically Dionysian effect. This effect, however, is so powerful that it finally forces the Apollonian drama itself into a sphere where it begins to speak with Dionysian wisdom, and even denies itself and its Apollonian clarity. So that the intricate relation of the Apollonian and the Dionysian in tragedy must really be symbolized by a fraternal union of the two deities: Dionysus speaks the language of Apollo, and Apollo finally speaks the language of Dionysus; and so the highest goal of tragedy and of art overall is attained.

Notes

1. From *Die Geburt der Tragödie aus dem Geiste der Musik* (Leipzig, 1872); tr. as *The Birth of Tragedy* in *The Complete Works of Friedrich Nietzsche*, ed. Oscar Levy (Edinburgh and London: T. N. Foulis, 18 vols., 1909-13), revised.

2. From Richard Wagner's opera *Die Meistersinger von Nürnberg* (1868). Set in the sixteenth century, Wagner's opera embodies ideas of Schopenhauer on music as the greatest of the arts; its hero is the modest, brilliant poet (and shoemaker) Hans Sachs.

3. Arthur Schopenhauer (1788–1860), German philosopher who contended that the world is not a rational place and who developed Plato's and Kant's philosophies into an instinct-recognizing and ascetic outlook. Throughout *The Birth of Tragedy* Nietzsche regularly quotes from Schopenhauer's 1819 masterwork *Die Welt als Wille und Vorstellung* (*The World as Will and Representation*), which emphasizes the human will's incessant, tragically unrealizable striving for satisfaction.

4. "Principle of individuation."

5. Babylonian and Persian winter solstice celebration, famous as a chaotic time of misrule.

6. Referring to the choral "Ode to Joy" that concludes Beethoven's Ninth Symphony; Nietzsche quotes the lines in question at the end of this paragraph.

7. Sanskrit term used in Hinduism for the illusory appearance of the physical world.

8.   The secret rituals of initiation to the cult of Demeter and Persephone at Eleusis in ancient Greece.

9.   Nietzsche here alludes to some major examples of divine violence in Greek mythology, from the Titans whom the Olympian gods overthrew, to the implacable Moira or three Fates, to the punishment of Prometheus, who brought fire to humanity and was sentenced to have his liver eternally gnawed by vultures, to the curses brought down upon Oedipus and the House of Atreus.

10.   Justification of the ways of God to humanity, term coined by the Enlightenment philosopher G. W. von Leibnitz in his book *Theodicy* (1710).

11.   When Odysseus visits the underworld in book 11 of *The Odyssey*, he meets the ghost of Achilles, who grimly declares that it would be better to live as a farmhand on earth than rule over the immortal dead.

12.   Friedrich von Schiller (1759–1805), German dramatist, poet, and historian, who wrote an influential aesthetic treatise *On Naïve and Sentimental Poetry*.

13.   Part novel and part philosophical treatise, Jean-Jacques Rousseau's *Émile: or On Education* (1762) champions a natural process of learning instead of formal schooling.

14.   These originary beings appear in Goethe's *Faust*, Part 2, Act 1.

15.   In the final centuries of the classical era, Egypt's Alexandria was famous for its great library, known as a center of preservation and commentary rather than of new artistic creation. By "Buddhistic" Nietzsche may mean "Brahmanic" (conflating Hinduism and Indian Buddhism).

16.   "God out of a machine," originally a mechanical device used by Euripides and other Greek playwrights to allow a god or goddess to descend onstage; the phrase became a metaphor for an unexpected or artificial character or event, introduced in a work to resolve a situation.

17.   Eternal truths.

18.   Quoting Goethe's *Faust*, pt. 2, lines 7438–39.

19.   Another reference to *Faust* (2:7697–7810), a scene in which the diabolical Mephistopheles is himself taken aback by the vampirish female spirits he has conjured up.

5

Present Tasks of Comparative Literature[1] (1877)

Hugo Meltzl

Principal editor of the first journal of comparative literature, Hugo Meltzl (1846–1908) grew up in a world of intertwined languages and cultures. His family belonged to the German-speaking minority in the Transylvanian region of Hungary, which was then part of the Austro-Hungarian Empire. Meltzl learned Hungarian only once he went to school. In college at Klausenburg—as it was known in German, or Kolosvár in Hungarian, or Cluj today in what is now Romania—he studied Romanian as well as Greek and Latin, then went on to study philology at Leipzig and Heidelberg Universities. At Leipzig he became friends with the young Friedrich Nietzsche, introducing him to the work of his favorite Hungarian poet, Sandor Petöfi, who had been a leading figure in nationalistic Hungarian Romanticism. Returning at age twenty-seven to take the Chair in German Language and Literature at Cluj, Meltzl joined forces in 1877 with an older colleague, Samuel Brassai, to found his pioneering journal, the *Acta Comparationis Litterarum Universarum*.

    Printed here is the programmatic essay that Meltzl wrote defining the purposes of the new journal, which was to have a global scope— visibly represented by the title page, which gave the journal's title in ten different languages. In principle, all ten languages were to be the "official" languages of the journal, but in practice most articles were written in German or in Hungarian, with some contributions in English, French, Italian, and Latin. Yet Meltzl and Brassai assembled an editorial board from around the globe, with contributing editors in India, Australia, the United

States, and Iceland, among many other countries, and during the journal's eleven-year life they published translations and discussions of literature in dozens of languages. In his introductory essay, Meltzl emphasizes "the principle of polyglottism," making a prescient comparison of less-spoken languages to endangered species and emphasizing that comparative literature should give equal attention to the world's folk poetry as well as to major literary masterpieces.

I.

Since our polyglot journal has been mistaken for a philological one by some philologists, it may not be superfluous to discuss briefly once more the tasks of our journal, which—being the very first such effort in this area—cannot rely on achievements of predecessors or other convenient advantages.

Comparative Literature—for which to our knowledge only the Germans, French and Italians already have an established designation—is nevertheless by no means a fully defined and established academic discipline. As a matter of fact, it is still far from that goal. The task, therefore, of an organ of this slowly emerging discipline of the future should not so much consist in definitely comparing the vast (though still insufficient) material at hand as in adding to it from all sides and in intensifying the effort, directly as well as indirectly. A journal like ours, then, must be devoted at the same time to the art of translation and to the Goethean *Weltliteratur* (a term which German literary historians, particularly Gervinus,[2] have thoroughly misunderstood). Literature and language are closely related; the latter being substantially subservient to the former, without which the servant would have not only no autonomy but no existence at all. Therefore it should be understood that linguistic problems will also be touched upon now and then (though not methodically discussed), particularly with regard to exotic peoples. For similar reasons Comparative Literature touches upon the fields of philosophy, aesthetics, even ethnology and anthropology. Without ethnological considerations, for instance, the literatures of remote regions could not be fully understood.[3]

To these tasks we have to add the *reform of literary history*, a reform long awaited and long overdue, which is possible only through an extensive application of the *comparative principle*. As every unbiased man of letters knows, modern literary history, as generally practiced today, is nothing but an *ancilla historiae politicae*, or even an *ancilla nationis*,[4] at best an *ancilla philologiae* (in the modern sense of the latter term). Literary historians have gone so far as to base their divisions into literary epochs on political events, sometimes on the death-years of—kings! For these and similar reasons, even the best and best-known presentations of the literary history of all languages are thoroughly unacceptable to the mature taste and are quite unprofitable for serious literary (not political and philological) purposes. Only extensive work in the comparative fields, particularly translation, can eliminate gradually many preconceptions. Of those many preconceptions, we may mention one in the field of modern German literary history. In Koberstein's monumental work,[5] which is on the whole justly famous (5th ed., by the conscientious Bartsch, Leipzig, 1872, Vol. I, p. 218, footnote 7), there is a lengthy discussion of the question whether the aubade was invented by Wolfram von Eschenbach or by the Provençal poets. Finally the author agrees with the "thorough and cautious" Lachmann that Wolfram is the inventor of this genre. With all their thoroughness and caution they do not consider the fact that Lieder of this type were sung eighteen centuries ago in China (as those contained in the *Shih Ching*) and are frequently found among the folksongs of modern peoples, for instance, the Hungarians.

There is no area of literary study today as overworked, unattractive and, in spite of this, frequented as that of literary history; and there is none that promises less. Lichtenberg already came to that conclusion before the writing of literary histories had properly begun. This is only confirmed by such rare exceptions as Scherr's and Minckwitz's historical works, which—in spite of occasionally fitting literary phenomena into conventional schemes derived from certain preconceptions of liberalism—at least compensate for it by a fresh, intelligent, and universal approach. There is no space here for an extensive discussion of these important questions.[6] Let us conclude by repeating what has been said earlier in this journal: our journal intends to be a meeting place of authors, translators and philosophers of all nations. The established disciplines are excluded, particularly since they serve, openly or not, only practical purposes. Besides, these disciplines have their share of scholarly journals. Only one discipline does not have its journal yet, the one we intend to cultivate: the art of translation as it has been accepted in its full significance only since Goethe—whose consequence is nothing less than the emerging discipline of the future: Comparative Literature. The scruple that a discipline still in the process of consolidation should not have its own journal would raise violent objections if directed at our older sister, Comparative Philology, which is also still consolidating itself, although it is already well-structured in many of its vast areas. Besides, comparative literary history is already practiced directly, even in the classrooms of German universities (e.g., Carriere in Munich). Among its indirect representatives belongs the impressive group of German translators of literature (and I am not talking about the mass of second and third rate translators).

II: The Principle of Polyglottism.

Our journal has changed its motto with the second volume. Instead of the beautiful one taken from Eötvös which is, after all, limited to the principle of true translation, we have found in Schiller's dictum a more precise and at the same time more universal expression of the tasks of this journal.[7] This seemingly unimportant change of mottoes alone may justify our returning to, or rather, our continuing the above discussion. Besides, much that is important had to be left unsaid on the last occasion for lack of space. We hope that nobody misunderstands our beautiful motto from Schiller.

The art of translation is, and will remain, one of the most important and attractive tools for the realization of our high comparative aims. But the means should not be mistaken for the end. Goethe was still able to conceive of his "Weltliteratur" as basically—or even exclusively?—(German) translation which for him was an end in itself.[8] To us today it can only be the means to a higher end.

True comparison is possible only when we have before us the objects of our comparison in their original form. Although translations facilitate the international traffic or distribution of literary products immensely (particularly in the German language, which is poetically more adaptable than any other modern language), nobody will dispute Schopenhauer's opinion that even the best translation leaves something to be desired and can never replace the original. Therefore, the *principle of translation* has to be not replaced but accompanied by a considerably more important comparative tool, the *principle of polyglottism*. The limited space of our journal, of course, permits us only a limited realization of this principle. But this modern principle has to be realized above all if literary comparison is to do more than scratch the surface. (Incidentally, polyglottism is not something entirely modern since we are indebted to it for two quite modern disciplines which both deal with the antiquity of human culture: Egyptology and Assyriology. Without the polyglottism of the tablets of Rashid and Nineveh our knowledge would be considerably poorer.)

The principle of translation is confined to the *indirect* commerce of literature in contrast to the principle of polyglottism which is the *direct* commerce itself. This already indicates the great importance of polyglottism, which can be applied in several ways. The most desirable and at the same time most practical way would be, for the time being, if the critical articles of a comparative journal would appear in that language with which they are principally concerned, so that, for instance, a Hungarian contribution to Camões scholarship would be written in Portuguese and a German contribution to Cervantes criticism would appear in Spanish. It should be obvious that in most cases this aim will remain an ideal and unattainable one for the time being. We on our part feel that we should strictly realize it at least with regard to Hungarian and German literature. (This is our reason for giving preference to German and Hungarian literature, which, besides, corresponds to our geographic and cultural situation; therefore the diglottism of the section *Revue*.) Also, a proper use of the principle of polyglottism should not exclude polyglot original production entirely.

It should be obvious, however, that these polyglot efforts have nothing in common with any kind of universal fraternization or similar international *nephelokokkugia*.[9] The ideals of Comparative Literature have nothing to do with foggy, "cosmopolitanizing" theories; the high aims (not to say tendencies) of a journal like ours would be gravely misunderstood or intentionally misrepresented if anybody expected us to infringe upon the national uniqueness of a people. To attempt that would be, for more than one reason, a ludicrous undertaking which even an association of internationally famous scholars would have to consider doomed from the start—supposing such an association would be foolish enough to get together for such a purpose. It can safely be assumed that the purposes of Comparative Literature are more solid than that. It is, on the contrary, the *purely national of all nations* that Comparative Literature means to cultivate lovingly—here within the narrow framework of a journal where every nation is made to institute healthy (or just attractive) comparisons, which would not result from other approaches. Our secret motto is: nationality as individuality of a people should be regarded as sacred and inviolable. Therefore, a people, be it ever so insignificant politically, is and will remain, from the standpoint of Comparative Literature, as important as the largest nation. The most unsophisticated language may offer us most precious and informative subjects for comparative philology. The same is true for the spiritual life of "literatureless peoples," as we might call them, whose ethnic individuality should not be impinged upon by the wrong kind of missionary zeal; rather, it is our duty to protect it honestly and preserve it, if possible, in its purity. (From this comparative-polyglot standpoint should be considered the *ukaz* of the Censorship Office of the Russian Ministry of the Interior of May 16, 1876—mentioned already on page 30—which prohibits the literary use of the Ukrainian language. It would appear as the greatest sin against the Holy Spirit even if it were directed only against the folksongs of an obscure horde of Kirghizes instead of a people of fifteen million.) To impede the folk literature of a people would mean to destroy arbitrarily an important expression of the human spirit. In a time when certain animal species such as the mountain goat and the European bison are protected against extinction by elaborate and strict laws, the willful extinction of a human species (or its literature, which amounts to the same thing) should be impossible.

In this sense we want understood the term "world literature" which, along with the art of translation, we intend to cultivate, particularly since the latter has not yet had a journal to itself, while the former has been well represented for some time now by such good, fully recognized and elaborate journals as the *Magazin für die Litteratur des Auslands* and Herrig's *Archiv für das Studium der neueren Sprachen* in Berlin. In England and France, too, it has always been cultivated by all major journals with praiseworthy zeal and good success. However, it cannot be denied that the so-called "world literature" is generally misunderstood, as has been indicated above. For today every nation demands its own "world literature" without quite knowing what is meant by it. By now, every nation considers itself, for one good reason or another, superior to all other nations, and this hypothesis, worked out into a complete theory of *suffisance*[10] is even the basis of much of modern pedagogy, which today practically everywhere strives to be "national." This unhealthy "national principle" therefore constitutes the fundamental premise of the entire spiritual life of modern Europe—which may take such peculiar forms as the "national ethic" of a Viennese high school teacher who exhibits no little satisfaction with his achievement. In this way, all sound conceptions are undermined from the start, even with regard to the highest spiritual concerns which could otherwise have immeasurably rich consequences considering today's wonderfully intensified commerce of ideas in the world. Instead of giving free rein to polyglottism and reaping the fruits in the future (fruits that it would certainly bring), every nation today insists on the strictest monoglottism, by considering its own language superior or even destined to rule supreme. This is a childish competition whose result will finally be that all of them remain—inferior. The brilliant Dora d'Istria, in the foreword to her fine book *La Poésie des*

Ottomans (the second edition appeared recently) confirms our opinion by exclaiming impatiently:

> Nous vivons en effet dans une époque fort peu littéraire, et l'Europe livrée aux haines des partis, aux luttes des races, aux querelles des sectes, aux rivalités des classes, n'attache qu'une médiocre importance aux questions qui semblaient, il y a quelques années, capables d'occuper tous les esprits cultivés. Trop de pays chrétiens ressemblent maintenant à la Turquie du XVIIIe siècle.[11]

True "world literature," therefore, in our opinion, can only remain an unattainable ideal in the direction of which, nevertheless, all independent literatures, i.e., all nations, should strive. They should use, however, only those means which we have called the two most important comparative principles, translation and polyglottism, never acts of violence or barbaric hypotheses which will be profitable for nobody but which unfortunately appear occasionally even in the great European journals. It is therefore particularly satisfying to hear a voice from Ultima Thule which I may be permitted to quote here. Our collaborator in Iceland writes us in German (July 29):

> I have always considered it desirable that there would be a journal which would bring together the writers, or all thinkers, of various nations; or, better still, that they would form an international society against the barbaric powers of our time. An important step in this direction seems to be this journal, as a focal point for writers and thinkers, or, to put it humorously, an exhibition of the spirit.

This noble voice of the Icelandic translator of Shakespeare, Steingrimur Thorsteinsson, moves us to submit the following proposal to our collaborators: For a small journal like ours to bring together at least a small number of "writers and thinkers of various nations" effectively, we intend to begin, starting with our next number, a small polyglot parliament on various problems of Comparative Literature, including practical ones. After all, it is necessary to assemble stone by stone the edifice of the future which may be of profit only to future generations.[12]

Notes

1. First published in German in *Acta Comparationis Litterarum Universarum* 1:9 (May 1877) and 1:15 (October 1877). Translated by Hans-Joachim Schulz and

Phillip H. Rhein in *Comparative Literature: The Early Years* (Chapel Hill: University of North Carolina Press, 1973), 53–62. A few notes by Meltzl on contemporary scholarly works are omitted here.

2. Georg Gottfried Gervinus (1805–71), author of a five-volume history of German literature. He used the idea of *Weltliteratur* to celebrate Germany's literary influence abroad and German writers' ability to make creative use of foreign material.

3. Philosophy, particularly modern inductive philosophy, is even the most natural point of departure of literary history, and it is difficult to imagine that it has so far remained *terra incognita* for literary historians. History in the widest sense, especially the so-called universal history, political science, theology, philology, all have the privilege to lead to literary history; but how long will a philosophy with a sound scientific-ethnological basis continue to be dictated by their literary history and their "car tel est notre plaisir"? [Author's note]

4. A handmaiden to political history or even to the nation.

5. August Koberstein, *Grundriss der Geschichte der deutschen national Literatur* (1827).

6. However, I have already discussed, in 1874, the reform of literary history in a lecture delivered at Klausenburg University, which was later published under the title *A kritikai irodalomtörtenelem fogalmarol (On the Concept of a Critical Literary History)*, Vienna: Faesy and Frick, Budapest: Rosenberg, 1875. [Au.]

7. The Eötvös motto is from *Gondolatok (Thoughts)* and may be translated as follows: "Let us study but not imitate the great authors of other ages and nations. The seed which grew into a tree elsewhere may sprout in our soil also, but the full-grown tree, if transplanted, would wither and perish the sooner and the more certainly the greater and more splendid it was in its original place." The Schiller motto is from a letter to Gottfried Körner, October 13, 1789: "It would be a pitiful, petty ideal to write for one nation only; for a philosophical spirit this limitation would be unbearable. He could not confine himself to such a changeable, accidental, and arbitrary form of humanity, a fragment—what is the greatest nation but a fragment?" [Translators' note.]

8. In the light of this fact, the "patriotic" misunderstanding of Goethe's "world literature" in Gervinus, Koberstein and their successors is all the more absurd. [Au.]

9. "Cloud-Cuckoo-Land," the ethereal dwelling-place of philosophers in Aristophanes' satiric play *The Clouds*.

10. Self-sufficiency.

11. "We live in effect in an epoch that is hardly literary at all, and Europe—given over to party hatreds, to the battles of races, to sectarian quarrels, to class conflict—attaches little importance to questions that only a few years ago had seemed capable of occupying every cultivated spirit. Too many Christian countries today resemble the Turkey of the 18th century."

12.   In the third part of his essay, entitled "The Decaglottism," Meltzl proposes to reduce the number of working languages of his journal to ten: German, French, English, Italian, Spanish, Portuguese, Dutch, Swedish, Icelandic and Hungarian. His criterion for designating these as languages that have genuinely contributed to the literature of an international *niveau* is that in these literatures "classicism" has been achieved. (The term is not defined in the essay.) Portuguese achieved this standard with Camões, Dutch with *Reinaert de Vos*, Swedish with Tegnér, Icelandic with the *Edda*, Hungarian with Eötvös and Petöfi. Meltzl denies Russian literature any importance comparable to Russia's political role, although he admits Pushkin to be an "isolated phenomenon of praiseworthy independence." The inclusion of non-Western languages in the future Meltzl considers possible only when "Asian literatures will finally come around to accepting our alphabet." [Tr.]

6

The Comparative Method and Literature[1] (1886)

Hutcheson Macaulay Posnett

A pioneering scholar of comparative literature—who claimed to have given the field its name in English—Hutcheson Macaulay Posnett was deeply interested in the relation of literature to social life. Trained as a barrister in his native Dublin, Posnett published studies of political economy before turning his attention to comparative literary studies. The fruit of ten years' labor, his book *Comparative Literature* was published in 1886, just after its author had sailed to New Zealand, where he had accepted a post as professor of Classics and English at the University of Auckland. This move from Ireland to New Zealand—from the inner to the outer margins of the British Empire—was appropriate for someone of Posnett's global perspective. In his book, he devotes substantial space not only to Western European literature and to the Greek and Roman classics in which he had been trained in school, but also to many other literatures, including Arabic, Hebrew, Sanskrit, Persian, Chinese, Japanese, Russian, and Eastern European literatures. He worked as needed in translation and read all the specialized scholarship he could get hold of for each area.

Posnett organized his globe-spanning discussion by the rigorous application of the social science methods of his day; his book was published, in fact, in a British "International Science Series," together with volumes on funguses, international law, volcanoes, socialism, and one titled *Jelly Fish, Star Fish and Sea Urchins*. Posnett derived his approach from the economist and political scientist Herbert Spencer, a social Darwinist who looked for evolutionary patterns in social life. Posnett argued that literary forms develop in tandem with the broader social evolution from the tribe to the city to the nation and beyond. He described this process as "the relativity of literature," challenging conceptions of literature as a transcendent aesthetic order. In his chapter "The Comparative Method and Literature," given here, Posnett stresses that comparative study should be a scientific enterprise focused on broad literary and social movements rather than on a Romantic-style appreciation for the outpourings of individual genius.

Posnett's evolutionary scheme can look somewhat mechanical today, but his emphasis on literary relativity enabled him to appreciate an exceptionally wide range of materials, from Sanskrit epics to Persian ghazals to gypsy folk songs to modern French novels, as he sought to determine the varied social settings to which each body of material responds. In "The Comparative Method and Literature" he makes an eloquent case for the importance of comparative study, both as an analytical tool and as a counter to narrow nationalism, even as he recognizes the nation as the fundamental basis of modern literary life.

The comparative method of acquiring or communicating knowledge is in one sense as old as thought itself, in another the peculiar glory of our nineteenth century. All reason, all imagination, operate subjectively, and pass from man to man objectively, by aid of comparisons and differences. The most colourless proposition of the logician is either the assertion of a comparison, A is B, or the denial of a comparison, A is not B; and any student of Greek thought will remember how the confusion of this simple process by mistakes about the nature of the copula (ἐστι) produced a flood of so-called "essences" (οὐσίαι) which have done more to mislead both ancient and modern philosophy than can be easily estimated. But not only the colourless propositions of logic, even the highest and most brilliant flights of oratorical eloquence or poetic fancy are sustained by this rudimentary structure of comparison and difference, this primary scaffolding, as we may call it, of human thought. If sober experience works out scientific truths in propositions affirming or denying comparison, imagination even in the richest colours works under the same elementary forms. Athenian intellect and Alexandrian reflection failed to perceive this fundamental truth, and the failure is attributable in the main to certain social characteristics of the Greeks. Groups, like individuals, need to project themselves beyond the circle of their own associations if they wish to understand their own nature; but the great highway which has since led to comparative philosophy was closed against the Greek by his contempt for any language but his own. At the same time, his comparisons of his own social life, in widely different stages, were narrowed partially by want of monuments of his past, much more by contempt for the less civilised Greeks, such as the Macedonians, and especially by a mass of myth long too sacred to be touched by science, and then too tangled to be profitably loosed by the hands of impatient sceptics. Thus, deprived of the historical study of their own past and circumscribed within the comparisons and distinctions their own adult language permitted, it is not surprising that the Greeks made poor progress in comparative thinking, as a matter not merely of unconscious action but of conscious reflection. This conscious reflection has been the growth of European thought during the past five centuries, at first indeed a weakling, but, from causes of recent origin, now flourishing in healthy vigour.

When Dante wrote *De Eloquio Vulgari*[2] he marked the starting-point of our modern comparative science—the nature of language, a problem not to be lightly overlooked by the peoples of modern Europe inheriting, unlike Greek or Hebrew, a literature written in a tongue whose decomposition had plainly gone to make up the elements of their own living speech. The Latin, followed at an interval by the Greek, Renaissance laid the foundations of comparative reflection in the mind of modern Europe. Meanwhile the rise of European nationalities was creating new standpoints, new materials, for comparison in modern institutions and modes of thought or sentiment. The discovery of the New World brought this new European civilisation face to face with primitive life, and awakened men to contrasts with their own associations more striking than Byzantine or even Saracen could offer. Commerce, too, was now bringing the rising nations of Europe into rivalry with, and knowledge of, each other, and, more than this, giving a greater degree of personal freedom to the townsmen of the West than they had ever possessed before. Accompanying the increase of wealth and freedom came an awakening of individual opinion among men, even an uprising of it against authority which has since been called the Reformation, but an uprising which, in days of feudal, monarchical, and "popular" conflict, in days when education was the expensive luxury of the few, and even the communication of work-a-day ideas was as slow and irregular as bad roads and worse banditti could make it, was easily checked even in countries where it was supposed to have done great things. Individual inquiry, and with it comparative thinking, checked within the domain of social life by constant collisions with theological dogma, turned to the material world, began to build up the vast stores of modern material knowledge, and only in later days of freedom began to construct from this physical side secular views of human origin and destiny which on the social side had been previously curbed by dogma. Meanwhile European knowledge of man's social life in its myriad varieties was attaining proportions such as neither Bacon nor Locke had contemplated. Christian missionaries were bringing home the life and literature of China so vividly to Europeans that neither the art nor the scepticism of Voltaire disdained to borrow from the Jesuit Prémare's translation of a Chinese drama published in 1735. Then Englishmen in India learned of that ancient language [Sanskrit] which Sir William Jones, toward the close of the eighteenth century, introduced to European scholars; and soon the points of resemblance between this language and the languages of Greeks and Italians, Teutons and Celts, were observed, and used like so many stepping-stones upon which men passed in imagination over the flood of time which separates the old Aryans from their modern offshoots in the West. Since those days the method of comparison has been applied to many subjects besides language; and many new influences have combined to make the mind of Europe more ready to compare and to contrast than it ever was before. The steam-engine, telegraph, daily press, now bring the local and central, the popular and the cultured, life of each European country and the general actions of the entire world face to face; and habits of comparison have arisen such as never before prevailed so widely and so vigorously. But, while we may call *consciously* comparative thinking the great glory of our nineteenth century, let us not forget that such thinking is largely due to mechanical improvements, and that long before our comparative philologists, jurists, economists, and the rest, scholars like Reuchlin[3] used the same method less consciously, less accurately, yet in a manner from the first foreshadowing a vast outlook instead of the exclusive views of Greek criticism. Here, then, is a rapid sketch of comparative thought in its European history. How is such thought, how is its method, connected with our subject, "Literature"?

It has been observed that imagination no less than experience works through the medium of comparisons; but it is too often forgotten that the range of these comparisons is far from being unlimited in space and time, in social life and physical environment. If scientific imagination, such as Professor Tyndall once explained and illustrated, is strictly bound by the laws of hypothesis, the magic of the literary artist which looks so free is as strictly bound within the range of ideas already marked out by the language of his group. Unlike the man of science, the man of literature cannot coin words for a currency of new ideas; for his verse or prose, unlike the discoveries of the man of science, must reach average, not specialised, intelligence. Words must pass from special into general use before they can be used by him; and, just in proportion as special kinds of knowledge (legal, commercial, mechanical, and the like) are developed, the more striking is the difference between the language of literature and that of science, the language and ideas of the community contrasted with those of its specialised parts. If we trace the rise of any civilised community out of isolated clans or tribes, we may observe a twofold development closely connected with the language and ideas of literature—expansion of the group outwards, a process attended by expansions of thought and sentiment; and specialisation of activities within, a process upon which depends the rise of a leisure-enjoying literary class, priestly or secular. The latter is the process familiar to economists as division of labour, the former that familiar to antiquaries as the fusion of smaller into larger social groups. While the range of comparison widens from clan to national and even world-wide associations and sympathies, the specialising process separates ideas, words, and forms of writing from the proper domain of literature. Thus, in the Homeric age the speech in the Agora has nothing professional or specialised about it, and is a proper subject of poetry; but in the days of professional Athenian oratory the speech is out of keeping with the drama, and smacks too much of the rhêtor's school. Arabic poets of the "Ignorance"[4] sing of their clan life; Spenser glows with warmly national feelings; Goethe and Victor Hugo rise above thoughts of even national destiny. It is due to these two processes of expansion and specialisation that the language and ideas of literature gradually shade off from the special language and special ideas of certain classes in any highly developed community, and literature comes to differ from science not only by its imaginative character, but by the fact that its language and ideas belong to no special class. In fact, whenever literary language and ideas cease to be in a manner common property, literature tends either towards imitation work or to become specialised, to become science in a literary dress,—as not a little of our metaphysical poetry has been of late. Such facts as these bring out prominently the relation of comparative thinking and of the comparative method to literature. Is the circle of common speech and thought, the circle of the group's comparative thinking, as narrow as a tribal league? Or, have many such circles combined into a national group? Are the offices of priest and singer still combined in a kind of magic ritual? Or, have professions and trades been developed, each, so to speak, with its own technical dialect for practical purposes? Then we must remember that these external and internal evolutions of social life, take place often unconsciously, making comparisons and distinctions without reflecting on their nature or limits; we must remember that it is the business of reflective comparison, of the comparative method, to retrace this development *consciously,* and to seek the causes which have produced it. Let us now look at the literary use of such comparison in a less abstract, a more lifelike form.

When Mr. Matthew Arnold defines the function of criticism as "a disinterested endeavour to learn and propagate the best that is known and thought in the world,"[5] he is careful to add that much of this best knowledge and thought is not of English but foreign growth. The English critic in these times of international literature must deal largely with foreign fruit and flower, and thorn-pieces sometimes. He cannot rest content with the products of his own country's culture, though they may vary from the wild fruits of the Saxon wilderness to the rude plenty of the Elizabethan age, from the courtly neatness of Pope to the democratic tastes of to-day. M. Demogeot has lately published an interesting study[6] of the influences exerted by Italy, Spain, England, and Germany on the literature of France; our English critic must do likewise for the literature of his own country. At every stage in the progress of his country's literature he is, in fact, forced to look more or less beyond her sea-washed shores. Does he accompany Chaucer on his pilgrimage and listen to the pilgrims' tales? The scents of the lands of the South fill the atmosphere of the Tabard Inn, and on the road to Canterbury waft him in thought to the Italy of Dante and of Petrarch and Boccaccio. Does he watch the hardy crews of Drake and Frobisher unload in English port the wealth of Spanish prize, and listen to the talk of great sea-captains full of phrases learned from the gallant subjects of Philip II? The Spain of Cervantes and Lope de Vega rises before his eyes, and the new physical and mental wealth of Elizabethan England bears him on the wings of commerce or of fancy to the noisy port of Cadiz and the palaces of Spanish grandees. Through the narrow and dirty streets of Elizabethan London fine gentlemen with Spanish rapiers at their sides and Spanish phrases in their mouths, pass to and fro in the dress admired by Spanish taste. The rude theatres resound with Spanish allusions. And, were it not for the deadly strife of Englishman and Spaniard on the seas, and the English dread of Spain as the champion of Papal interference, England's Helicon[7] might forget the setting sun of the Italian republics to enjoy the full sunshine of Spanish influences. But now our critic stands in the Whitehall of Charles II., or lounges at Will's Coffee-House, or enters the theatres whose recent restoration cuts to the heart his Puritan friends. Everywhere it is the same. Spanish phrases and manners have been forgotten. At the court, Buckingham and the rest perfume their licentious wit with French *bouquet.* At Will's,

Dryden glorifies the rimed tragedies of Racine; and theatres, gaudy with scenic contrivances unknown to Shakespeare, are filled with audiences who in the intervals chatter French criticism, and applaud with equal fervour outrageous indecencies and formal symmetry. Soon the English Boileau will carry the culture of French exotics as far as the English hothouse will allow; soon that scepticism which the refined immorality of the court, the judges, and the Parliament renders fashionable among the few who as yet guide the destinies of the English nation, shall pass from Bolingbroke to Voltaire, and from Voltaire to the Revolutionists. We need not accompany our critic to Weimar, nor seek with him some sources of German influence on England in English antipathies to France and her revolution. He has proved that the history of our country's literature cannot be explained by English causes alone, any more than the origin of the English language or people can be so explained. He has proved that each national literature is a centre towards which not only national but also international forces gravitate. We thank him for this glimpse of a growth so wide, so varying, so full of intricate interaction; it is an aspect of literature studied comparatively, but, in spite of its apparent width, it is only one aspect. National literature has been developed from within as well as influenced from without; and the comparative study of this internal development is of far greater interest than that of the external, because the former is less a matter of imitation and more an evolution directly dependent on social and physical causes.

To the internal sources of national development, social or physical, and the effect of different phases of this development on literature, the student will therefore turn as the true field of scientific study. He will watch the expansion of social life from narrow circles of clans or tribal communities, possessed of such sentiments and thoughts as could live within such narrow spheres, and expressing in their rude poetry their intense feelings of brotherhood, their weak conceptions of personality. He will watch the deepening of personal sentiments in the isolated life of feudalism which ousts the communism of the clan, the reflection of such sentiments in songs of personal heroism, and the new aspects which the life of man, and of nature, and of animals—the horse, the hound, the hawk in feudal poetry, for example—assumes under this change in social organisation. Then he will mark the beginnings of a new kind of corporate life in the cities, in whose streets sentiments of clan exclusiveness are to perish, the prodigious importance of feudal personality is to disappear, new forms of individual and collective character are to make their appearance, and the drama is to take the place of the early communal chant or the song of the chieftain's hall. Next, the scene will change into the courts of monarchy. Here the feelings of the cities and of the seigneurs are being focussed; here the imitation of classical models supplements the influences of growing national union; here literature, reflecting a more expanded society, a deeper sense of individuality, than it ever did before, produces its masterpieces under the patronage of an Elizabeth or a Louis Quatorze. Nor, in observing such effects of social evolution on literature, will the student by any means confine his view to this or that country. He will find that if England had her clan age, so also had Europe in general; that if France had her feudal poetry, so also had Germany, and Spain, and England; that though the rise of the towns affected literature in diverse ways throughout Europe, yet there are general features common to their influences; and that the same may be said of centralism in our European nations. Trace the influence of the Christian pulpit, or that of judicial institutions, or that of the popular assembly, on the growth of prose in different European countries, and you soon find how similarly internal social evolution has reflected itself in the word and thought of literature; how essential it is that any accurate study of literature should pass from language into the causes which allowed language and thought to reach conditions capable of supporting a literature; and how profoundly this study must be one of comparison and contrast. But we must not underrate our difficulties in tracing the effects of such internal evolution on a people's verse and prose. We must rather admit at the outset that such evolution is liable to be obscured or altogether concealed by the imitation of foreign models. To an example of such imitation we shall now turn.

The cases of Rome and Russia are enough to prove that external influences, carried beyond a certain point, may convert literature from the outgrowth of the group to which it belongs into a mere exotic, deserving of scientific study only as an artificial production indirectly dependent on social life. Let an instrument of speech be formed, a social centre established, an opportunity for the rise of a literary class able to depend upon its handiwork be given, and only a strong current of national ideas, or absolute ignorance of foreign and ancient models, can prevent the production of imitative work whose materials and arrangement, no matter how unlike those characteristic of the group, may be borrowed from climates the most diverse, social conditions the most opposite, and conceptions of personal character belonging to totally different epochs. Especially likely is something of this kind to occur when the cultured few of a people comparatively uncivilised become acquainted with the literary models of men who have already passed through many grades of civilisation, and who can, as it seems, save them the time and trouble of nationally repeating the same laborious ascent. The imitative literature of Rome is a familiar example of such borrowing; and that of Russia looked for a time as if it were fated to follow French models almost as closely as Rome once followed the Greek. How certain this imitation of French models was to conceal the true national spirit of Russian life, to throw a veil of contemptuous ignorance over her barbarous past, and to displace in her literature the development of the nation by the caprice of a Russo-Gallic clique, none can fail to perceive. In a country whose social life was, and is, so largely based on the communal organisation of the *Mir*, or village community, the strongly-individualised literature of France became such a favourite source of imitation as to throw into the background altogether those folk-songs which the reviving spirit of national literature in Russia, and that of social study in Europe generally, are at length beginning to examine. This Russian imitation of France may be illustrated by the works of Prince Kantemir (1709–43), who has been called "the first writer of Russia," the friend of Montesquieu, and the imitator of Boileau and Horace in his epistles and satires; by those of Lomonossoff (1711–65), "the first classical writer of Russia," the pupil of Wolff, the founder of the University of Moscow, the reformer of the Russian language, who by academical *Panegyrics* on Peter the Great and Elizabeth sought to supply the want of that truly oratorical prose which only free assemblies can foster, attempted an epic *Petreid,* in honour of the great Tsar, and modelled his odes on the French lyric poets and Pindar;[8] or by those of Soumarokoff, who, for the theatre of St. Petersburg established by Elizabeth, adapted or translated Corneille, Racine, Voltaire, much as Plautus and Terence had introduced the Athenian drama at Rome. As in Rome there had set in a conflict between old Roman family sentiments and the individualising spirit of the Greeks, as in Rome nobles of light and leading had been delighted to exchange archaic sentiments of family life and archaic measures like the Saturnian for the cultured thought and harmonious metres of Greece, so in Russia there set in a conflict between French individualism, dear to the court and nobles, and the social feelings of the Russian commune and family. The most ancient monuments of Russian thought—the Chronicle of the monk Nestor (1056–1116) and the *Song of Igor*—were as unlikely to attract the attention of such imitators as the *Builinas* and the folk-songs; and among a people who had never experienced the Western feudalism with its chivalrous poetry, to whom the Renaissance and Reformation had been unknown, came an imitation of Western progress which threatened for a time to prove as fatal to national literature as the imitation of Greek ideas had proved in Rome. In this European China, as Russia, with her family sentiments and filial devotion to the Tsar, has been called, French, and afterwards German and English, influences clearly illustrate the difficulties to which a scientific student of literature is exposed by imitative work out of keeping with social life; but the growing triumph of Russian national life as the true spring of Russian literature marks the want of real vitality in any literature dependent upon such foreign imitation.

These internal and external aspects of literary growth are thus objects of comparative inquiry, because literatures are not Aladdin's palaces raised by unseen hands in the twinkling of an eye, but the substantial results of causes which can be specified and described. The theory that literature is the detached life-work of individuals who are to be worshipped like images fallen down from heaven, not known as workers in the language and ideas of their age and place, and the kindred theory that imagination transcends the associations of space and time, have done much to conceal the relation of science to literature and to injure the works of both. But the "great-man theory" is really suicidal; for, while breaking up history and literature into biographies and thus preventing the recognition of any lines of orderly development, it would logically reduce not only what is known as "exceptional genius," but all men and women, so far as they possess personality at all, to the unknown, the causeless—in fact, would issue in a sheer denial of human knowledge, limited or unlimited. On the other hand, the theory that imagination works out of space and time (Coleridge, for example, telling us that "Shakspere is as much out of time as Spenser out of space") must not be repelled by any equally dogmatic assertion that it is limited by human experience, but is only to be refuted or established by such comparative studies as those on which we are about to enter.

The central point of these studies is the relation of the individual to the group. In the orderly changes through which this relation has passed, as revealed by the comparison of literatures belonging to different social states, we find our main reasons for treating literature as capable of scientific explanation. There are, indeed, other standpoints, profoundly interesting, from which the art and criticism of literature may also be explained—that of physical nature, that of animal life. But from these alone we shall not see far into the secrets of literary workmanship. We therefore adopt, with a modification hereafter to be noticed, the gradual expansion of social life, from clan to city, from city to nation, from both of these to cosmopolitan humanity, as the proper order of our studies in comparative literature.

Notes

1. From Hutcheson Macaulay Posnett, *Comparative Literature* (London: Kegan Paul, Trench, & Co., 1886), 73–86.

2. Usually known as *De Vulgari Eloquentia* (ca. 1300), Dante's treatise advocated the literary use of a purified, deregionalized Italian in place of Latin.

3. A German humanist and scholar of Greek and Latin (1455–1522).

4. Pre-Islamic poets, who wrote of tribal desert life.

5. Citing Arnold's influential essay "The Function of Criticism at the Present Time" (1865).

6. *Histoire des littératures étrangères* (Paris, 1880). [Author's note]

7. Greek mountain, supposed abode of the Muses.

8. The son of the fisherman of Archangel did much, no doubt, to create national literature, especially by his severance of the old Slavon of the Church from the spoken language; but his works contain evidences of French influence in spite of his national predilections. [Au.]

7

World Literature[1] (1899)

Georg Brandes

Georg Brandes (1842–1927) was both a major proponent of Scandinavian literature and a wide-ranging scholar of modern European writing. Born in Copenhagen to middle-class Jewish parents, Brandes studied law, philosophy, and aesthetics at the University of Copenhagen. Having decided to make literary studies his life's work, Brandes emphasized writers' social and political engagement, and he championed the new trends of realism and naturalism as vehicles for writers to discuss and influence contemporary society. Denied a professorship in Copenhagen by opponents who viewed him as too radical and possibly atheist, Brandes moved for several years to Germany, returning to Copenhagen in 1883 to become a leader of Danish literary life. Brandes discussed and influenced many Scandinavian writers, helping open their horizons to broader European trends. He championed the drama of Ibsen and the philosophy of Kierkegaard, while also writing widely on German, French, and English literature. Those three traditions became the focus of his magisterial four-volume study *Hauptströmungen der Litteratur des neunzehnten Jahrhunderts* (Major trends in nineteenth-century literature, 1872–75).

   In his 1899 essay on the concept of *Weltliteratur*, Brandes shows a keen awareness of the tension between literary quality at home and what becomes popular in the international marketplace. He discusses the advantage that writers in large countries have over those in smaller countries with less-spoken languages, and he expresses skepticism that translation can go very far to overcome this linguistic imbalance. Despite this skepticism, however, Brandes was himself a leading mediator between the smaller literary cultures of Scandinavia and the major literary markets of France, Germany, and England, and his essay gives insight into the opportunities and the challenges of comparative study across literary and linguistic borders.

The editors of this journal have asked me to express my views on the concept of world literature. I am afraid that I shall be unable to give a satisfactory response. I am aware that the term derives from Goethe, but at the moment the context in which he used it is not clear to me. I dimly recall that he prophesied a world literature in opposition to the previous national literatures.

But if I put to myself the question, "What is world literature?" without reference to the great inventor of the phrase, it appears to me that one must think in the first place of the works of discoverers and inventors in the natural sciences. The writings of Pasteur, Darwin, Bunsen or Helmholtz certainly belong to world literature; they apply directly to the human race and enrich humanity as a whole. Certain travel narratives like those of Stanley or Nansen also without a doubt make up part of world literature.

The works of historians—even the greatest among them—seem to me not wholly to belong to world literature in this way, since by the nature of their subject they are less final, they necessarily bear a strongly individual stamp and thus are better geared to the analogous personality of the author's compatriots. Despite all the learning and genius of their authors, such exceptional works as Carlyle's *Oliver Cromwell*, Michelet's *History of France*, or Mommsen's *Roman History* are not definitively works of scholarship, but can only be regarded as indissoluble wholes insofar as they are works of art—which does not hinder them from becoming familiar to the main nations of Europe and America, in the original as in translation. For when one speaks of world literature, one thinks primarily and principally of belles-lettres in all their forms.

Time itself has passed judgment on the literature of the past. A few writers out of many thousands, a few works from hundreds of thousands, are part of world literature. Everyone has the names of such writers and works on the tip of the tongue: the *Divine Comedy* belongs not to Italy alone, nor *Don Quixote* to Spain. Alongside the world-famous works, numberless others are preserved, loved and respected—and continuously read—in their countries of origin without being known abroad. Shakespeare is part of world literature, but his great contemporary Marlowe belongs to English literature. In the same way Klopstock is merely German, Coleridge merely English, Slovacky merely Polish. As far as the world is concerned, they do not exist.

Moreover a difference is to be observed between premodern and modern times, since nowadays foreign languages are studied better and more frequently and the activity of translation has gained such an extraordinary momentum; in no other language do translations play so great a role as in German.

Apart from all that is lost in translation, it is incontestable that writers of different countries and languages occupy enormously different positions where their chances of obtaining worldwide fame, or even a moderate degree of recognition, are concerned. The most favorably situated are the French writers, although the French language occupies only the fifth rank in terms of extension. When a writer has succeeded in France, he is known throughout the world. English and Germans, who can count on an immense public if they are successful, take second place. It is only writers from these three nations who can hope to be read in the original by the most educated people of all nations.

Italian and Spanish writers are far less fortunate, though they may be read by a significant number of readers outside their native lands. Such is not the case for Russian writers, although the Russian population with its millions compensates for this.

But whoever writes in Finnish, Hungarian, Swedish, Danish, Dutch, Greek or the like is obviously poorly placed in the universal struggle for fame. In this competition he lacks the major weapon, a language—which is, for a writer, almost everything.

It is impossible to write anything of artistic value in a language other than one's own. On that, everyone agrees. "But what about translations?" someone may object. I confess to the heresy that sees in them nothing but a lamentable necessity. Translations leave out the linguistic artistry whereby the writer affirms himself, and the better and greater he is in his own language, the more he loses in translation.

The inescapable incompleteness of translations is the reason that an author of the sixth rank who writes in a widely spoken world language can easily become better known than a second-rank author whose language is spoken by no more than a few million. Anyone who knows the literatures of smaller and larger countries will readily concede this point, though the inhabitants of large countries are as a rule slow to believe it.

The only concession made is this: lyric poems are hard to translate, always lose a great deal by it, and normally the attempt to translate them is abandoned because the results are not worth while. Germans can well conceive that anyone who knows Goethe's poems only through a prose translation must find them unworthy of admiration. A Frenchman is incapable of imagining the verses of Victor Hugo and Leconte de Lisle translated into a foreign language. Most consider that in the case of prose works, not so much is lost in translation; but that is an error. The difficulty is still enormous, immense, even if less apparent than with poetry. The selection and resonance of words, the singularities of linguistic expression, all vanish. Translations are never replicas.

Even someone who, recalling certain artistically executed versions, holds translators in high esteem will not deny that writers of different origins are unequally favored in the pursuit of worldwide fame.

It has nonetheless been observed that some authors who, like Ibsen, write in a language of small compass have succeeded in making themselves known everywhere—some of them far lesser spirits than Ibsen. Is fame in the present, fame among one's contemporaries, decisive? Are the author and the work therefore likely to endure in world literature? Only an optimist could think so. World fame seems to me too poor a measure to be useful.

In the first place, some win it without deserving it in any way. Where their level coincides with the level of general culture or of common taste, and if they belong to a major people, it is easy for them to become universally known. Georges Ohnet is read everywhere.[2] And to capture general attention, such a writer must not merely be inoffensive, he need not directly cater to dominant prejudices; he can do so indirectly, as when he crudely and superficially counters a banal idea with a banal idea of his own, for example, if he takes up arms against royalist, clerical or aristocratic prejudices. One has seen writers without the least artistic education or sense of craft who became famous for attacking the greatest artists, poets, or thinkers of their time with obstinate smugness and spoke of them condescendingly as empty-headed or insane. This act makes an impression on the greatest mass in most countries, and the fellow-traveler too is received into world literature.

On the other hand, it seems often to be a matter of sheer chance that this or that author of the first rank dies without fame and remains unknown after his death.

I find examples ready to hand from the literature that I know best. Of all the writers of Denmark in the nineteenth century, only one, Hans Christian Andersen, has achieved world fame. This has caused much amazement in Denmark. Among us Andersen is thought of as one among many, nothing more. He does not stand with our greatest; in his own lifetime he was never thought of as belonging to the first or second class. Nor, I might add, even after his death. As a thinker he was inconsequential and never had an intellectual influence. He was viewed as a gifted, childlike creature, and this estimation was not incorrect. But nonetheless he belongs to world literature, for he wrote fairy tales that made their way everywhere through their general comprehensibility.

At least a dozen of his literary colleagues in Denmark were far more important as individuals and no less well equipped as poets or writers. But they have never been translated. Remaining untranslated, they became local celebrities instead, and were far more cherished, indeed deified, in their home country. Who, outside the Scandinavian North, knows the name of Poul Möller, who in Denmark is revered like a demigod? Who knows Johan Ludvig Heiberg, who defined good taste in Denmark and Norway in near-dictatorial fashion? Who knows Christian Winther, the greatest lyric poet in Denmark between the 1830s and 1850s, and who is still far more beloved, recited and revered than Andersen?

But my intention is to restrict myself to the truly great alone. Søren Kierkegaard, the greatest religious thinker of the Scandinavian North, is unknown in Europe. One would think that every paladin of Christianity in Europe would have to engage with him, as with Pascal some centuries ago; but he has no place in world literature. This is unfortunate for world literature, though it represents no great loss to the dead philosopher. It would be good if a few of his works such as *Sickness unto Death*, *Stages on Life's Way*, or *Practice in Christianity*, were known everywhere. No one knows them.

There is no point in closing one's eyes to the fact that most of humanity is dull, ignorant, of limited judgment. The best is inaccessible to them, the finest is incomprehensible. They follow the loud market-crier and the charismatic charlatan. They demand success and obey fashion. What pleases mankind in one's own time will not necessarily become a lasting part of world literature.

At present there are in Europe, as far as I know, no poets and hardly any writers of the first rank. The best are no match for the great dead: neither Kipling in England nor d'Annunzio in Italy. But in all probability they are far more famous than the greatest of their predecessors ever were.

Something unprecedented has arisen in our time, precisely because writers see before them the possibility of being known and read throughout the whole world. People begin to write for an invisible, abstract public, and this does damage to literary production. Emile Zola provides an example. His great series of novels, *Les Rougon-Macquart*, was written for the French and is therefore carefully and concretely executed. His trilogy *Lourdes, Rome, Paris*, composed after he had achieved great fame, was written for the whole world, and for this reason is far more abstract than before. In this trilogy he wrote as Sarah Bernhardt acts—whether she is performing in Peru or in Chicago.[3] If a writer wants to have a powerful effect, he must have his surroundings before his eyes, he must be active there where he was born, he must write for his compatriots, whose stage of development he knows well. Whatever is written for the whole world sacrifices strength and vigor for the sake of universal comprehensibility, it no longer carries the flavor of the soil. If it were not so odious to name them, I could mention several great writers who, in the process of becoming first local, then worldwide celebrities, have done homage to an alien and ordinary taste as they had once embraced the taste of their own people. There is something dangerous in the courting of world fame and world literature.

On the other hand, it is obvious that one should not write for those who live in the same street or the same city as oneself, as polemical writers in particular try to do.

When Goethe coined the term "world literature," humanism and cosmopolitanism were still ideas that everyone held in honor. In the last years of the nineteenth century, an ever stronger and more jealous national sentiment has caused these ideas to recede almost everywhere. Today literature is becoming more and more national. But I do not believe that nationality and cosmopolitanism are incompatible. The world literature of the future will be all the more interesting, the more strongly its national stamp is pronounced and the more distinctive it is, even if, as art, it also has its international side; for that which is written directly for the world will hardly appear as a work of art. Truly, the work of art is a fortress, not an open city.

Notes

1. First published as "Weltliteratur" in the German journal *Das litterarische Echo* 2:1 (1899). Translated by Haun Saussy.

2. Ohnet (1848–1918) was a popular French novelist who rejected the realism that Brandes favored; he wrote a series of sentimental, action-packed novels in the 1880s under the overall title *Les Batailles de la vie* (Life's battles).

3. French actress Sarah Bernhardt (1844–1923) began her career in classical roles in Paris, but by the 1880s she had become an international celebrity for her performances on tour, often in popular melodramas.

8

From *What Is Comparative Literature?*[1] (1903)

Charles Mills Gayley

Charles Mills Gayley (1858–1932) was an influential figure for the establishment of comparative literature in the United States at the turn of the twentieth century. Born in China, the son of Irish American Presbyterian missionaries, he was raised in Ireland, then completed his primary and secondary education in England and his university degree at the University of Michigan. His earliest memory, according to his biographer, was of standing with a Chinese nurse in a courtyard and looking through a window upon his dead father, a victim of cholera. Best known during his lifetime for his scholarship on English literature and for his reform of the English curriculum, first at the University of Michigan and then at the University of California at Berkeley, he was also a vigorous proponent of the systematizing and scientific approach to comparative literature.

In 1894, he proposed the creation of a collaborative Society of Comparative Literature, each of whose members "should devote himself to the study of a given type or movement in a literature with which he is specially, and at first hand, familiar," gradually building a massive database of analysis from which future generations could discern the laws of genre and of literary evolution. "Of course the labor is arduous, and the limit undefined," Gayley allowed, but in time great results would be achieved: "The members of this Society of Comparative literature must be hewers of wood and drawers of water. Even though they cannot hope to see the completion of a temple of criticism, they may have the joy of construction: the reward of the philologist."[2]

Gayley expanded on his ideas in his programmatic 1903 essay on Comparative Literature, given here, which was published for a general highbrow audience in *The Atlantic Monthly*. In this essay he provides a concise and comprehensive overview of the dominant trends in the field over the nineteenth century and earlier. Like Posnett but with a wider disciplinary base, he advocates a "new science of literature" that would build on an array of modern disciplines (history, psychology, linguistics, and especially anthropology) and inductively derive the general laws of literature. Vast and comprehensive, this scientific endeavor requires a collaborative approach that Gayley hoped would be organized by a society of comparative literature. History, particularly an idea of uniform historical development or growth, is central to Gayley's literary science, as is his insistence that the field of comparative literature should be geographically inclusive and encompass all verbal expression "wherever found," including the oral expression of nonliterate peoples. The positivist and systematic approach to comparative literature was overtaken by other intellectual currents after the first European war and seemed outdated for most of the twentieth century. It has, however, gained a new purchase in the first decade of the twenty-first century in renewed attention to systematizing approaches for comparative literature developed in the work of scholars such as Franco Moretti and Pascale Casanova.

Some ten years ago, I made bold to publish a plea for the formation of a Society of Comparative Literature; and to call attention to the fact that the work which such a society might perform had not been undertaken by any English or American organization, or by any periodical or series of publications in the English language. I was then of the opinion, which I still hold, that the principles of literature and of criticism are not to be discovered in aesthetic theory alone, but in a theory which both impels and is corrected by scientific inquiry. No individual can gather from our many literatures the materials necessary for an induction to the characteristics of even one literary type; but an association, each member of which should devote himself to the study of a given type, species, movement, or theme, with which he was specially and at first hand familiar, might with some degree of adequacy prosecute a comparative investigation into the nature of literature, part by part. Thus, gradually, wherever the type or movement had existed, its quality and history might be observed. And in time, by systematization of results, scholarship might attain to the common, and probably some of the essential, characteristics of classified phenomena, to some of the laws actually governing the origin, growth, and differentiation of one and another of the component literary factors and kinds. A basis would correspondingly be laid for criticism not in the practice of one nationality or school, nor in aesthetics of sporadic theory, otherwise interesting and profitable enough, but in the common qualities of literature, scientifically determined. To adopt, as universal, canons of criticism constructed upon particular premises—by Boileau or Vida, Puttenham, Sidney, or Corneille, or even Lessing and Aristotle, and to apply them to types, or varieties of type, movement, or theme, with which these masters were unacquainted, is illogical, and therefore unhistorical. And still, that is precisely what the world of literary dictators persists in doing. *Alle Theorie ist grau.*[3] The principles of the drama cannot be derived from consideration of the Greek drama alone, nor of European drama, but of all drama, wherever found, European, Peruvian, Chinese; among aboriginal as well as among civilized peoples; and in all stages of its history. From such comparative formulation of results proceed the only trustworthy canons for that kind of composition; some of them general, some dependent upon conditions historically differenced. So also with the nature and laws of other types, movements or moods, forms or themes, and ultimately of literature as a unit. Our current aesthetic canons of judgment, based upon psychological and speculative premises that sometimes by accident fit the case, but more frequently upon historical inexperience, might thus be renovated and widened with the process of scientific knowledge.

That dream seems now in a fair way to be realized. The society is yet to be founded; but the periodical is on its feet. And it was in prospect of its first appearance that I asked myself some months ago, what this term "Comparative Literature" might now mean to me; and answered it in the manner that follows. Imperfect as the answer may be, it is possibly of interest, if for no other reason, that it makes a different approach to a subject which since then Professor Woodberry has discussed in the *Journal of Comparative Literature*.[4] To his significant and poetic utterance, I shall accordingly in due season recur.

What, then, is "Comparative Literature"? Of the name itself, I must say that I know of no occurrence in English earlier than 1886, when we find it used for the comparative study of literature, in the title of an interesting and suggestive volume by Professor H. M. Posnett.[5] The designation had apparently been coined in emulation of such nomenclatures as the *Vergleichende*

Grammatik of Bopp, or Comparative Anatomy, Comparative Physiology, Comparative Politics. If it had been so constructed as to convey the idea of a discipline or method, there would have been no fault to find. Before Posnett's book appeared, Carriere and others in Germany had spoken properly enough of *Vergleichende Literaturgeschichte*; and the French and Italians, not only of the comparative method or discipline, *l'histoire comparée des littératures, la storia comparata,* or, from the literary avenue of approach, *la littérature comparée, letteratura comparata.* At Turin and Genoa, the study had been listed under such captions long before the English misnomer was coined. Misnomer it, of course, is; for to speak of a comparative object is absurd. But since the name has some show of asserting itself, we may as well postpone consideration of a better, till we have more fully determined what the study involved, no matter how called, is ordinarily understood to be.

[Gayley goes on to survey the definitions offered by Posnett and others before him, as well as the first courses in the subject given in Europe and the United States. He then continues]:

This survey might be extended to the practice of our American philological journals and associations. The academic conception will, however, be found to be as I have stated it: Comparative Literature works in the history of national as well as of international conditions, it employs, more or less prominently, the comparative method, logical and historical, it presupposes, and results in, a conception of literature as a solidarity, and it seeks to formulate and substantiate a theory of literary development whether by evolution or permutation, in movements, types, and themes. With these main considerations it is but natural that scholars should associate the attempt to verify and systematize the characteristics common to literature in its various manifestations wherever found; to come by induction, for instance, at the *eidographic* or generic qualities of poetry,—the characteristics of the drama, epic, or lyric; at the *dynamic* qualities, those which characterize and differentiate the main literary movements, such as the classical and romantic; and at the *thematic,* the causes of persistence and modification in the history of vital subjects, situations, and plots. As to the growth, or development, of literature our survey shows that two distinct doctrines contend for acceptance: one, by evolution, which is an attempt to interpret literary processes in accordance with biological laws; the other, by what I prefer to call permutation. Since literature like its material, language, is not an organism, but a resultant medium, both product and expression of the society whence it springs, the former theory must be still in doubt. It can certainly not be available otherwise than metaphorically unless it be substantiated by just such methods—comparative and scientific—as those of which we have spoken.

How much of this is new, of the nineteenth century, for instance? Very little in theory; much, and that important, in discipline and fact. The *solidarity of literature* was long ago announced by Bacon, who in his *Advancement of Learning* says, "As the proficience of learning consisteth much in the orders and institutions of universities in the same states and kingdoms, so it would be yet more advanced if there were more intelligence mutual between the universities of Europe than there now is. . . . And surely as nature createth brotherhoods in families, and arts mechanical contract brotherhoods in communities, and the anointment of God superinduceth a brotherhood in kings and bishops, so in like manner there cannot but be a *fraternity in learning and illumination,* relating to that paternity which is attributed to God who is called the Father of illuminations or lights."[6] Bacon was the founder, in England, of that species of literary history which, as soon as national literatures were placed in comparison, could not but result in the conception of literary unity. He was our first distinguished advocate of the genetic method of critical research: the procedure by cause and effect to movement, influence, relation, change, decay, revival; and he emphasized the elasticity of literary forms and types,—ideas all essential to the understanding of literature as a growth. But he was not the only forerunner of the present movement. In one way or another the solidarity of literature, the theories of permutation or of evolution, sometimes crudely, sometimes with keen scientific insight, were anticipated by Englishmen, Germans, Frenchmen, Italians of note all the way from Dante, Scaliger, and Sidney down. In England, Webbe, Puttenham, and Meres, Ben Jonson, Edmund Bolton, prepared for Bacon; and Bacon was well followed by the Earl of Stirling (whose *Anacrisis* furnishes hints by the score for the comparative method of literary research), by Davenant in his *Preface to Gondibert,* by Cowley (a fine advocate of the analytical and historical methods); and by our prince of criticism, the perspicacious Dryden, who in his *Heads of an Answer to Rymer* insists upon a standard of literary judgment at once historical and logical, upon the recognition of development in literary types, the principles of *milieu* and national variety, and the adoption accordingly of criteria that shall allow for the diversity and gradual modification of literary conditions. Most worthy, too, of recognition which, I think, he has never fully obtained, is John Dennis; for in his *Remarks upon Blackmore's Prince Arthur* and in his *Advancement and Reformation of Modern Poetry* he more clearly than any predecessor foreshadows the theories of the early and middle nineteenth century concerning the influence of religious ideals in the permutations of literature. Shaftesbury, Bentley, Swift, the Wartons, Hurd, Addison, Hallam, Carlyle, and De Quincey,—it was not necessary that any of these should defer his birth till 1900 to appreciate what the comparative study of literature, in one or more of its phases, meant.

In Germany, Herder and Schiller may have been the first, as Professor Wetz has said, to give the science a comprehensive foundation. They, however, owed not a little to Bodmer and Breitinger and others of the Swiss school of 1740, to the *Æsthetica* of Baumgarten of 1750, and to Winckelmann's application of the historical method to the study of fine art. When we come down the line and add the contributions of Goethe, Richter, the Schlegels to literary science, and then of Gervinus, Boeckh, Paul, and Elze, we begin to wonder what there is left of system for the students of Comparative Literature to devise.

In France, likewise, there have been approaches to one or another side of the idea and discipline from the *Défense* of Joachim du Bellay, 1549, and the *Poetics* of Scaliger (one of the greatest comparers of literary history) down. The *Recueil* of Claude Fauchet, 1581, Pasquier's treatise on the Pléiade, Mairet's preface to *Sylvanire,* the early battles of Corneille with the Academy and Chapelain, all illustrate phases of this slowly maturing method of study. Rapin's *Poëtes Anciens et Modernes,* of 1674, aims not only to adapt Aristotle's *Poetics* to modern practice, but to teach the moderns that certain qualities of poetry, no matter what the conditions of the age, endure. And the age felt Rapin, especially the England of the age,—Dryden and his school. The scientific importance of literary history and the advantages of the comparative method in criticism were clearly apprehended by Saint-Evremond as early as by Rapin. Desmarets de Saint Sorlin had advanced to a conception of poetry as an institutional mouthpiece for society and religion as far back as 1657,—but nine years after Davenant's famous *Preface* on the same theory, and fully two hundred before its more distinguished elaboration by Carriere. That Perrault, Fontenelle, the Daciers, La Fontaine, Fénelon, indeed, and the younger heroes of the Battle of the Books, should by some be supposed to be the founders of the comparative method is extremely odd: they were anticipated not only by several whom I have mentioned and by the Pléiade in France, but by the *Areopagus* in England as well. Why multiply examples? I believe that without difficulty one could indicate a forerunner earlier than 1830 for every doctrine or ideal comprised to-day under the term Comparative Literature, except the theory of evolution on the Darwinian principle,—and for much of the method. Dubos, Batteux, Voltaire, Rousseau, Diderot, La Harpe, Madame de Staël, Chateaubriand, Ginguené, Baour-Lormian, Stendhal, Hugo,

Villemain,—a host of prophets before the immortal Sainte-Beuve and those Monday chats that gathered up in method and ideal all that was worth gathering and gave the impetus to most of the theory and method current to-day!

This cloud of witnesses is not produced, however, to discredit, but to confirm the scope and hope of the so-called Comparative Literature of to-day. They testify to the need of a science in the nature of things. They perform their service by anticipations in detail of a discipline that could not be designated a science until the sciences propaedeutic[7] thereto had been developed. The experimental stage of literary theory has by its antiquity, its persistence, and its faith, given proof of the naturalness and worth of the science that was to follow when experience should be ripe. Experimental efforts accomplished this much at least: they marked out the field,— the relativity of literature; they shadowed the substance and significance of the ideal of literary solidarity, and they foreshadowed that of spiritual community; they apprehended a comparative method of procedure, and applied it to some few objects of investigation, to the history of sources, for instance, and of themes; and to artistic and literary analogies with a view to inductive canons of criticism. But, on the other hand, the method as conceived was, in the nature of the case, but imperfectly scientific; and the objects of its application, the determination of literary types, their reality and characteristics, and the study of literary conditions antecedent and environing, were but vaguely comprehended. The facts were insufficient. As to a growth of literature, our earlier scholars utterly failed to elaborate a theory, failed generally to surmise; and that being so, a study of movements, national or international, and the moods that underlie them, was incapable of prosecution. How could they build a science the social and psychological foundations of which were not yet established?

Advances in historical method, in psychological, sociological, linguistic, and ethnological research have, now, furnished the discipline with an instrument unknown to its forebearers in critical procedure; and with fresh and rich materials for illumination from without. The conception of literature as a unit is no longer hypothetical; the comparison of national histories has proved it. The idea of a process by evolution may be unproved; but that some process, as by permutation, must obtain is recognized. We no longer look upon the poet as inspired. Literature develops with the entity which produces it,—the common social need and faculty of expression; and it varies according to *differentiae* of racial, physiographic, and social conditions, and of the inherited or acquired characteristics of which the individual author is constituted. The science of its production must analyze its component factors and determine the laws by which they operate. By a constant factor are fixed the only possible moulds or channels of expression, and, therefore, the integral and primary types, as, for instance, within the realm of poetry, the lyric, narrative, and dramatic. By the presence of other factors both inconstant, these types are themselves liable to modification. I refer, of course, to environment, that is to say, to the antecedent and contemporary condition of thought, social tendency, and artistic fashion; and to the associational congeries called the author. So far as physiological and psychological modes of expression may be submitted to objective and historical analysis, so far as the surrounding conditions which directly or indirectly affect the art in which the author works, and the work of the author in that art, may be inductively studied, and their nature interpreted and registered in relation to other products of society, such as language, religion, and government, so far is the discipline of which we speak legitimately scientific. And as rapidly as experimental psychology, anthropology, ethnology, or the history of art in general, prove their right to scientific recognition, they become instruments for the comparative investigation of the social phenomenon called literature. It is thus that the literary science, just now called Comparative Literature, improves upon the efforts of the former stylistic or poetics, largely traditional or speculative, and displaces the capricious matching of authors, the static or provincial view of history, and the appraisement lacking atmosphere.

While this science must exclude from the object under consideration the purely subjective element, and the speculative or so-called "judicial" *(me judice)* method from criticism and history, it need not ignore or disregard the unexplained quantity,—the imaginative. Its aim will be to explore the hitherto unexplained in the light of historical sequence and scientific cause and effect, physical, biological, psychological, or anthropological, to reduce the apparently unreasonable or magical element, and so to leave continually less to be treated in the old-fashioned inspirational or ecstatic manner. We shall simply cease to confound the science with the art. We no longer refer history to Clio, law to the tables of the Mount, or medicine to the Apollo-born sage of Epidaurus; but while we acknowledge the science, we none the less respect the genius,—the Herodotus, or Marshall, or Lorenz. Not only does literary science take up into itself the best methods that literary history has so far devised,—the analytical-critical of Dryden and Hegel and Taine, the psychological and cultural of Schiller, as expressed in his matchless essay on poetry naive and sentimental, and of Goethe in his "Deutsche Baukunst" and his *Dichtung und Wahrheit,* and the efforts at a comparative discipline exerted by Sainte-Beuve and Arnold,—it avails itself, as I have said, of the results, and so far as possible of the methods, of the sciences that most directly contribute to the comprehension of man the producer; it partly bases and partly patterns its procedure upon those other records of human consciousness, the histories of ethics and religion and society; it gathers hints from theories not yet scientific, but historically on the way,—theories of art in general, aesthetic, physiological, and psychological, or even speculative, if, as in the case of Winckelmann, the speculation be founded upon induction from facts historically considered. The more immediate advantages of the prosecution of literary research in such a way as this are an ever increasing knowledge of the factors that enter into world-literature and determine its growth,—its reasons, conditions, movements, and tendencies, in short, its laws; and a poetics capable not only of detecting the historical but also of appreciating the social accent in what is foreign and too often despised, or contemporary and too often overpraised if not ignored. The new science of literature will in turn throw light upon that which gave it birth; it will prove an index to the evolution of soul in the individual and in society; it will interpret that sphinx, national consciousness or the spirit of the race, or, mayhap, destroy it. It will in one case and in all assist a science of comparative ethics.

This is what Comparative Literature means to me. Before I attempt to show what the science should be called, let us see what it means to the editors of the new periodical. In his scholarly and poetic editorial in the first number of the *Journal of Comparative Literature,* Professor Woodberry, treating of what the subject already is, announces the method, the field, the theory of literary community substantially as we have already conceived them; save that under the objects of comparative investigation he does not explicitly include literary movements, and that in the category of forms he appears to assimilate the fundamental and generic modes of expression, lyric, drama, etc. with the extrinsic and more or less conventional and interchangeable trappings such as alliteration and rhyme. He fails consequently to attach to a particular phase, the comparative study of literary types or modes, the significance which, in my opinion, it possesses. That, however, matters little. His forecast of the course of the sciences is inspiring. "The study of forms," he says, "should result in a canon of criticism, which would mean a new and greater classicism; . . . the study of themes should reveal temperamentally, as form does structurally, the nature of the soul." "It is in temperament," he continues, "in moods, that romanticism, which is the life of all literature, has its dwelling-place. To disclose the necessary forms, the vital moods of the beautiful soul, is the far goal of our effort—to help in this, in the bringing of those spiritual unities in which human destiny is accomplished." With this the genuine student of literary science must agree. And yet it may strike him as peculiar, that in the outlook over literary theory the possibility of growth appears to be ignored. The omission can hardly be accidental. I take it to indicate non-acceptance of a theory of evolution such as Brunetière's, however, rather than rejection of all theory of development. Movements are the corollaries of the "vital moods in which is the life of literature"; and the life of literature changes with the gradual deepening and widening of the "beautiful soul" individual, racial, or integrally human. I find, therefore, a testimony to our theory of literary permutation in Professor Woodberry's reticence. I rejoice also to note his insistence upon a matter of method apparently minor but of importance to our comprehension of the discipline, namely, that the study of international relations and influences is but one of the objects of Comparative Literature: the study of a single literature may be just as scientifically comparative if it seeks the reason and law of the literature in the psychology of the race or of humanity.

Now what shall this science be called, since the name which it has is malformed and misleading? If it were not for traditional prejudice, the term stylistic should be recognized as of scientific quality, and it should cover the history as well as the theory of all kinds of writing. According to the older nomenclature, the individuality and the purpose of the author, the quality of his thought and the objective characteristics of literary species and form, are, all of them, factors of *style*. Elze, Boeckh, Maas, and others arrange the matter thus: Style is the form and method of expression in language. Stylistic is the general theory of style, and this general theory divides itself naturally into the theory of prose style or rhetoric and the theory of poetic style or poetics. I am not going to propose "stylistic." The old stylistic is limited by tradition, by its speculative quality, and by that well-worn and slippery dictum of Buffon,—style is of the individual. What is called Comparative Literature has, on the other hand, brought to the study of all kinds of writing a scientific objectivity and the historical method. It has taken up into itself what is objective and historical of the older stylistic: it aims to reject or confirm former theories but on purely scientific grounds. It is the transition from stylistic to a science of literature which shall still find room for aesthetics, but for aesthetics properly so called, developed, checked, and corrected by scientific procedure and by history.

Without our modern psychology, anthropology, linguistics, and the comparative sciences of society, religion, and art, literature could be studied neither in relation to its antecedents nor to its components. Otherwise our study would long ago have been known as comparative philology, a name improperly usurped by a younger branch of the philological discipline. Such indeed is the name by which Professor Whitney would have called the comparative study of the literatures of different countries had the discipline been prosecuted as a science when he wrote. Comparative Literature is a reaffirmation of that aspect of philology—the literary—which, both because it was eclipsed by, and dependent upon, the development of linguistics, has long ceased to be regarded as philology at all; save in Germany, where philological seminars have dealt not only with the phonology and history of language as they asserted themselves, but also as of old with whatever concerns the literary side of language as an expression of the national, or more broadly human spirit. Since all study of origins and growth, whether of one phenomenon or more than one, must be comparative if scientifically conducted, it is not necessary to characterize the literary science, of which we speak, by that particular adjective. More methods than the comparative enter into it, and it is more than a method: it is a theory of relativity and of growth; and its material is vertically as well as horizontally disposed. The Comparative Literature of to-day, based upon the sciences of which I have spoken and conducted in the scientific method, is literary philology,—nothing more nor less; it stands over against linguistic philology or glottology, and it deals genetically, historically, and comparatively with literature as a solidarity and as a product of the social individual, whether the point of view be national or universal. We welcome academic departments and journals, devoted to its interests, but literary philology is not and cannot be measured by the scope and effort of a distinct academic department, or of a specific journal, however excellent the latter, like this to which we wish Godspeed, may be. The new discipline is already the property and method of all scientific research in all literatures, ancient or modern, not only in their common but in their individual relations to the social spirit in which they live and move and have their being. The more we develop what now is called Comparative Literature, the more rapidly will each literature in turn seek its explanation in Literary Philology.

Notes

1. From the *Atlantic Monthly* 92 (1903), 56–68; reprinted in Hans-Joachim Schultz and Phillip H. Rhein, *Comparative Literature: The Early Years* (Chapel Hill: University of North Carolina Press, 1973), 79–105.
2. "A Society of Comparative Literature," *The Dial,* August 1, 1894, 57.

3. "All theory is grey."

4. George E. Woodberry, "Editorial." *Journal of Comparative Literature* 1 (1903), 3–9. Reprinted in Schultz and Rhein, *Comparative Literature,* 207–14.

5. See the selection from Posnett's *Comparative Literature,* chapter 6 in this volume.

6. Citing *The Proficience and Advancement of Learning* (1605) by the English statesman, philosopher, and scientist Sir Francis Bacon.

7. Preparatory.

PART TWO

The Years of Crisis

9

The Epic and the Novel[1] (1916)

Georg Lukács

Born in Budapest in 1885 to a German Jewish family, Georg (or György) Lukács spent his life mediating between the political and literary cultures of Eastern, Central, and Western Europe. The young Lukács became a socialist while still a teenager, with a keen interest in contemporary literature and drama, and spent several years in a modern theater group before going to Berlin and Heidelberg to study philosophy and aesthetics. He returned to Budapest in 1915 and founded a progressive literary circle, whose members debated the state of the world amid the crisis of the First World War. An outgrowth of these discussions, his book *The Theory of the Novel* (1916) is a foundational work for the historical grounding of literary form.

Elaborating a homology between forms of social life and literary genres, Lukács argues that the European novel is the literary form proper to an alienated modern social life, in a world no longer suffused with meaning or complete unto itself as was the world of epic. The novel carries on the epic's function in some ways, but instead of reflecting the "rounded totality" of immanent meaning, it strives to compensate for the absence of such meaning. The novel is thus at once a product of the human being's estrangement from society and a creative attempt to construct or reveal the lost totality. Ranging across the entire extent of the European tradition, from ancient Greek epic and tragedy to German lyric and to the Russian novel, Lukács proceeds quasi-associatively, according to what he calls the "method of abstract synthesis." The resulting lyrical abstraction of his prose makes for slow but rewarding reading, as will be seen in the section of the book given here.

With its object of historicizing aesthetic categories and in its concern with the unification of matter and spirit, *The Theory of the Novel* avowedly follows and also significantly advances the project of G.W.F. Hegel's *Aesthetics*. Lukács later disclaimed the idealist dimensions of *The Theory of the Novel* as reactionary when he turned decisively to Marxism and Bolshevism in his intellectual and political activities at the end of the First World War. He subsequently wrote a highly influential work of political theory, *History and Class Consciousness* (1920), in which he developed the theory of "reification." The most distinguished and prolific Marxist literary critic of his time, he wrote books on individual writers and thinkers (including Hegel, Marx, Nietzsche, Lenin, Dostoevsky, and Thomas Mann) and also important comparative studies focused on German, French, English, and Russian literature. He wrote extensively on realism in such works as *Studies in European Realism* (1948) and *The Historical Novel* (1955), polemicizing against modernist experiments with form and arguing for the value of an intimate linking of literary realism and social progress. The method and insights of *The Theory of the Novel* continue to inspire and inform materialist and historicizing approaches to the modern novel, from Bakhtin to Moretti and many others.

The epic and the novel, these two major forms of great epic literature, differ from one another not by their authors' fundamental intentions but by the given historico-philosophical realities with which the authors were confronted. The novel is the epic of an age in which the extensive totality of life is no longer directly given, in which the immanence of meaning in life has become a problem, yet which still thinks in terms of totality. It would be superficial—a matter of a mere artistic technicality—to look for the only and decisive genre-defining criterion in the question of whether a work is written in verse or prose.

Verse is not an ultimate constituent either of the epic or of tragedy, although it is indeed a profound symptom by which the true nature of these forms is most truly and genuinely revealed. Tragic verse is sharp and hard, it isolates, it creates distance. It clothes the heroes in the full depth of their solitude, which is born of the form itself; it does not allow of any relationships between them except those of struggle and annihilation; its lyricism can contain notes of despair or excitement about the road yet to be travelled and its ending, it can show glimpses of the abyss over which the essential is suspended, but a purely human understanding between the tragic characters' souls will never break through, as it sometimes does in prose; the despair will never turn into elegy, nor the excitement into a longing for lost heights; the soul can never seek to plumb its own depths with psychologistic vanity, nor admire itself in the mirror of its own profundity.

Dramatic verse, as Schiller wrote to Goethe, reveals whatever triviality there may be in the artistic invention: it has a specific sharpness, a gravity all its own, in face of which nothing that is merely lifelike—which is to say nothing that is dramatically trivial—can survive: if the artist's creative mentality has anything trivial about it, the contrast between the weight of the language and that of the content will betray him.

Epic verse, too, creates distances, but in the sphere of the epic (which is the sphere of life) distance means happiness and lightness, a loosening of the bonds that tie men and objects to the ground, a lifting of the heaviness, the dullness, which are integral to life and which are dispersed only in scattered happy moments. The created distances of epic verse transform such moments into the true level of life. And so the effect of verse is here the opposite just because its immediate consequence—that of abolishing triviality and coming closer to the essence—is the same. Heaviness is trivial in the sphere of life—the epic—just as lightness is trivial in tragedy. An objective guarantee that the complete removal of everything lifelike does not mean an empty abstraction from life but the becoming essence, can only be given the consistency with which these unlifelike forms are created; only if they are incomparably more fulfilled, more rounded, more fraught with substance than we could ever dream of in real life, can it be said that tragic stylisation has been successfully achieved. Everything light or pallid (which of course has nothing to do with the banal concept of unlifelikeness) reveals the absence of a normative tragic intention and so demonstrates the triviality of the work, whatever the psychological subtlety and/or lyrical delicacy of its parts.

In life, however, heaviness means the absence of present meaning, a hopeless entanglement in senseless casual connections, a withered sterile existence too close to the earth and too far from heaven, a plodding on, an inability to liberate oneself from the bonds of sheer brutal materiality, everything that, for the finest immanent forces of life, represents a challenge which must be constantly overcome—it is, in terms of formal value judgement, triviality. A pre-stabilised harmony decrees that epic verse should sing of the blessedly existent totality of life; the pre-poetic process of embracing all life in a mythology had liberated existence from all trivial heaviness; in Homer, the spring buds were only just opening, ready to blossom. Verse itself, however, can only tentatively encourage the bud to open; verse can only weave a garland of freedom round something that has already been liberated from all fetters. If the author's action consists in disclosing buried meaning, if his heroes must first break out of their prisons and, in desperate struggles or long, wearisome wanderings, attain the home of their dreams— their freedom from terrestrial gravity—then the power of verse, which can spread a carpet of flowers over the chasm, is not sufficient to build a practicable road across it. The lightness of great epic literature is only the concretely immanent Utopia of the historical hour, and the form-giving detachment which verse as a vehicle confers upon whatever it carries must, therefore, rob the epic of its great totality, its subjectlessness, and transform it into an idyll or a piece of playful lyricism. The lightness of great epic literature is a positive value and a reality-creating force only if the restraining bonds have really been thrown off. Great epic literature is never the result of men forgetting their enslavement in the lovely play of a liberated imagination or in tranquil retirement to happy isles not to be found on the map of this world of trivial attachment. In times to which such lightness is no longer given, verse is banished from the great epic, or else it transforms itself, unexpectedly and unintentionally, into lyric verse. Only prose can then encompass the suffering and the laurels, the struggle and the crown, with equal power; only its unfettered plasticity and its non-rhythmic rigour can, with equal power, embrace the fetters and the freedom, the given heaviness and the conquered lightness of a world henceforth immanently radiant with found meaning. It is no accident that the disintegration of a reality-become-song led, in Cervantes' prose, to the sorrowful lightness of a great epic, whereas the serene dance of Ariosto's verse remained mere lyrical play; it is no accident that Goethe, the epic poet, poured his idylls into the mould of verse but chose prose for the totality of his *Meister* (master) novel. In the world of distances, all epic verse turns into lyric poetry (*Don Juan* and *Onegin*, although written in verse, belong to the company of the great humorous novels), for, in verse, everything hidden becomes manifest, and the swift flight of verse makes the distance over which prose travels with its deliberate pace as it gradually approaches meaning appear naked, mocked, trampled, or merely a forgotten dream.

Dante's verse, too, is not lyrical although it is more lyrical than Homer's; it intensifies and concentrates the ballad tone into an epic one. The immanence of the meaning of life is present and existent in Dante's world, but only in the beyond: it is the perfect immanence of the transcendent.

Distance in the ordinary world of life is extended to the point where it cannot be overcome, but beyond that world every lost wanderer finds the home that has awaited him since all eternity; every solitary voice that falls silent on earth is there awaited by a chorus that takes it up, carries it towards harmony and, through it, becomes harmony itself.

The world of distances lies sprawling and chaotic beneath the radiant celestial rose of sense made sensuous; it is visible and undisguised at every moment. Every inhabitant of that home in the beyond has come from this world, each is bound to it by the indissoluble force of destiny, but each recognises it, sees it in its fragility and heaviness, only when he has travelled to the end of his path thereby made meaningful; every figure sings of its isolated destiny, the isolated event in which its apportioned lot was made manifest: a ballad. And just as the totality of the transcendent world-structure is the pre-determined sense-giving, all-embracing *a priori* of each individual destiny, so the increasing comprehension of this edifice, its structure and its beauty—the great experience of Dante the traveller—envelops everything in the unity of its meaning, now revealed. Dante's insight transforms the individual into a component of the whole, and so the ballads become epic songs. The meaning of this world becomes distanceless, visible and immanent only in the beyond. Totality, in this world, is bound to be a fragile or merely a longed-for one: the verse passages in Wolfram von Eschenbach or Gottfried von Strassburg are only lyrical ornaments to their novels,[2] and the ballad quality of the *Song of the Nibelungs* can be disguised by compositional means, but cannot be rounded so that it achieves world-embracing totality.

The epic gives form to a totality of life that is rounded from within; the novel seeks, by giving form, to uncover and construct the concealed totality of life. The given structure of the object (i.e. the search, which is only a way of expressing the subject's recognition that neither objective life nor its relationship to the subject is spontaneously harmonious in itself) supplies an indication of the form-giving intention. All the fissures and rents which are inherent in the historical situation must be drawn into the form-giving process and cannot nor should be disguised by compositional means. Thus the fundamental form-determining intention of the novel is objectivised as the psychology of the novel's heroes: they are seekers. The simple fact of seeking implies that neither the goals nor the way leading to them can be directly given, or else that, if they are given in a psychologically direct and solid manner, this is not evidence of really existent relations or ethical necessities but only of a psychological fact to which nothing in the world of objects or norms need necessarily correspond. To put it another way, this "givenness" may be crime or madness; the boundaries which separate crime from acclaimed heroism and madness from life-mastering wisdom are tentative, purely psychological ones, although at the end, when the aberration makes itself terribly manifest and clear, there is no longer any confusion.

In this sense, the epic and the tragedy know neither crime nor madness. What the customary concepts of everyday life call crime is, for them, either not there at all, or it is nothing other than the point, symbolically fixed and sensually perceptible from afar, at which the soul's relationship to its destiny, the vehicle of its metaphysical homesickness, becomes visible. The epic world is either a purely childlike one in which the transgression of stable, traditional norms has to entail vengeance which again must be avenged *ad infinitum,* or else it is the perfect theodicy in which crime and punishment lie in the scales of world justice as equal, mutually homogeneous weights.

In tragedy, crime is either nothing at all or a symbol—it is either a mere element of the action, demanded and determined by technical laws, or it is the breaking down of forms on this side of the essence, it is the entrance through which the soul comes into its own. Of madness the epic knows nothing, unless it be the generally incomprehensible language of a superworld that possesses no other means of expression. In non-problematic tragedy, madness can be the symbolic expression of an end, equivalent to physical death or to the living death of a soul consumed by the essential fire of selfhood. For crime and madness are objectivations of transcendental homelessness—the homelessness of an action in the human order of social relations, the homelessness of a soul in the ideal order of a supra-personal system of values. Every form is the resolution of a fundamental dissonance of existence; every form restores the absurd to its proper place as the vehicle, the necessary condition of meaning. When the peak of absurdity, the futility of genuine and profound human aspirations, or the possibility of the ultimate nothingness of man has to be absorbed into literary form as a basic vehicular fact, and when what is in itself absurd has to be explained and analysed and, consequently, recognised as being irreducibly *there,* then, although some streams within such a form may flow into a sea of fulfilment, the absence of any manifest aim, the determining lack of direction of life as a whole, must be the basic *a priori* constituent, the fundamental structural element of the characters and events within it.

Where no aims are directly given, the structures which the soul, in the process of *becoming-man,* encounters as the arena and sub-stratum of its activity among men lose their obvious roots in supra-personal ideal necessities; they are simply existent, perhaps powerful, perhaps frail, but they neither carry the consecration of the absolute within them nor are they the natural containers for the overflowing inferiority of the soul. They form the world of convention, a world from whose all-embracing power only the innermost recesses of the soul are exempt, a world which is present everywhere in a multiplicity of forms too complex for understanding. Its strict laws, both in becoming and in being, are necessarily evident to the cognisant subject, but despite its regularity, it is a world that does not offer itself either as meaning to the aim-seeking subject or as matter, in sensuous immediacy, to the active subject. It is a second nature, and, like nature (first nature), it is determinable only as the embodiment of recognised but senseless necessities and therefore it is incomprehensible, unknowable in its real substance. Yet for creative literature substance alone has existence and only substances which are profoundly homogeneous with one another can enter into the righting union of reciprocal compositional relationships.

Lyric poetry can ignore the phenomenalisation of the first nature and can create a protean mythology of substantial subjectivity out of the constitutive strength of its ignorance. In lyric poetry, only the great moment exists, the moment at which the meaningful unity of nature and soul or their meaningful divorce, the necessary and affirmed loneliness of the soul becomes eternal. At the lyrical moment the purest interiority of the soul, set apart from duration without choice, lifted above the obscurely determined multiplicity of things, solidifies into substance; whilst alien, unknowable nature is driven from within, to agglomerate into a symbol that is illuminated throughout. Yet this relationship between soul and nature can be produced only at lyrical moments. Otherwise, nature is transformed— because of its lack of meaning—into a kind of picturesque lumber-room of sensuous symbols for literature; it seems to be fixed in its bewitched mobility and can only be reduced to a meaningfully animated calm by the magic word of lyricism. Such moments are constitutive and form-determining only for lyric poetry; only in lyric poetry do these direct, sudden flashes of the substance become like lost original manuscripts suddenly made legible; only in lyric poetry is the subject, the vehicle of such experiences, transformed into the sole carrier of meaning, the only true reality. Drama is played out in a sphere that lies beyond such reality, and in the epic forms the subjective experience remains inside the subject: it becomes mood. And nature, bereft of its "senseless" autonomous life as well of its meaningful symbolism, becomes a background, a piece of scenery, an accompanying voice; it has lost its independence and is only a sensually perceptible projection of the essential—of interiority.

The second nature, the nature of man-made structures, has no lyrical substantiality; its forms are too rigid to adapt themselves to the symbol-creating moment; the content of the second nature, precipitated by its own laws, is too definite to be able to rid itself of those elements which, in lyric poetry, are bound to become essayistic; furthermore, these elements are so much at the mercy of laws, are so absolutely devoid of any sensuous valency of existence independent from laws, that without them they can only disintegrate into nothingness. This second nature is not dumb, sensuous and yet senseless like the first: it is a complex of senses—meanings—which has become rigid and strange, and which no longer awakens interiority; it is a charnel-house of long-dead interiorities; this second nature could only be brought to life—if this were possible—by the metaphysical act of reawakening the souls which, in an early or ideal existence, created or preserved it; it can never be animated by another interiority. It is too akin to the soul's aspirations to be treated by the soul as mere raw material for moods, yet too alien to those aspirations ever to become their appropriate and adequate expression. Estrangement from nature (the first nature), the modern sentimental attitude to nature, is only a projection of man's experience of his self-made environment as a prison instead of as a parental home.

When the structures made by man for man are really adequate to man, they are his necessary and native home; and he does not know the nostalgia that posits and experiences nature as the object of its own seeking and finding. The first nature, nature as a set of laws for pure cognition, nature as the bringer of comfort to pure feeling, is nothing other than the historico-philosophical objectivation of man's alienation from his own constructs.

When the soul-content of these constructs can no longer directly become soul, when the constructs no longer appear as the agglomerate and concentrate of interiorities which can at any moment be transformed back into a soul, then they must, in order to subsist, achieve a power which dominates men blindly, without exception or choice. And so men call "law" the recognition of the power that holds them in thrall, and they conceptualise as "law" their despair at its omnipotence and universality: conceptualise it into a sublime and exalting logic, a necessity that is eternal, immutable and beyond the reach of man.

The nature of laws and the nature of moods stem from the same *locus* in the soul: they presuppose the impossibility of an attained and meaningful substance, the impossibility of finding a constitutive object adequate to the constitutive subject. In its experience of nature, the subject, which alone is real, dissolves the whole outside world in mood, and itself becomes mood by virtue of the inexorable identity of essence between the contemplative subject and its object. The desire to know a world cleansed of all wanting and all willing transforms the subject into an a-subjective, constructive and constructing embodiment of cognitive functions. This is bound to be so, for the subject is constitutive only when it acts from within—i.e. only the ethical subject is constitutive. It can only avoid falling prey to laws and moods if the arena of its actions, the normative object of its actions, is made of the stuff of pure ethics: if right and custom are identical with morality: if no more of the soul has to be put into the man-made structures to make them serve as man's proper sphere of action than can be released, by action, from those structures. Under such conditions the soul has no need to recognise any laws, for the soul itself is the law of man and man will behold the same face of the same soul upon every substance against which he may have to prove himself. Under such conditions, it would seem petty and futile to try to overcome the strangeness of the non-human world by the mood-arousing power of the subject: the world of man that matters is the one where the soul, as man, god or demon, is at home: then the soul finds everything it needs, it does not have to create or animate anything out of its own self, for its existence is filled to overbrimming with the finding, gathering and moulding of all that is given as cognate to the soul.

The epic individual, the hero of the novel, is the product of estrangement from the outside world. When the world is internally homogeneous, men do not differ qualitatively from one another; there are of course heroes and villains, pious men and criminals, but even the greatest hero is only a head taller than the mass of his fellows, and the wise man's dignified words are heard even by the most foolish. The autonomous life of interiority is possible and necessary only when the distinctions between men have made an unbridgeable chasm; when the gods are silent and neither sacrifices nor the ecstatic gift of tongues can solve their riddle; when the world of deeds separates itself from men and, because of this independence, becomes hollow and incapable of absorbing the true meaning of deeds in itself, incapable of becoming a symbol through deeds and dissolving them in turn into symbols; when interiority and adventure are forever divorced from one another.

The epic hero is, strictly speaking, never an individual. It is traditionally thought that one of the essential characteristics of the epic is the fact that its theme is not a personal destiny but the destiny of a community. And rightly so, for the completeness, the roundness of the value system, which determines the epic cosmos creates a whole which is too organic for any part of it to become so enclosed within itself, so dependent upon itself, as to find itself as an interiority—i.e. to become a personality. The omnipotence of ethics, which posits every soul as autonomous and incomparable, is still unknown in such a world. When life *qua* life finds an immanent meaning in itself, the categories of the organic determine everything: an individual structure and physiognomy is simply the product of a balance between the part and the whole, mutually determining one another; it is never the product of polemical self-contemplation by the lost and lonely personality. The significance which an event can have in a world that is rounded in this way is therefore always a quantitative one; the series of adventures in which the event expresses itself has weight in so far as it is significant to a great organic life complex—a nation or a family.

Epic heroes have to be kings for different reasons from the heroes of tragedy (although these reasons are also formal). In tragedy the hero must be a king simply because of the need to sweep all the petty causalities of life from the ontological path of destiny—because the socially dominant figure is the only one whose conflicts, while retaining the sensuous illusion of a symbolic existence, grow solely out of the tragic problem; because only such a figure can be surrounded, even as to the forms of its external appearance, with the required atmosphere of significant isolation.

What is a symbol in tragedy becomes a reality in the epic: the weight of the bonds linking an individual destiny to a totality. World destiny, which in tragedy is merely the number of zeros that have to be added to 1 to transform it into a million, is what actually gives the events of the epic their content; the epic hero, as bearer of his destiny, is not lonely, for this destiny connects him by indissoluble threads to the community whose fate is crystallised in his own.

As for the community, it is an organic—and therefore intrinsically meaningful—concrete totality; that is why the substance of adventure in an epic is always articulated, never strictly closed; this substance is an organism of infinite interior richness, and in this is identical or similar to the substance of other adventure.

The way Homer's epics begin in the middle and do not finish at the end is a reflexion of the truly epic mentality's total indifference to any form of architectural construction, and the introduction of extraneous themes—such as that of Dietrich von Born in the *Song of the Nibelungs*—can never disturb this balance, for everything in the epic has a life of its own and derives its completeness from its own inner significance. The extraneous can calmly hold out its hand to the central; mere contact between concrete things creates concrete relationships, and the extraneous, because of its perspectival distance and its not yet realised richness, does not endanger the unity of the whole and yet has obvious organic existence.

Dante is the only great example in which we see the architectural clearly conquering the organic, and therefore he represents a historico-philosophical transition from the pure epic to the novel. In Dante there is still the perfect immanent distancelessness and completeness of the true epic, but his figures are already individuals, consciously and energetically placing themselves in opposition to a reality that is becoming closed to them, individuals who, through this opposition, become real personalities. The constituent principle of Dante's totality is a highly systematic one, abolishing the epic independence of the organic part-unities and transforming them into hierarchically ordered, autonomous parts. Such individuality, it is true, is found more in the secondary figures than in the hero. The tendency of each part-unity to retain its autonomous lyrical life (a category unknown and unknowable in the old epic) increases towards the periphery as the distance from the centre becomes greater.

The combination of the presuppositions of the epic and the novel and their synthesis to an *epopoeia*[3] is based on the dual structure of Dante's world: the break between life and meaning is surpassed and cancelled by the coincidence of life and meaning in a present, actually experienced transcendence. To the postulate-free organic nature of the older epics, Dante opposes a hierarchy of fulfilled postulates. Dante—and only Dante—did not have to endow his hero with visible social superiority or with a heroic destiny that codetermined the destiny of the community—because his hero's lived experience was the symbolic unity of human destiny in general.

Notes

1. From *The Theory of the Novel: A Historico-Philosophical Essay on the Forms of Great Epic Literature*, trans. Anna Bostock (Cambridge: M.I.T. Press, 1971). First published as *Die Theorie des Romans; ein geschichtsphilosophischer Versuch über die Formen der grossen Epik* (1917, repr. Berlin: Luchterhand, 1967).

2. The medieval poet Wolfram von Eschenbach is best known for his chivalric verse romance *Parzival*; his contemporary Gottfried von Strassburg wrote *Tristan*.

3. Epic poem.

10

Chaos in the Literary World[1] (1934)

Kobayashi Hideo

Born in Tokyo in 1902, Kobayashi emerged in the 1920s and 1930s as modern Japan's preeminent literary critic. He studied French literature at Tokyo University in the early 1920s, then went on to a varied career as a critic, book reviewer, translator, and university lecturer. In 1933 he was one of the founders of an important literary magazine, *Bungakkai*. He wrote extensively on modern European and Japanese literature, and published a biography of one of his heroes, Dostoevsky. In the postwar era, he also began to write about medieval Japanese literature and about European music and painting, including studies of Mozart and Van Gogh. In his seminal criticism of the 1930s, Kobayashi developed an unusually personal style as he sought to mediate between Japanese and Western traditions, and between political and aesthetic categories of thought.

In "Chaos in the Literary World" (1934), Kobayashi takes criticism itself as his theme, moving from responses to his own work to a far-reaching comparison of Japanese and European criticism and then a provocative account of the challenges facing contemporary novelists. His discussion of the intertwined literary and critical crises of his day bears comparison with Theodor Adorno's meditations on the ambiguous ideological role of artists and critics and with Edward Said's discussion of the fraught relations of world, text, and critic in the postwar era.

1. On Criticism

I thought of calling this piece "On the Literary Revival" but decided against it. Had I used such a title, surely someone would have piped up, absurdly but with great conviction, that "according to Kobayashi Hideo, literature has revived." Elsewhere, already, one smug critic has written: "Although I am quite dubious about the outcome, it would seem that voices calling for a rebirth of pure literature are rising, along with those who rejoice at the expected coming of the glorious day of literary revival." Stop posing, I want to tell this critic. Who, after all, has been calling for a rebirth of pure literature? Where, precisely, are the writers who are revealing their joy over a literary revival? Does a single critic exist who has written an essay heralding the dawn of this revival?

I am not suggesting that we try to get hold of the true shape of this phantom revival. I am saying that we should not create phantoms unnecessarily. Whether they are in sympathy with or scorn a revival, why don't critics start with plain, simple facts, such as the recent appearance of two or three more literary magazines? Who could possibly be impressed, not by such facts, but instead by the "analysis" of a phantom, built by a mob of spectators, that is made out to be either the vestige of some past or the sign of some present crisis? We have arrived at the height of absurdity when we start to suspect that this phantom is not the construction of a whole mob, but an invention made by a lone critic for his convenience. How warped indeed are the conditions of our criticism!

Each year, come December, the review sections of our newspapers and magazines present us with the seasonal spectacle of critic-poseurs. "Oh my," such critics exclaim, "how many wonderful things happened this year." What lies. Moreover, the makers of these claims never introduce us to literary issues of real importance and complexity. Indeed, isn't it the case that far from introducing us to such problems, they have instead killed them off?

It is characteristic of the anxiety of our age that one after another, at complete random, problems of all kinds should be spread before us. Again, it is characteristic of these problems that they should be presented in a form vulnerable to attack and destruction. Now it does not take much effort to twist or to kill. A given problem emerges, and everyone rushes toward it and begins to resolve it. And so something is being resolved, but we should observe that it never existed as a proper, formal problem in the first place. We have resolutions to problems, then, that have yet to take shape.

This is not wordplay on my part, but a faithful account of a situation that is truly strange.

There was the recent controversy over "the impotence of criticism." I know it well because I was made out to be a perpetrator of this condition. Charges against my useless, impotent criticism encircled an impressionistic piece I wrote in the August issue of *Kaizō*, titled "On Criticism." Now it had been my intention there to underscore the power and potency of criticism. But my manner of expression was admittedly subjective and somewhat perverse. Still, I did manage to express the following positive conviction: "Just as great writers are not necessarily aware of the methods by which they write, so too are distinguished critics unaware of the range of paradox contained within their critical methods. I long to see the emergence of a great critic whose strong critical practice will overcome the entanglements of method." Now for whatever reason, what I was saying here was misunderstood. As a matter of fact, I am not upset at the misunderstanding itself. Something even more lamentable is at stake. For isn't it shameful that any problem would be thought "resolved" by my admittedly slight essay?

No matter how orderly its structure, any problem as such will eventually die. No matter how modest its scale, any problem at the moment of its inception lives. If there is a vital issue to begin with, then it will be dispersed through every sentence that I write. Indeed, I consciously infuse it into my writing. But who will allow me to nurture this vitality as my own? Who will permit it to expand, deepen, and itself become a focus of critical discussion? As a critic, I should not have to waste my time worrying about whether my criticism will be judged "potent" or not.

Critics today pursue novelties, but do not seek true vitality. They are fond of building one new problem after another, but are not inclined to give new forms of expression to a given problem. They are fond of resolving random issues in the same way, but are not inclined to resolve each one in a new and distinctive way. This is because it is far more difficult to discern what constitutes the new or the old about a given problem than to address ready-made "new problems" or "old problems." The tendency to drift toward increasingly expedient critical methods is a strong inertial force within our literary world [*bundan*].[2] It is an illness easily transmitted to our critics. For any lazy critic who has climbed aboard this inertia, solving problems seems far less troublesome than introducing them properly. Indeed, we can say that only those problems are being introduced that have already been resolved. Many critics can only resolve problems that are introduced in this manner. This I do not call the real work of the critical spirit. Yet owing to such well-built solutions, how many really vital questions have been buried? How many intricate possibilities within a given problem have been ruled out at the halfway point? In this way, time and again, vital literary issues have become grist for a desiccated *bundan*. And so we hear them exclaim: "How many wonderful things happened this year." They are the voices of fools, or demons.

Yazaki Dan, in a critique of my work, writes that my spirit is one which abhors judgments. But does Yazaki know what a "spirit which abhors judgments" really is? Can he in good conscience say that he knows it? His argument makes no sense. And so I feel under no obligation, based on the connotations of his critical vocabulary, to accept his fashionable notion about my "spirit which abhors judgments."

I regard all things, not just criticism, skeptically. But I take no pleasure in my skepticism. In fact, I do not have the spiritual leisure to enjoy it. I am possessed only by an arrogant wish to pursue each and every possibility of which my spirit is capable. Indeed, it is this wish alone that drives my spirit toward skepticism. I do not wish to interpret my skepticism negatively or to have it be so interpreted.

I have come to value my consciousness before all else and am well aware that its present disorder does not lend itself to rearrangement. A useless, harmful complexity; unproductive subtlety; paradox, deception, intoxication, disillusionment—all these I know as well as I know objects before my eyes. Yet I have never felt shame. True, I have felt an inexplicable anxiety at those moments when it seemed all too natural to be living with a consciousness so full of confusion and contradiction. I may even have expressed what sounded like an admission of shame. But I never really felt that emotion and believe that any possible expression of my shame came from a consciousness that was insufficiently disordered. An orderly consciousness will grasp an orderly truth; a moderate consciousness, a moderate truth. In the world of literature, truths of this kind are but fairy tales.

Never before in the literary history of our country has criticism seemed to occupy such a prominent position. Again, never before has such critical chaos reigned. But whereas from a bird's-eye view the situation looks chaotic, up close, focusing on the details, it appears orderly, if in a close-fisted and grudging way. Some critics bemoan the loss of critical principles. But I would ask them, just once, to truly leave such principles behind.

At this moment when criticism is in chaos, who among our critics signals an awareness of how difficult it is to write criticism? The critical world is in turmoil, yet writing criticism seems to be as simple a task as it ever was. I want to focus on this bizarre situation. The crisis has nothing at all to do with any so-called loss of critical principles. Rather, what we see before us is a struggle among contending critics armed with a whole array of borrowed critical principles. Viewed from outside, the struggle looks chaotic. But does a sense of chaos exist within the spirit of each combatant? Does any real disorder exist there?

Since the appearance in the world of Aristotle's *Poetics,* the main thrust of his criticism was passed on from the Middle Ages through the Renaissance into modern times, without undergoing substantive change. The path taken by a host of critics had thus been an even one. Along this path, critics sang of the beauty of literary works classified by genre, or told the story of distinct aesthetic doctrines and principles. But with the emergence of the modern literary movement called Romanticism, it can be said that this level path ran into a mountain heretofore unknown.

The Romantics implanted the idea of relativism into literary criticism. No longer could critics see the crisp and clear outlines of a given literary work. Just behind the work loomed a human presence, as well as the place where that presence lived, and the history of its times. What had been an isolated and motionless literary work began to move before the critic's eye. The confusion thus visited on the practice of criticism lies at the origin of what we take to be literary criticism today. In other words, the determinedly modern, tragic shape assumed by Western literary criticism is a fact of past history and is already over a century old. It is no wonder, then, that critics, whose pronouncements were caught in the paradox-filled crosscurrents of the Romantic movement, who were passionate both to extol the creative freedom of the individual and to scientifically dispel all superstition, should have come to regard criticism itself with profound skepticism. It was startling for me to discover how closely related are the soliloquies of Sainte-Beuve and Gide.[3]

The complications that modern literary criticism faced from the moment of its birth—the rivalry between creative and scientific impulses within the critical spirit—have not been resolved satisfactorily even in our own day. Perhaps we should say that these contradictory impulses have driven literature to become more and more specialized by type, so that each impulse is nurtured by a distinctive kind of writing spirit, and each one carries out its own solutions to literary problems. Only observe the difference in critical spirit between Plekhanov and Friche on the one hand, or Gundolf and Gide on the other.

Have these general complications within the modern critical spirit cast any sort of shadow over literary criticism in our country? We cannot find them, for example, in the criticism of Mori Ōgai, the greatest of our importers of Western writing. Even as our earliest critical battles were being waged by Ōgai and [Tsubouchi] Shōyō on the pages of *Shigarami zōshi* and *Waseda bungaku,* over such issues as idealism or its negation, or deductive against inductive methods, in Europe Taine and Pater were about to close their eyes in death. Later, we would witness [Takayama] Chogyū's intoxication with Nietzsche, [Shimamura] Hōgetsu's application of Arnold, [Ueda] Bin's emulation of Pater. Yet amid all this critical activity, no one questioned what made a literary work "literary." Symons was known, as were Gourmont and Anatole France, but the basic optimism of our critics showed no evidence of slipping from its base. The fact that Romanticism wreaked havoc with the spirit of classical criticism had no deep bearing on the history of modern literary criticism in our country. It is no exaggeration to say that down to the present, even in the area of criticism, not to speak of literature in general, the hand of science has not been felt at all.

Such were the conditions of literary criticism in Japan when suddenly a radically scientific method was introduced. I refer of course to Marxism. Although the historical fact of its introduction is not surprising in the least, it struck the literary world as a stunning event. Everyone was caught off guard, and so the reaction was indeed exaggerated. Amid all the distortions and bombast that marked this reaction, both those who imported the Marxist approach and those who just received it forgot the fact that no method even remotely similar to this one had ever been part of the critical traditions of Japan. This was a situation peculiar to our country, yet not a single critic pointed it out. Until this peculiarity is explained, it will remain impossible to fathom that complex farce currently enacted on many stages, whereby a critic is accused of being a "bourgeois liberal," never once having regarded himself consciously as such, yet on being so accused proudly claims that truly his criticism must be that of a bourgeois liberal.

But the farce thus born in the chaos of our critical condition will surely meet a farcical end unless our critics raise their level of awareness to see that the chaos itself is a product of conflicting critical paths. If our critics persist in seeing disorder as but the momentary reflection of a fleeting crisis, the disorder may well pass, having given birth to nothing.

I want to penetrate to the core of this disorder. I want to seize chaos as an opportunity and not hesitate to reach down to the roots of a question that is being posed for the first time in our literary history: Why is criticism a difficult thing? I do not intend to let go of this question, no matter what the outcome may be.

I do not want words like "chaos" and "disorder" to be the only ones used to describe the state of Japanese criticism today. Nor do I want such words to merely outline a critical scene wherein there is more than one kind of critic and a broad range of issues to address. I do mean to regard such descriptive language as a real enemy and threat to my spirit, as something I must overthrow. Still, it is not my belief that living with confusion is preferable to observing it. I simply want to feel whatever chaos is within myself as a living thing. By whatever means possible, I want to grapple with it hand to hand.

It may turn out that the chaos of our critical world will become all the more intense. Even for critics who believe that the enemy to be fought exists outside themselves, the time may come when they must face a host of enemies within. Like it or not, we will then need to experience at a deep level the real chaos, the actual disorder of our critical spirit.

2. On 'Watakushi shōsetsu'

In his literary review column in the December issue of *Bungei*, Kawakami Tetsutarō addressed himself to the issue of the first-person novel [*watakushi shōsetsu*]. He cited a passage I had written in the inaugural issue of *Bungakkai*: "Balzac's novels are indeed fabricated, and precisely because they are fabricated, they are more splendid and more truthful than any confessional language about the artist's sufferings. Precisely because he overcame his self, and cast it aside, he discovered a path that was vital and alive within this fabrication." Kawakami went on to comment: "What is unfortunate is that Kobayashi concludes his essay with these words, when instead he should have begun his study of the *watakushi shōsetsu* with them." Kawakami is quite right. Still, my quoted words are extremely ambiguous. He might as well have criticized me, saying "Kobayashi should have begun his study of *orthodox realism* with them." At this point the issue suddenly expands, leaving us all in a stupefied haze. I lack the power, of course, to restore clarity, but reading Chikamatsu Shūkō's "Kukai" (Sea of troubles) in the December issue of *Chūō kōron*, I feel compelled to return to the issue of personal fiction and try to draw out a bit more from my earlier remarks.

Writing in the *Tōkyō Asahi*, Uno Kōji praised "Kukai" as the most moving piece he had read in the past month. I, too, thought it extraordinary. But my feelings upon reading the story were so tangled and complex that even I could make no sense of them. First of all, I recognize straightaway that certain objections to the work—its style is old, its setting is narrow—

are unsupportable, and that these very qualities make it plunge straight into the world of our emotions. At the same time, in the process of reading, I was aware of feeling somehow revolted and depressed. I will leave it to others to detail the extraordinary literary qualities of this story. However arrogant it may seem, I will try to focus on my feelings of depression.

Reading "Kukai," we understand the character of the man, Chikamatsu Shūkō.[4] The man Chikamatsu seems neither greater nor lesser than the figure Tawara in the story. In that sense, perhaps "Kukai" is a story that has no secrets. I have met Chikamatsu only once, at a literary gathering, but reading this work I was made to recall Chikamatsu's expressions and movements at that time, especially the way he used his hand to massage a cramp in his leg. And I was given naturally to imagine, however disrespectful it may sound, the author making the rounds of the magazine offices in an effort to sell his work. How will I further describe my anxious feelings about this story, and where they have taken me?

Some will say that just such an anxious response to the work is proof of its quality. Perhaps. But such a positive claim, given the difficulties experienced by the reader, seems empty and remote. Will it further be claimed that what defines literature is just such remoteness? If that were so, then I would have no faith in literature. There is nothing in "Kukai" to make the heart feel refreshed, nothing to enrich one's sense of human life. Needless to say, it is not the author's pessimistic spirit that leaves me dissatisfied. Even pessimism, so long as it is powerfully expressed, has the capacity to change lives. What I want to say is that in my reading experience, "Kukai" possesses neither the power nor the true beauty of such expression. The question is not whether a reading of "Kukai" should bring the reader salvation. Rather, I want to ask Chikamatsu himself if he felt a writer's joy as he wrote it? Perhaps the author would ask a question in turn— Who knows if literature is a way toward enlightenment or delusion? But after nearly forty years of life as a writer, it is unfortunate that joy, or if not joy, then a fierce pride becoming to a writer, should have left no mark on him. Of course we cannot say that there are many writers, who, having risked a lifetime of discontent, are unmistakably stamped with such a mark. But precisely because we know that they exist, we maintain hope in literature, knowing full well how much discontent it will continue to generate.

"Kukai" runs counter to such a hope. But would we be better off and feel less guilty, had we read a work possessing sweeter sentiments?

The progenitor of the I-novel was no doubt Jean-Jacques Rousseau. At least he was the first to be clearly conscious of the question of the confessional self, and to make it part of literature. The unhappiness he outlined in his *Confessions* is not that of a hero, but of a common man. Yet readers often find this unhappiness beyond their grasp. To put it another way, they sense in the writing a power that redeemed the author's unhappy existence. This power reveals an "I," and salvages something greater than "I." The author writes an autobiography, and turns it into literature. In other words, the objectivity of the *Confessions* rests on the author's belief in his unprecedented project: to speak without reserve about himself. And what inspired such belief was a prior conviction that if society was a problem for him, then a man like himself was surely a problem for society.

His strategy was a clear and simple one. To overcome himself, he would speak about himself as honestly as possible. Perhaps the magnificent drama enacted in the *Confessions* seems a bit too unadorned and simple to us, obsessed as we have become with theories about the *watakushi shōsetsu*. But we should also realize that all kinds of questions about the I-novel are strewn along a great road that begins and ends with Rousseau.

Kawakami Tetsutarō has described two conditions that spawned the I-novel. Of the first, he writes: "Among the various anxieties felt by the writer as he seeks ways to effectively depict a certain fictional persona, the clear majority owe less to the writer trying to break away from the persona than to his attempt to break away from himself. We can thus affirm a common phenomenon, whereby as art advances, the wish to break away from the self manifests a powerful latent energy." And of the second: "At the same time it can be said that the artist is obsessed with an inwardly glimpsed image of himself." Kawakami concludes, stating that "until now, our conception of the I-novel has been based on only the latter of these two conditions." I think this is a fair assessment, although these two conditions are so entangled that we cannot easily say which one is more dominant, because both are essential to the writer's spirit, trying to express itself by means of a certain fascination with the self. Here we grasp a double-edged sword. Thus, even within Kawakami's second condition, a double-sided outline appears.

However, reading a *watakushi shōsetsu*, I immediately gauge what might be called the distance between the real life of the author and the author of the work. The question is not one of depth, that is, the degree of sincerity an author conveys, but rather one of breadth—how wide is the gap, the distance between the two? If one focuses instead on depth of feeling, then immediately the question is rendered personal, and made more complicated. Take, for example, Hirotsu Kazuo's recent critique of the [Tokuda] Shusei story, "Shi ni shitashimu" (Intimate with death) in the November issue of *Bungei shunjū*, which follows this trajectory as far as

Hirotsu's curiosity takes him. But were we to see the question instead as one of writing, trying to gauge the gap between real life and the author, then we could clarify any number of abstract issues as they relate to the *watakushi shōsetsu*. The fact that I once praised Uno Kōji's "Ko no raireki" (Annals of a child) has less to do with the shadow cast on the story by the scenery of real life than with the distance between what the author of that work clearly felt and the personal life of Uno. It is a distance that is bracing, exhilarating. But in the case of "Shi ni shitashimu," there is less distance, and lesser still in "Kukai." As for the issue of the real feelings and sentiments of Shūkō, Shusei, or Uno—I have no idea whose run deepest.

In the headnote to his literary review in the *Tōkyō Asahi,* Uno cited the following passage from Shiga Naoya:[5] "As I gaze upon the Merciful Kannon at the Yumedono, it does not occur to me to ask who created this statue. This is because the statue possesses a life wholly apart from its creator. It is unique. If from literature I were able to create such a work, I would never think to attach my name to it." In these words of our preeminent author of *watakushi shōsetsu,* who combines a primitive desire for life with a classical sensibility, there is not the slightest metaphorical significance. Like Uno, I number these words among the most beautiful Shiga ever wrote, yet am not inclined to rummage through them for some significance that might resolve the "I-novel" controversy which presently besets us. In fact, Shiga's aesthetics are not strong enough to settle this question. It is also true that his aesthetics shape his moral understanding.

"I thought the work was interesting. But then I met the author, and found out he was a bore . . ." Statements like this abound, although I will not trade here in such critical vulgarities. Still, I question if in Japan today there are many writers whose fictional worlds have excavated a depth that is not wholly apparent in real life. Isn't it the case that for most of our writers, literature has not disentangled itself from real life? And isn't real life greater than fiction for most writers? Not only did such questions go unasked in the tradition of I-novel writing; they were avoided out of desperation. Our writers chewed real life to the bone, exhausting its possibilities, yet remain bewitched by their dream of "real life," and have now seized upon a territory called "deep feelings." But what are readers given to chew in these stories? To be blunt, we are being fed leftovers. Meanwhile, those who continued writing in bondage to real life knew that even as the plenitude of this real life was being depleted, so too were their dreams of literature. It was at this juncture that the Merciful Kannon of the Yumedono appeared.

I am neither contemptuous of the sphere of sensibility that our established writers attained, nor feel the least envy of their position. Nor do

I have any faith in Marxist literature, although I do value the ambition to create social novels, something Marxism evoked. I believe in the passion to write for others, having abandoned the self. Again, although I have no faith in psychological novels or in novels of ideas, I do believe that such novelists, whose dreams of creating a viable self-portrait were dashed as abruptly as were their dreams of suckling on real life, are still stirred by an ambition to break new literary ground. At present, the *watakushi shōsetsu* is being destroyed from two directions. The writer is either overcome by ideology and abandons his self without a fight before discovering any new face to portray in his work, or else he destroys his portrait under pressure from his surroundings and can find no inner imperative to build a new literature. The chaos thus loosed on our fiction is analogous to the chaos of our critical world and is becoming more and more intense. Seedlings and sprouts are everywhere. But nothing stands.

What should be the reply if asked what was the year's unequivocal masterpiece? I myself would agree with those who say it is Tanizaki's "Shunkinshō" (Portrait of Shunkin).[6] I would also admit to the strangeness of our times, the absurdity of our cultural situation, as well as to our unending hope.

I am moved to re-read all of Dostoevsky. This author did not utter a word about his real life, suffused though it was with a depth and range of vital experience. When he had exhausted the bounty of real life, he created a rich literature. All of his writing is replete with secrets drawn from real life, yet we cannot read his fiction without dismissing as abject lies the records of real life kept by his wife and daughter. In just such a writer I believe we find the richest, most fertile field wherein to explore issues of the I-novel. In every possible way, I want to engage the secrets of this writer.

Notes

1. First published as "Bungakkai no konran," *Bungei shunjū*, January 1934. From Paul Anderer ed. and trans., *Literature of the Lost Home: Kobayashi Hideo—Literary Criticism, 1924–1939* (Stanford: Stanford University Press, 1995), 55–66.

2. The term is conventionally used to describe the small group of writers, critics, and editors whose work and opinions have determined what qualifies as "literature" throughout the modern period. [Translator's note]

3. Charles-Augustin Sainte-Beuve (1804–69) was the leading French critic of the nineteenth century; committed to scientific principles and assembling the facts

of authors' lives, he might seem to be very different from the modernist novelist and memoirist André Gide (1869–1951).

4. Chikamatsu (1876–1944) was a naturalist writer, known for his confessional tales of betrayal and humiliation. [Tr.]

5. Shiga Naoya (1883–1971) was author of the most famous Japanese first-person novel, *Anya kōro* (*A Dark Night's Passing*). [Tr.]

6. Tanizaki Junichiro (1886–1965) became one of Japan's leading novelists, famous for his stylistic virtuosity in tales of decadent desire.

From *Epic and Novel*[1] (1941)

Mikhail Bakhtin

Spanning a turbulent period in Russian history, many of Bakhtin's works were published with great delay or not at all during his lifetime; they were not widely known outside the Soviet Union until the 1970s. Born in 1895, Mikhail Mikhailovich Bakhtin came of age amid the upheavals of the Russian Revolution and apparently never received any formal higher education. A voracious reader and a wide-ranging thinker from an early age, he began publishing essays on philosophical and cultural topics in 1919. The previous year, he and a group of friends had founded a philosophical and literary circle in Belorussia; in 1924 the group moved to Leningrad, where they debated ideas and championed radical artistic movements even as official Soviet policy was tending increasingly toward the promotion of socialist realism and an unquestioning loyalty to Stalin. The "Bakhtin Circle" was shattered in 1929 with the arrest of most of its members. Bakhtin was sent into internal exile, holding low-level posts in Kazakhstan and elsewhere, ultimately teaching at a provincial teacher's college until his retirement in 1961. A gradual cultural thaw following Stalin's death enabled him in the 1960s to revise and republish several of his major early works; he had achieved an international reputation by the time of his death in 1975.

Bakhtin is best known as a startlingly original theorist of the novel and its language. He developed his ideas in major books on Dostoevsky (*Problems of Dostoevsky's Poetics*, 1929, rev. 1972) and on Rabelais (*Rabelais and His World*, 1963), and in a series of long theoretical essays of the

1930s and 1940s. Central to his conception of novelistic language is what he calls "heteroglossia," which signifies the multiplicity of interwoven "socio-ideological" languages within any given culture: the language of college students, of epic poetry, of intellectuals, of war veterans. Heteroglossia highlights the constant tension in language between unbounded multiplicity on the one hand and centralization and unification on the other. The novel, according to Bakhtin, is the only genre that is genuinely heteroglossic. The lyric, the drama, and the epic might include a variety of languages, but they incorporate them into their own singular discourses. Only the novel allows each language to carry its own point of view and in so doing paradoxically defines itself as a genre by indeterminacy and open-endedness.

The long essay excerpted here, "Epic and Novel" (1941), develops this idea by contrasting the self-enclosure and archaism of epic to the incompleteness and contemporaneity of the novel. This comparison between ancient epic and the modern novel is indebted to Georg Lukács's argument in *The Theory of the Novel*, but Bakhtin takes it in a different direction. For Bakhtin, the novel is not a compensation for lost totality, but an expression of social dynamism and potentiality. With a characteristically capacious range of reference across the history of Western literature, Bakhtin emphasizes the novel's subversive and playful dimensions and foretells the "novelization" of all genres as the future of literature. His central concepts have exerted a powerful influence on a broad range of contemporary criticism, from genre theory, to semiotics, to postcolonial theory and cultural studies.

The study of the novel as a genre is distinguished by peculiar difficulties. This is due to the unique nature of the object itself: the novel is the sole genre that continues to develop, that is as yet uncompleted. The forces that define it as a genre are at work before our very eyes: the birth and development of the novel as a genre takes place in the full light of the historical day. The generic skeleton of the novel is still far from having hardened, and we cannot foresee all its plastic possibilities.

We know other genres, as genres, in their completed aspect, that is, as more or less fixed pre-existing forms into which one may then pour artistic experience. The primordial process of their formation lies outside historically documented observation. We encounter the epic as a genre that has not only long since completed its development, but one that is already antiquated. With certain reservations we can say the same for the other major genres, even for tragedy. The life they have in history, the life with which we are familiar, is the life they have lived as already completed genres, with a hardened and no longer flexible skeleton. Each of them has developed its own canon that operates in literature as an authentic historical force.

All these genres, or in any case their defining features, are considerably older than written language and the book, and to the present day they retain their ancient oral and auditory characteristics. Of all the major genres only the novel is younger than writing and the book: it alone is organically receptive to new forms of mute perception, that is, to reading. But of critical importance here is the fact that the novel has no canon of its own, as do other genres; only individual examples of the novel are historically active, not a generic canon as such. Studying other genres is analogous to studying dead languages; studying the novel, on the other hand, is like studying languages that are not only alive, but still young.

This explains the extraordinary difficulty inherent in formulating a theory of the novel. For such a theory has at its heart an object of study completely different from that which theory treats in other genres. The novel is not merely one genre among other genres. Among genres long since completed and in part already dead, the novel is the only developing genre. It is the only genre that was born and nourished in a new era of world history and therefore it is deeply akin to that era, whereas the other major genres entered that era as already fixed forms, as an inheritance, and only now are they adapting themselves—some better, some worse—to the new conditions of their existence. Compared with them, the novel appears to be a creature from an alien species. It gets on poorly with other genres. It fights for its own hegemony in literature; wherever it triumphs, the other older genres go into decline. Significantly, the best book on the history of the ancient novel—that by Erwin Rohde[2]—does not so much recount the history of the novel as it does illustrate the process of disintegration that affected all major genres in antiquity.

The mutual interaction of genres within a single unified literary period is a problem of great interest and importance. In certain eras—the Greek classical period, the Golden Age of Roman literature, the neoclassical period—all genres in "high" literature (that is, the literature of ruling social groups) harmoniously reinforce each other to a significant extent; the whole of literature, conceived as a totality of genres, becomes an organic unity of the highest order. But it is characteristic of the novel that it never enters into this whole, it does not participate in any harmony of the genres. In these eras the novel has an unofficial existence, outside "high" literature. Only already completed genres, with fully formed and well-defined generic contours, can enter into such a literature as a hierarchically organized, organic whole. They can mutually delimit and mutually complement each other, while yet preserving their own generic natures. Each is a unit, and all units are interrelated by virtue of certain features of deep structure that they all have in common.

The great organic poetics of the past—those of Aristotle, Horace, Boileau[3]—are permeated with a deep sense of the wholeness of literature and of the harmonious interaction of all genres contained within this whole. It is as if they literally hear this harmony of the genres. In this is their strength—the inimitable, all-embracing fullness and exhaustiveness of such poetics. And they all, as a consequence, ignore the novel. Scholarly poetics of the nineteenth century lack this integrity: they are eclectic, descriptive; their aim is not a living and organic fullness but rather an abstract and encyclopedic comprehensiveness. They do not concern themselves with the actual possibility of specific genres coexisting within the living whole of literature in a given era; they are concerned rather with their coexistence in a maximally complete anthology. Of course these poetics can no longer ignore the novel—they simply add it (albeit in a place of honor) to already existing genres (and thus it enters the roster as merely one genre among many; in literature conceived as a living whole, on the other hand, it would have to be included in a completely different way).

We have already said that the novel gets on poorly with other genres. There can be no talk of a harmony deriving from mutual limitation and complementariness. The novel parodies other genres (precisely in their role as genres); it exposes the conventionality of their forms and their language; it squeezes out some genres and incorporates others into its own peculiar structure, reformulating and re-accentuating them. Historians of literature sometimes tend to see in this merely the struggle of literary tendencies and schools. Such struggles of course exist, but they are peripheral phenomena and historically insignificant. Behind them one must be sensitive to the deeper and more truly historical struggle of genres, the establishment and growth of a generic skeleton of literature.

Of particular interest are those eras when the novel becomes the dominant genre. All literature is then caught up in the process of "becoming" and in a special kind of "generic criticism." This occurred several times in the Hellenic period, again during the late Middle Ages and the Renaissance, but with special force and clarity beginning in the second half of the eighteenth century. In an era when the novel reigns supreme, almost all the remaining genres are to a greater or lesser extent "novelized": drama (for example Ibsen, Hauptmann,[4] the whole of Naturalist drama), epic poetry (for example, *Childe Harold* and especially Byron's *Don Juan),* even lyric poetry (as an extreme example, Heine's[5] lyrical verse). Those genres that stubbornly preserve their old canonic nature begin to appear stylized. In general any strict adherence to a genre begins to feel like a stylization, a stylization taken to the point of parody despite the artistic intent of the author. In an environment where the novel is the dominant genre, the conventional languages of strictly canonical genres begin to sound in new ways, which are quite different from the ways they sounded in those eras when the novel was *not* included in "high" literature.

Parodic stylizations of canonized genres and styles occupy an essential place in the novel. In the era of the novel's creative ascendancy—and even more so in the periods of preparation preceding this era—literature was flooded with parodies and travesties of all the high genres (parodies precisely of genres, and not of individual authors or schools)—parodies that are the precursors, "companions" to the novel, in their own way studies for it. But it is characteristic that the novel does not permit any of these various individual manifestations of itself to stabilize. Throughout its entire history there is a consistent parodying or travestying of dominant or fashionable novels that attempt to become models for the genre: parodies on the chivalric romance of adventure (*Dit d'aventures*, the first such parody, belongs to the thirteenth century), on the Baroque novel, the pastoral novel (Sorel's *Le Berger extravagant*),[6] the Sentimental novel (Fielding, and *The Second Grandison* of Musäus[7]) and so forth. This ability of the novel to criticize itself is a remarkable feature of this ever-developing genre.

What are the salient features of this novelization of other genres suggested by us above? They become more free and flexible, their language renews itself by incorporating extraliterary heteroglossia and the "novelistic" layers of literary language, they become dialogized, permeated with laughter, irony, humor, elements of self-parody and finally—this is the most important thing—the novel inserts into these other genres an indeterminacy, a certain semantic open-endedness, a living contact with unfinished, still-evolving contemporary reality (the open-ended present). As we will see below, all these phenomena are explained by the transposition of other genres into this new and peculiar zone for structuring artistic models (a zone of contact with the present in all its open-endedness), a zone that was first appropriated by the novel.

It is of course impossible to explain the phenomenon of novelization purely by reference to the direct and unmediated influence of the novel itself. Even where such influence can be precisely established and demonstrated, it is intimately interwoven with those direct changes in reality itself that also determine the novel and that condition its dominance in a given era. The novel is the only developing genre and therefore it reflects more deeply, more essentially, more sensitively and rapidly, reality itself in the process of its unfolding. Only that which is itself developing can comprehend development as a process. The novel has become the leading hero in the drama of literary development in our time precisely because it best of all reflects the tendencies of a new world still in the making; it is, after all, the only genre born of this new world and in total affinity with it. In many respects the novel has anticipated, and continues to anticipate, the future development of literature as a whole. In the process of becoming the dominant genre, the novel sparks the renovation of all other genres, it infects them with its spirit of process and inconclusiveness. It draws them ineluctably into its orbit precisely because this orbit coincides with the basic direction of the development of literature as a whole. In this lies the exceptional importance of the novel, as an object of study for the theory as well as the history of literature. [. . .]

We speak of the epic as a genre that has come down to us already well defined and real. We come upon it when it is already completely finished, a congealed and half-moribund genre. Its completedness, its consistency and its absolute lack of artistic naïveté bespeak its old age as a genre and its lengthy past. We can only conjecture about this past, and we must admit that so far our conjectures have been rather poor. Those hypothetical primordial songs that preceded both the epic and the creation of a generic epic tradition, songs about contemporaries that directly echoed events that had just occurred—such songs we do not know, although we must presume they existed. We can only guess at the nature of those original aëdonic songs, or of the cantilenas.[8] And we have no reason to assume that they are any more closely related to the later and better-known epic songs than to our topical feuilletons or popular ditties. Those heroicized epic songs about contemporaries that *are* available to us and that we *do* know existed arose only after the epic was already an established form, and arose on the basis of an already ancient and powerful epic tradition. These songs transfer to contemporary events and contemporaries the ready-made epic form; that is, they transfer to these events the time-and-value contour of the past, thus

attaching them to the world of fathers, of beginnings and peak times—
canonizing these events, as it were, while they are still current. In a patriarchal social structure the ruling class does, in a certain sense, belong to
the world of "fathers" and is thus separated from other classes by a distance
that is almost epic. The epic incorporation of the contemporary hero into
a world of ancestors and founders is a specific phenomenon that developed
out of an epic tradition long since completed, and that therefore is as little
able to explain the origin of the epic as is, say, the neoclassical ode.

Whatever its origins, the epic as it has come down to us is an absolutely completed and finished generic form, whose constitutive feature
is the transferral of the world it describes to an absolute past of national
beginnings and peak times. The absolute past is a specifically evaluating
(hierarchical) category. In the epic world view, "beginning," "first," "founder,"
"ancestor," "that which occurred earlier" and so forth are not merely temporal categories but *valorized* temporal categories, and valorized to an extreme degree. This is as true for relationships among people as for relations
among all the other items and phenomena of the epic world. In the past,
everything is good: all the really good things (i.e., the "first" things) occur
only in this past. The epic absolute past is the single source and beginning
of everything good for all later times as well.

In ancient literature it is memory, and not knowledge, that serves
as the source and power for the creative impulse. That is how it was, it is
impossible to change it: the tradition of the past is sacred. There is as yet
no consciousness of the possible relativity of any past.

The novel, by contrast, is determined by experience, knowledge
and practice (the future). In the era of Hellenism a closer contact with the
heroes of the Trojan epic cycle began to be felt; epic is already being transformed into novel. Epic material is transposed into novelistic material,
into precisely that zone of contact that passes through the intermediate
stages of familiarization and laughter. When the novel becomes the dominant genre, epistemology becomes the dominant discipline.

The epic past is called the "absolute past" for good reason: it is
both monochronic and valorized (hierarchical); it lacks any relativity, that
is, any gradual, purely temporal progressions that might connect it with
the present. It is walled off absolutely from all subsequent times, and above
all from those times in which the singer and his listeners are located. This
boundary consequently is immanent in the form of the epic itself and is felt
and heard in its every word.

To destroy this boundary is to destroy the form of the epic as a
genre. But precisely because it is walled off from all subsequent times, the

epic past is absolute and complete. It is as closed as a circle; inside it everything is finished, already over. There is no place in the epic world for any open-endedness, indecision, indeterminacy. There are no loopholes in it through which we glimpse the future; it suffices unto itself, neither supposing any continuation nor requiring it. Temporal and valorized definitions are here fused into a single inseparable whole (as they are also fused in the semantic layers of ancient languages). Everything incorporated into this past was simultaneously incorporated into a condition of authentic essence and significance, but therefore also took on conclusiveness and finality, depriving itself, so to speak, of all rights and potential for a real continuation. Absolute conclusiveness and closedness is the outstanding feature of the temporally valorized epic past. [. . .]

This idealization of the past in high genres has something of an official air. All external expressions of the dominant force and truth (the expression of everything conclusive) were formulated in the valorized-hierarchical category of the past, in a distanced and distant image (everything from gesture and clothing to literary style, for all are symbols of authority). The novel, however, is associated with the eternally living element of unofficial language and unofficial thought (holiday forms, familiar speech, profanation).

The dead are loved in a different way. They are removed from the sphere of contact, one can and indeed must speak of them in a different style. Language about the dead is stylistically quite distinct from language about the living.

In the high genres all authority and privilege, all lofty significance and grandeur, abandon the zone of familiar contact for the distanced plane (clothing, etiquette, the style of a hero's speech and the style of speech about him). It is in this orientation toward completeness that the classicism of all non-novel genres is expressed.

Contemporaneity, flowing and transitory, "low," present—this "life without beginning or end" was a subject of representation only in the low genres. Most importantly, it was the basic subject matter in that broadest and richest of realms, the common people's creative culture of laughter. In the aforementioned work[9] I tried to indicate the enormous influence exercised by this realm—in the ancient world as well as the Middle Ages—on the birth and formation of novelistic language. It was equally significant for all other historical factors in the novelistic genre, during their emergence and early formation. Precisely here, in popular laughter, the authentic folkloric roots of the novel are to be sought. The present, contemporary life as such, "I myself" and "my contemporaries," "my time"—all these concepts were originally the objects of ambivalent laughter, at the same time cheerful and annihilating. It is precisely here that a fundamentally new attitude toward language and toward the word is generated. Alongside direct representation—laughing at living reality—there flourish parody and travesty of all high genres and of all lofty models embodied in national myth. The "absolute past" of gods, demigods and heroes is here, in parodies and even more so in travesties, "contemporized": it is brought low, represented on a plane equal with contemporary life, in an everyday environment, in the low language of contemporaneity.

In classical times this elemental popular laughter gave rise directly to a broad and varied field of ancient literature, one that the ancients themselves expressively labeled *spoudogeloion,* that is, the field of "serio-comical." The weakly plotted mimes of Sophron, all the bucolic poems, the fable, early memoir literature (the *Epidēmiai* of Ion of Chios, the *Homilae* of Critias),[10] pamphlets all belong to this field; here the ancients themselves included the "Socratic dialogues" (as a genre), here belong Roman satire (Lucilius, Horace, Persius, Juvenal), the extensive literature of the "Symposia" and finally Menippean satire (as a genre) and dialogues of the Lucianic type.[11] All these genres, permeated with the "serio-comical," are authentic predecessors of the novel. In addition, several of these genres are thoroughly novelistic, containing in embryo and sometimes in developed form the basic elements characteristic of the most important later prototypes of the European novel. The authentic spirit of the novel as a developing genre is present in them to an incomparably greater degree than in the so-called Greek novels (the sole ancient genre bearing the name). The Greek novel [Greek romance] had a powerful influence on the European novel precisely in the Baroque era, that is, precisely at that time when novel theory was beginning to be reworked (Abbé Huet)[12] and when the very term "novel" was being tightened and made more precise. Out of all novelistic works of antiquity, the term "novel" was, therefore, attached to the Greek novel alone. Nevertheless, the serio-comical genres mentioned above anticipate the more essential historical aspects in the development of the novel in modern times, even though they lack that sturdy skeleton of plot and composition that we have grown accustomed to demand from the novel as a genre. This applies in particular to the Socratic dialogues, which may be called—to rephrase Friedrich Schlegel—"the novels of their time," and also to Menippean satire (including the *Satyricon* of Petronius), whose role in the history of the novel is immense and as yet inadequately appreciated by scholarship. These serio-comical genres were the first authentic and essential step in the evolution of the novel as the genre of becoming.

Precisely what is this novelistic spirit in these serio-comical genres, and on what basis do we claim them as the first step in the development of the novel? It is this: contemporary reality serves as their subject, and—even more important—it is the starting point for understanding, evaluating and formulating such genres. For the first time, the subject of serious literary representation (although, it is true, at the same time comical) is portrayed without any distance, on the level of contemporary reality, in a zone of direct and even crude contact. Even where the past or myth serves as the subject of representation in these genres there is no epic distance, and contemporary reality provides the point of view. Of special significance in this process of demolishing distance is the comical origin of these genres: they derive from folklore (popular laughter). It is precisely laughter that destroys the epic, and in general destroys any hierarchical (distancing and valorized) distance. As a distanced image a subject cannot be comical; to be made comical, it must be brought close. Everything that makes us laugh is close at hand, all comical creativity works in a zone of maximal proximity. Laughter has the remarkable power of making an object come up close, of drawing it into a zone of crude contact where one can finger it familiarly on all sides, turn it upside down, inside out, peer at it from above and below, break open its external shell, look into its center, doubt it, take it apart, dismember it, lay it bare and expose it, examine it freely and experiment with it. Laughter demolishes fear and piety before an object, before a world, making of it an object of familiar contact and thus clearing the ground for an absolutely free investigation of it. Laughter is a vital factor in laying down that prerequisite for fearlessness without which it would be impossible to approach the world realistically. As it draws an object to itself and makes it familiar, laughter delivers the object into the fearless hands of investigative experiment—both scientific and artistic—and into the hands of free experimental fantasy. Familiarization of the world through laughter and popular speech is an extremely important and indispensable step in making possible free, scientifically knowable and artistically realistic creativity in European civilization. [. . .]

The destruction of epic distance and the transferal of the image of an individual from the distanced plane to the zone of contact with the inconclusive events of the present (and consequently of the future) result in a radical re-structuring of the image of the individual in the novel—and consequently in all literature. Folklore and popular-comic sources for the novel played a huge role in this process. Its first and essential step was the comic familiarization of the image of man. Laughter destroyed epic distance; it began to investigate man freely and familiarly, to turn him inside out, expose the disparity between his surface and his center, between his potential and his reality. A dynamic authenticity was introduced into the image of man, dynamics of inconsistency and tension between various factors of this image; man ceased to coincide with himself, and consequently men ceased to be exhausted entirely by the plots that contain them. Of these inconsistencies and tensions laughter plays up, first of all, the comic sides (but not only the comic sides); in the serio-comical genres of antiquity, images of a new order emerge—for example, the imposing, newly and more complexly integrated heroic image of Socrates.

Characteristic here is the artistic structuring of an image out of durable popular masks—masks that had great influence on the novelistic image of man during the most important stages of the novel's development (the serio-comical genres of antiquity, Rabelais, Cervantes). Outside his destiny, the epic and tragic hero is nothing; he is, therefore, a function of the plot fate assigns him; he cannot become the hero of another destiny or another plot. On the contrary, popular masks—Maccus, Pulcinello, Harlequin—are able to assume any destiny and can figure into any situation (they often do so within the limits of a single play), but they cannot exhaust their possibilities by those situations alone; they always retain, in any situation and in any destiny, a happy surplus of their own, their own rudimentary but inexhaustible human face. Therefore these masks can function and speak independent of the plot; but, moreover, it is precisely in these excursions outside the plot proper—in the Atellan *trices*, in the *lazzi* of Italian comedy[13]—that they best of all reveal a face of their own. Neither an epic nor a tragic hero could ever step out in his own character during a pause in the plot or during an intermission: he has no face for it, no gesture, no language. In this is his strength and his limitation. The epic and tragic hero is the hero who, by his very nature, must perish. Popular masks, on the contrary, never perish: not a single plot in Atellan, Italian or Italianized French comedies provides for, or could ever provide for, the actual death of a Maccus, a Pulcinello or a Harlequin. However, one frequently witnesses their fictive comic deaths (with subsequent resurrections). These are heroes of free improvisation and not heroes of tradition, heroes of a life process that is imperishable and forever renewing itself, forever contemporary—these are not heroes of an absolute past.

These masks and their structure (the non-coincidence with themselves, and with any given situation—the surplus, the inexhaustibility of their self and the like), have had, we repeat, an enormous influence on the development of the novelistic image of man. This structure is preserved even in the novel, although in a more complex, deeply meaningful and serious (or serio-comical) form.

One of the basic internal themes of the novel is precisely the theme of the hero's inadequacy to his fate or his situation. The individual is either greater than his fate, or less than his condition; as a man. He cannot become once and for all a clerk, a landowner, a merchant, a fiancé, a jealous lover, a father and so forth. If the hero of a novel actually becomes something of the sort—that is, if he completely coincides with his situation and his fate (as do generic, everyday heroes, the majority of secondary characters in a novel)—then the surplus inhering in the human condition is realized in the main protagonist. The way in which this surplus will actually be realized grows out of the author's orientation toward form and content, that is, the ways he sees and depicts individuals. It is precisely the zone of contact with an inconclusive present (and consequently with the future) that creates the necessity of this incongruity of a man with himself. There always remains in him unrealized potential and unrealized demands. The future exists, and this future ineluctably touches upon the individual, has its roots in him.

An individual cannot be completely incarnated into the flesh of existing sociohistorical categories. There is no mere form that would be able to incarnate once and forever all of his human possibilities and needs, no form in which he could exhaust himself down to the last word, like the tragic or epic hero; no form that he could fill to the very brim, and yet at the same time not splash over the brim. There always remains an unrealized surplus of humanness; there always remains a need for the future, and a place for this future must be found. All existing clothes are always too tight, and thus comical, on a man. But this surplus of un-fleshed-out humanness may be realized not only in the hero, but also in the author's point of view (as, for example, in Gogol). Reality as we have it in the novel is only one of many possible realities; it is not inevitable, not arbitrary, it bears within itself other possibilities.

The epic wholeness of an individual disintegrates in a novel in other ways as well. A crucial tension develops between the external and the internal man, and as a result the subjectivity of the individual becomes an object of experimentation and representation—and first of all on the humorous familiarizing plane. Coordination breaks down between the various aspects: man for himself alone and man in the eyes of others. This disintegration of the integrity that an individual had possessed in epic (and in tragedy) combines in the novel with the necessary preparatory steps toward a new, complex wholeness on a higher level of human development.

Finally, in a novel the individual acquires the ideological and linguistic initiative necessary to change the nature of his own image (there is a new and higher type of individualization of the image). In the antique stage of novelistic development there appeared remarkable examples of such hero-ideologues—the image of Socrates, the image of a laughing Epicurus in the so-called "Hypocratic" novel, the deeply novelized image of Diogenes in the thoroughly dialogized literature of the cynics and in Menippean satire (where it closely approximates the image of the popular mask) and, finally, the image of Menippius in Lucian. As a rule, the hero of a novel is always more or less an ideologue.

What all this suggests is a somewhat abstract and crude schematization for restructuring the image of an individual in the novel.

We will summarize with some conclusions.

The present, in its all open-endedness, taken as a starting point and center for artistic and ideological orientation, is an enormous evolution in the creative consciousness of man. In the European world this reorientation and destruction of the old hierarchy of temporalities received its crucial generic expression on the boundary between classic antiquity and Hellenism, and in the new world during the late Middle Ages and Renaissance. The fundamental constituents of the novel as a genre were formed in these eras, although some of the separate elements making up the novel were present much earlier, and the novel's roots must ultimately be sought in folklore. In these eras all other major genres had already long since come to completion, they were already old and almost ossified genres. They were all permeated from top to bottom with a more ancient hierarchization of temporalities. The novel, from the very beginning, developed as a genre that had at its core a new way of conceptualizing time. The absolute past, tradition, hierarchical distance played no role in the formation of the novel as a genre (such spatiotemporal categories did play a role, though insignificant, in certain periods of the novel's development, when it was slightly influenced by the epic—for example in the Baroque novel). The novel took shape precisely at the point when epic distance was disintegrating, when both the world and man were assuming a degree of comic familiarity, when the object of artistic representation was being degraded to the level of a contemporary reality that was inconclusive and fluid. From the very beginning the novel was structured not in the distanced image of the absolute past but in the zone of direct contact with inconclusive present-day reality. At its core lay personal experience and free creative imagination. Thus a new, sober artistic-prose novelistic image and a new critical scientific perception came into being simultaneously. From the very beginning, then, the novel was made of different clay than the other already completed genres; it is a different breed, and with it and in it is born the future of all literature. Once it came into being, it could never be merely one genre among others, and it could not erect rules for interrelating with others in peaceful and harmonious co-existence. In the presence of the novel, all other genres somehow have a different resonance. A lengthy battle for the novelization of the other genres began, a battle to drag them into a zone of contact with reality. The course of this battle has been complex and tortuous.

The novelization of literature does not imply attaching to already completed genres a generic canon that is alien to them, not theirs. The novel, after all, has no canon of its own. It is, by its very nature, not canonic. It is plasticity itself. It is a genre that is ever questing, ever examining itself and subjecting its established forms to review. Such, indeed, is the only possibility open to a genre that structures itself in a zone of direct contact with developing reality. Therefore, the novelization of other genres does not imply their subjection to an alien generic canon; on the contrary, novelization implies their liberation from all that serves as a brake on their unique development, from all that would change them along with the novel into some sort of stylization of forms that have outlived themselves.

I have developed my various positions in this essay in a somewhat abstract way. There have been few illustrations, and even these were taken only from an ancient period in the novel's development. My choice was determined by the fact that the significance of that period has been greatly underestimated. When people talk about the ancient period of the novel they have traditionally had in mind the "Greek novel" alone. The ancient period of the novel is enormously significant for a proper understanding of the genre. But in ancient times the novel could not really develop all its potential; this potential came to light only in the modern world. We indicated that in several works of antiquity, the inconclusive present begins to sense a greater proximity to the future than to the past. The absence of a temporal perspective in ancient society assured that this process of reorientation toward a real future could not complete itself; after all, there was no real concept of a future. Such a reorientation occurred for the first time during the Renaissance. In that era, the present (that is, a reality that was contemporaneous) for the first time began to sense itself not only as an incomplete continuation of the past, but as something like a new and heroic beginning. To reinterpret reality on the level of the contemporary present now meant not only to degrade, but to raise reality into a new and heroic sphere. It was in the Renaissance that the present first began to feel with great clarity and awareness an incomparably closer proximity and kinship to the future than to the past.

The process of the novel's development has not yet come to an end. It is currently entering a new phase. For our era is characterized by an extraordinary complexity and a deepening in our perception of the world; there is an unusual growth in demands; on human discernment, on mature objectivity and the critical faculty. These are features that will shape the further development of the novel as well.

Notes

1. From M. M. Bakhtin, *The Dialogic Imagination: Four Essays*, ed. Michael Holquist, trans. Caryl Emerson and Michael Holquist. Austin: University of Texas Press, 1981.

2. Erwin Rohde's *Der Griechesche Roman und seine Vorläufer* (1876), one of the greatest monuments of nineteenth-century classical scholarship in Germany. [Translator's note]

3. Nicolas Boileau-Despréaux, French poet and critic who deployed his wit to criticize the bad taste of his time in *Satires* (1666) and *L'Art poétique* (1674).

4. Henrik Ibsen, Norwegian playwright who promoted realism in modern drama, in such plays as *A Doll's House* (1873). Gerhart Hauptmann, German playwright, novelist and poet who inaugurated the naturalist movement in Germany with *Before Dawn* (1889).

5. Heinrich Heine (1797–1856), journalist, essayist, and one of the most important German Romantic poets.

6. Charles Sorel (1599–1674), an important figure in the reaction to the *preciosité* of such figures as Honoré d'Urfé (1567–1625), whose *L'Astrée*, a monstrous 5,500-page volume overflowing with high-flown language, is parodied in *Le Berger extravagant* (1627). The latter book's major protagonist is a dyed-in-the-wool Parisian who reads too many pastoral novels; intoxicated by these, he attempts to live the rustic life as they describe it—with predictably comic results. [Tr.]

7. Henry Fielding parodied Samuel Richardson's moralizing novel *Pamela: or, Virtue Rewarded* in his *Shamela* (1741); in *Grandison der Zweite* (1762), J.K.A. Musäus satirized Richardson's later novel *The History of Sir Charles Grandison*.

8. Aëdonic songs: folk songs. Cantilenas: ballads.

9. Bakhtin's essay "From the Prehistory of Novelistic Discourse," included in *The Dialogic Imagination*, 41–83.

10. Sophron (fl. fifth century BCE) wrote mimes based on everyday life. Ion of Chios (490–421 BCE) wrote a memoir that included a vivid description of an evening

with Sophocles. Critias (460–403 BCE), one of the Thirty Tyrants of Athens, also wrote elegies and tragedies. His rambling *Homilai* ("discussions") survive only in fragments.

11.   Menippus was a Greek cynic and satirist of the third century BCE, credited as the founder of the genre of episodic Menippean satire. Lucian (ca. 125–180) was a Greek satirist whose works include *Dialogues of the Dead*.

12.   Abbé Huet, bishop of Avranches and a prolific scholar, whose *Traité de l'origine des romans* (1670) was first published as an introduction to Mme de Lafayette's *Zaïde,* a novel written while its author was still influenced by ideas of the *précieux* society.

13.   *Trices* are thought to have been interludes in the action of the Atellanae (Roman farces) during which the masks often stepped out of character. *Lazzi* were what we might now call "routines" or "numbers" that were not part of the ongoing action of the plot. [Tr.]

12

Preface to *European Literature and the Latin Middle Ages*[1] (1948)

Ernst Robert Curtius

Born and raised in Alsace, a disputed territory that passed back and forth between the French and German states from the seventeenth to the twentieth century, Ernst Robert Curtius (1886–1956) was one of the most distinguished literary scholars of his generation. For the greater part of his professional life, he held a professorship in Romance Philology at the University of Bonn. He first became known for his extensive writings on modern French, English, and Spanish literature, but his *magnum opus* is *European Literature and the Latin Middle Ages* (1948). Emphasizing the common culture fostered by the Latin language rather than the emerging vernaculars that would develop into separate national languages, this work powerfully asserts the unity of European literature and the grounds of its continuity from its origins in Greek and Roman antiquity.

Curtius has come under criticism, like all intellectuals who remained in Nazi Germany and maintained their posts, but he had strongly protested the cultural program of the rising Nazi movement in a book published just before Hitler came to power, *Deutscher Geist in Gefahr* (The German spirit/intellect in danger, 1932). Unable to voice objections openly after Hitler became chancellor of Germany in 1933, Curtius turned to the study of the Middle Ages, in a project that was at once conservative and subversive. The result was *European Literature and the Latin Middle Ages*, a work that stands alongside Erich Auerbach's *Mimesis* (1946) as a testament to the unity of European humanist culture that was gravely—some would say terminally—threatened by the conflict tearing Europe apart. The project of cultural synthesis and retrieval was made all the more historically urgent by the murderous, racialized nationalism of the "German catastrophe," a sentiment eloquently articulated by Curtius in 1953 in the preface to the English translation of his study.

For the English edition of this book a few words of explanation will perhaps be welcomed.

My central field of study is the Romance languages and literatures. After the war of 1914–18 I saw it as my task to make modern France understood in Germany through studies of Rolland, Gide, Claudel, Péguy (*Die literarischen Wegbereiter des neuen Frankreich* [1919]); of Barrès (1922) and Balzac (1923); of Proust, Valéry, Larbaud (*Französischer Geist im neuen Europa* [1925]). This cycle was closed with a study of French culture (*Einführung in die französische Kultur* [1930]). By that time I had already begun studying English and American authors. An essay on T. S. Eliot (with a translation of *The Waste Land*) appeared in 1927, a study of James Joyce in 1929. Studies published during the last twenty-five years are collected in my *Kritische Essays zur europäischen Literatur* (1950). This contains essays on Virgil, Goethe, Friedrich Schlegel, Emerson, Stefan George, Hofmannsthal, Unamuno, Ortega y Gasset, Eliot, Toynbee.

Virgil and Dante have long had a place in the innermost circle of my admiration. What were the roads that led from the one to the other? This question increasingly preoccupied me. The answer could not but be found in the Latin continuity of the Middle Ages. And that in turn was a portion of the European tradition, which has Homer at its beginning and at its end, as we see today, Goethe.

This tradition of thought and art was severely shaken by the war of 1914–18 and its aftermath, especially in Germany. In 1932 I published my polemical pamphlet *Deutscher Geist in Gefahr*. It attacked the barbarization of education and the nationalistic frenzy which were the forerunners of the Nazi regime. In it I pleaded for a new Humanism, which should integrate the Middle Ages, from Augustine to Dante. I had undergone the influence of a great American book: *Founders of the Middle Ages* by Edward Kennard Rand (1871–1945).

When the German catastrophe came, I decided to serve the idea of a medievalistic Humanism by studying the Latin literature of the Middle Ages. These studies occupied me for fifteen years. The result of them is the present book. It appeared in 1948. I put it forth with trepidation, for I did not believe that I could count upon its arousing any response. It was not in line with any of the scientific, scholarly, or philosophic trends which governed contemporary thought. That it nevertheless aroused attention and sympathy was a gratifying surprise to me.

What I have said will have made it clear that my book is not the product of purely scholarly interests, that it grew out of a concern for the preservation of Western culture. It seeks to serve an understanding of the Western cultural tradition in so far as it is manifested in literature. It attempts to illuminate the unity of that tradition in space and time by the application of new methods. In the intellectual chaos of the present it has become necessary, and happily not impossible, to demonstrate that unity. But the demonstration can only be made from a universal standpoint. Such a standpoint is afforded by Latinity. Latin was the language of the educated during the thirteen centuries which lie between Virgil and Dante. Without this Latin background, the vernacular literatures of the Middle Ages are incomprehensible. Some of my critics have objected that important phenomena of medieval literature (e.g., the *Song of Roland*, the troubadours, the drama) do not appear in my book. Perhaps these critics did not read its title. It treats of the *Latin* Middle Ages, not of the Middle Ages in general. There is no lack of good books on the vernacular literatures of France, Germany, Italy, Spain. My book does not undertake to compete with them, but to provide what they do not provide.

The Latin Middle Ages is one focus of the ellipse here under consideration. The other focus is European literature. Hence much will be said concerning Greek and Roman Antiquity, together with much concerning schools and works of the sixteenth and seventeenth centuries. I venture to hope that even specialists in these periods will find something useful in my book. My book, however, is not addressed to scholars, but to lovers of literature, that is, to those who are interested in literature as literature. In the preface to his *History of Criticism* George Saintsbury says: "A friend who is at once friendly, most competent, and of a different complexion in critical thought, objected to me that 'I treat literature as something by itself.' I hastened to admit the impeachment, and to declare that this is the very postulate of my book." Of course literature cannot be absolutely isolated, as Saintsbury well knew. In my book there will also be found things which I could not have seen without C. G. Jung; problems in the history of civilization and in the history of philosophy will also be touched upon; something is said about the seven liberal arts, the universities, and so on. But the spotlight of observation is always upon literature; its themes, its techniques, its biology, its sociology.

The reader can find information here on where the word *literature* comes from and what meaning it had originally; what a canon of writers is; how the concept of the classic author was formed and how it developed. The recurrent or constant phenomena of literary biology are investigated; the opposition between "ancients" and "moderns"; the anticlassical trends which are today called Baroque and for which I prefer the name Mannerism. Poetry is investigated in its relation to philosophy and theology. The question is raised by what means it has idealized human life (the hero, the shepherd) and nature (description of landscape), and what fixed types it has developed for the purpose. All these and other questions are prolegomena to what I should like to call a phenomenology of literature. This appears to me something different from literary history, comparative literature, and "Literaturwissenschaft"[2] as they are practiced today.

Contemporary archaeology has made surprising discoveries by means of aerial photography at great altitudes. Through this technique it has succeeded, for example, in recognizing for the first time the late Roman system of defense works in North Africa. A person standing on the ground before a heap of ruins cannot see the whole that the aerial photograph reveals. But the next step is to enlarge the aerial photograph and compare it with a detailed map. There is a certain analogy to this procedure in the technique of literary investigation here employed. If we attempt to embrace two or two and a half millenniums of Western literature in one view, we can make discoveries which are impossible from a church steeple. Yet we can do so only when the parochialism of the specialists has provided careful detailed studies. All too often, to be sure, such studies are lacking, and from a more elevated standpoint we see tasks which would promise a rich yield to individual research. The historical disciplines will progress wherever specialization and contemplation of the whole are combined and interpenetrate. The two require each other and stand in a complementary relation. Specialization without universalism is blind. Universalism without specialization is inane.

But as far as viewing the whole in the field of literature is concerned, Saintsbury's axiom is valid: "Ancient without Modern is a stumbling block, Modern without Ancient is foolishness utter and irremediable." My book, as I said, is not the product of purely scholarly interests. It grew out of vital urges and under the pressure of a concrete historical situation. But in order to convince, I had to use the scientific technique which is the foundation of all historical investigation: philology. For the intellectual sciences it has the same significance as mathematics has for the natural sciences. As Leibniz[3] taught, there are two kinds of truths: on the one hand, those which are only arrived at by reason and which neither need nor are capable of empirical confirmation; on the other hand, those which are recognized through experience and which are logically indemonstrable; necessary truths and accidental truths, or, as Leibniz also puts it, *vérités éternelles et vérités de fait*. The accidental truths of fact can only be established by philology. Philology is the handmaid of the historical disciplines. I have attempted to employ it with something of the precision with which the natural sciences employ their methods. Geometry demonstrates with figures, philology with texts. But philology too ought to give results which are verifiable.

But if the subject of this book is approached through philological technique, it is nevertheless clear, I hope, that philology is not an end in itself. What we are dealing with is literature—that is, the great intellectual and spiritual tradition of Western culture as given form in language. It contains imperishable treasures of beauty, greatness, faith. It is a reservoir of spiritual energies through which we can flavor and ennoble our present-day life.[4]

Notes

1. From *European Literature and the Latin Middle Ages*, trans. Willard R. Trask (New York: Pantheon,1953, reprinted Princeton University Press, 1973). Originally published as *Europäische Literatur und lateinisches Mittelalter* (Bern: A. Francke, 1948).

2. Positivistic literary studies.

3. Gottfried Wilhelm Leibniz (1646–1716), one of the leading rationalist philosophers of the Enlightenment.

4. [Curtius concludes his preface with a final note]: I attempted some suggestions in this direction in 1949 at Aspen, Colorado, where, on the occasion of the Goethe Bicentennial Convocation, I spoke on "The Medieval Bases of Western Thought." This lecture supplements my book and hence, with the publisher's permission, is here included as an appendix.

13

Philology and *Weltliteratur*[1] (1952)

Erich Auerbach

One of the most influential comparatists of the twentieth century, Erich Auerbach continues to attract readers by his remarkable range, his erudition, and the melancholy eloquence of his style. Born in Berlin in 1892, he took a degree in law at Heidelberg in 1913. After serving in the German army during World War I, he shifted from law to the field of romance philology, earning his doctorate in 1921 with a dissertation on the early novel in France and Italy. He worked for several years as a librarian before becoming professor of Romance Philology at the University of Marbourg. Together with his friends and rivals Ernst Robert Curtius and Leo Spitzer, Auerbach broadened philological study into a deep engagement with literary works through close attention to style. Auerbach was particularly fascinated to explore the roots of novelistic realism. In a major essay entitled "Figura," for instance, he argued that medieval allegory gained its power by fusing transcendent religious meaning with concrete earthly realities; this perspective informed his influential early book *Dante, Poet of the Earthly World* (1929).

Auerbach's peaceful career as a German academic was disrupted by the rise of the Nazis to power. Stripped of his professorship in 1935 during a purge of Jewish academics, Auerbach followed the lead of Leo Spitzer and took a post at Istanbul State University, where he remained until the end of the war. There he composed his masterpiece, *Mimesis: Dargestellte Wirklichkeit in der abendländischen Literatur* (1946), translated in 1953 as *Mimesis: The Representation of Reality in Western Literature*. An account of the rise of novelistic realism from antiquity to the twentieth century, *Mimesis* presented dazzling close readings of exemplary passages in the Bible, Homer, Dante, Rabelais, and many more writers up through Proust and Virginia Woolf. Squarely focused on issues of style, Auerbach's analyses penetrate to the soul of each work, and in its magisterial sweep, *Mimesis* became a compelling example of the ability of a cultivated mind to bring back together the cultural traditions of a Europe shattered by successive world wars. *Mimesis* is at once a meditation on literature's transcendence of local circumstances and also a product of Auerbach's own precarious position in exile during the war.

After the war ended, Auerbach left Europe for America, holding professorships first at Pennsylvania State University and then at Yale, where he worked on studies that would be published after his death in 1957 under the titles *Literary Language and Its Public in Late Antiquity and in the Middle Ages* (1958) and *Scenes from the Drama of European Literature* (1959). In his 1952 essay "Philology and *Weltliteratur*" Auerbach discusses his methods in the context of broad historical movements. He emphasizes the double-edged quality of the emerging world order of postwar modernity: we can read and appreciate a greater range of literatures than ever before, even as globalization threatens to produce a unitary world culture radically different from anything experienced before. The individual scholar has the responsibility, and the opportunity, to counter both the multiplicity of the past and the massification of the present through a blend of intuition, reading, and research—a combination that Auerbach compellingly embodied in his own writing.

———————

Nonnulla pars inventionis est nosse quid quaeras.[2]
—Augustine, Quest. in Hept, Prooem.

It is time to ask what meaning the word *Weltliteratur* can still have if we relate it, as Goethe did, both to the past and to the future. Our earth, the domain of *Weltliteratur*, does not merely refer to what is generically common and human; rather it considers humanity to be the product of fruitful intercourse between its members. The presupposition of *Weltliteratur* is a *felix culpa*: mankind's division into many cultures. Today, however, human life is becoming standardized. The process of imposed uniformity, which originally derived from Europe, continues its work, and hence serves to undermine all individual traditions. To be sure, national wills are stronger and louder than ever, yet in every case they promote the same standards and forms for modern life; and it is clear to the impartial observer that the inner bases of national existence are decaying. The European cultures, which have long enjoyed their fruitful interrelation, and which have always been supported by the consciousness of their worth, these cultures still retain their individualities. Nevertheless, even among them the process of leveling proceeds with a greater rapidity than ever before. Standardization, in short, dominates everywhere. All human activity is being concentrated into European-American or into Russian-Bolshevik patterns; no matter how great they seem to us, the differences between the two patterns are comparatively minimal when they are both contrasted with the basic patterns underlying the Islamic, Indian or Chinese traditions. Should mankind succeed in withstanding so mighty and rapid a process of concentration— for which the spiritual preparation has been poor—then man will have to accustom himself to existence in a standardized world, to a single literary culture, only a few literary languages and perhaps even a single literary language. And herewith the notion of *Weltliteratur* would now be at once realized and destroyed.

If I assess it correctly, in its compulsion and in its dependence on mass movements, this contemporary situation is not what Goethe had in mind. For he gladly avoided thoughts about what later history has made inevitable. He occasionally acknowledged the depressing tendencies of our world, yet no one could then suspect how radically, how unexpectedly, an unpleasant potential could be realized. His epoch was brief indeed; and yet those of us who are members of an older generation actually experienced its passing away. It is approximately five hundred years since the national European literatures won their self-consciousness from and their superiority over Latin civilization; scarcely two hundred years have passed since the awakening of our sense of historicism, a sense that permitted the formation of the concept of *Weltliteratur*. By the example and the stimulation of his work Goethe himself, who died one hundred and twenty years ago, contributed decisively to the development of historicism and to the philological research that was generated out of it. And already in our own time a world is emerging for which this sense no longer has much practical significance.

Although the period of Goethean humanism was brief indeed, it not only had important contemporary effects but it also initiated a great deal that continues, and is ramifying today. The world literatures that were available to Goethe at the end of his life were more numerous than those which were known at the time of his birth; compared to what is available to us today, however, the number was small. Our knowledge of world literatures is indebted to the impulse given that epoch by historicist humanism; the concern of that humanism was not only the overt discovery of materials and the development of methods of research, but beyond that their penetration and evaluation so that an inner history of mankind—which thereby created a conception of man unified in his multiplicity—could be written. Ever since Vico and Herder[3] this humanism has been the true purpose of philology: because of this purpose philology became the dominant branch of the humanities. It drew the history of the arts, the history of religion, law, and politics after itself, and wove itself variously with them into certain fixed aims and commonly achieved concepts of order. What was thereby gained, in terms of scholarship and synthesis, need not be recalled for the present reader.

Can such an activity be continued with meaning in wholly changed circumstances and prospects? The simple fact that it is continued, that it continues to be widespread, should not be overstressed. What has once become a habit or an institution continues for a long time, especially if those who are aware of a radical change in the circumstances of life are often neither ready nor able to make their awareness practically operative. There is hope to be gained from the passionate commitment to philological and historicist activity of a small number of young people who are distinguished for their talent and originality. It is encouraging to hope that their instinct for this work of theirs does not betray them, and that this activity still has relevance for the present and the future.

A scientifically ordered and conducted research of reality fills and rules our life; it is, if one wishes to name one, our Myth: we do not possess another that has such general validity. History is the science of reality that affects us most immediately, stirs us most deeply, and compels us most forcibly to a consciousness of ourselves. It is the only science in which human beings step before us in their totality. Under the rubric of history one is to understand not only the past, but the progression of events in general; history therefore includes the present. The inner history of the last thousand years is the history of mankind achieving self-expression: this is what philology, a historicist discipline, treats. This history contains the records of man's mighty, adventurous advance to a consciousness of his human condition and to the realization of his given potential; and this advance, whose final goal (even in its wholly fragmentary present form) was barely imaginable for a long time, still seems to have proceeded as if according to a plan, in spite of its twisted course. All the rich tensions of which our being is capable are contained within this course. An inner dream unfolds whose scope and depth entirely animate the spectator, enabling him at the same time to find peace in his given potential by the enrichment he gains from having witnessed the drama. The loss of such a spectacle—whose appearance is thoroughly dependent on presentation and interpretation—would be an impoverishment for which there can be no possible compensation. To be sure, only those who have not totally sustained this loss would be aware of privation. Even so, we must do everything within our power to prevent so grievous a loss. If my reflections on the future, with which I began this essay, have any validity, then the duty of collecting material and forming it into a whole that will continue to have effect is an urgent one. For we are still basically capable of fulfilling this duty, not only because we have a great deal of material at our disposal, but above all because we also have inherited the sense of historic perspectivism which is so necessary for the job. The reason we still possess this sense is that we live the experience of historical multiplicity, and without this experience, I fear, the sense would quickly lose its living concreteness. It also appears to me that we live at a time (*Kairos*)[4] when the fullest potential of reflective historiography is capable of being realized; whether many succeeding generations will still be part of such a time is questionable. We are already threatened with the impoverishment that results from an ahistorical system of education; not only does that threat exist but it also lays claim to dominating us. Whatever we are, we became in history, and only in history can we remain the way we are and develop therefrom: it is the task of philologists, whose province is the world of human history, to demonstrate this so that it penetrates our lives unforgettably. At the end of the chapter called "The Approach" in Adalbert Stifter's *Nachsommer* one of the characters says: "The highest of wishes is to imagine that after human life had concluded its period on earth, a spirit might survey and summarize all of the human arts from their inception to their disappearance." Stifter, however, only refers to the fine arts. Moreover, I do not believe it possible now to speak of the conclusion of human life. But it is correct to speak of our time as a period of conclusive change in which a hitherto unique survey appears to have become possible.

This conception of *Weltliteratur* and its philology seems less active, less practical and less political than its predecessor. There is no more talk now—as there had been—of a spiritual exchange between peoples, of the refinement of customs and of a reconciliation of races. In part these goals have failed of attainment, in part they have been superseded by historical developments. Certain distinguished individuals, small groups of highly cultivated men always have enjoyed, under the auspices of these goals, an organized cultural exchange: they will continue to do so. Yet this sort of activity has little effect on culture or on the reconciliation of peoples: it cannot withstand the storm of opposed vested interests—from which an intensified propaganda emerges—and so its results are immediately dissipated. An exchange that is effective is the kind that takes place between partners already brought together into a rapport based on political developments: such a cultural dialogue has an internally cohesive effect, hastens mutual understanding and serves a common purpose. But for those cultures not bound together thus there has been a disturbing (to a humanist with Goethean ideals) general rapport in which the antitheses that persist nonetheless [as those, for example, between differing national identities] are not being resolved except, paradoxically, through ordeals of sheer strength. The conception of *Weltliteratur* advocated in this essay—a conception of the diverse background of a common fate—does not seek to affect or alter that which has already begun to occur, albeit contrary to expectation; the present conception accepts as an inevitable fact that world-culture is being standardized. Yet this conception wishes to render precisely and, so that it may be retained, consciously to articulate the fateful coalescence of cultures for those people who are in the midst of the terminal phase of fruitful multiplicity: thus this coalescence, so rendered and articulated, will become their myth. In this manner, the full range of the spiritual movements of the last thousand years will not atrophy within them. One cannot speculate with much result about the future effects of such an effort. It is our task to create the possibility for such an effect; and only this much can be said, that for an age of transition such as ours the effect could be very significant. It may well be that this effect might also help to make us accept our fate with more equanimity so that we will not hate whoever opposes us—even when we are forced into a posture of antagonism. By token of this, our conception of *Weltliteratur* is no less human, no less humanistic, than its antecedent; the implicit comprehension of history—which underlies this conception of *Weltliteratur*—is not the same as the former one, yet it is a development of it and unthinkable without it.

II

It was noted above that we are fundamentally capable of performing the task of a philology of *Weltliteratur* because we command unlimited, steadily growing material, and because of our historic perspectivist sense, which is our heritage from the historicism of Goethe's time. Yet no matter how hopeful the outlook seems for such a task, the practical difficulties are truly great. In order for someone to penetrate and then construct an adequate presentation of the material of *Weltliteratur* he must command that material—or at least a major part of it—himself. Because, however, of the superabundance of materials, of methods and of points of view, a mastery of that sort has become virtually impossible. We possess literatures ranging over six thousand years, from all parts of the world, in perhaps fifty literary languages. Many cultures known to us today were unknown a hundred years ago; many of the ones already known to us in the past were known only partially. As for those cultural epochs most familiar to scholars for hundreds of years, so much that is new has been found out about them that our conception of these epochs has been radically altered—and entirely new problems have arisen. In addition to all of these difficulties, there is the consideration that one cannot concern himself solely with the literature of a given period; one must study the conditions under which this literature developed; one must take into account religion, philosophy, politics, economics, fine arts and music; in every one of these disciplines there must be sustained, active and individual research. Hence more and more exact specialization follows; special methods evolve, so that in each of the individual fields—even within each special point of view on a given field—a kind of esoteric language is generated. This is not all. Foreign, nonphilological or scientific methods and concepts begin to be felt in philology: sociology, psychology, certain kinds of philosophy, and contemporary literary criticism figure prominently among these influences from the outside. Thus all these elements must be assimilated and ordered even if only to be able to demonstrate, in good conscience, the uselessness of one of them for philology. The scholar who does not consistently limit himself to a narrow field of specialization and to a world of concepts held in common with a small circle of likeminded colleagues, lives in the midst of a tumult of impressions and claims on him: for the scholar to do justice to these is almost impossible. Still, it is becoming increasingly unsatisfactory to limit oneself to only one field of specialization. To be a Provençal specialist in our day and age, for example, and to command only the immediately relevant linguistic, paleological and historical facts, is hardly enough to be a good specialist. On the other hand, there are fields of specialization that have become so widely various that their mastery has become the task of a lifetime. Such fields are, for instance, the study of Dante (who can scarcely be called a "field of specialization" since doing him justice takes one practically everywhere), or the courtly romance, with its three related (and problematic) subtopics, courtly love, Celtic matter and Grail literature. How many scholars have really made one of these fields entirely their own? How can anyone go on to speak of a scholarly and synthesizing philology of *Weltliteratur*?

A few individuals today do have a commanding overview of the European material; so far as I know, however, they all belong to the generation that matured before the two World Wars. These scholars cannot be replaced very easily, for since their generation the academic study of Greek, Latin and the Bible—which was a mainstay of the late period of bourgeois humanistic culture—has collapsed nearly everywhere. If I may draw conclusions from my own experiences in Turkey, then it is easy to note corresponding changes in non-European, but equally ancient, cultures. Formerly, what could be taken for granted in the university (and, in the English-speaking countries, at the post-graduate level) must now be acquired there; most often such acquirements are either made too late or they are inadequate. Moreover, the intellectual center of gravity within the university or graduate school has shifted; there is a greater emphasis on the most modern literature and criticism, and, when earlier periods are favored with scholarly attention, they are usually periods like the baroque, which have been recently rediscovered, perhaps because they lie within the scope of modern literary prejudices and catchalls. It is obviously from within the situation and mentality of our own time that the whole of history has to be comprehended if it is to have significance for us. But a talented student possesses and is possessed by the spirit of his own time anyway: it seems to me that he should not need academic instruction in order to appropriate the work of Rilke or Gide or Yeats. He does need instruction, however, to understand the verbal conventions and the forms of life of the ancient world, the Middle Ages, the Renaissance, and also to learn to know the methods and means for exploring earlier periods. The problematics and the ordering categories of contemporary literary criticism are always significant, not only because they often are ingenious and illuminating in themselves, but also because they express the inner will of their period. Nevertheless only a few of them have an immediate use in historicist philology or as substitutes for genuinely transmitted concepts. Most of them are too abstract and ambiguous, and frequently they have too private a slant. They confirm a temptation to which neophytes (and acolytes) are frequently inclined to submit: the desire to master a great mass of material through the introduction of hypostatized, abstract concepts of order; this leads to the effacement of what is being studied, to the discussion of illusory problems and finally to bare juggling of terms.

Though they appear to be disturbing, such scholarly tendencies do not strike me as being truly dangerous, at least not for the sincere and gifted student of literature. Furthermore, there are talented people who manage to acquire for themselves whatever is indispensable for historical and philological study, and who also manage to adopt the proper attitudes of open-mindedness and independence toward modish intellectual currents. In many respects these young people have a distinct advantage over their predecessors. During the past forty years events have enlarged our intellectual perspectives, new outlooks on history and on reality have been revealed, and the view of the structure of interhuman processes has been enriched and renewed. We have participated—indeed, we are still participating—in a practical seminar on world history; accordingly, our insight and our conceptual powers with regard to historical matters have developed considerably. Thus even many extraordinary works, which had previously seemed to us to be outstanding philological achievements of late bourgeois humanism, now appear unrealistic and restricted in their positing of the problems they set themselves. Today we have it somewhat easier than forty years ago.

But how is the problem of synthesis to be solved? A single lifetime seems too short to create even the preliminaries. The organized work of a group is no answer, even if a group has high uses otherwise. The historical synthesis of which I am speaking, although it has significance only when it is based on a scholarly penetration of the material, is a product of personal intuition and hence can only be expected from an individual. Should it succeed perfectly we would be given a scholarly achievement and a work of art at the same time. Even the discovery of a point of departure [*Ansatzpunkt*] —of which I shall speak later—is a matter of intuition: the performance of the synthesis is a form which must be unified and suggestive if it is to fulfill its potential. Surely the really noteworthy achievement of such a work is due to a uniting intuition; in order to achieve its effect historical synthesis must in addition appear to be a work of art. The traditional protestation, that literary art must possess the freedom to be itself—which means that it must not be bound to scientific truth—can scarcely be voiced: for as they present themselves today historical subjects offer the imagination quite enough freedom in the questions of choice, of the problems they seem to generate, of their combination with each other, and of their formulation. One can say in fact that scientific truth is a good restriction on the philologist; scientific truth preserves and guarantees the probable in the "real," so that the great temptation to withdraw from reality (be it by trivial glossing or by shadowy distortion) is thereby foiled, for reality is the criterion of the probable. Besides, we are concerned with the need for a synthetic history-from-within, with history, that is, as the *genos* [class, family] of the European tradition of literary art: the historiography of classical antiquity was a literary *genos*, for example, and similarly the philosophic and historicist criticism created by German Classicism and Romanticism strove for its own form of literary art and expression.

III

Thus we return to the individual. How is he to achieve synthesis? It seems to me that he certainly cannot do it by encyclopedic collecting. A wider perspective than mere fact gathering is an imperative condition, but it should be gained very early in the process, unintentionally, and with an instinctive personal interest for its only guidepost. Yet the experience of recent decades has shown us that the accumulation of material in one field, an accumulation that strives for the exhaustiveness of the great handbooks that treat a national literature, a great epoch or a literary *genos*, can hardly lead to synthesis and formulation. The difficulty lies not only in the copiousness of the material that is scarcely within the grasp of a single individual (so much so that a group project seems to be required), but also in the structure of the material itself. The traditional divisions of the material, chronological, geographical or typological, are no longer suitable and cannot guarantee any sort of energetic, unified advance. The fields covered by such divisions do not coincide with the problematic areas with which the synthesis is coping. It has even become a matter of some doubt to me whether monographs—and there are many excellent ones—on single, significant authors are suited to be points of departure for the kind of synthesis that I have been speaking about. Certainly a single author embodies as complete and concrete a unity of life as any, and this is always better than an invented unity; but at the same time such a unity is finally ungraspable because it has passed into the ahistorical inviolability into which individuality always flows.

The most impressive recent book in which a synthesizing historical view is accomplished is Ernst Robert Curtius's book on European literature and the Latin Middle Ages. It seems to me that this book owes its success to the fact that despite its comprehensive, general title, it proceeds from a clearly prescribed, almost narrow, single phenomenon: the survival of the scholastic rhetorical tradition. Despite the monstrosity of the materials it mobilizes, in its best parts this book is not a mere agglomeration of many items, but a radiation outwards from a few items. Its general subject is the survival of the ancient world in the Latin Middle Ages, and the effect on the new European literature of the medieval forms taken by classical culture. When one has so general and comprehensive an intention one can at first do nothing. The author, who in the earliest stages of his project intends only the presentation of so broadly stated a theme, stands before an unsurveyable mass of various material that defies order. If it were to be collected mechanistically—for example, according to the survival of a set of individual writers, or according to the survival of the whole ancient world in the succession of one medieval century after another—the mere outlines of such a bulk would make a formulated intention towards this material impossible. Only by the discovery of a phenomenon at once firmly circumscribed, comprehensible and central enough to be a point of departure (in this case, the rhetorical tradition, and especially the *topoi*) was the execution of Curtius's plan made possible. Whether Curtius's choice for a point of departure was satisfactory, or whether it was the best of all possible choices for his intention, is not being debated; precisely because one might contend that Curtius's point of departure was inadequate one ought to admire the resulting achievement all the more. For Curtius's achievement is obligated to the following methodological principle: in order to accomplish a major work of synthesis it is imperative to locate a point of departure, a handle, as it were, by which the subject can be seized. The point of departure must be the election of a firmly circumscribed, easily seen, set of phenomena whose interpretation is a radiation out from them and which orders and interprets a greater region than they themselves occupy.

This method has been known to scholars for a long time. The discipline of stylistics, for example, has long availed itself of the method in order to describe a style's individuality in terms of a few fixed characteristics. Yet it seems to me to be necessary to emphasize the method's general significance, which is that it is the only method that makes it possible for us now to write a history-from-within against a broader background, to write synthetically and suggestively. The method also makes it possible for a younger scholar, even a beginner, to accomplish that end; a comparatively modest general knowledge buttressed by advice can suffice once intuition has found an auspicious point of departure. In the elaboration of this point of departure, the intellectual perspective enlarges itself both sufficiently and naturally, since the choice of material to be drawn is determined by the point of departure. Elaboration therefore is so concrete, its component parts hang together with such necessity, that what is thereby gained cannot easily be lost: the result, in its ordered exposition, possesses unity and universality.

Of course in practice the general intention does not always precede the concrete point of departure. Sometimes one discovers a single point of departure that releases the recognition and formulation of the general problem. Naturally, this can only occur when a predisposition for the problem already exists. It is essential to remark that a general, synthetic intention or problem does not suffice in and of itself. Rather, what needs to be found is a partially apprehendable phenomenon that is as circumscribed and concrete as possible, and therefore describable in technical, philological terms. Problems will therefore roll forth from it, so that a formulation of one's intention can become feasible. At other times, a single point of departure will not be sufficient—several will be necessary; if the first one is present, however, others are more easily available, particularly as they must be of the kind that not only links itself to others, but also converges on a central intention. It is therefore a question of specialization—not a specializing of the traditional modes of classifying material—but of the subject at hand, which needs constant rediscovery.

Points of departure can be very various; to enumerate all the possibilities here is quite impracticable. The characteristic of a good point of departure is its concreteness and its precision on the one hand, and on the other, its potential for centrifugal radiation. A semantic interpretation, a rhetorical trope, a syntactic sequence, the interpretation of one sentence, or a set of remarks made at a given time and in a given place—any of these can be a point of departure, but once chosen it must have radiating power, so that with it we can deal with world history. If one were to investigate the position of the writer in the nineteenth century—in either one country or in the whole of Europe—the investigation would produce a useful reference book (if it contained all the necessary material for such a study) for which we would be very grateful. Such a book has its uses, but the synthesis of which we have been speaking would more likely be achieved if one were to proceed from a few remarks made by writers about the public. Similarly, such subjects as the enduring reputation (*la fortuna*) of various poets can only be studied if a concrete point of departure is found to coerce the general theme. Existing works on Dante's reputation in various countries are certainly indispensable: a still more interesting work would emerge (and I am indebted to Erwin Panofsky for this suggestion) were one to trace the interpretation of individual portions of the *Commedia* from its earliest commentators to the sixteenth century, and then again since Romanticism. That would be an accurate type of spiritual history [*Geistesgeschichte*].

A good point of departure must be exact and objective; abstract categories of one sort or another will not serve. Thus concepts like "the Baroque" or "the Romantic," "the dramatic" or "the idea of fate," "intensity" or "myth," or "the concept of time" and "perspectivism" are dangerous. They can be used when their meaning is made clear in a specific context, but they are too ambiguous and inexact to be points of departure. For a point of departure should not be a generality imposed on a theme from the outside, but ought rather to be an organic inner part of the theme itself. What is being studied should speak for itself, but that can never happen if the point of departure is neither concrete nor clearly defined. In any event, a great deal of skill is necessary—even if one has the best point of departure possible—in order to keep oneself focused on the object of study. Ready-made, though rarely suitable, concepts whose appeal is deceptive because it is based on their attractive sound and their modishness, lie in wait, ready to spring in on the work of a scholar who has lost contact with the energy of the object of study. Thus the writer of a scholarly work is often tricked into accepting the substitution of a cliché for the true object; surely a great many readers can also be deceived. Since readers are all too prone to this sort of substitution, it is the scholar's job to make such evasions impossible. The phenomena treated by the philologist whose intention is synthesis contain their own objectivity, and this objectivity must not disappear in the synthesis: it is most difficult to achieve this aim. Certainly one ought not to aim at a complacent exultation in the particular, but rather at being moved and stirred by the movement of a whole. Yet the movement can be discovered in its purity only when all the particulars that make it up are grasped as essences.

So far as I know we possess no attempts at a philological synthesis of *Weltliteratur*; only a few preliminary efforts in this direction are to be found within Western culture. But the more our earth grows closer together, the more must historicist synthesis balance the contraction by expanding its activity. To make men conscious of themselves in their own history is a great task, yet the task is small—more like a renunciation—when one considers that man not only lives on earth, but that he is in the world and in the universe. But what earlier epochs dared to do—to designate man's place in the universe—now appears to be a very far-off objective.

In any event, our philological home is the earth; it can no longer be the nation. The most priceless and indispensable part of a philologist's heritage is still his own nation's culture and language. Only when he is first separated from this heritage, however, and then transcends it does it become truly effective. We must return, in admittedly altered circumstances, to the knowledge that prenational medieval culture already possessed: the knowledge that the spirit [*Geist*] is not national. *Paupertas* and *terra aliena*:[5] this, or something to this effect, can be read in Bernard of Chartres, John of Salisbury, Jean de Meun and many others. *Magnum virtutis principium est*, Hugo of St. Victor writes (Didascalicon III, 20), *ut discat paulatim exercitatus animus visibilia haec et transitoria primum commutare, ut postmodum possit etiam derelinquere. Delicatus ille est adhuc cui patria dulcis est, fortis autem cui omne solum patria est, perfectus vero cui mundus totus exilium est.*[6] Hugo intended these lines for one whose aim is to free himself from a love of the world. But it is a good way also for one who wishes to earn a proper love for the world.

—————

Notes

1. From *Centennial Review* 13:1 (1969), 1–17, translated by M. and E. W. Said. First published as "Philologie der Weltliteratur" in *Weltliteratur: Festgabe für Fritz Strich zum 70. Geburtstag*, ed. Walter Muschg and Emil Staiger (Bern: Francke, 1952), 39–50, a collection in honor of Fritz Strich, author of *Goethe und die Weltliteratur* (1946), a work written like *Mimesis* during the war years.

2. "It is no small part of discovery to know what you are looking for."

3. For Herder, see the selection in this volume. The Enlightenment-era philosopher Giambattista Vico argued in his *La Scienza nuova* (*The New Science*, 1725) that human history and institutions must be understood in secular rather than theological terms. Vico's project, with its close attention to legal and literary language, deeply inspired Auerbach; see his essay "Vico and Aesthetic Historicism," *Journal of Aesthetics and Art Criticism* 8 (1950), 110–18.

4. The Greek term *kairos* refers to a favorable time or opportunity, as opposed to mere chronology; in Christian theology it came to be used especially for times of crisis and the ushering in of a new order of things.

5. "Poverty and foreign ground."

6. "The great basis of virtue . . . is for the practiced mind to learn, bit by bit, first to change about in visible and transitory things, so that afterwards it may be able to leave them behind altogether. He who finds his homeland sweet is still a tender beginner; he to whom every soil is as his homeland is yet stronger; but he is perfect to whom the entire world is a place of exile."

14

From *Minima Moralia*[1] (1951)

Theodor Adorno

Theodor Adorno was one of the most influential critical thinkers of the twentieth century, a philosopher whose multifaceted works combine aesthetics, sociology, political theory, music criticism, and literary analysis. Born in Frankfurt in 1903 as Theodor Wiesengrund, he was the son of a prosperous German Jewish wine merchant and a talented musician from a Catholic family in Corsica; he later took his mother's maiden name for his own. Adorno divided his university studies between philosophy and musical composition. Though he chose philosophy as his profession, he was an accomplished pianist and wrote often on music as well as literature.

Having completed a dissertation on Kierkegaard's aesthetic theory in 1931, Adorno began a university career but was dismissed two years later when the Nazis came to power and began purging the universities of people of Jewish descent. He moved to Oxford, then New York and Los Angeles, returning to Germany in 1949. He became closely associated with the Institute for Social Research in Frankfurt, long headed by his close friend and collaborator Max Horkheimer; Adorno himself directed the institute from 1958 until his death in 1969. The interdisciplinary sociological, philosophical, and cultural-critical projects of the Frankfurt School have had a major impact on contemporary discussions of culture and society.

Among the most important of Adorno's projects was *Dialectic of Enlightenment* (1947), written with Horkheimer in California during the war. Horkheimer and Adorno argued that the evils of Nazi repression and genocide did not represent a flight from reason so much as a vicious mutation of reason itself—the Enlightenment search for a perfect order corrupted by fear and hatred of the unknown and the unfamiliar. In that book and in works such as *Negative Dialectics*, Adorno mounted a powerful critique of twentieth-century culture as in thrall to industrial capitalism, with all aspects of culture increasingly commodified or "reified" (a term he adopted from the Marxist thought of Georg Lukács). Adorno's numerous writings on literature, music, and aesthetic theory probe the possibility of art—and criticism itself—to resist being swallowed up by "commodity fetishism" and to challenge the domination of the weak by those in political and economic power.

Adorno's wartime writings include one of his greatest works, *Minima Moralia*—dedicated to Horkheimer—a loosely connected set of meditations on the role of culture, and of the cultural critic, in a time of crisis. *Minima Moralia* represents an act of cultural retrieval comparable to Erich Auerbach's *Mimesis*, though through opposite means, embracing the anxiety and fragmentation of the wartime world and not exempting the artist and the critic from responsibility, even culpability. *Minima Moralia*—whose title can be translated "Ethics in a minor mode"—is composed of 153 mini-essays ranging from a paragraph to a few pages in length. Adorno's observations are grouped in three sections dated 1944, 1945, and 1946–47, with fifty entries per section (plus three postscripts), a tripartite division that forms an ironic version of a Hegelian process of thesis, antithesis, and synthesis, while also recalling another exile's voyage through an infernal world, Dante's *Commedia*. In the eight entries given here, Adorno interweaves French and German poetry, Nietzsche, Marx, Freud, Proust, Kafka, and comments on popular culture and European opera in an objective critique that is also a deeply personal confession.

1: For Marcel Proust.—The son of well-to-do parents who, whether from talent or weakness, engages in a so-called intellectual profession, as an artist or a scholar, will have a particularly difficult time with those bearing the distasteful title of colleagues. It is not merely that his independence is envied, the seriousness of his intentions mistrusted, and that he is suspected of being a secret envoy of the established powers. Such suspicions, though betraying a deep-seated resentment, would usually prove well-founded. But the real resistances lie elsewhere. The occupation with things of the mind has by now itself become "practical," a business with strict division of labour, departments and restricted entry. The man of independent means who chooses it out of repugnance for the ignominy of earning money will not be disposed to acknowledge the fact. For this he is punished. He is not a "professional," is ranked in the competitive hierarchy as a dilettante no matter how well he knows his subject, and must, if he wants to make a career, show himself even more resolutely blinkered than the most inveterate specialist. The urge to suspend the division of labour which, within certain limits, his economic situation enables him to satisfy, is thought particularly disreputable: it betrays a disinclination to sanction the operations imposed by society, and domineering competence permits no such idiosyncrasies. The departmentalization of mind is a means of abolishing mind where it is not exercised *ex officio*, under contract. It performs this task all the more reliably since anyone who repudiates the division of labour—if only by taking pleasure in his work—makes himself vulnerable by its standards in ways inseparable from elements of his superiority. Thus is order ensured: some have to play the game because they cannot otherwise live, and those who could live otherwise are kept out because they do not want to play the game. It is as if the class from which independent intellectuals have defected takes its revenge, by pressing its demands home in the very domain where the deserter seeks refuge.

137: Small sorrows, great songs.[2]—Contemporary mass-culture is historically necessary not merely as a result of the encompassment of life in its totality by monster enterprises, but as a consequence of what seems most utterly opposed to the standardization of consciousness predominant today, aesthetic subjectivism. True, the more artists have journeyed into the interior, the more they have learned to forgo the infantile fun of imitating external reality. But at the same time, by dint of reflecting on the psyche, they have found out more and more how to control themselves. The progress in technique that brought them ever greater freedom and independence of anything heterogeneous, has resulted in a kind of reification, technification of the inward as such. The more masterfully the artist expresses himself, the less he has to "be" what he expresses, and the more what he expresses, indeed the content of subjectivity itself, becomes a mere function of the production process. Nietzsche had an inkling of this when he taxed Wagner, that tamer of expression, with hypocrisy, without perceiving that this was not a matter of psychology but of a historical tendency.[3] The transformation of expressive content from an undirected impulse into material for manipulation makes it palpable, exhibitable, saleable. The lyrical subjectivism of Heine, for example, does not stand in simple contradiction to his commercial traits; the saleable is itself subjectivity administered by subjectivity. The virtuoso use of the "scale" characteristic of nineteenth-century performers is transformed by an internal impulsion, without any need for betrayal, into journalism, spectacle, calculation. The law of motion of art, which amounts to the control and therefore the objectification of the subject by itself, means its downfall: the hostility to art of film, which passes in administrative review all materials and emotions in order to sell them most effectively to the public, the second stage of externality, has its source in art, in the growing domination over inner nature. The much-lauded play-acting of modern artists, their exhibitionism, is the gesture whereby they put themselves as goods on the market.

138: *Who is who.*—The artist's or scholar's flattering conviction of his own naivety and purity is prolonged in his propensity to explain difficulties by the devious interests, the practical, calculating mentality of those who contract his services. But just as every construction that acquits oneself and convicts the world, all insistence on one's own qualifications, tends precisely to acquit the world in oneself, so the same holds good for the antithesis of pure intentions and cunning. Premeditating, guided by a thousand political and tactical considerations, cautious and suspicious—just such is the attitude adopted today by the intellectual outsider who knows what to expect. The insiders, however, whose realm has long since coalesced across party frontiers into "living-space," no longer need the calculation ascribed to them. They are so dependably committed to the rules of reason's game, their interests have so unquestionably sedimented in their thinking, that they have again become ingenuous. In seeking out their dark designs, one's judgement is indeed metaphysically true, in that they are akin to the sombre course of the world, but psychologically false: one succumbs to the objective increase of persecution-mania. They who, through their function, commit base and treacherous acts, who sell themselves and their friends to power, need no cunning or *arrière-pensée*,[4] no plans elaborated by the ego, rather they need only give way to their own reactions, unthinkingly satisfy the demands of the moment, to perform effortlessly what others could achieve only by unfathomable scheming. They inspire trust just by proclaiming it. They see their own advantage, live from hand to mouth and commend themselves as both unegoistic and subscribers to a state of things which can be relied on to let them go short of nothing. Because all pursue without conflict solely their own particular interests, these appear in turn as universal and, in this way, disinterested. Their gestures are candid, spontaneous, disarming. They are nice and their opponents unpleasant. Since they no longer have the independence to perform an act in opposition to their interests, they rely on the goodwill of others, and themselves radiate it. Abstract interest, being wholly mediated, creates a second immediacy, while the man not yet wholly encompassed compromises himself as unnatural. If he is not to come to grief he must ceremoniously outdo the world in worldliness and is easily convicted of his maladroit excess. Suspicion, power-greed, lack of comradeship, deceit, vanity and inconsistency are a compelling reproach to him. Social witchcraft inescapably turns him who does not play the game into a self-seeker, and he who, lacking a self, lives by the principle of reality, is called selfless.

141: La nuance/encor'.[5]—The demand that thinking and information dispense with nuances cannot be summarily dismissed as bowing to the prevalent obtuseness. Were linguistic nuance no longer perceptible, it would be itself implicated, not merely reception. Language is by its own objective substance social expression, even where it has abruptly severed itself from society as individual. Changes that it undergoes in communication involve the writer's uncommunicative material. Words and phrases spoilt by use do not reach the secluded workshop intact. And the historical damage cannot be repaired there. History does not merely touch on language, but takes place in it. What continues to be used in spite of usage smacks of simple-minded provincialism or cosy restoration. So thoroughly have all nuances been perverted and sold off as "flavour" that even advanced literary subtleties recall debased words like "gloaming," "pensive," "verdant," "fragrant." The measures against banality are becoming banal, arty-crafty, with an undertone of moping consolation from that womanly world whose soulfulness, complete with lutes and traditional costume, was politically coordinated in Germany. In the cultivated superior trash with which the intellectuals who survive there happily compete for the vacant posts of culture, what yesterday had a linguistically conscious air hostile to convention, reads today as olde-worlde prettifying. German culture seems faced with the alternative between a loathsome second *Biedermeier*[6] or paper administrative philistinism. Yet this simplification, suggested not only by market interests but by cogent political motives and finally by the historical state of the language itself, does not so much overcome nuances as it tyrannically furthers their decay. It offers sacrifices to omnipotent society. But the latter, by virtue of its very omnipotence, is as incommensurable and alien to the subject of knowledge and expression as it ever was in the milder days when it spurned the language of common speech. The fact that human beings are absorbed by the totality without being humanly equal to it, makes institutionalized linguistic forms as vacuous as naively individualistic tone-values, and equally fruitless is the attempt to turn the tables on the former by admitting them to the literary medium: people incapable of reading a diagram posing as engineers. The collective language attractive to the writer who suspects his isolation of romanticism, is no less romantic: he usurps the voice of those for whom he cannot speak directly, as one of them, because his language, through reification, is as divorced from them as all are from each other; because the present form of the collective is in itself speechless. No collective entrusted today with expressing the subject, thereby becomes a subject. He who does not chime in with the official hymnic tone of festivals to liberation supervised by totalitarians, but seriously espouses the *aridité* recommended ambiguously enough by Roger Caillois,[7] merely submits to an objective discipline as privation, without receiving anything concrete and general in exchange. The contradiction between the abstractness of the language that wants to do away with bourgeois subjectivism, and its emphatically concrete objects, does not reside in the incapacity of writers but in a historical antinomy. The subject wants to cede himself to the collective without being cancelled by it. Therefore his very forfeiture of the private becomes private, chimerical. His language, imitating single-handed the taut construction of society, fondly believes it has wakened cement to speech. As punishment, this unauthorized communal language commits incessant *faux pas,* matter-of-factness at the expense of matter and fact, not so very different from a bourgeois waxing eloquent. The conclusion to be drawn from the decay of nuance is not to cling obstinately to forms that have decayed, nor yet to extirpate them altogether, but rather to try to out-nuance them, to push them to the point where from subjective shading they switch to being a pure, specific definition of the object. The writer must combine the tightest control in ensuring that the word refers, without sidelong glances, to the matter alone, with the shedding of all phrases, the patient effort to detect what linguistically, in itself, carries meaning and what does not. But those in fear of falling in spite of everything behind the *Zeitgeist,* of being cast on the refuse-heap of discarded subjectivity, should be reminded that *arriviste* timeliness and progressive content are no longer the same. In an order which liquidates the modern as backward, this backwardness, once condemned, can be invested with the truth over which the historical process obliviously rolls. Because no other truth can be expressed than that which is able to fill the subject, anachronism becomes the refuge of modernity.

142: By this does German song abide.[8]—Free verse was rejected by artists like George as a miscarried form, a hybrid between metre and prose.[9] They are refuted by Goethe and by Hölderlin's late hymns. Their technical eye takes free verse at face value. They stop their ears to history by which free verse is stamped. Only in the period of their decay are free rhythms no more than prose periods printed one below the other, in elevated tone. Where free verse proves a form in its own right, it has emerged from the metrical strophe, transcending subjectivity. It turns the pathos of metre against its own claims, a strict negation of ultimate strictness, just as musical prose, emancipated from the symmetry of the eight-beat rhythm, owes its existence to the implacable principles of construction which matured in the articulation of tonal regularity. In free rhythms the ruins of the artistically rhymeless classical strophe grow eloquent. Jutting their alien contours into the newer languages, they are suited by their strangeness to express what is not exhausted by communication. But they yield, unrescuable, to the flood of the languages in which they once stood erect. Only brokenly, marooned in the realm of communication and distinguishable from it by no capricious convolutions, do they signify distance and stylization, as if incognito, and without privilege, until in poetry like Trakl's the waves of dream close over the helpless verses.[10] Not without reason was the epoch of free rhythms that of the French Revolution, the solemn entrance of human dignity and equality. But does not the conscious practice of such verses resemble the law followed by language as a whole in its unconscious history? Is not all carefully-fashioned prose really a system of free rhythms, an attempt to make the magic charm of the absolute coincide with the negation of its appearance, an effort of the mind to save the metaphysical power of expression by means of its own secularization? Were this so, a ray of light would fall on the sisyphean burden that every prose-writer has shouldered, now that demythologization has led to the destruction of language itself. Linguistic quixotry has become obligatory, since the putting-together of each sentence contributes to the decision whether language as such, ambiguous since primeval times, will succumb to commercialism and the consecrated lie that is a part of it, or whether it will make itself a sacred text by diffidence towards the sacral element on which it lives. Prose isolates itself so ascetically from poetry for the sake of invoking song.

143: In nuce.[11]—The task of art today is to bring chaos into order.

Artistic productivity is the capacity for being voluntarily involuntary.

Art is magic delivered from the lie of being truth.

Since works of art are sprung, for better or worse, from fetishes —are artists to be blamed if their attitude to their products is slightly fetishistic?

The art-form which has from earliest times laid the highest claims to spirituality, as representation of Ideas, drama, depends equally, by its innermost presuppositions, on an audience.

Just as, according to Benjamin, painting and sculpture translate the mute language of things into a higher but similar one, so it might be supposed that music rescues name as pure sound—but at the cost of severing it from things.

Perhaps the strict and pure concept of art is applicable only to music, while great poetry or great painting—precisely the greatest—necessarily brings with it an element of subject-matter transcending aesthetic confines, undissolved in the autonomy of form. The more profound and consequential an aesthetic theory, the more inappropriate it becomes to such works as the major novels of the nineteenth century. Hegel seized this advantage in his polemic against Kant.[12]

The belief put about by aesthetic theorists that a work of art is to be understood as an object of immediate contemplation, purely on its own terms, is unsound. It is limited not merely by the cultural presuppositions of each work, its "language," which only the initiate can follow. Even where there are no such difficulties, the work of art demands more than that one should merely abandon oneself to it. Anyone wishing to find the *Fledermaus* beautiful must know that it is the *Fledermaus*: [13] his mother must have told him that it is not about the winged animal but a fancy-dress costume; he must remember having been told: tomorrow you can go to see the *Fledermaus*. To be within tradition used to mean: to experience the work of art as something sanctioned, valid: to participate through it in all the reactions of those who had seen it previously. Once this falls away, the work is exposed in its nakedness and fallibility. The plot, from a ritual, becomes idiocy, the music, from a canon of significant figures, flat and stale. It is really no longer so beautiful. From this mass-culture draws its right of adaptation. The weakness of all traditional culture outside its tradition provides the pretext for improving, and so barbarically mutilating it.

The comfort that flows from great works of art lies less in what they express than in the fact that they have managed to struggle out of existence. Hope is soonest found among the comfortless.

Kafka: the solipsist without ipseity.[14]

Kafka, though an avid reader of Kierkegaard, is connected with existentialist philosophy only to the extent that one speaks of down-and-outs as "annihilated existences."

Surrealism breaks the *promesse du bonheur*.[15] It sacrifices, to the appearance of happiness transmitted by any integral form, concern for its truth.

144: *Magic Flute*.[16]—The ideology of cultural conservatism which sees enlightenment and art as simple antitheses is false, among other reasons, in overlooking the moment of enlightenment in the genesis of beauty. Enlightenment does not merely dissolve all the qualities that beauty adheres to, but posits the quality of beauty in the first place. The disinterested pleasure that according to Kant is aroused by works of art, can only be understood by virtue of historical antitheses still at work in each aesthetic object. The thing disinterestedly contemplated pleases because it once claimed the utmost interest and thus precluded contemplation. The latter is a triumph of enlightened self-discipline. Gold and precious stones, in the perception of which beauty and luxury still coexist undistinguished, were honoured as magical. The radiance they reflect was thought their own essence. Under their power falls whatever is touched by their light. This was early used in the mastering of nature. Jewels were seen as instruments for subjugating the course of the world by its own cunningly usurped power. The magic adhered to the illusion of omnipotence. This illusion was dispelled by mind's self-enlightenment, but the magic has survived as the power of radiant things over men, in whom they once instilled a dread that continues to hold their eyes spellbound, even after they have seen through its claim to domination. Contemplation, as a residue of fetishist worship, is at the same time a stage in overcoming it. As radiant things give up their magic claims, renounce the power with which the subject invested them and hoped with their help himself to wield, they become transformed into images of gentleness, promises of a happiness cured of domination over nature. This is the primeval history of luxury, that has migrated into the meaning of all art. In the magic of what reveals itself in absolute powerlessness, of beauty, at once perfection and nothingness, the illusion of omnipotence is mirrored negatively as hope. It has escaped every trial of strength. Total purposelessness gives the lie to the totality of purposefulness in the world of domination, and only by virtue of this negation, which consummates the established order by drawing the conclusion from its own principle of reason, has existing society up to now become aware of another that is possible.

The bliss of contemplation consists in disenchanted charm. Radiance is the appeasement of myth.

153: Finale.—The only philosophy which can be responsibly practised in the face of despair is the attempt to contemplate all things as they would present themselves from the standpoint of redemption.[17] Knowledge has no light but that shed on the world by redemption: all else is reconstruction, mere technique. Perspectives must be fashioned that displace and estrange the world, reveal it to be, with its rifts and crevices, as indigent and distorted as it will appear one day in the messianic light. To gain such perspectives without velleity or violence, entirely from felt contact with its objects—this alone is the task of thought. It is the simplest of all things, because the situation calls imperatively for such knowledge, indeed because consummate negativity, once squarely faced, delineates the mirror-image of its opposite. But it is also the utterly impossible thing, because it presupposes a stance removed, even though by a hair's breadth, from the scope of existence, whereas we well know that any possible knowledge must not only be first wrested from what is, if it shall hold good, but is also marked, for this very reason, by the same distortion and indigence which it seeks to escape. The more passionately thought denies its conditionality for the sake of the unconditional, the more unconsciously, and so calamitously, it is delivered up to the world. Even its own impossibility it must at last comprehend for the sake of the possible. But beside the demand thus placed on thought, the question of the reality or unreality of redemption itself hardly matters.

Notes

1. From *Minima Moralia: Reflections on a Damaged Life*, trans. E.F.N. Jephcott (London and New York: Verso, 1974). First published as *Minima Moralia: Reflexionen aus dem beschädigten Leben* (Berlin: Suhrkampf, 1951). Adorno's title ironically echoes Aristotle's *Magna Moralia* or "Great Ethics."

2. Adorno here plays on a passage from the nineteenth-century German Jewish poet Heinrich Heine: "From my great sorrows, / I make small songs" (*Lyrisches Intermezzo*, 36).

3. Having lavishly praised Wagner in *The Birth of Tragedy*, Nietzsche turned on him in later works such as "The Case of Wagner," disgusted with what he saw as Wagner's increasing embrace of conservative and Christian values in operas such as *Parsifal*.

4. Second thoughts or mental reservations.

5. Quoting lines from Paul Verlaine's poem *Art poétique*: "For we want nuance once again, / No colors, nothing but nuance!"

6. The ornate Biedermeier style of home décor had come to be seen as bourgeois kitsch.

7. In *L'Aridité* (1938), the leftist critic Roger Callois had argued in favor of a spare, "arid" literary style, against the extravagances and hermeticism of much Surrealist writing.

8. Quoting the final line of Friedrich Hölderlin's poem *Patmos*.

9. The poet and critic Stefan George (1868–1933) was the center of an influential artistic circle in Berlin; George favored the use of classical poetic forms.

10. The young Austrian expressionist poet Georg Trakl published his sole volume of verse in 1913, committing suicide the next year.

11. In a nutshell.

12. Whereas Immanuel Kant had argued in *The Critique of Judgment* (1790) that artworks are "purposive without purpose," to be understood purely in aesthetic terms, in his *Philosophy of Fine Art* Hegel insisted on the equal importance of understanding a work's engagement with its times. In the next section, Adorno returns to a qualified defense of Kantian disinterestedness and the liberating value of beauty.

13. "The Bat" (1874), a comic opera by Richard Strauss centered on a masked ball.

14. A pervasive, stable sense of self.

15. The promise of satisfaction or happiness that art was traditionally expected to provide.

16. Title of Mozart's last opera (*Die Zauberflöte*, 1791), which presents music as the ideal vehicle for redemption in the demystified world of the Enlightenment.

17. In his conclusion, Adorno is in dialogue with the late reflections on messianic redemption by his close friend Walter Benjamin, who had committed suicide when blocked from escaping Nazi Germany. See Benjamin's "On the Concept of History," in *Selected Writings*, ed. Howard Eiland and Michael W. Jennings (Cambridge: Harvard University Press, 2003), 4:389–400.

15

Poetry, Society, State[1] (1956)

Octavio Paz

Celebrated Mexican essayist, poet, and diplomat, Octavio Paz (1914–98) was born and raised on the outskirts of Mexico City until his family was forced into exile in the United States, as a result of his father's legal work for Emiliano Zapata's uprising against powerful landowners and the government that supported them. On returning to Mexico, as an adolescent Paz was imbued with the classic European and Mexican literature in the library of his grandfather, a journalist and novelist. Paz wrote his first poems as a teenager and published his first collection of poems in 1932. He began studying law, but interrupted his studies to become a teacher in a school for poor children in Yucatan, where he began his first long poem *Entre la piedra y la flor* (Between the stone and the flower), which describes the exploitation of Mexican peasants. After studying for two years in the United States, Paz joined the Mexican diplomatic corps in 1945. His life thereafter alternated between periods in Mexico and extensive travels and residence in many parts of the globe.

He was stationed in New York and then in Paris, where he wrote his now classic exploration of Mexican history and identity, *El laberinto de la soledad* (*The Labyrinth of Solitude*, 1950). After travels in India, Japan, and Switzerland, he returned to Mexico, where he wrote *Piedra de sol* (*Sunstone*, 1957), a long poem that borrows its structure from the Aztec calendar. He subsequently became Mexican ambassador to India, where he served until he resigned from the diplomatic corps in 1968 to protest the Mexican government's violent suppression of student protests in Mexico City. Thereafter, Paz lectured widely and founded several cultural publications, winning numerous awards, including the Nobel Prize for literature in 1990, eight years before his death.

Paz's poetry draws from many sources and models—Surrealism, Buddhism, painting, Aztec culture—which it combines in highly original ways. His prose similarly ranges widely from cultural and philosophical questions to topical issues relating to economics, politics, and sexuality. With an erudite multiplicity of examples, in this selection from *El arco y la lira* (*The Bow and the Lyre*, 1956), Paz deploys a comparative literary study to mount an argument for the independence of art from the pernicious influence of state power—an independence needed especially for artists, such as Paz himself, whose work confronts social and political issues in fundamental ways that reach beyond the boundaries of political discourse and established social relations.

There is no more pernicious and barbarous prejudice than that of attributing to the state powers in the sphere of artistic creation. Political power is sterile, because its essence is the domination of men, whatever the ideology that may mask it. Although there has never been absolute freedom of expression—freedom is always defined in relation to certain obstacles and within certain limits: we are free in relation to this or that—it would not be difficult to show that where power invades every human activity, art languishes or is transformed into a servile and mechanical activity. An artistic style is a living thing, a continuous invention within a certain direction. Never imposed from without, born of the profound tendencies of society, that direction is to a certain extent unpredictable, as is the growth of the tree's branches. On the other hand, the official style is the negation of creative spontaneity: great empires tend to have a leveling effect on man's changing face and to transform it into a mask that is repeated indefinitely. Power immobilizes, stabilizes life's variety in a single gesture—grandiose, terrible, or theatrical and, in the end, simply monotonous. "I am the state" is a formula that signifies the alienation of human faces, supplanted by the stony features of an abstract self that is changed, until the end of time, into the model of a whole society. The style that, like a melody, advances and weaves new combinations, utilizing some of the same elements, is degraded into mere repetition.

There is nothing more urgent than the need to dispel the confusion that has been established between the so-called "communal" or "collective" art and the official art. One is art that is inspired by the beliefs and ideals of a society; the other, art subjected to the rules of a tyrannical power. Diverse ideas and spiritual tendencies—the cult of the *polis*, Christianity, Buddhism, Islam, and so on—have been incarnated in powerful states and empires. But it would be a mistake to regard Gothic or Romanesque art as creations of the papacy, or the sculpture of Mathura as the expression of the empire founded by Kanishka.[2] Political power can channel, utilize, and—in certain cases—stimulate an artistic current. It can never create it. What is more: in the long run it generally has a sterilizing effect. Art is always nourished from the social language. That language is, likewise and above all, a vision of the world. Like the arts, states live by that language and sink their roots in that vision of the world. The papacy did not create Christianity, but the other way around; the liberal state is the offshoot of the bourgeoisie, not the latter of the former. The examples can be multiplied. And when a conqueror imposes his vision of the world on a people—for example: Islam in Spain—the foreign state and its whole culture remain as alien superimpositions until the people have truly made that religious or political conception their own. Only then, that is to say when the new vision of the world becomes a shared belief and a common language, will there be an art or a poetry in which society recognizes itself. Thus, the state can impose one vision of the world, prevent others from emerging, and exterminate those that obscure it, but it lacks the fecundity to create such a vision. And the same thing happens with art: the state does not create it, it can hardly encourage it without corrupting it and, more frequently, as soon as it tries to utilize it, it deforms it, suffocates it, or converts it into a mask.

Egyptian and Aztec art, the art of the Spanish baroque and the Grand Century of France—to cite the best-known examples—seem to belie these ideas. They all coincide with the noonday of absolute power. Thus, it is not strange that many see in their light a reflection of the state's splendor. A brief examination of some of these cases will help to correct the error.

Like every art of the so-called "ritualistic civilizations," Aztec art is religious. Aztec society was submerged in the atmosphere, alternately somber and luminous, of the sacred. Every act was impregnated with religion. The state itself was an expression of it. Moctezuma was more than a chief: he was a priest. War was a rite: the representation of the solar myth in which Huitzilopochtli, the invincible Sun, armed with his *xiuhcóatl*, defeated Coyolxauhqui and his column of stars, the Centzonhiznahua. The same quality characterized other human activities: politics and art, commerce and artisanship, foreign and family relations issued from the matrix of the sacred. Public and private life were two sides of the same vital current, not separate worlds. Dying or being born, going to war or to a festival were religious acts. Therefore, it is a grave error to classify Aztec art as a state or political art. The state and politics had not achieved their autonomy; power was still tinged with religion and magic. Aztec art does not in fact express the tendencies of the state but those of religion. One will say that this is a play on words, since the religious nature of the state does not limit but rather strengthens its power. The observation is unjust: a religion that is incarnated in a state, as occurs with the Aztec, is not the same as a state that is served by religion, as happens with the Romans. The difference is so important that without it one could not understand the Aztec policy toward Cortés. And one thing more: Aztec art is, literally, religion. Sculpture, poem, and painting are not "works of art"; neither are they representations, but rather incarnations, living manifestations of the sacred. And similarly: the absolute, total, and totalitarian character of the Mexican state is not political but religious. The state is religion: chiefs, warriors, and simple *mecehuales* [commoners] are religious categories. The forms in which Aztec art is expressed, as well as the political expressions, constitute a sacred language shared by the whole society.

The contrast between Romans and Aztecs shows the difference between sacred and official art. The art of the Romans aspires to the sacred. But if the passage from the sacred to the profane, from the mythical to the political—as is seen in ancient Greece or at the end of the Middle Ages—is natural, the leap in the opposite direction is not. In reality, what we are dealing with here is not a religious state but rather a state religion. Augustus or Nero, Marcus Aurelius or Caligula, "delights of mankind" or "out-and-out monsters," are feared or beloved beings, but they are not gods. And the images with which they aim to make themselves eternal are not divine either. Imperial art is an official art. Although Virgil has his eye on Homer and Greek antiquity, he knows that the original unity has been broken forever. The urban desert of the metropolis follows the universe of federations, alliances, and rivalries of the classic *polis*; the state religion replaces the communal religion; the inner attitude of the philosophers supplants the old piety, which worships at the public altars, as in the age of Sophocles; the public rite becomes an official function, and the real religious attitude is expressed as solitary contemplation; philosophical and mystical sects proliferate. The splendor of the age of Augustus—and, later, of the Antonines—must not cause us to forget that there are brief periods of rest and respite. But neither the learned benevolence of some men, nor the will of others—be they named Augustus or Trajan—can resuscitate the dead. An official art, at its best and highest moments Roman art is an art of the court, aimed at a select minority. The attitude of the poets of that time can be exemplified in these verses by Horace:

> *Odi profanum vulgus et arceo. Favete linguis: carmina non prius*
> *audita Musarum sacerdos virginibus puerisque canto . . .*[3]

As to the Spanish literature of the sixteenth and seventeenth centuries and its relation to the house of Austria: almost all the artistic forms of that period are born at the moment when Spain opens up to Renaissance culture, feels the influence of Erasmus, and participates in the tendencies that prepare the way for the modern epoch (*La Celestina*, Nebrija, Garcilaso, Vives, the Valdés brothers, and so on). Even the artists who belong to what Valbuena Prat calls the "mystic reaction" and the "national period," whose common attribute is opposition to the Europeanism and "modernism" of the epoch of the emperor, merely develop the tendencies and forms that Spain appropriated some years earlier. Saint John imitates Garcilaso (possibly through the "Garcilaso a lo divino" of Sebastián de Córdoba); Fray Luis de León cultivates Renaissance poetic forms exclusively, and in his thought Plato and Christianity are allied; Cervantes—figure between two epochs and example of a secular writer in a society of clerics and theologians—"absorbs the Erasmist ferments of the sixteenth century,"[4] besides being directly influenced by the culture and free life of Italy. The state and the church channel, limit, prune, and utilize those tendencies, but do not create them. And if attention is focused on Spain's most purely national creation—the theater—the astonishing thing is, precisely, its freedom and spontaneity within the conventions of the time. In short, the Austrian monarchy did not create Spanish art and, on the other hand, it separated Spain from the incipient modernity.

Nor does the French example show convincing proof of the supposed relation of cause and effect between the centralization of political power and artistic greatness. As in the case of Spain, the "classicism" of the period of Louis XIV was brought about by the extraordinary philosophical, political, and vital unrest of the sixteenth century. The intellectual freedom of Rabelais and Montaigne, the individualism of the highest figures of the lyric—from Marot and Scève to Jean de Sponde, Desportes, and Chassignet, and including Ronsard and d'Aubigné—the eroticism of Louise Labé and the "Blasonneurs du corps féminin" bear witness to spontaneity, ease, and free creation. The same must be said of the other arts and even the very life of that individualistic and anarchical century. Nothing could be further from an official style, imposed by a state, than the art of the Valois period,[5] which is invention, sensuality, whim, movement, passionate and lucid curiosity. This current penetrates the seventeenth century. But everything changes as soon as the monarchy is consolidated. After the founding of the Academy, poets not only have to contend with the vigilance of the Church, but also with that of a State grown grammatical. The sterilization process culminates, years later, with the revocation of the Edict of Nantes and the triumph of the Jesuit party. From this perspective alone the dispute over *Le Cid* and Corneille's difficulties, Molière's troubles and bitterness, La Fontaine's solitude and, finally, Racine's silence—a silence that merits something more than a simple psychological explanation and seems to me like a symbol of France's spiritual situation in the "Grand Century"— acquire true meaning. These examples show that the arts must fear rather than be grateful for a protection that ends by suppressing them on the pretext of giving them guidance. The Sun King's "classicism" sterilized France. And it is not an exaggeration to say that the romanticism, realism, and symbolism of the nineteenth century are a profound negation of the spirit of the "Grand Century" and an attempt to resume the free tradition of the sixteenth.

Ancient Greece reveals that communal art is spontaneous and free. It is impossible to compare the Athenian *polis* with the Caesarean state, the papacy, the absolute monarchy, or modern totalitarian states. The supreme authority of Athens is the assembly of citizens, not a remote group of bureaucrats supported by the army and the police. The violence with which the tragedy and the Old Comedy treat of the affairs of the *polis* helps to explain the attitude of Plato, who desired "the intervention of the state in the freedom of poetic creation." One has only to read the tragedians—especially Euripides—or Aristophanes to note the incomparable freedom and grace of these artists. That freedom of expression was grounded on political liberty. And it may even be said that the root of the Greeks' conception of the world was the sovereignty and freedom of the *polis*. "The same year that Aristophanes staged his *Clouds*," says Burckhardt in his *History of Greek Culture*, "there appeared the earliest political memoir surviving anywhere on earth, *On the Athenian State*." Political reflection and artistic creation live in the same climate. Painters and sculptors enjoyed similar freedom, within the limitations of their calling, and the conditions under which they were employed. Unlike what occurs in our own time, the politicians of that period had the good sense to abstain from legislating on artistic styles.

Greek art participated in the debates of the city because the very constitution of the *polis* required citizens' free opinion on public affairs. A "political" art can only spring up where there is the possibility of expressing political opinions, that is, where freedom of speech and thought prevails.

In this sense, Athenian art was "political," but not in the base contemporary acceptance of the word. Read *The Persians* to learn what it is to view one's adversary with eyes undefiled by the distortions of propaganda. And Aristophanes' ferocity was always unleashed against his fellow citizens; the extremes he resorted to in order to ridicule his enemies were part of the nature of Old Comedy. This political belligerence of art was born of freedom. No one thought of persecuting Sappho because she sang about love instead of the struggles of the city. It was necessary to wait until the sectarian and shabby twentieth century to know this kind of a disgrace.

Gothic art was not the work of popes or emperors, but of the cities and religious orders. The same may be said of the typical intellectual institution of the Middle Ages, the university. Like the latter, the cathedral was the creation of the urban communes. It has often been said that in their vertical thrust those churches express the Christian aspiration toward the hereafter. It must be added that if the direction of the building, tense and seemingly thrown to heaven, incarnates the *meaning* of medieval society, its structure reveals the *composition* of that same society. Indeed, everything is thrown upward, toward heaven; but, at the same time, each part of the edifice has a life of its own, individuality and character, but that plurality does not break the unity of the whole. The arrangement of the cathedral seems like a living materialization of that society in which, against the backdrop of monarchical and feudal power, communities and guilds form a complicated solar system of federations, leagues, pacts, and contracts. The free spontaneity of the communes, not the authority of popes and emperors, gives Gothic art its double movement: on the one hand, thrown upward like an arrow; on the other, spread out horizontally, sheltering and covering but not oppressing every genus and species and individual in creation. The great art of the papacy is truly that of the baroque period and its typical representative is Bernini.

The relations between the state and artistic creation depend, in each case, on the nature of the society to which they belong. But in general—insofar as it is possible to reach conclusions in a sphere so vast and contradictory—historical examination corroborates the fact that not only has the state never been the creator of an art of real value, but that each time it tries to transform art into a tool for its own purposes, it ends by denaturalizing and degrading that art. Thus, "art for the few" is almost always the bold answer of a group of artists who, openly or with caution, oppose an official art or the decomposition of the social language. Góngora in Spain, Seneca and Lucan in Rome, Mallarmé before the Philistines of the Second Empire and the Third Republic, are examples of artists who, affirming their solitude and repudiating the public of their time, achieve a communication that is the highest to which a creator can aspire: the communication with posterity. Thanks to their efforts, language is not dispersed as a jargon or petrified in a formula but concentrated, acquiring consciousness of itself and its powers of liberation.

Their hermetism—never completely impenetrable, but always open to the one who will venture to cross the undulant and spiny wall of words—is like that of the seed. Immured within it sleeps the life to come. Centuries after their death, the obscurity of these poets becomes light. And their influence is so profound that, more than poets of poems, they can be called poets or creators of poets. The phoenix, the pomegranate, and the Eleusinian corn always figure on their escutcheon.

Notes

1. From *El Arco y la lyra* (1956), trans. Ruth L. C. Simms as *The Bow and the Lyre: The Poem, the Poetic Revelation, Poetry and History* (Austin: University of Texas Press, 1973).

2. King of the Kushan Empire in South Asia in the second century CE; his empire included Mathura, the reputed birthplace of Krishna.

3. "I despise the vulgar rabble and I warn them off. Observe a reverent silence! I, priest of the Muses, sing songs never before heard for maidens and boys" (Horace, *Carmina* 3.1).

4. Angel Valbuena Prat, *Historia de la literatura española* (1946).

5. French art of the late 1400s and early 1500s.

16

Preface to *La Littérature comparée*[1] (1951)

Jean-Marie Carré

Jean-Marie Carré long held the chair of "Littératures modernes comparées" at the Sorbonne. A specialist in literary relations among France,
Germany, and England, Carré was known for studies of travel writing and
accounts of writers' influence abroad, such as *Goethe en Angleterre* (1920).
Carré gave a pointed expression of his perspective in his preface to a
1951 survey of comparative literature by his former student Marius-
François Guyard. Here Carré strongly—even sternly—emphasizes that
comparatists should focus on "rapports de fait" or concrete literary
relations between writers and cultures, rather than on more general
patterns or parallels. Carré's preface was reprinted the following year in
the inaugural issue of the American *Yearbook of Comparative and General
Literature*, whose editor praised Carré for his success in "summing up the
quintessence of Comparative Literature." Though Carré's approach was
positivistic in nature, he loved to explore the transformations, distortions,
even hallucinations that result when a culture becomes a "mirage" seen
through foreign eyes.

Comparative Literature is enjoying a vogue these days in France which is at
once encouraging and troubling. (More than two hundred thesis proposals

have been registered at the Sorbonne since Liberation.)[2] This so stimulating infatuation threatens to become anarchic. We must thus be grateful to M. M.-F. Guyard for taking stock of the situation. His lucid exposition is a clarification—and a warning.

The concept of comparative literature needs, once more, to be spelled out.[3] It does not do to compare just anything with anything, no matter when and no matter where.

Comparative literature is not literary comparison. It is not a matter of simply transposing to the plane of foreign literatures the old rhetoricians' parallels between Corneille and Racine, Voltaire and Rousseau, etc. We do not much love to dwell on the resemblances and differences between Tennyson and Musset, Dickens and Daudet, etc.

Comparative literature is a branch of literary history. It is the study of international intellectual relations, of the actual connections that existed between Byron and Pushkin, Goethe and Carlyle, Walter Scott and Vigny—between the works, the inspirations, or even the lives of writers belonging to various literatures.

This study does not fundamentally consider works in their original worth, but concerns itself above all with the transformations that each nation and each author impose on what they borrow. In speaking of influence, one often speaks of interpretation, reaction, resistance, combat. "Nothing more original," Valéry writes, "nothing more true to oneself, than to nourish oneself on others. But it is necessary to digest. The lion is made of assimilated sheep."

What is more, there has perhaps been too great a rush into studies of influence. They are difficult to conduct, often deceptive. One sometimes risks attempting to weigh imponderables. More certain is the history of the success of works, of a writer's fortunes, a great figure's destiny, the reciprocal interpretation of peoples, travels, mirages—how we see each other among ourselves, English and French, French and Germans, etc.

Finally, comparative literature is not general literature.[4] It can ultimately lead there; some consider that it must. But these grand parallelisms (and also synchronisms)—such as Humanism, Classicism, Romanticism, Realism, Symbolism—run the risk of becoming too systematic, too spread out in space and time, becoming attenuated in abstraction, arbitrariness, or mere terminology. Though it can prepare the way for them, comparative literature cannot afford to wait for these grand syntheses. The movement proves itself by advancing. What is needed is not to advance in ragged formation but to discipline our forward march. M. M.-F. Guyard's book will show us the way.

Notes

1. From M.-F. Guyard, *La Littérature comparée* (Paris: Presses Universitaires de France, 1951). Translated by David Damrosch.

2. The Allies had liberated Paris from German occupation in 1945, six years before Carré wrote his preface, a fact that may be echoed in the military language of his concluding sentences.

3. The first general exposition was provided by our teacher Fernand Baldensperger in 1921 (first issue of the *Revue de Littérature Comparée*). See also P. Van Tieghem, *La Littérature comparée* (1931; reprint, 1946). [Au.]

4. A subject taught in the United States. [Au.]

17

The Crisis of Comparative Literature[1] (1959)

René Wellek

One of the eminent European scholars who spearheaded the study of comparative literature in the United States after the Second World War, René Wellek was born in Vienna in 1903 of Czech parents. He was educated in Vienna and then in Prague, where he pursued a doctorate in philology at Charles University. While later holding a teaching post there, he joined Roman Jakobson, Nikolai Trubetskoy, and others as a member of the Prague linguistic circle. This group was instrumental in extending the insights of structural linguistics to literature. The war's outbreak sent him into exile in the United States, where he eventually became a professor of Slavic and Comparative Literature at Yale University. With Austin Warren, he co-authored *Theory of Literature* (1949), a pioneering and highly influential approach to the study of comparative literature in which history, theory and criticism are intimately linked. Sympathetic to New Criticism's critique of historical and biographical approaches to literature, Wellek nonetheless advocates a more synoptic view of literature, and he himself attempted a sweeping overview in his massive, unfinished eight-volume *History of Modern Criticism*, on which he worked from the mid-1950s until his death in 1995 at the age of ninety-two.

Throughout the 1950s and 1960s, Wellek made a great impact on comparative studies through a series of searching, polemical essays on problems of defining literary terms and the discipline of literary studies. In "The Crisis of Comparative Literature" (1959), Wellek defends a broad and multivalent definition of the discipline against the strict emphasis on the study of direct and verifiable influences, represented by such scholars as Marius-François Guyard and Jean-Marie Carré. The essay became a manifesto of sorts for what came to be known as the "American School" of comparative literature, which emphasized the importance of literary theory and championed cosmopolitan humanism over cultural nationalism.

———————

The world (or rather our world) has been in a state of permanent crisis since, at least, the year 1914. Literary scholarship, in its less violent, muted ways, has been torn by conflicts of methods since about the same time. The old certainties of nineteenth-century scholarship, its ingenuous belief in the accumulations of facts, any facts, in the hope that these bricks will be used in the building of the great pyramid of learning, its trust in causal explanation on the model of the natural sciences, had been challenged sharply even before: by Croce in Italy, by Dilthey and others in Germany. Thus no claim can be made that recent years have been exceptional or even that the crisis of literary scholarship has reached anywhere a point of solution or even temporary accommodation. Still, a re-examination of our aims and methods is needed. There is something symbolic to the passing, in the last decade, of several of the masters: Van Tieghem, Farinelli, Vossler, Curtius, Auerbach, Carré, Baldensperger, and Spitzer.

The most serious sign of the precarious state of our study is the fact that it has not been able to establish a distinct subject matter and a specific methodology. I believe that the programmatic pronouncements of Baldensperger, Van Tieghem, Carré, and Guyard have failed in this essential task. They have saddled comparative literature with an obsolete methodology and have laid on it the dead hand of nineteenth-century factualism, scientism, and historical relativism.

Comparative literature has the immense merit of combating the false isolation of national literary histories: it is obviously right (and has brought a mass of evidence to support this) in its conception of a coherent Western tradition of literature woven together in a network of innumerable interrelations. But I doubt that the attempt to distinguish between "comparative" and "general" literature, made by Van Tieghem,[2] can succeed. According to Van Tieghem "comparative" literature is confined to the study of interrelations between *two* literatures while "general" literature is concerned with the movements and fashions which sweep through *several* literatures. Surely this distinction is quite untenable and impracticable. Why should, say, the influence of Walter Scott in France be considered "comparative" literature while a study of the historical novel during the Romantic age be "general" literature? Why should we distinguish between a study of the influence of Byron on Heine and the study of Byronism in Germany? The attempt to narrow "comparative literature" to a study of the "foreign trade" of literatures is surely unfortunate. Comparative literature would be, in subject matter, an incoherent group of unrelated fragments: a network of relations which are constantly interrupted and broken off from meaningful wholes. The *comparatiste* qua *comparatiste* in this narrow sense could study only sources and influences, causes and effects, and would be even prevented from investigating a single work of art in its totality as no work can be reduced entirely to foreign influences or considered as a radiating point of influence only toward foreign countries. Imagine that similar restrictions would be imposed on the study of the history of music, the fine arts, or philosophy! Could there be a congress or even a periodical exclusively devoted to such a mosaic of questions as, say, the influence of Beethoven in France, of Raphael in Germany, or even Kant in England? These related disciplines have been much wiser: there are musicologists, art historians, historians of philosophy, and they do not pretend that there are special disciplines such as comparative painting, music, or philosophy. The attempt to set up artificial fences between comparative and general literature must fail because literary history and literary scholarship have one subject: literature. The desire to confine "comparative literature" to the study of the foreign trade of two literatures limits it to a concern with externals, with second-rate writers, with translations, travel books, "intermediaries"; in short, it makes "comparative literature" a mere subdiscipline investigating data about the foreign sources and reputations of writers.

The attempt to set apart not only the subject matter but also the methods of comparative literature has failed even more signally. Van Tieghem sets up two criteria which supposedly distinguish comparative literature from the study of national literatures. Comparative literature is concerned, he tells us, with the myths and legends which surround the poets and it is preoccupied with minor and minimal authors. But it is impossible to see why a student of a single national literature should not do the same: the image of Byron or Rimbaud in England or France has been successfully described without much regard to other countries and, say, Daniel Mornet in France or Josef Nadler in Germany have shown us that one can write national literary history with full attention to ephemeral and forgotten writers.

Nor can one be convinced by recent attempts by Carré and Guyard to widen suddenly the scope of comparative literature in order to include a study of national illusions, of fixed ideas which nations have of each other. It may be all very well to hear what conceptions Frenchmen had about Germany or about England—but is such a study still literary scholarship? Is it not rather a study of public opinion useful, for instance, to a program director in the Voice of America and its analogues in other countries? It is national psychology, sociology, and, as literary study, nothing else but a revival of the old *Stoffgeschichte*.[3] "England and the English in the French novel" is hardly better than "the Irishman on the English stage" or "the Italian in Elizabethan drama." This extension of comparative literature implies a recognition of the sterility of the usual subject matter—at the price, however, of dissolving literary scholarship into social psychology and cultural history.

All these flounderings are only possible because Van Tieghem, his precursors and followers conceive of literary study in terms of nineteenth-century positivistic factualism, as a study of sources and influences. They believe in causal explanation, in the illumination which is brought about by tracing motifs, themes, characters, situations, plots, etc., to some other chronologically preceding work. They have accumulated an enormous mass of parallels, similarities, and sometimes identities, but they have rarely asked what these relationships are supposed to show except possibly the fact of one writer's knowledge and reading of another writer. Works of art, however, are not simply sums of sources and influences: they are wholes in which raw materials derived from elsewhere cease to be inert matter and are assimilated into a new structure. Causal explanation leads only to a *regressus ad infinitum* and besides, in literature, seems hardly ever unequivocally successful in establishing what one would consider the first requirement of any causal relationship: "when X occurs, Y must occur." I am not aware that any literary historian has given us proof of such a necessary relationship or that he even could do so, as the isolation of such a cause has been impossible with works of art which are wholes, conceived in the free imagination, whose integrity and meaning are violated if we break them up into sources and influences.

The concept of source and influence has of course worried the more sophisticated practitioners of comparative literature. For instance, Louis Cazamian, commenting on Carré's book *Goethe en Angleterre,* sees that there is "no assurance that this particular action made this particular difference." He argues that M. Carré is wrong in speaking of Goethe's "having, indirectly, provoked the English romantic movement" merely because Scott translated *Goetz von Berlichingen*.[4] But Cazamian can only make a gesture toward the idea, familiar since Bergson, of flux and becoming. He recommends the study of individual or collective psychology which, with Cazamian, means an elaborate, totally unverifiable theory of the oscillations of the rhythm of the English national soul.

Similarly also, Baldensperger,[5] in his programmatic introduction to the first number of *Revue de littérature comparée* (1921) saw the dead end of literary scholarship preoccupied with tracing the history of literary themes. They can never establish, he admits, clear and complete sequences. He rejects also the rigid evolutionism propounded by Brunetière.[6] But he can substitute for it only the suggestion that literary study should be widened to include minor writers and should pay attention to contemporaneous evaluations. Brunetière is too much concerned with masterpieces. "How can we know that Gessner played a role in general literature, that Destouches charmed the Germans more than Molière, that Delille was considered as a perfect and supreme poet in his time as Victor Hugo was later and that Heliodorus counted perhaps as much as Aeschylus in the heritage of antiquity?" (p. 24). Baldensperger's remedy is thus again attention to minor authors and to the bygone fashions of literary taste. A historical relativism is implied: we should study the standards of the past in order to write "objective" literary history. Comparative literature should plant itself "behind the scenes and not in front of the stage" as if in literature the play were not the thing. Like Cazamian, Baldensperger makes a gesture toward Bergson's becoming, the incessant movement, the "realm of universal variation" for which he quotes a biologist as a parallel. In the conclusion of his manifesto Baldensperger abruptly proclaims comparative literature a preparation for a New Humanism. He asks us to ascertain the spread of Voltaire's skepticism, of Nietzsche's faith in the superman, of the mysticism of Tolstoy: to know why a book considered a classic in one nation is rejected as academic in another, why a work despised in one country is admired elsewhere. He hopes that such researches will furnish our dislocated humanity with a "less uncertain core of common values" (p. 29). But why should such erudite researches into the geographical spread of certain ideas lead to anything like a definition of the patrimony of humanity? And even if such a definition of the common core were successful and would be generally accepted, would it mean an effective New Humanism?

There is a paradox in the psychological and social motivation of "comparative literature" as practiced in the last fifty years. Comparative literature arose as a reaction against the narrow nationalism of much nineteenth-century scholarship, as a protest against the isolationism of many historians of French, German, Italian, English, etc., literature. It was cultivated often by men who stood themselves at the crossroads of nations or, at least, on the borders of one nation. Louis Betz was born in New York of German parents and went to Zürich to learn and teach. Baldensperger was of Lothringian origin and spent a decisive year in Zürich. Ernst Robert Curtius was an Alsatian convinced of the need of better German-French understanding. Arturo Farinelli was an Italian from Trento, then still "irredenta,"[7] who taught at Innsbruck. But this genuine desire to serve as a mediator and conciliator between nations was often overlaid and distorted by the fervent nationalism of the time and situation. Reading Baldensperger's autobiography, *Une Vie parmi d'autres* (1940, actually written in 1935), we feel the basic patriotic impulse behind his every activity: his pride in foiling German propaganda at Harvard in 1914, in refusing to meet Brandes in 1915 in Copenhagen, in going to liberated Strasbourg in 1920. Carré's book on *Goethe in England* contains an introduction arguing that Goethe belongs to all the world and to France in particular as a son of the Rhineland. After the second World War Carré wrote *Les Écrivains français et le mirage allemand* (1947) where he tried to show how the French nourished illusions about the two Germanies and were always taken in at the end. Ernst Robert Curtius thought of his first book, *Die literarischen Wegbereiter des neuen Frankreichs* (1918), as a political action, as instruction for Germany. In a postscript to a new edition written in 1952, Curtius declared his early concept of France an illusion. Romain Rolland was not the voice of the new France as he had thought. Like Carré, Curtius discovered a "mirage" but this time it was a French *mirage*. Even in that early book Curtius had defined his conception of a good European: "Ich weiss nur eine Art ein guter Europäer zu sein: mit Macht die Seele seiner Nation haben, und sie mit Macht nähren von allem, was es Einzigartiges gibt in der Seele der anderen Nationen, der befreundeten oder der feindlichen."[8] A cultural power politics is recommended: everything serves only the strength of one's nation.

I am not suggesting that the patriotism of these scholars was not good or right or even high-minded. I recognize civic duties, the necessity of making decisions, of taking sides in the struggles of our time. I am acquainted with Mannheim's sociology of knowledge, his *Ideology and Utopia*, and understand that proof of motivation does not invalidate the work of a man. I clearly want to distinguish these men from the base corruptors of scholarship in Nazi Germany or from the political doctrinaires in Russia who, for a time, declared "comparative literature" taboo and called anybody who would say in print that Pushkin drew the story of "The Golden Cockerel" from Washington Irving a "rootless cosmopolitan kowtowing to the West."

Still, this basically patriotic motivation of many comparative literature studies in France, Germany, Italy, and so on, has led to a strange system of cultural bookkeeping, a desire to accumulate credits for one's nation by proving as many influences as possible on other nations or, more subtly, by proving that one's own nation has assimilated and "understood" a foreign master more fully than any other. This is almost naïvely displayed in the table of M. Guyard's little handbook for students: it has neat empty boxes for the unwritten *thèses* on Ronsard in Spain, Corneille in Italy, Pascal in Holland, etc.[9] This type of cultural expansionism can be found even in the United States which, on the whole, has been immune to it partly because it had less to boast of and partly because it was less concerned with cultural politics. Still, for instance, the excellent cooperative *Literary History of the United States* (ed. R. Spiller, W. Thorp, et al., 1948) blithely claims Dostoevsky as a follower of Poe and even of Hawthorne. Arturo Farinelli, a comparatist of the purest water, described this situation in an article contributed to the *Mélanges Baldensperger* (1930) entitled "Gl'influssi letterari e l'insuperbire delle nazioni."[10] Farinelli very appropriately comments on the absurdity of such computations of cultural riches, of the whole creditor and debtor calculus in matters of poetry. We forget that "the destinies of poetry and art are fulfilled only in the intimate life and the secret accords of the soul."[11] In an interesting article Professor Chinard has most opportunely pronounced the principle of "no debts" in the comparison of literatures and quoted a fine passage from Rabelais on an ideal world without debtors and creditors.[12]

An artificial demarcation of subject matter and methodology, a mechanistic concept of sources and influences, a motivation by cultural nationalism, however generous—these seem to me the symptoms of the long-drawn-out crisis of comparative literature.

A thorough reorientation is needed in all these three directions. The artificial demarcation between "comparative" and "general" literature should be abandoned. "Comparative" literature has become an established term for any study of literature transcending the limits of one national literature. There is little use in deploring the grammar of the term and to insist that it should be called "the comparative study of literature," since everybody understands the elliptic usage. "General" literature has not caught on, at least in English, possibly because it has still its old connotation of referring to poetics and theory. Personally I wish we could simply speak of the study of literature or of literary scholarship and that there were, as Albert Thibaudet proposed, professors of literature just as there are professors of philosophy and of history and not professors of the history of English philosophy even though the individual may very well specialize in this or that particular period or country or even in a particular author. Fortunately, we still have no professors of English eighteenth-century literature or of Goethe philology. But the naming of our subject is an institutional matter of academic interest in the most literal sense. What matters is the concept of literary scholarship as a unified discipline unhampered by linguistic restrictions. I cannot thus agree with Friederich's view that comparatists "cannot and dare not encroach upon other territories," i.e. those of the students of English, French, German, and other national literatures. Nor can I see how it is even possible to follow his advice not to "poach in each other's territory."[13] There are no proprietary rights and no recognized "vested interests" in literary scholarship. Everybody has the right to study any question even if it is confined to a single work in a single language and everybody has the right to study even history or philosophy or any other topic. He runs of course the risk of criticism by the specialists, but it is a risk he has to take. We comparatists surely would not want to prevent English professors from studying the French sources of Chaucer, or French professors from studying the Spanish sources of Corneille, etc., since we comparatists would not want to be forbidden to publish on topics confined to specific national literatures. Far too much has been made of the "authority" of the specialist who often may have only the bibliographical knowledge or the external information without necessarily having the taste, the sensibility, and the range of the non-specialist whose wider perspective and keener insight may well make up for years of intense application. There is nothing presumptuous or arrogant in advocating a greater mobility and ideal universality in our studies. The whole conception of fenced-off reservations with signs of "no trespassing" must be distasteful to a free mind. It can arise only within the limits of the obsolete methodology preached and practiced by the standard theorists of comparative literature who assume that "facts" are to be discovered like nuggets of gold for which we can stake out prospectors' claims.

But true literary scholarship is not concerned with inert facts, but with values and qualities. That is why there is no distinction between literary history and criticism. Even the simplest problem of literary history requires an act of judgment. Even such a statement that Racine influenced Voltaire or Herder influenced Goethe requires, to be meaningful, a knowledge of the characteristics of Racine and Voltaire, Herder and Goethe, and hence a knowledge of the context of their traditions, an unremitting activity of weighing, comparing, analyzing, and discriminating which is essentially critical. No literary history has ever been written without some principle of selection and some attempt at characterization and evaluation. Literary historians who deny the importance of criticism are themselves unconscious critics, usually derivative critics who have merely taken over traditional standards and accepted conventional reputations. A work of art cannot be analyzed, characterized, and evaluated without recourse to critical principles, however unconsciously held and obscurely formulated. Norman Foerster in a still pertinent booklet, *The American Scholar,* said very cogently that the literary historian "must be a critic *in order* to be a historian."[14] In literary scholarship theory, criticism, and history collaborate to achieve its central task: the description, interpretation, and evaluation of a work of art or any group of works of art. Comparative literature which, at least with its official theorists has shunned this collaboration and has clung to "factual relations," sources and influences, intermediaries and reputations as its only topics, will have to find its way back into the great stream of contemporary literary scholarship and criticism. In its methods and methodological reflections comparative literature has become, to put it bluntly, a stagnant backwater. We can think of many scholarly and critical movements and groupings during this century quite diverse in their aims and methods—Croce and his followers in Italy, Russian formalism and its offshoots and developments in Poland and Czechoslovakia, German *Geistesgeschichte*[15] and stylistics which have found such an echo in the Spanish-speaking countries, French and German existentialist criticism, the American "New Criticism," the myth criticism inspired by Jung's archetypal patterns, and even Freudian psychoanalysis or Marxism: all these are, whatever their limitations and demerits, united in a common reaction against the external factualism and atomism which is still fettering the study of comparative literature.

Literary scholarship today needs primarily a realization of the need to define its subject matter and focus. It must be distinguished from the study of the history of ideas, or religious and political concepts and sentiments which are often suggested as alternatives to literary studies. Many eminent men in literary scholarship and particularly in comparative literature are not really interested in literature at all but in the history of public opinion, the reports of travelers, the ideas about national character—in short, in general cultural history. The concept of literary study is broadened by them so radically that it becomes identical with the whole history of humanity. But literary scholarship will not make any progress, methodologically, unless it determines to study literature as a subject distinct from other activities and products of man. Hence we must face the problem of "literariness," the central issue of aesthetics, the nature of art and literature.

In such a conception of literary scholarship the literary work of art itself will be the necessary focus and we will recognize that we study different problems when we examine the relations of a work of art to the psychology of the author or to the sociology of his society. The work of art, I have argued, can be conceived as a stratified structure of signs and meanings which is totally distinct from the mental processes of the author at the time of composition and hence of the influences which may have formed his mind. There is what has been rightly called an "ontological gap" between the psychology of the author and a work of art, between life and society on the one hand and the aesthetic object. I have called the study of the work of art "intrinsic" and that of its relations to the mind of the author, to society, etc., "extrinsic." Still, this distinction cannot mean that genetic relations should be ignored or even despised or that intrinsic study is mere formalism or irrelevant aestheticism. Precisely the carefully worked out concept of a stratified structure of signs and meanings attempts to overcome the old dichotomy of content and form. What is usually called "content" or "idea" in a work of art is incorporated into the structure of the work of art as part of its "world" of projected meanings. Nothing would be further from my mind than to deny the human relevance of art or to erect a barrier between history and formal study. While I have learned from the Russian formalists and German *Stilforscher*,[16] I would not want to confine the study of literature either to the study of sound, verse, and compositional devices or to elements of diction and syntax; nor would I want to equate literature with language. In my conception these linguistic elements form, so to say, the two bottom strata: the sound stratum and that of the units of meaning. But from them there emerges a "world" of situations, characters, and events which cannot be identified with any single linguistic element or, least of all, with any element of external ornamental form. The only right conception seems to me a resolutely "holistic" one which sees the work of art as a diversified totality, as a structure of signs which, however, imply and require meanings and values. Both a relativistic antiquarianism and an external formalism are mistaken attempts to dehumanize literary study. Criticism cannot and must not be expelled from literary scholarship.

If such a change and liberation, such a reorientation toward theory and criticism, toward critical history should take place, the problem of motivation will take care of itself. We still can remain good patriots and even nationalists, but the debit and credit system will have ceased to matter. Illusions about cultural expansion may disappear as may also illusions about world reconciliation by literary scholarship. Here, in America, looking from the other shore at Europe as a whole we may easily achieve a certain detachment, though we may have to pay the price of uprootedness and spiritual exile. But once we conceive of literature not as an argument in the warfare of cultural *prestige,* or as a commodity of foreign trade or even as an indicator of national psychology we shall obtain the only true objectivity obtainable to man. It will not be a neutral scientism, an indifferent relativism and historicism but a confrontation with the objects in their essence: a dispassionate but intense contemplation which will lead to analysis and finally to judgments of value. Once we grasp the nature of art and poetry, its victory over human mortality and destiny, its creation of a new world of the imagination, national vanities will disappear. Man, universal man, man everywhere and at any time, in all his variety, emerges and literary scholarship ceases to be an antiquarian pastime, a calculus of national credits and debts and even a mapping of networks of relationships. Literary scholarship becomes an act of the imagination, like art itself, and thus a preserver and creator of the highest values of mankind.

Notes

1. First published in *Proceedings of the Second International Congress of Comparative Literature*, ed. Werner P. Friederich (Chapel Hill: University of North Carolina Press, 1959), 148–59. Reprinted in Wellek's *Concepts of Criticism*, ed. Stephen G. Nichols, Jr. (New Haven and London: Yale University Press, 1963), 282–95.

2. Paul Van Tieghem, a French comparatist specializing in European Romanticism, had made this distinction in his widely used survey *Littérature comparée* (1931).

3. History of themes and motifs.

4. "Goethe en Angleterre, quelques réflexions sur les problèmes d'influence," *Revue Germanique* 12 (1921), 374–75.

5. Fernand Baldensperger (1871–1958), French comparatist who taught in France and the United States, and co-founded the *Revue de littérature comparée*.

6. In *L'Évolution des genres dans l'histoire de la littérature* (1890), Ferdinand Brunetière offered a Darwinian narrative of the development of literature.

7. "Unredeemed," the name for a nineteeth-century Italian nationalist movement that argued for the unification of all territories where Italian was the predominant language.

8. "I only know one way to be a good European: to powerfully possess the soul of one's nation, and to nourish oneself powerfully with everything distinctive to be found in the souls of other nations, whether friends or foes." *Französischer Geist im zwanzigsten Jahrhundert* (Bern, 1952), 237.

9. M.-F. Guyard, *La Littérature comparée* (Paris, 1951), 124–25.

10. Literary influences and national pride.

11. *Mélanges d'histoire littéraire, générale et comparée, offerts à Fernand Baldensperger,* 2 vols. (Paris: H. Champion, 1930), 1:273.

12. "La Littérature comparée et l'histoire des idées dans l'étude des relations franco-américaines," *Proceedings of the Second Congress of the International Comparative Literature Association,* ed. Werner P. Friederich (Chapel Hill: University of North Carolina Press, 1959), 349–69.

13. *Yearbook of Comparative and General Literature* 4 (1955), 57.

14. (Chapel Hill: University of North Carolina Press, 1929), 36.

15. History of ideas.

16. Researchers on stylistics.

PART THREE

The Theory Years

18

The Structuralist Activity[1] (1963)

Roland Barthes

One of the leading thinkers of the twentieth century, French literary and social critic Roland Barthes was central to making structuralism a dominant intellectual movement of the 1960s and 1970s. Born in 1915 in the town of Cherbourg in Normandy, Barthes was brought up by his mother following the early death of his father. Barthes's studies and early career were hampered by periodic bouts of tuberculosis; he studied Classics, French literature, grammar, and philology at the Sorbonne before teaching in various schools in France, Romania, and Egypt between 1939 and 1952. He settled in 1952 at the Centre National de Recherche Scientifique in Paris, where he worked in an unusual combination of fields, principally sociology and lexicography; in 1960 he moved to the École Pratique des Hautes Études. In 1975 he was appointed to the prestigious Collège de France, where a chair in Semiology was created for him; he remained there until his death in 1980.

Ceaselessly productive as a writer, Barthes published innumerable essays, many collected within the covers of some of his seventeen books. His first book, *Writing Degree Zero* (1953), was a response to the dissatisfaction Jean-Paul Sartre had expressed in *What Is Literature?* (1947) with the limited political engagement of both established writers and particularly the avant-garde. In his book Barthes introduced the concept of *écriture* ("writing"—the heightened manipulation of conventions of style) as the creative aspect of a writer's practice as opposed to a merely conventional use of language and style. A champion of the experimental

French *nouveau roman*, Barthes argued that even seemingly apolitical writing could have a revolutionary impact in destabilizing the established social, political, and sexual codes of bourgeois society, showing the constructedness and contingency of ideas and customs widely taken to be natural and universal.

Semiotics, the study of signifying systems, became a principal means by which Barthes pursued his analyses of nonverbal as well as verbal patterns of meaning. Drawing on the work of the structural linguist Ferdinand de Saussure, he considered a literary text as a system of signs whose structure forms the work's meaning. His most developed application of structural linguistics came in his book *S/Z* (1970), a sentence-by-sentence reading of Balzac's story "Sarrasine" that teases out the various social and narrative "codes" embedded in the story. In *The Pleasure of the Text* (1973) he considered personal impulses in relation to a text, an approach that was sometimes criticized as being too subjective but that contributed to a new interest in the reader's role in creating a work's meaning.

In "The Structuralist Activity" (1963), Barthes articulates his vision of structuralism's ways of making the world intelligible, illustrating his argument with examples of contemporaries who were doing what he considered structuralist work. Barthes boldly associates a wide range of thinkers in such disparate fields as linguistics, anthropology, economics, and history of religion with the structural experiments of avant-garde artists such as the abstract painter Piet Mondrian, the serialist composer Pierre Boulez, and the experimental novelist Michel Butor.

What is structuralism? Not a school, nor even a movement (at least, not yet), for most of the authors ordinarily labeled with this word are unaware of being united by any solidarity of doctrine or commitment. Nor is it a vocabulary. *Structure* is already an old word (of anatomical and grammatical provenance), today quite overworked: all the social sciences resort to it abundantly, and its use can distinguish no one, except to polemicize about the content assigned to it; *functions, forms, signs,* and *significations* are scarcely more pertinent: they are, today, words in common use from which one asks (and obtains) whatever one wants, notably the camouflage of the old determinist schema of cause and product; we must doubtless resort to pairings like those of *signifier/signified* and *synchronic/diachronic* in order to approach what distinguishes structuralism from other modes of thought: the first because it refers to the linguistic model as originated by Saussure and because, along with economics, linguistics is, in the present state of affairs, the true science of structure; the second, more decisively, because it seems to imply a certain revision of the notion of history, insofar as the idea of synchrony (although in Saussure this is a pre-eminently operational concept) accredits a certain immobilization of time, and insofar as diachrony tends to represent the historical process as a pure succession of forms.[2] This second pairing is all the more distinctive in that the chief resistance to structuralism today seems to be of Marxist origin and in that it focuses on the notion of history (and not of structure); whatever the case, it is probably the serious recourse to the nomenclature of signification (and not to the word itself, which is, paradoxically, not at all distinctive) which we must ultimately take as structuralism's spoken sign: watch who uses *signifier* and *signified, synchrony* and *diachrony,* and you will know whether the structuralist vision is constituted.

This is valid for the intellectual metalanguage, which explicitly employs methodological concepts. But since structuralism is neither a school nor a movement, there is no reason to reduce it a priori, even in a problematical way, to the activity of philosophers; it would be better to try and find its broadest description (if not its definition) on another level than that of reflexive language. We can in fact presume that there exist certain writers, painters, musicians in whose eyes a certain exercise of structure (and no longer merely its thought) represents a distinctive experience, and that both analysts and creators must be placed under the common sign of what we might call *structural man,* defined not by his ideas or his languages, but by his imagination—in other words, by the way in which he mentally experiences structure.

So the first thing to be said is that in relation to all its users, structuralism is essentially an *activity,* i.e., the controlled succession of a certain number of mental operations: we might speak of structuralist activity as we once spoke of surrealist activity (surrealism, moreover, may well have produced the first experience of structural literature, a possibility which must some day be explored). But before seeing what these operations are, we must say a word about their goal.

The goal of all structuralist activity, whether reflexive or poetic, is to reconstruct an "object" in such a way as to manifest thereby the rules of functioning (the "functions") of this object. Structure is therefore actually a *simulacrum* of the object, but a directed, *interested* simulacrum, since the imitated object makes something appear which remained invisible or, if one prefers, unintelligible in the natural object. Structural man takes the real, decomposes it, then recomposes it; this appears to be little enough (which makes some say that the structuralist enterprise is "meaningless," "uninteresting," "useless," etc.). Yet from another point of view, this "little enough" is decisive: for between the two objects, or the two tenses, of structuralist activity, there occurs something new, and what is new is nothing less than the generally intelligible: the simulacrum is intellect added to object, and this addition has an anthropological value, in that it is man himself, his history, his situation, his freedom, and the very resistance which nature offers to his mind.

We see, then, why we must speak of a structuralist *activity*: creation or reflection are not, here, an original "impression" of the world, but a veritable fabrication of a world which resembles the primary one, not in order to copy it but to render it intelligible. Hence one might say that structuralism is essentially *an activity of imitation,* which is also why there is, strictly speaking, no *technical* difference between structuralism as an intellectual activity, on the one hand, and literature in particular, art in general, on the other: both derive from a *mimesis,* based not on the analogy of substances (as in so-called realist art), but on the analogy of functions (what Lévi-Strauss calls *homology).* When Troubetskoy reconstructs the phonetic object as a system of variations; when Dumézil elaborates a functional mythology; when Propp constructs a folk tale resulting by structuration from all the Slavic tales he has previously decomposed; when Lévi-Strauss discovers the homologic functioning of the totemic imagination, or Granger the formal rules of economic thought, or Gardin the pertinent features of prehistoric bronzes; when Richard decomposes a poem by Mallarmé into its distinctive vibrations—they are all doing nothing different from what Mondrian, Boulez, or Butor are doing when they articulate a certain object —what will be called, precisely, a *composition*—by the controlled manifestation of certain units and certain associations of these units. It is of little consequence whether the initial object submitted to the simulacrum activity is given by the world in an already assembled fashion (in the case of the structural analysis made of a constituted language or society or work) or is still dispersed (in the case of the structural "composition"); whether this initial object is drawn from a social reality or an imaginary reality. It is not the nature of the copied object which defines an art (though this is a tenacious prejudice in all realism), it is the fact that man adds to it in reconstructing it: technique is the very being of all creation. It is therefore to the degree that the goals of structuralist activity are indissolubly linked to a certain technique that structuralism exists in a distinctive fashion in relation to other modes of analysis or creation: we recompose the object in order to make certain functions appear, and it is, so to speak, the way that makes the work; this is why we must speak of the structuralist activity rather than the structuralist work.

The structuralist activity involves two typical operations: dissection and articulation. To dissect the first object, the one which is given to the simulacrum-activity, is to find in it certain mobile fragments whose differential situation engenders a certain meaning; the fragment has no meaning in itself, but it is nonetheless such that the slightest variation wrought in its configuration produces a change in the whole; a *square* by Mondrian, a *series* by Pousseur, a *versicle* of Butor's *Mobile*, the "mytheme" in Lévi-Strauss, the phoneme in the work of the phonologists, the "theme" in certain literary criticism—all these units (whatever their inner structure and their extent, quite different according to cases) have no significant existence except by their frontiers: those which separate them from other actual units of the discourse (but this is a problem of articulation) and also those which distinguish them from other virtual units, with which they form a certain class (which linguistics calls a *paradigm*); this notion of a paradigm is essential, apparently, if we are to understand the structuralist vision: the paradigm is a group, a reservoir—as limited as possible—of objects (of units) from which we summon, by an act of citation, the object or unit we wish to endow with an actual meaning; what characterizes the paradigmatic object is that it is, vis-à-vis other objects of its class, in a certain relation of affinity and of dissimilarity: two units of the same paradigm must resemble each other somewhat *in order* that the difference which separates them be indeed evident: s and z must have both a common feature (dentality) and a distinctive feature (presence or absence of sonority) so that we cannot, in French, attribute the same meaning to *poisson* and *poison*;[3] Mondrian's squares must have both certain affinities by their shape as squares, and certain dissimilarities by their proportion and color; the American automobiles (in Butor's *Mobile)* must be constantly regarded in the same way, yet they must differ each time by both their make and color; the episodes of the Oedipus myth (in Lévi-Strauss's analysis) must be both identical and varied—in order that all these languages, these works may be intelligible. The dissection-operation thus produces an initial dispersed state of the simulacrum, but the units of the structure are not at all anarchic: before being distributed and fixed in the continuity of the composition, each one forms with its own virtual group or reservoir an intelligent organism, subject to a sovereign motor principle: that of the least difference.

Once the units are posited, structural man must discover in them or establish for them certain rules of association: this is the activity of articulation, which succeeds the summoning activity. The syntax of the arts and of discourse is, as we know, extremely varied; but what we discover in every work of structural enterprise is the submission to regular constraints whose formalism, improperly indicted, is much less important than their stability; for what is happening, at this second stage of the simulacrum-activity, is a kind of battle against chance; this is why the constraint of recurrence of the units has an almost demiurgic value: it is by the regular return of the units and of the associations of units that the work appears constructed, i.e., endowed with meaning; linguistics calls these rules of combination *forms,* and it would be advantageous to retain this rigorous sense of an overtaxed word: form, it has been said, is what keeps the contiguity of units from appearing as a pure effect of chance: the work of art is what man wrests from chance. This perhaps allows us to understand on the one hand why so-called nonfigurative works are nonetheless to the highest degree works of art, human thought being established not by the analogy of copies and models but by the regularity of assemblages; and on the other hand why these same works appear, precisely, fortuitous and thereby useless to those who discern in them no form: in front of an abstract painting, Khrushchev is certainly wrong to see only the traces of a donkey's tail whisked across the canvas; at least he knows in his way, though, that art is a certain conquest of chance (he simply forgets that every rule must be learned, whether one wants to apply or interpret it).

The simulacrum, thus constructed, does not render the world as it has found it, and it is here that structuralism is important. First of all, it manifests a new category of the object, which is neither the real nor the rational, but the *functional,* thereby joining a whole scientific complex which is being developed around information theory and research. Subsequently and especially, it highlights the strictly human process by which men give meaning to things. Is this new? To a certain degree, yes; of course the world has never stopped looking for the meaning of what is given it and of what it produces; what is new is a mode of thought (or a "poetics") which seeks less to assign completed meanings to the objects it discovers than to know how meaning is possible, at what cost and by what means. Ultimately, one might say that the object of structuralism is not man endowed with meanings but man fabricating meanings, as if it could not be the *content* of meanings which exhausted the semantic goals of humanity, but only the act by which these meanings, historical and contingent variables, are produced. *Homo significans*: such would be the new man of structural inquiry.[4]

According to Hegel, the ancient Greek was amazed by the natural in nature; he constantly listened to it, questioned the meaning of mountains, springs, forests, storms; without knowing what all these objects were telling him by name, he perceived in the vegetal or cosmic order a tremendous shudder of meaning, to which he gave the name of a god: *Pan*. Subsequently, nature has changed, has become social: everything given to man is already human, down to the forest and the river which we cross when we travel. But confronted with this social nature, which is quite simply culture, structural man is no different from the ancient Greek: he too listens for the natural in culture, and constantly perceives in it not so much stable, finite, "true" meanings as the shudder of an enormous machine which is humanity tirelessly undertaking to create meaning, without which it would no longer be human. And it is because this fabrication of meaning is more important, to its view, than the meanings themselves, it is because the function is extensive with the works, that structuralism constitutes itself as an activity, and refers the exercise of the work and the work itself to a single identity: a serial composition or an analysis by Lévi-Strauss are not objects except insofar as they have been made: their present being *is* their past act: they are *having-been-mades*; the artist, the analyst recreates the course taken by meaning, he need not designate it: his function, to return to Hegel's example, is a *manteia*;[5] like the ancient soothsayer, he speaks the locus of meaning but does not name it. And it is because literature, in particular, is a mantic activity that it is both intelligible and interrogating, speaking and silent, engaged in the world by the course of the meaning which it remakes with the world, but disengaged from the contingent meanings which the world elaborates: an answer to the man who consumes it yet always a question to nature, an answer which questions and a question which answers.

How then does structural man deal with the accusation of "unreality" which is sometimes flung at him? Are not forms in the world? Are not forms responsible? Was it really his Marxism that was revolutionary in Brecht? Was it not rather the decision to link to Marxism, in the theater, the placing of a spotlight or the deliberate fraying of a costume? Structuralism does not withdraw history from the world: it seeks to link to history not only certain contents (this has been done a thousand times) but also certain forms, not only the material but also the intelligible, not only the ideological but also the esthetic. And precisely because all thought about the historically intelligible is also a participation in that intelligibility, structural man is scarcely concerned to last; he knows that structuralism, too, is a certain form of the world, which will change with the world; and just as he experiences his validity (but not his truth) in his power to speak the old languages of the world in a new way, so he knows that it will suffice that a new language rise out of history, a new language which speaks *him* in his turn, for his task to be done.

Notes

1. First published as "L'Activité structuraliste" (1963), reprinted in *Essais critiques* (Paris: Seuil, 1964) and in *Oeuvres complètes* (Paris: Seuil, 1993); translated by Richard Howard as "The Structuralist Activity," *Partisan Review* 34 (Winter 1973), 82–88.

2. In the lectures collected as *Course in General Linguistics* (1916), Saussure had broken with the dominant historical linguistics of the nineteenth century, which had focused on the evolution of languages over time. Instead, he emphasized the "synchronic" workings of a language as spoken by a given community, exploring the complex relations of words to one another and to the things signified.

3. "Fish" and "poison."

4. In place of *homo sapiens* ("the man who knows"), Barthes proposes to define the human as "the one who creates signs."

5. A prophecy.

19

Women's Time[1] (1977)

Julia Kristeva

Born in Bulgaria in 1941, Julia Kristeva completed college at the University of Sofia and wrote for a communist newspaper before coming to Paris in 1965 for further study. Her early Marxist training in Bulgaria left Kristeva deeply engaged in struggles for social equality—and with a lasting interest in the politics of language. In Paris, she rapidly became active in leftist literary and political circles, joining the editorial board of the radical cultural journal *Tel Quel* while also studying with Roland Barthes and others and completing a doctorate in linguistics. In her doctoral thesis— published in 1974 as *Revolution de langue poétique* (*Revolution in Poetic Language*)—she focused on intersections of politics, psychology, and linguistics, moving from structuralist ideas to a poststructuralist emphasis on the multiplicity of identity and the shifting ability of language both to order reality and to resist the status quo.

Kristeva built on the work of the psychologist Jacques Lacan, whose seminars she attended for several years; in 1979 Kristeva herself became certified as a psychoanalyst and has maintained a psychoanalytic practice since then, while also writing many theoretical works and several novels. In her theoretical writings, Kristeva takes up Lacan's claim that the unconscious is structured like a language. Yet whereas Lacan, like Freud before him, had emphasized the crucial role of the child's relation to the often distant and forbidding father, Kristeva stressed the importance of the prelinguistic bond to the mother, arguing for a sense of the self as composed of drives originally experienced in terms of unfettered pleasure (*jouissance*) and close emotional connection. Language itself, in Kristeva's view, is created through the double action of the rational, ordered, grammatical processes of language (what she calls the "symbolic" order) and of the discharge of bodily drives in the rhythms and tones of language (the "semiotic" order). This distinction can be compared to Nietzsche's dual Apollonian and Dionysian forces, as well as to the deconstructive effect of rhetoric on grammar in the work of Jacques Derrida and Paul de Man, though unlike them Kristeva believed in the ability of language to construct a viable if constantly transforming self and to create revolutionary alternatives to the status quo.

Kristeva's 1977 essay "Women's Time" describes three generations of feminist thought: an early phase up to the midtwentieth century in which feminists sought to erase gender differences on the basis of universal, Enlightenment-era ideals of humanity; a second phase, prominent in the 1960s, in which feminists argued for the fundamental difference of the sexes, seeking the specificity of women's experience in an essentialist mode; and a third phase, just coming into being, that would move beyond essentialism to promote sexual equality (and social equality generally) on the basis of a nonessentialist sense of the self and its many investments, including the maternal role. This wide-ranging, controversial essay shows Kristeva's ability to both build on and challenge figures from Jacques Lacan to contemporary French and American feminists. The essay remains of special interest for its early discussion of the intertwined problematic of woman and nation, even including a section on women and terrorism, and for Kristeva's emphasis on the crucial role that literature can play in transforming the self and society alike.

The nation—dream and reality of the nineteenth century—seems to have reached both its apogee and its limits when the 1929 crash and the National-Socialist apocalypse demolished the pillars that, according to Marx, were its essence: economic homogeneity, historical tradition, and linguistic unity. It could indeed be demonstrated that World War II, though fought in the name of national values (in the above sense of the term), brought an end to the nation as a reality: It was turned into a mere illusion which, from that point forward, would be preserved only for ideological or strictly political purposes, its social and philosophical coherence having collapsed. To move quickly toward the specific problematic that will occupy us in this article, let us say that the chimera of economic *homogeneity* gave way to *interdependence* (when not submission to the economic superpowers), while *historical* tradition and *linguistic* unity were recast as a broader and deeper determinant: what might be called a *symbolic denominator*, defined as the cultural and religious memory forged by the interweaving of history and geography. The variants of this memory produce social territories which then redistribute the cutting up into political parties which is still in use but losing strength. At the same time, this memory or symbolic denominator, common to them all, reveals beyond economic globalization and/or uniformization certain characteristics transcending the nation that sometimes embrace an entire continent. A new social ensemble superior to the nation has thus been constituted, within which the nation, far from losing its own traits, rediscovers and accentuates them in a strange temporality, in a kind of "future perfect," where the most deeply repressed past gives a distinctive character to a logical and sociological distribution of the most modern type. For this memory or symbolic common denominator concerns the response that human groupings, united in space and time, have given not to the problems of the *production* of material goods (i.e., the domain of the economy and of the human relationships it implies, politics, etc.) but, rather, to those of *reproduction*, survival of the species, life and death, the body, sex, and symbol. If it is true, for example, that Europe is representative of such a sociocultural ensemble, it seems to me that its existence is based more on this "symbolic denominator," which its art, philosophy, and religions manifest, than on its economic profile, which is certainly interwoven with collective memory but whose traits change rather rapidly under pressure from its partners.

It is clear that a social ensemble thus constituted possesses both a *solidity* rooted in a particular mode of reproduction and its representations through which the biological species is connected to its humanity, which is a tributary of time; as well as a certain *fragility* as a result of the fact that, through its universality, the symbolic common denominator is necessarily echoed in the corresponding symbolic denominator of another sociocultural ensemble. Thus, barely constituted as such, Europe finds itself being asked to compare itself with, or even to recognize itself in, the cultural, artistic, philosophical, and religious constructions belonging to other supranational sociocultural ensembles. This seems natural when the entities involved were linked by history (e.g., Europe and North America, or Europe and Latin America), but the phenomenon also occurs when the universality of this denominator we have called symbolic juxtaposes modes of production and reproduction apparently opposed in both the past and the present (e.g., Europe and India, or Europe and China). In short, with socio-cultural ensembles of the European type, we are constantly faced with a double problematic: that of their *identity* constituted by historical sedimentation, and that of their *loss of identity* which is produced by this connection of memories which escape from history only to encounter anthropology. In other words, we confront two temporal dimensions: the time of linear history, or *cursive time* (as Nietzsche called it), and the time of another history, thus another time, *monumental time* (again according to Nietzsche),[2] which englobes these supranational, sociocultural ensembles within even larger entities.

I should like to draw attention to certain formations which seem to me to summarize the dynamics of a sociocultural organism of this type. The question is one of sociocultural groups, that is, groups defined according to their place in production, but especially according to their role in the mode of reproduction and its representations, which, while bearing the specific sociocultural traits of the formation in question, are *diagonal* to it and connect it to other sociocultural formations. I am thinking in particular of sociocultural groups which are usually defined as age groups (e.g., "young people in Europe"), as sexual divisions (e.g., "European women"), and so forth. While it is obvious that "young people" or "women"" in Europe have their own particularity, it is nonetheless just as obvious that what defines them as "young people" or as "women" places them in a diagonal relationship to their European "origin" and links them to similar categories in North America or in China, among others. That is, insofar as they also belong to "monumental history," they will not be only European "young people" or "women" of Europe but will echo in a most specific way the universal traits of their structural place in reproduction and its representations.

Consequently, the reader will find in the following pages, first, an attempt to situate the problematic of women in Europe within an inquiry on time: that time which the feminist movement both inherits and modifies. Second, I will attempt to distinguish two phases or two generations of women which, while immediately universalist and cosmopolitan in their demands, can nonetheless be differentiated by the fact that the first generation is more determined by the implications of a national problematic (in the sense suggested above), while the second, more determined by its place within the "symbolic denominator," is European *and* trans-European. Finally, I will try, both through the problems approached and through the type of analysis I propose, to present what I consider a viable stance for a European—or at least a European woman—within a domain which is henceforth worldwide in scope.

Which Time?

"Father's time, mother's spacies," as Joyce put it;[3] and, indeed, when evoking the name and destiny of women, one thinks more of the *space* generating and forming the human species than of *time*, becoming, or history. The modern sciences of subjectivity, of its genealogy and accidents, confirm in their own way this intuition, which is perhaps itself the result of a sociohistorical conjuncture. Freud, listening to the dreams and fantasies of his patients, thought that "hysteria was linked to place."[4] Subsequent studies on the acquisition of the symbolic function by children show that the permanence and quality of maternal love condition the appearance of the first spatial references which induce the child's laugh and then induce the entire range of symbolic manifestations which lead eventually to sign and syntax.[5] Moreover, antipsychiatry and psychoanalysis as applied to the treatment of psychoses, before attributing the capacity for transference and communication to the patient, proceed to the arrangement of new places, gratifying substitutes that repair old deficiencies in the maternal space. I could go on giving examples. But they all converge on the problematic of space, which innumerable religions of matriarchal (re)appearance attribute to "woman," and which Plato, recapitulating in his own system the atomists of antiquity, designated by the aporia of the *chora*, matrix space, nourishing, unnameable, anterior to the One, to God and, consequently, defying metaphysics.[6]

As for time, female subjectivity would seem to provide a specific measure that essentially retains *repetition* and *eternity* from among the multiple modalities of time known through the history of civilizations. On the one hand, there are cycles, gestation, the eternal recurrence of a biological rhythm which conforms to that of nature and imposes a temporality whose stereotyping may shock, but whose regularity and unison with what is experienced as extrasubjective time, cosmic time, occasion vertiginous visions and unnameable *jouissance*. On the other hand, and perhaps as a consequence, there is the massive presence of a monumental temporality, without cleavage or escape, which has so little to do with linear time (which passes) that the very word "temporality" hardly fits: All-encompassing and infinite like imaginary space, this temporality reminds one of Kronos in Hesiod's mythology, the incestuous son whose massive presence covered all of Gea in order to separate her from Ouranos, the father. Or one is reminded of the various myths of resurrection which, in all religious beliefs, perpetuate the vestige of an anterior or concomitant maternal cult, right up to its most recent elaboration, Christianity, in which the body of the Virgin Mother does not die but moves from one spatiality to another within the same time via dormition (according to the Orthodox faith) or via assumption (the Catholic faith).[7]

The fact that these two types of temporality (cyclical and monumental) are traditionally linked to female subjectivity insofar as the latter is thought of as necessarily maternal should not make us forget that this repetition and this eternity are found to be the fundamental, if not the sole, conceptions of time in numerous civilizations and experiences, particularly mystical ones.[8] The fact that certain currents of modern feminism recognize themselves here does not render them fundamentally incompatible with "masculine" values.

In return, female subjectivity as it gives itself up to intuition becomes a problem with respect to a certain conception of time: time as project, teleology, linear and prospective unfolding; time as departure, progression, and arrival—in other words, the time of history. It has already been abundantly demonstrated that this kind of temporality is inherent in the logical and ontological values of any given civilization, that this temporality renders explicit a rupture, an expectation, or an anguish which other temporalities work to conceal. It might also be added that this linear time is that of language considered as the enunciation of sentences (noun + verb; topic-comment; beginning-ending), and that this time rests on its own stumbling block, which is also the stumbling block of that enunciation —death. A psychoanalyst would call this "obsessional time," recognizing in the mastery of time the true structure of the slave. The hysteric (either male or female) who suffers from reminiscences would, rather, recognize his or her self in the anterior temporal modalities: cyclical or monumental. This antinomy, one perhaps embedded in psychic structures, becomes, nonetheless, within a given civilization, an antinomy among social groups and ideologies in which the radical positions of certain feminists would rejoin the discourse of marginal groups of spiritual or mystical inspiration and, strangely enough, rejoin recent scientific preoccupations. Is it not true that the problematic of a time indissociable from space, of a space-time in infinite expansion, or rhythmed by accidents or catastrophes, preoccupies both space science and genetics? And, at another level, is it not true that the contemporary media revolution, which is manifest in the storage and reproduction of information, implies an idea of time as frozen or exploding according to the vagaries of demand, returning to its source but uncontrollable, utterly bypassing its subject and leaving only two preoccupations to those who approve of it: Who is to have power over the origin (the programming) and over the end (the use)?

It is for two precise reasons, within the framework of this article, that I have allowed myself this rapid excursion into a problematic of unheard-of complexity. The reader will undoubtedly have been struck by a fluctuation in the term of reference: mother, woman, hysteric. . . . I think that the apparent coherence which the term "woman" assumes in contemporary ideology, apart from its "mass" or "shock" effect for activist purposes, essentially has the negative effect of effacing the differences among the diverse functions or structures which operate beneath this word. Indeed, the time has perhaps come to emphasize the multiplicity of female expressions and preoccupations so that from the intersection of these differences there might arise, more precisely, less commercially, and more truthfully, the real *fundamental difference* between the two sexes: a difference that feminism has had the enormous merit of rendering painful, that is, productive of surprises and of symbolic life in a civilization which, outside the stock exchange and wars, is bored to death.

It is obvious, moreover, that one cannot speak of Europe or of "women in Europe" without suggesting the time in which this sociocultural distribution is situated. If it is true that a female sensibility emerged a century ago, the chances are great that by introducing *its own* notion of time, this sensibility is not in agreement with the idea of an "eternal Europe" and perhaps not even with that of a "modern Europe." Rather, through and with the European past and present, as through and with the ensemble of "Europe," which is the repository of memory, this sensibility seeks its own trans-European temporality. There are, in any case, three attitudes on the part of European feminist movements toward this conception of linear temporality, which is readily labeled masculine and which is at once both civilizational and obsessional.

Two Generations

In its beginnings, the women's movement, as the struggle of suffragists and of existential feminists, aspired to gain a place in linear time as the time of project and history. In this sense, the movement, while immediately universalist, is also deeply rooted in the sociopolitical life of nations. The political demands of women; the struggles for equal pay for equal work, for taking power in social institutions on an equal footing with men; the rejection, when necessary, of the attributes traditionally considered feminine or maternal insofar as they are deemed incompatible with insertion in that history—all are part of the *logic of identification* with certain values: not with the ideological (these are combated, and rightly so, as reactionary) but, rather, with the logical and ontological values of a rationality dominant in the nation-state. Here it is unnecessary to enumerate the benefits which this logic of identification and the ensuing struggle have achieved and continue to achieve for women (abortion, contraception, equal pay, professional recognition, etc.); these have already had or will soon have effects even more important than those of the Industrial Revolution. Universalist in its approach, this current in feminism *globalizes* the problems of women of different milieux, ages, civilizations, or simply of varying psychic structures, under the label "Universal Woman." A consideration of *generations* of women can only be conceived of in this global way as a succession, as a progression in the accomplishment of the initial program mapped out by its founders.

In a second phase, linked, on the one hand, to the younger women who came to feminism after May 1968 and, on the other, to women who had an aesthetic or psychoanalytic experience, linear temporality has been almost totally refused, and as a consequence there has arisen an exacerbated distrust of the entire political dimension. If it is true that this more recent current of feminism refers to its predecessors and that the struggle for sociocultural recognition of women is necessarily its main concern, this current seems to think of itself as belonging to another generation—qualitatively different from the first one—in its conception of its own identity and, consequently, of temporality as such. Essentially interested in the specificity of female psychology and its symbolic realizations, these women seek to give a language to the intrasubjective and corporeal experiences left mute by culture in the past. Either as artists or writers, they have undertaken a veritable exploration of the *dynamic of signs*, an exploration which relates this tendency, at least at the level of its aspirations, to all major projects of aesthetic and religious upheaval. Ascribing this experience to a new generation does not only mean that other, more subtle problems have been added to the demands for sociopolitical identification made in the beginning. It also means that, by demanding recognition of an irreducible identity, without equal in the opposite sex and, as such, exploded, plural, fluid, in a certain way nonidentical, this feminism situates itself outside the linear time of identities which communicate through projection and revindication. Such a feminism rejoins, on the one hand, the archaic (mythical) memory and, on the other, the cyclical or monumental temporality of marginal movements. It is certainly not by chance that the European and trans-European problematic has been posited as such at the same time as this new phase of feminism.

Finally, it is the mixture of the two attitudes—insertion into history and the radical *refusal* of the subjective limitations imposed by this history's time on an experiment carried out in the name of the irreducible difference—that seems to have broken loose over the past few years in European feminist movements, particularly in France and in Italy.

If we accept this meaning of the expression "a new generation of women," two kinds of questions might then be posed. What sociopolitical processes or events have provoked this mutation? What are its problems: its contributions as well as dangers?

Socialism and Freudianism

One could hypothesize that if this new generation of women shows itself to be more diffuse and perhaps less conscious in the United States and more massive in Western Europe, this is because of a veritable split in social relations and mentalities, a split produced by socialism and Freudianism. I mean by *socialism* that egalitarian doctrine which is increasingly broadly disseminated and accepted as based on common sense, as well as that social practice adopted by governments and political parties in democratic regimes which are forced to extend the zone of egalitarianism to include the distribution of goods as well as access to culture. By *Freudianism* I mean that lever, inside this egalitarian and socializing field, which once again poses the question of sexual difference and of the difference among subjects who themselves are not reducible one to the other.

Western socialism, shaken in its very beginnings by the egalitarian or differential demands of its women (e.g., Flora Tristan), quickly got rid of those women who aspired to recognition of a specificity of the female role in society and culture, only retaining from them, in the egalitarian and universalistic spirit of Enlightenment Humanism, the idea of a necessary identification between the two sexes as the only and unique means for liberating the "second sex."[9] I shall not develop here the fact that this "ideal" is far from being applied in practice by these socialist-inspired movements and parties and that it was in part from the revolt against this situation that the new generation of women in Western Europe was born after May 1968.

Let us just say that in theory, and as put into practice in Eastern Europe, socialist ideology, based on a conception of the human being as determined by its place in *production* and the *relations of production*, did not take into consideration this same human being according to its place in *reproduction*, on the one hand, or in the *symbolic order*, on the other. Consequently, the specific character of women could only appear as nonessential or even nonexistent to the totalizing and even totalitarian spirit of this ideology.[10] We begin to see that this same egalitarian and in fact censuring treatment has been imposed, from Enlightenment Humanism through socialism, on religious specificities and, in particular, on Jews.[11]

What has been achieved by this attitude remains nonetheless of capital importance for women, and I shall take as an example the change in the destiny of women in the socialist countries of Eastern Europe. It could be said, with only slight exaggeration, that the demands of the suffragists and existential feminists have, to a great extent, been met in these countries, since three of the main egalitarian demands of early feminism have been or are now being implemented despite vagaries and blunders: economic, political, and professional equality. The fourth, sexual equality, which implies permissiveness in sexual relations (including homosexual relations), abortion, and contraception, remains stricken by taboo in Marxian ethics as well as for reasons of state. It is, then, this fourth equality which is the problem and which therefore appears *essential* in the struggle of a new generation. But simultaneously and as a consequence of these socialist accomplishments—which are in fact a total deception—the struggle is no longer concerned with the quest for equality but, rather, with difference and specificity. It is precisely at this point that the new generation encounters what might be called the symbolic question. Sexual difference—which is at once biological, physiological, and relative to reproduction—is translated by and translates a difference in the relationship of subjects to the symbolic contract which is the social contract: a difference, then, in the relationship to power, language, and meaning. The sharpest and most subtle point of feminist subversion brought about by the new generation will henceforth be situated on the terrain of the inseparable conjunction of the sexual and the symbolic, in order to try to discover, first, the specificity of the female, and then, in the end, that of each individual woman.

A certain saturation of socialist ideology, a certain exhaustion of its potential as a program for a new social contract (it is obvious that the effective realization of this program is far from being accomplished, and I am here treating only its system of thought) makes way for . . . Freudianism. I am, of course, aware that this term and this practice are somewhat shocking to the American intellectual consciousness (which rightly reacts to a muddled and normatizing form of psychoanalysis) and, above all, to the feminist consciousness. To restrict my remarks to the latter: Is it not true that Freud has been seen only as a denigrator or even an exploiter of women? as an irritating phallocrat in a Vienna which was at once Puritan and decadent—a man who fantasized women as sub-men, castrated men?

Castrated and/or Subject to Language

Before going beyond Freud to propose a more just or more modern vision of women, let us try, first, to understand his notion of castration. It is, first of all, a question of an *anguish* or *fear* of castration, or of correlative penis *envy*; a question, therefore, of *imaginary* formations readily perceivable in the *discourse* of neurotics of both sexes, men and women. But, above all, a careful reading of Freud, going beyond his biologism and his mechanism, both characteristic of his time, brings out two things. First, as presupposition for the "primal scene," the castration fantasy and its correlative (penis envy) are hypotheses, a priori suppositions intrinsic to the theory itself, in the sense that these are not the ideological fantasies of their inventor but, rather, logical necessities to be placed at the "origin" in order to explain what unceasingly functions in neurotic discourse. In other words, neurotic discourse, in man and woman, can only be understood in terms of its own logic when its fundamental causes are admitted as the fantasies of the primal scene and castration, even if (as may be the case) nothing renders them present in reality itself. Stated in still other terms, the reality of castration is no more real than the hypothesis of an explosion which, according to modern astrophysics, is at the origin of the universe: Nothing proves it, in a sense it is an article of faith, the only difference being that numerous phenomena of life in this "big-bang" universe are explicable only through this initial hypothesis. But one is infinitely more jolted when this kind of intellectual method concerns inanimate matter than when it is applied to our own subjectivity and thus, perhaps, to the fundamental mechanism of our epistemophilic thought.

Moreover, certain texts written by Freud (*The Interpretation of Dreams*, but especially those of the second topic, in particular the *Metapsychology*) and their recent extensions (notably by Lacan), imply that castration is, in sum, the imaginary construction of a radical operation which constitutes the symbolic field and all beings inscribed therein. This operation constitutes signs and syntax; that is, language, as a *separation* from a presumed state of nature, of pleasure fused with nature so that the introduction of an articulated network of differences, which refers to objects henceforth and only in this way separated from a subject, may constitute *meaning.* This logical operation of separation (confirmed by all psycholinguistic and child psychology) which preconditions the binding of language which is already syntactical, is therefore the common destiny of the two sexes, men and women. That certain biofamilial conditions and relationships cause women (and notably hysterics) to deny this separation and the language which ensues from it, whereas men (notably obsessionals) magnify both and, terrified, attempt to master them—this is what Freud's discovery has to tell us on this issue.

The analytic situation indeed shows that it is the penis which, becoming the major referent in this operation of separation, gives full meaning to the *lack* or to the *desire* which constitutes the subject during his or her insertion into the order of language. I should only like to indicate here that, in order for this operation constitutive of the symbolic and the social to appear in its full truth and for it to be understood by both sexes, it would be just to emphasize its extension to all that is privation of fulfillment and of totality; exclusion of a pleasing, natural, and sound state: in short, the break indispensable to the advent of the symbolic.

It can now be seen how women, starting with this theoretical apparatus, might try to understand their sexual and symbolic difference in the framework of social, cultural, and professional realization, in order to try, by seeing their position therein, either to fulfill their own experience to a maximum or—but always starting from this point—to go further and call into question the very apparatus itself.

Living the Sacrifice

In any case, and for women in Europe today, whether or not they are conscious of the various mutations (socialist and Freudian) which have produced or simply accompanied their coming into their own, the urgent question on our agenda might be formulated as follows: *What can be our place in the symbolic contract?* If the social contract, far from being that of equal men, is based on an essentially sacrificial relationship of separation and articulation of differences which in this way produces communicable meaning, what is our place in this order of sacrifice and/or of language? No longer wishing to be excluded or no longer content with the function which has always been demanded of us (to maintain, arrange, and perpetuate this sociosymbolic contract, as wives, nurses, doctors, teachers . . .), how can we reveal our place, first as it is bequeathed to us by tradition, and then as we want to transform it?

It is difficult to evaluate what in the relationship of women to the symbolic as it reveals itself now arises from a sociohistorical conjuncture (patriarchal ideology, whether Christian, humanist, socialist or so forth), and what arises from a structure. We can speak only about a structure observed in a sociohistorical context, which is that of Christian, Western civilization and its lay ramifications. In this sense of psychosymbolic structure, women, "we" (is it necessary to recall the warnings we issued at the beginning of this article concerning the totalizing use of this plural?) seem to feel that they are the casualties, that they have been left out of the sociosymbolic contract, of language as the fundamental social bond. They find no affect there, no more than they find the fluid and infinitesimal significations of their relationships with the nature of their own bodies, that of the child, another woman, or a man. This frustration, which to a certain extent belongs to men also, is being voiced today principally by women, to the point of becoming the essence of the new feminist ideology. A therefore difficult, if not impossible, identification with the sacrificial logic of separation and syntactical sequence at the foundation of language and the social code leads to the rejection of the symbolic—lived as the rejection of the paternal function and ultimately generating psychoses.

But this limit, rarely reached as such, produces two types of counterinvestment of what we have termed the sociosymbolic contract. On the one hand, there are attempts to take hold of this contract, to possess it in order to enjoy it as such or to subvert it. How? The answer remains difficult to formulate (since, precisely, any formulation is deemed frustrating, mutilating, sacrificial) or else is in fact formulated using stereotypes taken from extremist and often deadly ideologies. On the other hand, another attitude is more lucid from the beginning, more self-analytical which—without refusing or sidestepping this sociosymbolic order—consists in trying to explore the constitution and functioning of this contract, starting less from the knowledge accumulated about it (anthropology, psychoanalysis, linguistics) than from the very personal affect experienced when facing it as subject and as a woman. This leads to the active research, still rare, undoubtedly hesitant but always dissident, being carried out by women in the human sciences;[12] particularly those attempts, in the wake of contemporary art, to break the code, to shatter language, to find a specific discourse closer to the body and emotions, to the unnameable repressed by the social contract. I am not speaking here of a "woman's language," whose (at least syntactical) existence is highly problematical and whose apparent lexical specificity is perhaps more the product of a social marginality than of a sexual-symbolic difference.[13]

Nor am I speaking of the aesthetic quality of productions by women, most of which—with a few exceptions (but has this not always been the case with both sexes?)—are a reiteration of a more or less euphoric or depressed romanticism and always an explosion of an ego lacking narcissistic gratification. What I should like to retain, nonetheless, as a mark of collective aspiration, as an undoubtedly vague and unimplemented intention, but one which is intense and which has been deeply revealing these past few years, is this: The new generation of women is showing that its major social concern has become the sociosymbolic contract as a sacrificial contract. If anthropologists and psychologists, for at least a century, have not stopped insisting on this in their attention to "savage thought," wars, the discourse of dreams, or writers, women are today affirming—and we consequently face a mass phenomenon—that they are forced to experience this sacrificial contract against their will. Based on this, they are attempting a revolt which they see as a resurrection but which society as a whole understands as murder. This attempt can lead us to a not less and sometimes more deadly violence. Or to a cultural innovation. Probably to both at once. But that is precisely where the stakes are, and they are of epochal significance.

The Terror of Power or the Power of Terrorism

First in socialist countries (such as the USSR and China) and increasingly in Western democracies, under pressure from feminist movements, women are being promoted to leadership positions in government, industry, and culture. Inequalities, devalorizations, underestimations, even persecution of women at this level continue to hold sway in vain. The struggle against them is a struggle against archaisms. The cause has nonetheless been understood, the principle has been accepted. What remains is to break down the resistance to change. In this sense, this struggle, while still one of the main concerns of the new generation, is not, strictly speaking, its problem. In relationship to power, its problem might rather be summarized as follows: What happens when women come into power and identify with it?

What happens when, on the contrary, they refuse power and create a parallel society, a counter-power which then takes on aspects ranging from a club of ideas to a group of terrorist commandos?

The assumption by women of executive, industrial, and cultural power has not, up to the present time, radically changed the nature of this power. This can be clearly seen in the East, where women promoted to decision-making positions suddenly obtain the economic as well as the narcissistic advantages refused them for thousands of years and become the pillars of the existing governments, guardians of the status quo, the most zealous protectors of the established order.[14] This identification by women with the very power structures previously considered as frustrating, oppressive, or inaccessible has often been used in modern times by totalitarian regimes: the German National-Socialists and the Chilean junta are examples of this.[15] The fact that this is a paranoid type of counterinvestment in an initially denied symbolic order can perhaps explain this troubling phenomenon; but an explanation does not prevent its massive propagation around the globe, perhaps in less dramatic forms than the totalitarian ones mentioned above, but all moving toward leveling, stabilization, conformism, at the cost of crushing exceptions, experiments, chance occurrences.

Some will regret that the rise of a libertarian movement such as feminism ends, in some of its aspects, in the consolidation of conformism; others will rejoice and profit from this fact. Electoral campaigns, the very life of political parties, continue to bet on this latter tendency. Experience proves that too quickly even the protest or innovative initiatives on the part of women inhaled by power systems (when they do not submit to them right off) are soon credited to the system's account; and that the long-awaited democratization of institutions as a result of the entry of women most often comes down to fabricating a few "chiefs" among them. The difficulty presented by this logic of integrating the second sex into a value system experienced as foreign and therefore counterinvested is how to avoid the centralization of power, how to detach women from it, and how then to proceed, through their critical, differential, and autonomous interventions, to render decision-making institutions more flexible.

Then there are the more radical feminist currents which, refusing homologation to any role of identification with existing power no matter what the power may be, make of the second sex a *countersociety*. A "female society" is then constituted as a sort of alter ego of the official society, in which all real or fantasized possibilities for *jouissance* take refuge. Against the sociosymbolic contract, both sacrificial and frustrating, this countersociety is imagined as harmonious, without prohibitions, free and fulfilling.

In our modern societies which have no hereafter or, at least, which are caught up in a transcendency either reduced to this side of the world (Protestantism) or crumbling (Catholicism and its current challenges), the counter-society remains the only refuge for fulfillment since it is precisely an a-topia, a place outside the law, utopia's floodgate.

As with any society, the countersociety is based on the expulsion of an excluded element, a scapegoat charged with the evil of which the community duly constituted can then purge itself;[16] a purge which will finally exonerate that community of any future criticism. Modern protest movements have often reiterated this logic, locating the guilty one—in order to fend off criticism—in the foreign, in capital alone, in the other religion, in the other sex. Does not feminism become a kind of inverted sexism when this logic is followed to its conclusion? The various forms of marginalism—according to sex, age, religion, or ideology—represent in the modern world this refuge for *jouissance*, a sort of laicized transcendence. But with women, and insofar as the number of those feeling concerned by this problem has increased, although in less spectacular forms than a few years ago, the problem of the countersociety is becoming massive: It occupies no more and no less than "half of the sky."

It has, therefore, become clear, because of the particular radicalization of the second generation, that these protest movements, including feminism, are not "initially libertarian" movements which only later, through internal deviations or external chance manipulations, fall back into the old ruts of the initially combated archetypes. Rather, the very logic of counterpower and of countersociety necessarily generates, by its very structure, its essence as a simulacrum of the combated society or of power. In this sense and from a viewpoint undoubtedly too Hegelian, modern feminism has only been but a moment in the interminable process of coming to consciousness about the implacable violence (separation, castration, etc.) which constitutes any symbolic contract.

Thus the identification with power in order to consolidate it or the constitution of a fetishist counterpower—restorer of the crises of the self and provider of a *jouissance* which is always already a transgression—seem to be the two social forms which the face-off between the new generation of women and the social contract can take. That one also finds the problem of terrorism there is structurally related.

The large number of women in terrorist groups (Palestinian commandos, the Baader-Meinhoff Gang, Red Brigades, etc.) has already been pointed out, either violently or prudently according to the source of information. The exploitation of women is still too great and the traditional prejudices against them too violent for one to be able to envision this phenomenon with sufficient distance. It can, however, be said from now on that this is the inevitable product of what we have called a denial of the sociosymbolic contract and its counterinvestment as the only means of self-defense in the struggle to safeguard an identity. This paranoid-type mechanism is at the base of any political involvement. It may produce different civilizing attitudes in the sense that these attitudes allow a more or less flexible reabsorption of violence and death. But when a subject is too brutally excluded from this sociosymbolic stratum; when, for example, a woman feels her affective life as a woman or her condition as a social being too brutally ignored by existing discourse or power (from her family to social institutions); she may, by counterinvesting the violence she has endured, make of herself a "possessed" agent of this violence in order to combat what was experienced as frustration—with arms which may seem disproportional, but which are not so in comparison with the subjective or more precisely narcissistic suffering from which they originate. Necessarily opposed to the bourgeois democratic regimes in power, this terrorist violence offers as a program of liberation an order which is even more oppressive, more sacrificial than those it combats. Strangely enough, it is not against totalitarian regimes that these terrorist groups with women participants unleash themselves but, rather, against liberal systems, whose essence is, of course, exploitative, but whose expanding democratic legality guarantees relative tolerance. Each time, the mobilization takes place in the name of a nation, of an oppressed group, of a human essence imagined as good and sound; in the name, then, of a kind of fantasy of archaic fulfillment which an arbitrary, abstract, and thus even bad and ultimately discriminatory order has come to disrupt. While that order is accused of being oppressive, is it not actually being reproached with being too weak, with not measuring up to this pure and good, but henceforth lost, substance? Anthropology has shown that the social order is sacrificial, but sacrifice orders violence, binds it, tames it. Refusal of the social order exposes one to the risk that the so-called good substance, once it is unchained, will explode, without curbs, without law or right, to become an absolute arbitrariness.

Following the crisis of monotheism, the revolutions of the past two centuries, and more recently fascism and Stalinism, have tragically set in action this logic of the oppressed goodwill which leads to massacres. Are women more apt than other social categories, notably the exploited classes, to invest in this implacable machine of terrorism? No categorical response, either positive or negative, can currently be given to this question. It must be pointed out, however, that since the dawn of feminism, and certainly before, the political activity of exceptional women, and thus in a certain sense of liberated women, has taken the form of murder, conspiracy, and crime. Finally, there is also the connivance of the young girl with her mother, her greater difficulty than the boy in detaching herself from the mother in order to accede to the order of signs as invested by the absence and separation constitutive of the paternal function. A girl will never be able to reestablish this contact with her mother—a contact which the boy may possibly rediscover through his relationship with the opposite sex—except by becoming a mother herself, through a child, or through a homosexuality which is in itself extremely difficult and judged as suspect by society; and, what is more, why and in the name of what dubious symbolic benefit would she want to make this detachment so as to conform to a symbolic system which remains foreign to her? In sum, all of these considerations— her eternal debt to the woman-mother—make a woman more vulnerable within the symbolic order, more fragile when she suffers within it, more virulent when she protects herself from it. If the archetype of the belief in a good and pure substance, that of utopias, is the belief in the omnipotence of an archaic, full, total, englobing mother with no frustration, no separation, with no break-producing symbolism (with no castration, in other words), then it becomes evident that we will never be able to defuse the violences mobilized through the counterinvestment necessary to carrying out this phantasm, unless one challenges precisely this myth of the archaic mother. It is in this way that we can understand the warnings against the recent invasion of the women's movements by paranoia,[17] in Lacan's scandalous sentence "There is no such thing as Woman."[18] Indeed, she does not exist with a capital "W," possessor of some mythical unity—a supreme power, on which is based the terror of power and terrorism as the desire for power. But what an unbelievable force for subversion in the modern world! And, at the same time, what playing with fire!

Creators: Male and Female

The desire to be a mother, considered alienating and even reactionary by the preceding generation of feminists, has obviously not become a standard for the present generation. But we have seen in the past few years an increasing number of women who not only consider their maternity compatible with their professional life or their feminist involvement (certain improvements in the quality of life are also at the origin of this: an increase in the number of day-care centers and nursery schools, more active participation of men in child care and domestic life, etc.) but also find it indispensable to their discovery, not of the plenitude, but of the complexity of the female experience, with all that this complexity comprises in joy and pain. This tendency has its extreme: in the refusal of the paternal function by lesbian and single mothers can be seen one of the most violent forms taken by the rejection of the symbolic outlined above, as well as one of the most fervent divinizations of maternal power—all of which cannot help but trouble an entire legal and moral order without, however, proposing an alternative to it. Let us remember here that Hegel distinguished between female right (familial and religious) and male law (civil and political). If our societies know well the uses and abuses of male law, it must also be recognized that female right is designated, for the moment, by a blank. And if these practices of maternity, among others, were to be generalized, women themselves would be responsible for elaborating the appropriate legislation to check the violence to which, otherwise, both their children and men would be subject. But are they capable of doing so? This is one of the important questions that the new generation of women encounters, especially when the members of this new generation refuse to ask those questions, seized by the same rage with which the dominant order originally victimized them.

Faced with this situation, it seems obvious—and feminist groups become more aware of this when they attempt to broaden their audience— that the refusal of maternity cannot be a mass policy and that the majority of women today see the possibility for fulfillment, if not entirely at least to a large degree, in bringing a child into the world. What does this desire for motherhood correspond to? This is one of the new questions for the new generation, a question the preceding generation had foreclosed. For want of an answer to this question, feminist ideology leaves the door open to the return of religion, whose discourse, tried and proved over thousands of years, provides the necessary ingredients for satisfying the anguish, the suffering, and the hopes of mothers. If Freud's affirmation—that the desire for a child is the desire for a penis and, in this sense, a substitute for phallic and symbolic dominion—can be only partially accepted, what modern women have to say about this experience should nonetheless be listened to attentively. Pregnancy seems to be experienced as the radical ordeal of the splitting of the subject: redoubling up of the body, separation and coexistence of the self and of an other, of nature and consciousness, of physiology and speech. This fundamental challenge to identity is then accompanied by a fantasy of totality—narcissistic completeness—a sort of instituted, socialized, natural psychosis. The arrival of the child, on the other hand, leads the mother into the labyrinths of an experience that, without the child, she would only rarely encounter: love for an other. Not for herself, nor for an identical being, and still less for another person with whom "I" fuse (love or sexual passion). But the slow, difficult, and delightful apprenticeship in attentiveness, gentleness, forgetting oneself. The ability to succeed in this path without masochism and without annihilating one's affective, intellectual, and professional personality—such would seem to be the stakes to be won through guiltless maternity. It then becomes a creation in the strong sense of the term. For this moment, utopian?

On the other hand, it is in the aspiration toward artistic and, in particular, literary creation that woman's desire for affirmation now manifests itself. Why literature?

Is it because, faced with social norms, literature reveals a certain knowledge and sometimes the truth itself about an otherwise repressed, nocturnal, secret, and unconscious universe? Because it thus redoubles the social contract by exposing the unsaid, the uncanny? And because it makes a game, a space of fantasy and pleasure, out of the abstract and frustrating order of social signs, the words of everyday communication? Flaubert said, "Madame Bovary, c'est moi." Today many women imagine, "Flaubert, c'est moi." This identification with the potency of the imaginary is not only an identification, an imaginary potency (a fetish, a belief in the maternal penis maintained at all costs), as a far too normative view of the social and symbolic relationship would have it. This identification also bears witness to women's desire to lift the weight of what is sacrificial in the social contract from their shoulders, to nourish our societies with a more flexible and free discourse, one able to name what has thus far never been an object of circulation in the community: the enigmas of the body, the dreams, secret joys, shames, hatreds of the second sex.

It is understandable from this that women's writing has lately attracted the maximum attention of both "specialists" and the media. The pitfalls encountered along the way, however, are not to be minimized: For example, does one not read there a relentless belittling of male writers whose books, nevertheless, often serve as "models" for countless productions by women? Thanks to the feminist label, does one not sell numerous works whose naive whining or market-place romanticism would otherwise have been rejected as anachronistic? And does one not find the pen of many a female writer being devoted to phantasmic attacks against Language and Sign as the ultimate supports of phallocratic power, in the name of a semiaphonic corporality whose truth can only be found in that which is "gestural" or "tonal"?

And yet, no matter how dubious the results of these recent productions by women, the symptom is there—women are writing, and the air is heavy with expectation: What will they write that is new?

In the Name of the Father, the Son . . . and the Woman?

These few elements of the manifestations by the new generation of women in Europe seem to me to demonstrate that, beyond the sociopolitical level where it is generally inscribed (or inscribes itself), the women's movement —in its present stage, less aggressive but more artful—is situated within the very framework of the religious crisis of our civilization. I call "religion" this phantasmic necessity on the part of speaking beings to provide themselves with a *representation* (animal, female, male, parental, etc.) in place of what constitutes them as such, in other words, symbolization— the double articulation and syntactic sequence of language, as well as its preconditions or substitutes (thoughts, affects, etc.). The elements of the current practice of feminism that we have just brought to light seem precisely to constitute such a *representation* which makes up for the frustrations imposed on women by the anterior code (Christianity or its lay humanist variant). The fact that this new ideology has affinities, often revindicated by its creators, with so-called matriarchal beliefs (in other words, those beliefs characterizing matrilinear societies) should not overshadow its radical novelty. This ideology seems to me to be part of the broader antisacrificial current which is animating our culture and which, in its protest against the constraints of the sociosymbolic contract, is no less exposed to the risks of violence and terrorism. At this level of radicalism, it is the very principle of sociality which is challenged.

Certain contemporary thinkers consider, as is well known, that modernity is characterized as the first epoch in human history in which human beings attempt to live without religion. In its present form, is not feminism in the process of becoming one? Or is it, on the contrary and as avant-garde feminists hope, that having started with the idea of difference, feminism will be able to break free of its belief in Woman, Her power, Her writing, so as to channel this demand for difference into each and every element of the female whole, and, finally, to bring out the singularity of each woman, and beyond this, her multiplicities, her plural languages, beyond the horizon, beyond sight, beyond faith itself?

A factor for ultimate mobilization? Or a factor for analysis?

Imaginary support in a technocratic era where all narcissism is frustrated? Or instruments fitted to these times in which the cosmos, atoms, and cells—our true contemporaries—call for the constitution of a fluid and free subjectivity? The question has been posed. Is to pose it already to answer it?

Another Generation Is Another Space

If the preceding can be *said*—the question whether all this is *true* belongs to a different register—it is undoubtedly because it is now possible to gain some distance on these two preceding generations of women. This implies, of course, that a *third* generation is now forming, at least in Europe. I am not speaking of a new group of young women (though its importance should not be underestimated) or of another "mass feminist movement" taking the torch passed on from the second generation. My usage of the word "generation" implies less a chronology than a *signifying space*, a both corporeal and desiring mental space. So it can be argued that as of now a third attitude is possible, thus a third generation, which does not exclude—quite to the contrary—the *parallel* existence of all three in the same historical time, or even that they be interwoven one with the other.

In this third attitude, which I strongly advocate—which I imagine? —the very dichotomy man/woman as an opposition between two rival entities may be understood as belonging to metaphysics. What can "identity," even "sexual identity," mean in a new theoretical and scientific space where the very notion of identity is challenged?[19] I am not simply suggesting a very hypothetical bisexuality which, even if it existed, would only, in fact, be the aspiration toward the totality of one of the sexes and thus an effacing of difference. What I mean is, first of all, the demassification of the problematic of *difference*, which would imply, in a first phase, an apparent de-dramatization of the "fight to the death" between rival groups and thus between the sexes. And this not in the name of some reconciliation—feminism has at least had the merit of showing what is irreducible and even deadly in the social contract—but in order that the struggle, the implacable difference, the violence be conceived in the very place where it operates with the maximum intransigence, in other words, in personal and sexual identity itself, so as to make it disintegrate in its very nucleus.

It necessarily follows that this involves risks not only for what we understand today as "personal equilibrium" but also for social equilibrium itself, made up as it now is of the counterbalancing of aggressive and murderous forces massed in social, national, religious, and political groups. But is it not the insupportable situation of tension and explosive risk that the existing "equilibrium" presupposes which leads some of those who suffer from it to divest it of its economy, to detach themselves from it, and to seek another means of regulating difference?

To restrict myself here to a personal level, as related to the question of women, I see arising, under the cover of a relative indifference toward the militance of the first and second generations, an attitude of retreat from sexism (male as well as female) and, gradually, from any kind of anthropomorphism. The fact that this might quickly become another form of spiritualism turning its back on social problems, or else a form of repression ready to support all status quos, should not hide the radicalness of the process. This process could be summarized as an *interiorization of the founding separation of the sociosymbolic contract*, as an introduction of its cutting edge into the very interior of every identity whether subjective, sexual, ideological, or so forth. This in such a way that the habitual and increasingly explicit attempt to fabricate a scapegoat victim as foundress of a society or a countersociety may be replaced by the analysis of the potentialities of *victim/executioner* which characterize each identity, each subject, each sex.

What discourse, if not that of a religion, would be able to support this adventure which surfaces as a real possibility, after both the achievements and the impasses of the present ideological reworkings, in which feminism has participated? It seems to me that the role of what is usually called "aesthetic practices" must increase not only to counterbalance the storage and uniformity of information by present-day mass media databank systems, and, in particular, modern communications technology, but also to demystify the identity of the symbolic bond itself, to demystify, therefore, the *community* of language as a universal and unifying tool, one which totalizes and equalizes. In order to bring out—along with the *singularity* of each person and, even more, along with the multiplicity of every person's possible identifications (with atoms, e.g., stretching from the family to the stars)—the *relativity of his/her symbolic as well as biological existence*, according to the variation in his/her specific symbolic capacities. And in order to emphasize the *responsibility* which all will immediately face of putting this fluidity into play against the threats of death which are unavoidable whenever an inside and an outside, a self and an other, one group and another, are constituted. At this level of interiorization with its social as well as individual stakes, what I have called "aesthetic practices" are undoubtedly nothing other than the modern reply to the eternal question of morality. At least, this is how we might understand an ethics which, conscious of the fact that its order is sacrificial, reserves part of the burden for each of its adherents, therefore declaring them guilty while immediately affording them the possibility for *jouissance*, for various productions, for a life made up of both challenges and differences.

Spinoza's question can be taken up again here: Are women subject to ethics? If not to that ethics defined by classical philosophy—in relationship to which the ups and downs of feminist generations seem dangerously precarious—are women not already participating in the rapid dismantling that our age is experiencing at various levels (from wars to drugs to artificial insemination) and which poses the demand for a new ethics? The answer to Spinoza's question can be affirmative only at the cost of considering feminism as but a *moment* in the thought of that anthropomorphic identity which currently blocks the horizon of the discursive and scientific adventure of our species.

Notes

1. From *Signs: Journal of Women in Culture and Society* 7:1 (1981), 13–35. Translated by Alice Jardine and Harry Blake. First published as "Le Temps des femmes," *34/44: Cahiers de recherche de sciences des textes et documents* 5 (1979), 5–19. Except as indicated, notes are the author's.

2. In his 1874 essay "The Uses and Abuses of History for Life," Friedrich Nietzsche distinguished among three kinds of history: antiquarian (based in empty, linear time), monumental (based on eternal or recurrent models from the past) and critical (a dynamic, fragmented, deconstructive approach to the past). [Ed.]

3. "Father Time and Mother Spacies boil their kettle with their crutch" (James Joyce, *Finnegans Wake* [New York: Viking, 1958], 600), referring to the lovemaking of the primordial parents, HCE and ALP.

4. Sigmund Freud and Carl G. Jung, *Correspondance* (Paris: Gallimard, 1975), 1:87.

5. R. Spitz, *La Première année de la vie de l'enfant* (Paris: PUF, 1958); D. W. Winnicott, *Playing and Reality* (New York: Basic Books, 1971); "Place Names" in Julia Kristeva, *Desire in Language* (New York: Columbia University Press, 1980).

6. For Plato, the chora is the dreamlike space where the Forms materialize. In her psychoanalytical writings, Kristeva uses the term to designate the prelinguistic stage of psychosexual development, a time of undifferentiated closeness to the mother and of pure experience of drives. [Ed.]

7. See Julia Kristeva, "Hérétique de l'amour," *Tel Quel* 74 (1977), 30–49.

8. See H. C. Puech, *La Gnose et la temps* (Paris: Gallimard, 1977).

9. A reference to Simone de Beauvoir's *The Second Sex* (1949); Flora Tristan (1803–44) was a pioneering socialist and feminist writer and activist. [Ed.]

10. See D. Desanti, "L'Autre Sexe des bolcheviks," *Tel Quel*, no. 76 (1978); Julia Kristeva, *On Chinese Women*, trans. Anita Barrows (New York: Urizen Press, 1977).

11. See Arthur Hertzberg, *The French Enlightenment and the Jews* (New York: Columbia University Press, 1968); *Les Juifs et la révolution française*, ed. B. Blumenkranz and A. Seboul (Paris: Edition Privat, 1976).

12. This work is periodically published in various academic women's journals, one of the most prestigious being *Signs: Journal of Women in Culture and Society*, University of Chicago Press. Also of note are the special issues: "Ecriture, féminité, féminisme," *La Revue des sciences humaines* (Lille III), 4 (1977); and "Les Femmes et la philosophie," *Le Doctrinal de sapience* (Editions Solin), 3 (1977).

13. See linguistic research on "female language": Robin Lakoff, *Language and Women's Place* (New York: Harper and Row, 1974); Mary R. Key, *Male/Female Language* (Metuchen, N.J.: Scarecrow Press, 1973); A. M. Houdebine, "Les Femmes et la langue," *Tel Quel* 74 (1977), 84–95.

14. See Julia Kristeva, *On Chinese Women*.

15. See M. A. Macciocchi, *Eléments pour une analyse du fascisme* (Paris: 10/18, 1976); Michele Mattelart, "Le Coup d'état au féminin," *Les Temps modernes* (January 1975).

16. The principles of a "sacrificial anthropology" are developed by René Girard in *La Violence et le sacré* (Paris: Grasset, 1972) and especially in *Des choses cachées depuis la fondation du monde* (Paris: Grasset, 1978).

17. Cf. Micheline Enriquez, "Fantasmes paranoiaques: Differénces des sexes, homosexualité, loi du père," *Topiques*, 13 (1974).

18. See Jacques Lacan, "Dieu et la jouissance de la femme" in *Encore* (Paris: Seuil, 1975), 61–71.

19. See Seminar on *Identity* directed by Levi-Strauss (Paris: Grasset and Fasquelle, 1977).

20

Semiology and Rhetoric[1] (1973)

Paul de Man

Born in Antwerp, Belgium, in 1919, Paul Adolph Michel de Man studied engineering and chemistry before the outbreak of World War II and began a journalistic career, writing on literature in the periodicals *Cahiers du libre examen* and *Jeudi*. Following the war, he settled in the United States and pursued literary studies at Harvard. De Man's life in Belgium was to remain obscure during his life as a Romanticist and literary theorist based first at Cornell and then at Yale. After his death, however, de Man became a figure of controversy with the discovery of essays he wrote for collaborationist newspapers in Belgium during World War II.

De Man achieved prominence in the 1970s as a member of the Yale School of deconstruction. Alongside J. Hillis Miller, Harold Bloom, and Geoffrey Hartman, he sought to create a sophisticated rhetoric for reading that approaches a text without any presuppositions and constantly calls its own assumptions into question. De Man was closely associated with the French philosopher Jacques Derrida, who explored tensions and contradictions in a text by way of questioning the hierarchical ordering of pairs of concepts that has been at the center of Western philosophy since the Greeks. De Man began applying deconstructive techniques to the analysis of the writings of philosophers and literary theorists; his collection *Blindness and Insight* (1971) trenchantly dissected the work of a range of influential figures, arguing that their insights stemmed from premises that their own theories, rigorously understood, should undermine.

De Man applied his method particularly to Romanticism and post-Romantic works in a series of important essays, some of which were collected in *Allegories of Reading: Figural Language in Rousseau, Nietzsche, Rilke, and Proust* (1979). In the essays de Man reckons with the problematics of reading, drawing from French semiology to investigate not what words mean, but how they mean. In his later career, de Man continued to explore the ambiguous interrelations of literature and theory, notably in the essays posthumously collected in *The Resistance to Theory* (1986). In "Semiology and Rhetoric" (1973), one of his best-known articles, de Man argues for the primacy of figural language, or rhetoric, over connected narrative and its grammar. This essay is both an exercise in comparative close reading, focused on passages from Proust and Yeats, and a formidable challenge to critics to become more self-aware of what they do to texts when they read them. With devastating rigor, sly irony, and a dizzying series of reversals of terms and direction, de Man deconstructs critics' common desire to elucidate a clear meaning, or moral, or social purpose from literary works, whether that meaning is seen to reside in a work's form or in its content.

To judge from various recent publications, the spirit of the times is not blowing in the direction of formalist and intrinsic criticism. We may no longer be hearing too much about relevance but we keep hearing a great deal about reference,[2] about the non-verbal "outside" to which language refers, by which it is conditioned and upon which it acts. The stress falls not so much on the fictional status of literature—a property now perhaps somewhat too easily taken for granted—but on the interplay between these fictions and categories that are said to partake of reality, such as the self, man, society, "the artist, his culture and the human community," as one critic puts it. Hence the emphasis on hybrid texts considered to be partly literary and partly referential, on popular fictions deliberately aimed towards social and psychological gratification, on literary autobiography as a key to the understanding of the self, and so on. We speak as if, with the problems of literary form resolved once and forever, and with the techniques of structural analysis refined to near-perfection, we could now move "beyond formalism" towards the questions that really interest us and reap, at last, the fruits of the ascetic concentration on techniques that prepared us for this decisive step.

With the internal law and order of literature well policed, we can now confidently devote ourselves to the foreign affairs, the external politics of literature. Not only do we feel able to do so, but we owe it to ourselves to take this step: our moral conscience would not allow us to do otherwise. Behind the assurance that valid interpretation is possible, behind the recent interest in writing and reading as potentially effective public speech acts, stands a highly respectable moral imperative that strives to reconcile the internal, formal, private structures of literary language with their external, referential and public effects.

I want, for the moment, to consider briefly this tendency in itself, as an undeniable and recurrent historical fact, without regard for its truth or falseness or for its value as desirable or pernicious. It is a fact that this sort of thing happens, again and again, in literary studies. On the one hand, literature cannot merely be received as a definite unit of referential meaning that can be decoded without leaving a residue. The code is unusually conspicuous, complex and enigmatic; it attracts an inordinate amount of attention to itself and this attention has to acquire the rigor of a method. The structural moment of concentration on the code for its own sake cannot be avoided and literature necessarily breeds its own formalism. Technical innovations in the methodical study of literature only occur when this kind of attention predominates. It can legitimately be said, for example, that, from a technical point of view, very little has happened in American criticism since the innovative works of New Criticism. There certainly have been numerous excellent books of criticism since, but in none of them have the techniques of description and interpretation evolved beyond the techniques of close reading established in the thirties and the forties. Formalism, it seems, is an all-absorbing and tyrannical muse; the hope that one can be at the same time technically original and discursively eloquent is not borne out by the history of literary criticism.

On the other hand—and this is the real mystery—no literary formalism, no matter how accurate and enriching in its analytic powers, is ever allowed to come into being without seeming reductive. When form is considered to be the external trappings of literary meaning or content, it seems superficial and expendable. The development of intrinsic, formalist criticism in the twentieth century has changed this model: form is now a solipsistic category of self-reflection and the referential meaning is said to be extrinsic. The polarities of inside and outside have been reversed, but they are still the same polarities that are at play: internal meaning has become outside reference and the outer form has become the intrinsic structure. A new version of reductiveness at once follows this reversal: formalism now-

adays is mostly described in an imagery of imprisonment and claustropho-
bia: the "prison house of language,"[3] "the impasse of formalist criticism,"
etc. Like the grandmother in Proust's novel ceaselessly driving the young
Marcel out into the garden, away from the unhealthy inwardness of his
closeted reading, critics cry out for the fresh air of referential meaning.
Thus, with the structure of the code so opaque, but the meaning so anxious to blot out the obstacle of form, no wonder that the reconciliation of
form and meaning would be so attractive. The attraction of reconciliation
is the elective breeding-ground of false models and metaphors; it accounts
for the metaphorical model of literature as a kind of box that separates
an inside from an outside, and the reader or critic as the person who opens
the lid in order to release in the open what was secreted but inaccessible
inside. It matters little whether we call the inside of the box the content or
the form, the outside the meaning or the appearance. The recurrent debate
opposing intrinsic to extrinsic criticism stands under the aegis of an inside/
outside metaphor that is never being seriously questioned.

Metaphors are much more tenacious than facts and I certainly don't
expect to dislodge this age-old model in one short expository talk. I merely
wish to speculate on a different set of terms, perhaps less simple in their
differential relationship than the strictly polar, binary opposition between
inside and outside and therefore less likely to enter into the easy play of
chiasmic reversals. I derive these terms (which are as old as the hills) prag-
matically from the observation of developments and debates in recent critical methodology.

One of the most controversial among these developments coincides
with a new approach to poetics or, as it is called in Germany, poetology, as
a branch of general semiotics. In France, a semiology of literature comes
about as the outcome of the long-deferred but all the more explosive encounter of the nimble French literary mind with the category of form.
Semiology, as opposed to semantics, is the science or study of signs as signifiers; it does not ask what words mean but how they mean. Unlike American New Criticism, which derived the internalization of form from the
practice of highly self-conscious modern writers, French semiology turned
to linguistics for its model and adopted Saussure and Jakobson[4] rather
than Valéry or Proust for its masters. By an awareness of the arbitrariness
of the sign (Saussure) and of literature as an autotelic statement "focused
on the way it is expressed" (Jakobson) the entire question of meaning can
be bracketed, thus freeing the critical discourse from the debilitating burden of paraphrase. The demystifying power of semiology, within the context of French historical and thematic criticism, has been considerable. It

demonstrated that the perception of the literary dimensions of language is largely obscured if one submits uncritically to the authority of reference. It also revealed how tenaciously this authority continues to assert itself in a variety of disguises, ranging from the crudest ideology to the most refined forms of aesthetic and ethical judgment. It especially explodes the myth of semantic correspondence between sign and referent, the wishful hope of having it both ways, of being, to paraphrase Marx in the German Ideology, a formalist critic in the morning and a communal moralist in the afternoon,[5] of serving both the technique of form and the substance of meaning. The results, in the practice of French criticism, have been as fruitful as they are irreversible. Perhaps for the first time since the late eighteenth century, French critics can come at least somewhat closer to the kind of linguistic awareness that never ceased to be operative in its poets and novelists and that forced all of them including Sainte-Beuve to write their main works "contre Sainte-Beuve."[6] The distance was never so considerable in England and the United States, which does not mean, however, that we may be able, in this country, to dispense with a preventative semiological hygiene altogether.

One of the most striking characteristics of literary semiology as it is practiced today, in France and elsewhere, is the use of grammatical (especially syntactical) structures conjointly with rhetorical structures, without apparent awareness of a possible discrepancy between them. In their literary analyses, Barthes, Genette, Todorov, Greimas[7] and their disciples all simplify and regress from Jakobson in letting grammar and rhetoric function in perfect continuity, and in passing from grammatical to rhetorical structures without difficulty or interruption. Indeed, as the study of grammatical structures is refined in contemporary theories of generative, transformational and distributive grammar, the study of tropes and of figures (which is how the term rhetoric is used throughout this paper, and not in the derived sense of comment or of eloquence or persuasion) becomes a mere extension of grammatical models, a particular subset of syntactical relations. In the recent *Dictionnaire encyclopédique des sciences du langage,* Ducrot and Todorov write that rhetoric has always been satisfied with a paradigmatic view over words (words substituting for each other), without questioning their syntagmatic relationship (the contiguity of words to each other). There ought to be another perspective, complementary to the first, in which metaphor, for example, would not be defined as a substitution but as a particular type of combination. Research inspired by linguistics or, more narrowly, by syntactical studies, has begun to reveal this possibility—but it remains to be explored. Todorov, who calls one of his books a *Grammar of the Decameron,* rightly thinks of his own work and that of his associates as first explorations in the elaboration of a systematic grammar of literary modes, genres and also of literary figures. Perhaps the most perceptive work to come out of this school, Genette's studies of figural modes, can be shown to be assimilations of rhetorical transformations or combinations to syntactical, grammatical patterns. Thus a recent study, now printed in *Figures III* and entitled *Metaphor and Metonymy in Proust,* shows the combined presence, in a wide and astute selection of passages, of paradigmatic, metaphorical figures with syntagmatic, metonymic structures. The combination of both is treated descriptively and non-dialectically without suffering the possibility of logical tensions.

One can ask whether this reduction of figure to grammar is legitimate. The existence of grammatical structures, within and beyond the unit of the sentence, in literary texts is undeniable, and their description and classification are indispensable. The question remains if and how figures of rhetoric can be included in such a taxonomy. This question is at the core of the debate going on, in a wide variety of apparently unrelated forms, in contemporary poetics, but I do not plan to make clear the connection between this "real" problem and the countless pseudo-problems that agitate literary studies. The historical picture of contemporary criticism is too confused to make the mapping out of such a topography a useful exercise. Not only are these questions mixed in and mixed up within particular groups or local trends, but they are often co-present, without apparent contradiction, within the work of a single author.

Neither is the theory of the question suitable for quick expository treatment. To distinguish the epistemology of grammar from the epistemology of rhetoric is a redoubtable task. On an entirely naïve level, we tend to conceive of grammatical systems as tending towards universality and as simply generative, i.e. as capable of deriving an infinity of versions from a single model (that may govern transformations as well as derivations) without the intervention of another model that would upset the first. We therefore think of the relationship between grammar and logic, the passage from grammar to propositions, as being relatively un-problematic: no true propositions are conceivable in the absence of grammatical consistency or of controlled deviation from a system of consistency no matter how complex. Grammar and logic stand to each other in a dyadic relationship of unsubverted support. In a logic of acts rather than of statements, as in Austin's theory of speech acts,[8] that has had such a strong influence on recent American work in literary semiology, it is also possible to move between speech acts and grammar without difficulty. The performance of what is called illocutionary acts such as ordering, questioning, denying, assuming etc. within the language is congruent with the grammatical structures of syntax in the corresponding imperative, interrogative, negative, optative sentences. "The rules for illocutionary acts," writes Richard Ohman in a recent paper, "determine whether performance of a given act is well-executed, in just the same way as *grammatical* rules determine whether the product of a locutionary act—a sentence—is well formed [. . .]. But whereas the rules of grammar concern the relationships among sound, syntax, and meaning, the rules of illocutionary acts concern relationships among people" ("Speech, Literature, and the Space in between," *New Literary History* IV, No. 1 [Autumn 1972]; p. 50). And since rhetoric is then conceived exclusively as persuasion, as actual action upon others (and not as an intralinguistic figure or trope), the continuity between the illocutionary realm of grammar and the perlocutionary realm of rhetoric is self-evident. It becomes the basis for a new rhetoric that, exactly as is the case for Todorov and Genette, would also be a new grammar.

Without engaging the substance of the question, it can be pointed out, without having to go beyond recent and American examples, and without calling upon the strength of an age-old tradition, that the continuity here assumed between grammar and rhetoric is not borne out by theoretical and philosophical speculation. Kenneth Burke mentions *Deflection* (which he compares structurally to Freudian displacement), defined as "any slight bias or even unintended error," as the rhetorical basis of language, and deflection is then conceived as a dialectical subversion of the consistent link between sign and meaning that operates within grammatical patterns; hence Burke's well-known insistence on the distinction between grammar and rhetoric.[9] Charles Sanders Peirce who, with Nietzsche and Saussure, laid the philosophical foundation for modern semiology, stressed the distinction between grammar and rhetoric in his celebrated and so suggestively unfathomable definition of the sign.[10] He insists, as is well known, on the necessary presence of a third element, called the interpretant, within any relationship that the sign entertains with its object. The sign is to be interpreted if we are to understand the idea it is to convey, and this is so because the sign is not the thing but a meaning derived from the thing by a process here called representation that is not simply generative, i.e. dependent on a univocal origin. The interpretation of the sign is not, for Peirce, a meaning but another sign; it is a reading, not a decodage, and this reading has, in its turn, to be interpreted into another sign, and so on *ad infinitum*. Peirce calls this process by means of which "one sign gives birth to another" pure rhetoric, as distinguished from pure grammar, which postulates the possibility of unproblematic, dyadic meaning and pure logic, which postulates the possibility of the universal truth of meanings. Only if the sign engendered meaning in the same way that the object engenders the sign, that is, by representation, would there be no need to distinguish between grammar and rhetoric.

These remarks should indicate at least the existence and the difficulty of the question, a difficulty which puts its concise theoretical exposition beyond my powers. I must retreat therefore into a pragmatic discourse and try to illustrate the tension between grammar and rhetoric in a few specific textual examples. Let me begin by considering what is perhaps the most commonly known instance of an apparent symbiosis between a grammatical and a rhetorical structure, the so-called rhetorical question, in which the figure is conveyed directly by means of a syntactical device. I take the first example from the sub-literature of the mass media: asked by his wife whether he wants to have his bowling shoes laced over or laced under, Archie Bunker answers with a question: "What's the difference?"[11] Being a reader of sublime simplicity, his wife replies by patiently explaining the difference between lacing over and lacing under, whatever this may be, but provokes only ire. "What's the difference" did not ask for difference but means instead "I don't give a damn what the difference is." The same grammatical pattern engenders two meanings that are mutually exclusive: the literal meaning asks for the concept (difference) whose existence is denied by the figurative meaning. As long as we are talking about bowling shoes, the consequences are relatively trivial; Archie Bunker, who is a great believer in the authority of origins (as long, of course, as they are the right origins),[12] muddles along in a world where literal and figurative meanings get in each others' way, though not without discomforts. But suppose that it is a *de*-bunker rather than a "Bunker," and a de-bunker of the arche (or origin), an Archie Debunker such as Nietzsche or Jacques Derrida for instance, who asks the question "What is the Difference"[13]—and we cannot even tell from his grammar whether he "really" wants to know "what" difference is or is just telling us that we shouldn't even try to find out. Confronted with the question of the difference between grammar and rhetoric, grammar allows us to ask the question, but the sentence by means of which we ask it may deny the very possibility of asking. For what is the use of asking, I ask, when we cannot even authoritatively decide whether a question asks or doesn't ask?

The point is as follows. A perfectly clear syntactical paradigm (the question) engenders a sentence that has at least two meanings of which the one asserts and the other denies its own illocutionary mode. It is not so that there are simply two meanings, one literal and the other figural, and that we have to decide which one of these meanings is the right one in this particular situation. The confusion can only be cleared up by the intervention of an extra-textual intention, such as Archie Bunker putting his wife straight; but the very anger he displays is indicative of more than impatience; it reveals his despair when confronted with a structure of linguistic meaning that he cannot control and that holds the discouraging prospect of an infinity of similar future confusions, all of them potentially catastrophic in their consequences. Nor is this intervention really a part of the mini-text constituted by the figure which holds our attention only as long as it remains suspended and unresolved. I follow the usage of common speech in calling this semiological enigma "rhetorical." The grammatical model of the question becomes rhetorical not when we have, on the one hand, a literal meaning and on the other hand a figural meaning, but when it is impossible to decide by grammatical or other linguistic devices which of the two meanings (that can be entirely contradictory) prevails. Rhetoric radically suspends logic and opens up vertiginous possibilities of referential aberration. And although it would perhaps be somewhat more remote from common usage, I would not hesitate to equate the rhetorical, figural potentiality of language with literature itself. I could point to a great number of antecedents to this equation of literature with figure; the most recent reference would be to Monroe Beardsley's insistence in his contribution to the *Essays* to honor William Wimsatt, that literary language is characterized by being "distinctly above the norm in ratio of implicit (or, I would say rhetorical) to explicit meaning" (p. 37).[14]

Let me pursue the question of the rhetorical question through one more example. Yeats's poem "Among School Children" ends with the famous line: "How can we know the dancer from the dance?" Although there are some revealing inconsistencies within the commentaries, the line is usually interpreted as stating, with the increased emphasis of a rhetorical device, the potential unity between form and experience, between creator and creation. It could be said that it denies the discrepancy between the sign and the referent from which we started out. Many elements in the imagery and the dramatic development of the poem strengthen this traditional reading; without having to look any further than the immediately preceding lines, one finds powerful and consecrated images of the continuity from part to whole that makes synecdoche into the most seductive of metaphors: the organic beauty of the tree, stated in the parallel syntax of a similar rhetorical question, or the convergence, in the dance, of erotic desire with musical form:

O chestnut tree, great rooted blossomer
Are you the leaf, the blossom or the bole?
O body swayed to music, O brightening glance
How can we know the dancer from the dance?

A more extended reading, always assuming that the final line is to be read as a rhetorical question, reveals that the thematic and rhetorical grammar of the poem yields a consistent reading that extends from the first line to the last and that can account for all the details in the text. It is equally possible, however, to read the last line literally rather than figuratively, as asking with some urgency the question we asked at the beginning of this talk within the context of contemporary criticism: *not* that sign and referent are so exquisitely fitted to each other that all difference between them is at times blotted out but, rather, since the two essentially different elements, sign and meaning, are so intricately intertwined in the imagined "presence" that the poem addresses, how can we possibly make the distinctions that would shelter us from the error of identifying what cannot be identified? The clumsiness of the paraphrase reveals that it is not necessarily the literal reading which is simpler than the figurative one, as was the case in our first example; here, the figural reading, which assumes the question to be rhetorical, is perhaps naïve, whereas the literal reading leads to greater complication of theme and statement. For it turns out that the entire scheme set up by the first reading can be undermined, or deconstructed, in the terms of the second, in which the final line is read literally as meaning that, since the dancer and the dance are not the same, it might be useful, perhaps even desperately necessary—for the question can be given a ring of urgency, "Please tell me, how *can* I know the dancer from the dance"—to tell them apart. But this will replace the reading of each symbolic detail by a divergent interpretation. The oneness of trunk, leaf and blossom, for example, that would have appealed to Goethe, would find itself replaced by the much less reassuring Tree of Life from the Mabinogion that appears in the poem "Vacillation," in which the fiery blossom and the earthly leaf are held together, as well as apart, by the crucified and castrated God Attis, of whose body it can hardly be said that it is "not bruised to pleasure soul." This hint should suffice to suggest that two entirely coherent but entirely incompatible readings can be made to hinge on one line, whose grammatical structure is devoid of ambiguity, but whose rhetorical mode turns the mood as well as the mode of the entire poem upside down. Neither can we say, as was already the case in the first example, that the poem simply has two meanings that exist side by side. The two readings have to engage each other in direct confrontation, for the one reading is precisely the error denounced by the other and has to be undone by it. Nor can we in any way make a valid decision as to which of the readings can be given priority over the other; none can exist in the other's absence. There can be no dance without a dancer, no sign without a referent. On the other hand, the authority of the meaning engendered by the grammatical structure is fully obscured by the duplicity of a figure that cries out for the differentiation that it conceals.

Yeats' poem is not explicitly "about" rhetorical questions but about images or metaphors, and about the possibility of convergence between experiences of consciousness such as memory or emotions—what the poem calls passion, piety and affection—and entities accessible to the senses such as bodies, persons or icons. We return to the inside/outside model from which we started out and which the poem puts into question by means of a syntactical device (the question) made to operate on a grammatical as well as on a rhetorical level. The couple grammar/rhetoric, certainly not a binary opposition since they in no way exclude each other, disrupts and confuses the neat antithesis of the inside/outside pattern. We can transfer this scheme to the act of reading and interpretation. By reading we get, as we say, inside a text that was first something alien to us and which we now make our own by an act of understanding. But this understanding becomes at once the representation of an extra-textual meaning; in Austin's terms, the illocutionary speech act becomes a perlocutionary actual act—in Frege's terms, *Bedeutung* becomes *Sinn*.[15] Our recurrent question is whether this transformation is semantically controlled along grammatical or along rhetorical lines. Does the metaphor of reading really unite outer meaning with inner understanding, action with reflection, into one single totality? The assertion is powerfully and suggestively made in a passage from Proust that describes the experience of reading as such a union. It describes the young Marcel, near the beginning of "Combray,"[16] hiding in the closed space of his room in order to read. The example differs from the earlier ones in that we are not dealing with a grammatical structure that also functions rhetorically but have instead the representation, the dramatization, in terms of the experience of a subject, of a rhetorical structure—just as, in many other passages, Proust dramatizes tropes by means of landscapes or descriptions of objects. The figure here dramatized is that of metaphor, an inside/outside correspondence as represented by the act of reading. The reading scene is the culmination of a series of actions taking place in enclosed spaces and leading up to the "dark coolness" of Marcel's room.

> *I had stretched out on my bed, with a book, in my room which sheltered, tremblingly, its transparent and fragile coolness against the afternoon*

sun, behind the almost closed blinds through which a glimmer of
daylight had nevertheless managed to push its yellow wings, remaining
motionless between the wood and the glass, in a corner, poised like a
butterfly. It was hardly light enough to read, and the sensation of the
light's splendor was given me only by the noise of Camus [. . .] hammer-
ing dusty crates; resounding in the sonorous atmosphere that is peculiar
to hot weather, they seemed to spark off scarlet stars: and also by the
flies executing their little concert, the chamber music of summer:
evocative not in the manner of a human tune that, heard perchance
during the summer, afterwards reminds you of it: it is connected to
summer by a more necessary link: born from beautiful days, resurrect-
ing only when they return, containing some of their essence, it does not
only awaken their image in our memory; it guarantees their return,
their actual, persistent, unmediated presence.

The dark coolness of my room related to the full sunlight of the
street as the shadow relates to the ray of light, that is to say it was just as
luminous and it gave my imagination the total spectacle of the summer,
whereas my senses, if I had been on a walk, could only have enjoyed it
by fragments; it matched my repose which (thanks to the adventures
told by my book and stirring my tranquility) supported, like the quiet
of a motionless hand in the middle of a running brook the shock and
the motion of a torrent of activity. (Swann's Way. Paris: Pléiade, 1954;
p. 83. Author's translation.)

From the beginning of the passage, inwardness is valorized positively as something desirable that has to protect itself against the intrusion
of outside forces, but that nevertheless has to borrow, as it were, some of its
constitutive properties from the outside. A chain of binary properties is set
up and antithetically differentiated in terms of the inside/outside polarity:
properties of coolness, darkness, repose, silence, imagination and totality,
associated with inwardness, contrast with the heat, the light, the activity,
the sounds, the senses and the fragmentation that govern the outside. By
the act of reading, these static oppositions are put in motion, thus allowing
for the play of substitutions by means of which the claim for totalization can
be made. Thus, in a beautifully seductive effect of chiaroscuro, mediated
by the metaphor of light as a poised butterfly, the inner room is convinc-
ingly said to acquire the amount of light necessary to reading. In the wake
of this light, warmth can also enter the room, incarnate in the auditive
synaesthesia of the various sounds. According to the narrator, these metaphorical substitutions and reversals render the presence of Summer in the

room more complete than the actual experience of Summer in the outside world could have done. The text achieves this synthesis and comments on it in normative terms, comparable to the manner in which treatises of practical rhetorics recommend the use of one figure in preference to another in a given situation: here it is the substitutive totalization by metaphor which is said to be more effective than the mere contiguity of metonymic association. As opposed to the random contingency of metonymy ("par hasard"), the metaphor is linked to its proper meaning by, says Proust, the "necessary link" that leads to perfect synthesis. In the wake of this synthesis, the entire conceptual vocabulary of metaphysics enters the text: a terminology of generation, of transcendental necessity, of totality, of essence, of permanence and of unmediated presence. The passage acts out and asserts the priority of metaphor over metonymy in terms of the categories of metaphysics and with reference to the act of reading.

The actual test of the truth of the assertion comes in the second paragraph when the absurd mathematical ratio set up at the beginning has to be verified by a further substitution. This time, what has to be exchanged are not only the properties of light and dark, warm and cool, fragment and totality (part and whole), but the properties of action and repose. The full seduction of the text can only come into being when the formal totalization of light and dark is completed by the transfer from rest to action that represents the extra-textual, referential moment. The text asserts the transfer in the concluding sentence: "The dark coolness of my room [. . .] supported, like the quiet of a motionless hand in the middle of a running brook, the shock and the motion of a torrent of activity." The verb "to support" here carries the full weight of uniting rest and action ("repos et activité"), fiction and reality, as firmly as the base supports the column. The transfer, as is so often the case in Proust, is carried out by the liquid element of the running brook. The natural, representational connotation of the passage is with coolness, so particularly attractive within the predominant summer-mood of the entire *Recherche*. But coolness, it will be remembered, is one of the characteristic properties of the "inside" world. It cannot therefore by itself transfer us into the opposite world of activity. The movement of the water evokes a freshness which in the binary logic of the passage is associated with the inward, imaginary world of reading and fiction. In order to accede to action, it would be necessary to capture one of the properties belonging to the opposite chain such as, for example, warmth. The mere "cool" action of fiction cannot suffice: it is necessary to reconcile the cool immobility of the hand with the heat of action if the claim made by the sentence is to stand up as true. This transfer is carried out, always within the same sentence, when it is said that repose supports "a torrent of activity." The expression "*torrent d'activité*" is not, or no longer, a metaphor in French: it is a cliché, a dead, or sleeping metaphor that has lost the suggestive, connotative values contained in the word "torrent." It simply means "a great deal of activity," the amount of activity that is likely to agitate one to the point of getting hot. Heat is thus surreptitiously smuggled into the passage from a cold source, closing the ring of antithetical properties and allowing for their exchange and substitution: from the moment tranquility can be active and warm without losing its cool and its distinctive quality of repose, the fragmented experience of reality can become whole without losing its quality of being real.

The transfer is made to seem convincing and seductive by the double play on the cliché "torrent of activity." The proximate, contiguous image of the brook awakens, as it were, the sleeping beauty of the dozing metaphor which, in its common use, had become the metonymic association of two words united by sheer habit and no longer by the inner necessity, the necessary link of a transcendental signification. "Torrent" functions in a double semantic register: in its reawakened literal meaning it relays the attribute of coolness that is actually part of the running water, whereas in its figural non-meaning it designates the quantity of activity connotative of the contrary property of warmth.

The rhetorical structure of this sentence is therefore not simply metaphorical. It is at least doubly metonymic, first because the coupling of words, in a cliché, is not governed by the necessary link that reveals their potential identity but by the contingent habit of proximity; second, because the reawakening of the metaphorical term "torrent" is carried out by a statement that happens to be in the vicinity, but without there being any necessity for this proximity on the level of the referential meaning. The most striking thing is that this doubly metonymic structure is found in a text that also contains highly seductive and successful metaphors (as in the chiaroscuro effect of the beginning, or in the condensation of light in the butterfly image) and that explicitly asserts the superiority of metaphor over metonymy in terms of metaphysical categories.

That these metaphysical categories do not remain unaffected by such a reading would become clear from an inclusive reading of Proust's novel or would become even more explicit in a language-conscious philosopher such as Nietzsche who, as a philosopher, has to be concerned with the epistemological consequences of the kind of rhetorical seductions exemplified by the Proust passage. It can be shown that the systematic critique of the main categories of metaphysics undertaken by Nietzsche in his late work, the critique of the concepts of causality, of the subject, of identity, of referential and revealed truth, etc. occurs along the same pattern of deconstruction that was operative in Proust's text; and it can also be shown that this pattern exactly corresponds to Nietzsche's description, in texts that precede *The Will to Power* by more than fifteen years, of the structure of the main rhetorical tropes. The key to this critique of metaphysics, which is itself a recurrent gesture throughout the history of thought, is the rhetorical model of the trope or, if one prefers to call it that, literature. It turns out that, in these innocent-looking didactic exercises we are in fact playing for very sizeable stakes.

It is therefore all the more necessary to know what is linguistically involved in a rhetorically conscious reading of the type here undertaken on a brief fragment from a novel and extended by Nietzsche to the entire text of post-Hellenic thought. Our first examples dealing with the rhetorical questions were rhetorizations of grammar, figures generated by syntactical paradigms, whereas the Proust example could be better described as a grammatization of rhetoric. By passing from a paradigmatic structure based on substitution, such as metaphor, to a syntagmatic structure based on contingent association such as metonymy, the mechanical, repetitive aspect of grammatical forms is shown to be operative in a passage that seemed at first sight to celebrate the self-willed and autonomous inventiveness of a subject. Figures are assumed to be inventions, the products of a highly particularized individual talent, whereas no one can claim credit for the programmed pattern of grammar. Yet, our reading of the Proust passage shows that precisely when the highest claims are being made for the unifying power of metaphor, these very images rely in fact on the deceptive use of semi-automatic grammatical patterns. The de-construction of metaphor and of all rhetorical patterns such as mimesis, paranomasia[17] or personification that use resemblance as a way to disguise differences, takes us back to the impersonal precision of grammar and of a semiology derived from grammatical patterns. Such a deconstruction puts into question a whole series of concepts that underlie the value judgments of our critical discourse: the metaphors of primacy, of genetic history and, most notably, of the autonomous power to will of the self.

There seems to be a difference, then, between what I called the rhetorization of grammar (as in the rhetorical question) and the grammatization of rhetoric, as in the de-constructive readings of the type sketched out in the passage from Proust. The former end up in indetermination, in a suspended uncertainty that was unable to choose between two modes of reading, whereas the latter seems to reach a truth, albeit by the negative road of exposing an error, a false pretense. After the de-constructive reading of the Proust passage, we can no longer believe the assertion made in this passage about the intrinsic, metaphysical superiority of metaphor over metonymy. We seem to end up in a mood of negative assurance that is highly productive of critical discourse. The further text of Proust's novel, for example, responds perfectly to an extended application of this de-constructive pattern: not only can similar gestures be repeated throughout the novel, at all the crucial articulations or all passages where large aesthetic and metaphysical claims are being made—the scenes of involuntary memory, the workshop of Elstir, the septette of Vinteuil, the convergence of author and narrator at the end of the novel—but a vast thematic and semiotic network is revealed that structures the entire narrative and that remained invisible to a reader caught in naïve metaphorical mystification. The whole of literature would respond in similar fashion, although the techniques and the patterns would have to vary considerably, of course, from author to author. But there is absolutely no reason why analyses of the kind here suggested for Proust would not to be applicable, with proper modifications of technique, to Milton or to Dante or to Hölderlin. This will in fact be the task of literary criticism in the coming years.

It would seem that we are saying that criticism is the deconstruction of literature, the reduction to the rigors of grammar of rhetorical mystifications. And if we hold up Nietzsche as the philosopher of such a critical deconstruction, then the literary critic would become the philosopher's ally in his struggle with the poets. Criticism and literature would separate around the epistemological axis that distinguishes grammar from rhetoric. It is easy enough to see that this apparent glorification of the critic-philosopher in the name of truth is in fact a glorification of the poet as the primary source of this truth; if truth is the recognition of the systematic character of a certain kind of error, then it would be fully dependent on the prior existence of this error. Philosophers of science like Bachelard or Wittgenstein are notoriously dependent on the aberrations of the poets. We are back at our unanswered question: does the grammatization of rhetoric end up in negative certainty or does it, like the rhetorization of grammar, remain suspended in the ignorance of its own truth or falsehood?

Two concluding remarks should suffice to answer the question. First of all, it is not true that Proust's text can simply be reduced to the mystified assertion (the superiority of metaphor over metonymy) that our reading deconstructs. The reading is not "our" reading, since it uses only the linguistic elements provided by the text itself; the distinction between author and reader is one of the false distinctions that the deconstruction makes evident. The deconstruction is not something we have added to the text but it constituted the text in the first place. A literary text simultaneously asserts and denies the authority of its own rhetorical mode and by reading the text as we did, we were only trying to come closer to being as rigorous a reader as the author had to be in order to write the sentence in the first place. Poetic writing is the most advanced and refined mode of deconstruction; it may differ from critical or discursive writing in the economy of its articulation, but not in kind.

But if we recognize the existence of the deconstructive moment as constitutive of all literary language, we have surreptitiously reintroduced the categories that this deconstruction was supposed to eliminate and that have merely been displaced. We have, for example, displaced the question of the self from the referent into the figure of the narrator, who then becomes the *signifié* of the passage. It becomes again possible to ask such naïve questions as what Proust's, or Marcel's, motives may have been in thus manipulating language: was he fooling himself, or was he represented as fooling himself and fooling us into believing that fiction and action are as easy to unite, by reading, as the passage asserts? The pathos of the entire section, which would have been more noticeable if the quotation had been a little more extended, the constant vacillation of the narrator between guilt and well-being, invites such questions. They are absurd questions, of course, since the reconciliation of fact and fiction occurs itself as a mere assertion made in a text, and is thus productive of more text at the moment when it asserts its decision to escape from textual confinement. But even if we free ourselves of all false questions of intent and rightfully reduce the narrator to the status of a mere grammatical pronoun, without which the deconstructive narrative could not come into being, this subject remains endowed with a function that is not grammatical but rhetorical, in that it gives voice, so to speak, to a grammatical syntagm.[18] The term voice, even when used in a grammatical terminology as when we speak of the passive or interrogative voice is, of course, a metaphor inferring by analogy the intent of the subject from the structure of the predicate. In the case of the deconstructive discourse that we call literary, or rhetorical, or poetic, this creates a distinctive complication illustrated by the Proust passage. The deconstructive reading revealed a first paradox: the passage valorizes metaphor as being the "right" literary figure, but then proceeds to constitute itself by means of the epistemologically incompatible figure of metonymy. The deconstructive critical discourse reveals the presence of this delusion and affirms it as the irreversible mode of its truth. It cannot pause there however. For if we then ask the obvious and simple next question, whether the rhetorical mode of the text in question is that of metaphor or metonymy, it is impossible to give an answer. Individual metaphors, such as the chiaroscuro effect or the butterfly, are shown to be subordinate figures in a general clause whose syntax is metonymic; from this point of view, it seems that the rhetoric is superseded by a grammar that de-constructs it. But this metonymic clause has as its subject a voice whose relationship to this clause is again metaphorical. The narrator who tells us about the impossibility of metaphor is himself, or itself, a metaphor, the metaphor of a grammatical syntagm whose meaning is the denial of metaphor stated, by antiphrasis,[19] as its priority. And this subject-metaphor is, in its turn, open to the kind of deconstruction to the second degree, the rhetorical deconstruction of psycholinguistics, in which the more advanced investigations of literature are presently engaged, against considerable resistance.

We end up therefore, in the case of the rhetorical grammatization of semiology, just as in the grammatical rhetorization of illocutionary phrases, in the same state of suspended ignorance. Any question about the rhetorical mode of a literary text is always a rhetorical question which does not even know whether it is really questioning. The resulting pathos is an anxiety (or bliss, depending on one's momentary mood or individual temperament) of ignorance, not an anxiety of reference— as becomes thematically clear in Proust's novel when reading is dramatized, in the relationship between Marcel and Albertine, not as an emotive reaction to what language does, but as an emotive reaction to the impossibility of knowing what it might be up to.[20] Literature as well as criticism—the difference between them being delusive—are condemned (or privileged) to be forever the most rigorous and, consequently, the most unreliable language in terms of which man names and modifies himself.

Notes

1. First published in *Diacritics* 3:3 (1973), 27–33.

2. De Man here suggests that an emphasis on social context and political impact is a new form of calls in the 1960s for art and education to be "relevant."

3. Fredric Jameson's influential book *The Prison-House of Language: A Critical Account of Structuralism and Russian Formalism* (1973) argued that the Russian Formalists of the earlier twentieth century should be understood as political thinkers and not seen as paving the way for a socially disengaged structuralism of the 1960s.

4. The Swiss linguist Ferdinand de Saussure developed his theory of the arbitrariness of the sign in lectures collected as *Course in General Linguistics* (1917). In a multitude of publications, the linguist Roman Jakobson gave close attention to

literary language. At several points de Man has in mind Jakobson's essay "The Metaphoric and the Metonymic Poles," in which Jakobson describes language as operating along two axes, a "vertical" one of metaphoric substitution and a "horizontal" or narrative axis of metonymic progression from one item to the next.

5. In *The German Ideology*, Marx says that Communism would make it possible "for me to do one thing today and another tomorrow, to hunt in the morning, fish in the afternoon, rear cattle in the evening, criticize after dinner, just as I have a mind, without ever becoming hunter, fisherman, shepherd, or critic."

6. Charles Augustin Sainte-Beuve was one of the most influential French critics of the 19th century. In *Contre Sainte-Beuve* Marcel Proust argued against Sainte-Beuve's stress on writers' personal lives and social standing.

7. All leading figures in French structuralism. For Barthes, see the selection in this volume. Tzvetan Todorov's works include an important essay collection, *Poétique de la prose* (1971), as well as the works de Man goes on to mention; Gérard Genette has published widely on language and literature, including a three-volume series of books entitled *Figures*; the linguist A. J. Greimas's works include *Essais de sémiotique poétique* (1972).

8. For J. L. Austin's speech act theory, see his *How To Do Things with Words* (1962).

9. Kenneth Burke developed this distinction most fully in *A Rhetoric of Motives* (1950) and *A Grammar of Motives* (1952).

10. Semiotic essays by the philosopher and logician Charles Sanders Peirce have been collected in *Peirce on Signs: Writings on Semiotic*, ed. James Hoopes (1991).

11. Archie Bunker was the crude, plain-spoken, working-class hero of the sitcom *All in the Family* (1971–79). It was the top-ranked show on television at the time of de Man's essay.

12. In the show, Archie is endlessly suspicious of immigrants moving into his neighborhood and taking jobs away from white Americans.

13. *Archē* is the ancient Greek term for "origin." In his essay "Différance" (English trans. in *Margins of Philosophy*, 1982), Jacques Derrida developed a punning transformation of the French term "différence," changing the second "e" to an "a" to produce a term that simultaneously means "to differ" and "to defer."

14. In Frank Brady et al., eds., *Literary Theory and Structure: Essays in Honor of William K. Wimsatt* (1973).

15. "Meaning" becomes "sense"; a distinction made by the philosopher Gottlob Frege (1848–1925).

16. The first section of Proust's *A la Recherche du temps perdu*.

17. Puns.

18. A sequence of words in a sentence.

19. A rhetorical figure: implying something by saying its opposite.

20. In the *Recherche*, Proust's hero is constantly obsessing about what his lover Albertine is up to when away from him and what she is communicating or concealing when they are together.

21

Writing[1] (1990)

Barbara Johnson

Barbara Johnson completed her Ph.D. at Yale under the direction of Paul de Man in 1977. Her critical practice was thus forged in the early days of the "Yale School," and her early writings lucidly elaborate the intellectual genealogy of deconstruction as a new approach to reading literature. Her translation of Jacques Derrida's *Dissemination* (1981) with a critical introduction and annotations was a milestone in the American reception of the work of this pre-eminent poststructuralist philosopher. Johnson's *Défigurations du langage poétique* (1979) and *The Critical Difference* (1980) demonstrate the powerful insights to be gained for the reading of literature with the combined aid of structuralist linguistics, poststructuralist philosophy, and psychoanalysis. Tracking the play of the signifier against the grain of the meaning it points to, Johnson's essays on Baudelaire, Barthes, Mallarmé, Melville, and Poe analyze how various manifestations of internal difference—distance, deferral, disjunction—subvert the unity and therefore the authority of singular meaning.

During the next decades Johnson extended deconstruction's critical difference to the analysis of the worldly manifestations of exclusionary and univocal authority represented in the predominantly white male literary canon. The essays collected in *A World of Difference* (1987) take on the complex play of difference and exclusion in the binary oppositions underlying gender and racial difference; these essays established her as an important voice at the intersection of deconstruction and contemporary feminism and multiculturalism. In subsequent work, she has extended the purview of her analysis to film, popular culture, and law, moving beyond the close focus on literary and philosophical language seen in the earlier deconstructive work of figures such as Paul de Man.

Johnson's 1990 essay "Writing" provides a good example of her compelling blend of linguistic and cultural analysis. Beginning with a concise introduction to the genealogy of deconstruction through a discussion of the reflexivity of writing itself, Johnson goes on to sketch the link between writing and other structures of authority, demonstrating the rich possibilities of deconstruction for cultural politics.

How is it that the word "writing" has come to be considered a critical term? Isn't "writing" simply one of those aspects of literature that can be taken for granted? Isn't it merely the medium through which a reader encounters words on a page—for example, these?

Every essay in this volume communicates to some extent *by means of* the very thing it is talking *about*. Nowhere is this more obvious than in the case of writing. An essay about writing, therefore, is an unclosable loop: it is an attempt to comprehend that which it is comprehended by. The non-Euclidean logic of such reciprocal inclusion has often itself been an object of attention in recent theoretical discussions of writing. That is only one of the consequences that the study of writing has entailed.

Writing about writing is hardly a new phenomenon, however. From Omar Khayyám's moving finger to Rousseau's trembling hand, from the broken tablets of Moses to the purloined letters of Poe and Alice Walker, from Borges's encyclopedia to Wordsworth's lines left upon a seat in a yew tree, images of writing in writing testify to an enduring fascination with the mechanics and materiality of the written word. A comprehensive treatment of the question of writing is obviously beyond the scope of the present essay. I will therefore concentrate on a particular recent moment of reflection about writing—the theoretical "revolution" in France in 1967—which has had a decisive impact upon the shape of literary studies today.

Writing (*l'écriture*) came to philosophical, psychoanalytic, and literary prominence in France in the 1960s, primarily through the work of Jacques Derrida, Roland Barthes, and other writers who were at that time associated with the journal *Tel Quel*. Philippe Sollers, in a "Program" that heads the group's collective theoretical volume, proclaimed in 1967: "A comprehensive theory arising out of a thought about the practice of writing cries out for elaboration." Writing, it seemed, was to become the key to all mythologies. The sudden spectacular interest in writing sprang from many different sources, some of which I will outline quickly here.

As early as 1953, in *Writing Degree Zero*, Roland Barthes had investigated the paradoxical relationship that existed in the nineteenth century in France between the development of a concept of Literature (with a capital *L*) and the growing sense of a breakdown in the representational capacities of language. Literature was in some ways being exalted as a substitute religion, but it was a religion whose high priests seemed only to proclaim the obscurity, imperfection, or unreliability of their own medium. The proper names associated with the elaboration of *both* sides of this phenomenon are Flaubert and Mallarmé. These writers, says Barthes, *constructed* the object Literature in the very act of announcing its death. In later essays, Barthes lays out a theory of literature based on a split between the classic notion of a *work* (*oeuvre*)—considered as a closed, finished, reliable representational *object*—and the modern notion of a *text*—considered as an open, infinite *process* that is both meaning-generating and meaning-subverting. "Work" and "text" are thus not two different kinds of object but two different ways of viewing the written word. What interests Barthes is the *tension* between the concept of Literature and the concept of textuality. While Literature is seen as a series of discrete and highly meaningful Great Works, textuality is the manifestation of an open-ended, heterogeneous, disruptive force of signification and erasure that transgresses all closure—a force that is operative even within the Great Works themselves.

Closure versus subversion, product versus practice, meaning-containing object versus significance-scattering process: Barthes' theory of writing owes a great deal, as we shall see, both to Marxism and to psychoanalysis. But the *Tel Quel* writers' involvement with Marxism and psychoanalysis takes on its particular coloring, strangely enough, through the mediation of Saussurian linguistics. How does this happen?

In his *Course in General Linguistics* (first published by his students in 1916, with new editions in 1948 and 1966), Ferdinand de Saussure mapped out a science of linguistics based not on the historical ("diachronic") development of families of languages but on the structural ("synchronic") properties of language "as such," frozen in time as a *system*. This "structuralist" perspective, also developed in the 1950s in anthropology by Claude Lévi-Strauss, involves viewing the system as a set of relations among elements governed by rules. The favorite analogy for such systems is chess: whatever the particular properties of an individual "man" (ivory, wood, plastic), the "man" is involved in a system of moves and relations that can be known and manipulated in themselves. From the structural point of view, there is no difference between ivory and plastic. There is difference between king, queen, and knight, or between white and black.

Saussure's most enduring contribution has been his description of the *sign* as the unit of the language system. The sign is composed of two parts: a mental image or concept (the "signified"), and a phonic or graphic vehicle (the "signifier"). The sign is thus both conceptual and material, sense and sound, spirit and letter at once. The existence of numerous languages indicates that the relation between the signifier and the signified in any given sign is arbitrary (there is no natural resemblance between sound and idea), but once fixed, that relation becomes a convention that cannot be modified at will by any individual speaker. By thus deciding that what is relevant to a structural study of language is neither history ("diachrony") nor reality (the "referent") but rather the system of differential relations among signs, Saussure set up a tremendously enabling, as well as limiting, heuristic perspective for analysis. And by asserting that signs signify not as independently meaningful units corresponding to external objects but as elements whose value is generated by their difference from neighboring elements in the system, Saussure put forth a notion of *difference* (not identity) as the origin of meaning.

Saussure's suspension of interest in history and the external world would seem to place him at the farthest remove from Marxism. But theorists of writing saw a connection between the signifier/signified relation and the materialism/idealism relation. If the signifier was the material condition of the existence of ideas, then the privileging of the signified resembled the fetishization of commodities resulting from bourgeois idealism's blindness to labor and to the material conditions of economic existence. The liberation of the signifier, the rebellion against idealist repressions, and the unleashing of the forces of difference and desire against the law and order of identity were all part of the program for change that developed in France in the 1960s. Whether linguistic materiality and economic materiality are linked *only* by analogy, or whether there is some profound interimplication between them, is still a subject for debate today. But whatever the case, the repressive return to order that followed the strikes and demonstrations in France in May 1968 squelched the optimism of those who might have believed in any simple connection between liberating the signifier and changing the class structure of society.[2]

The understanding of what it might mean to liberate the signifier also had roots in the psychoanalytic theory of Jacques Lacan. For many years prior to the 1966 publication of his *Écrits* (*Writings*), Lacan had been conducting a seminar in which he attempted to work out a radically new way of reading Freud. What he emphasized in Freud's writing was the discovery that "the unconscious is structured like a language." The unconscious is *structured*. It is not a reservoir of amorphous drives and energies but a system of articulations through which repressed ideas return in displaced form. Freud's comparison of a dream to a rebus is extended as an analogy for all effects of the unconscious: just as each element in a rebus must be translated separately in order to decipher the total message, so each element in a dream is a knot of associations that must be explored without regard for the dream's surface coherence. Dreams, slips of the tongue, parapraxes, hysterical symptoms, and other expressions of the unconscious are for Lacan manifestations of a "signifying chain," a structure of associations that resembles an unconscious foreign language. Consciousness attempts to disregard this language in order to control and define the identity of the self, but the psychoanalyst's task is to attempt to hear that language despite the ego's efforts to scramble it. Using the terminology of Saussure, Lacan calls the units of unconscious expression "signifiers," linked to repressed "signifieds." But the search for the signified can only take the form of a sliding along the chain of signifiers. In other words, there is no one-to-one link between signifier and signified but rather an "effect of signified" generated by the movement from one signifier to another. Freud never comes to the end of his dream analyses, never "solves" their enigma, but it feels as though something like insight is achieved by following out the dreamer's chains of associations.

Lacan's troubling of Saussure's one-to-one link between signifiers and signifieds actually turns out to have its counterpart in Saussure's own work. Beginning in 1964, Jean Starobinski began publishing strange notebooks in which Saussure attempted to prove that certain late Latin poems contained hidden proper names anagrammatically dispersed throughout their texts. The poems, in other words, contained extra signifiers, readable only to those in the know. Whether or not these anagrams were a secret key to late Latin poetics, the notion that the signifier could take the lead in creating poetic effects appealed to students of poetry. Saussure's anagrams prompted Julia Kristeva, among others, to theorize an anagrammatic (or paragrammatic) functioning in poetic language as such.

The claim that signifiers can generate effects even when the signified is unknown serves as the basis for Lacan's famous reading of Poe's story "The Purloined Letter." In that story, an unscrupulous minister steals a compromising letter from the queen under the unsuspecting eyes of the king. An amateur detective, Dupin, is commissioned by the stymied prefect of police to get the letter back. Dupin suspects that the minister has hidden the letter in plain sight, just as it had been when he stole it. Dupin then repeats the minister's act and steals the letter back for the queen. Lacan emphasizes the way in which the characters' actions are determined by the position of the letter among them. Neither the letter's contents (the never-revealed "signified") nor the individual identities of the people (the psychological equivalent of Saussure's ivory and wood chessmen) determine the course of the plot. It is the movement of the letter that dictates the characters' actions.

The rebus, the anagram, and the letter are clearly all manifestations of *writing*. They are graphic, articulated, material instantiations of systems of marks that simultaneously obscure and convey meaning. They are also something other than mere transcriptions of the spoken word. In other words, they are not examples of *phonetic* writing. It is this "something other" that must be kept in mind as we now turn to the work of the most important French theorist of writing, Jacques Derrida.

It was in 1967 that Derrida published three major books devoted to the question of writing: *Writing and Difference, Of Grammatology,* and *Speech and Phenomena.* Derrida's project in these writings is to reevaluate the structuring principles of Western metaphysics. Western philosophy, writes Derrida, has analyzed the world in terms of binary oppositions: mind vs. body, good vs. evil, man vs. woman, presence vs. absence. Each of these pairs is organized hierarchically: the first term is seen as higher or better than the second. According to Derrida, the opposition between speech and writing has been structured similarly: speech is seen as immediacy, presence, life, and identity, whereas writing is seen as deferment, absence, death, and difference. Speech is primary; writing secondary. Derrida calls this privileging of speech as self-present meaning "logocentrism."

In his three volumes of 1967, Derrida gives rigorous attention to the paradox that the Western tradition (the "Great Books") is filled with *writings* that privilege *speech.* By closely analyzing those writings, Derrida attempts to uncover the ways in which the Great Books rebel against their own stated intention to say that speech is better than writing. What his analyses reveal is that even when a text *tries to* privilege speech as immediacy, it cannot completely eliminate the fact that speech, like writing, is based on a *différance* (a Derridean neologism meaning both "deferment" and "difference") between signifier and signified inherent in the sign. Speakers do not beam meanings directly from one mind to another. Immediacy is an illusion. Properties normally associated with writing inevitably creep into a discussion designed to privilege speech. Thus, for example, although Saussure wishes to treat speech as primary and writing as secondary for an understanding of language, he describes language as a "dictionary in the head" or as "linear"—a spatial term more applicable to writing than to speech. Or, to take another example, when Socrates tells Phaedrus that proper teaching must take place orally rather than in writing, he nevertheless ends up describing the truths such teaching is supposed to reach as being "*inscribed* in the soul." Because a gap of heterogeneity and distance is fundamental to the structure of language, Derrida sees "speech" as being ultimately structured like "writing." This emphasis on writing as the more originary category is designed to counter the history of logocentrism and to track the functioning of *différance* in structures of signification.

Many literary texts seem in fact to stage some version of this encounter between the search for spoken immediacy or identity and the recourse to writing and difference. The following poem by Edward Taylor (ca. 1642–1729), for example, does not seem to expect to end up talking about writing:

> Meditation 6
> Am I thy gold? Or purse, Lord, for thy wealth,
>   Whether in mine or mint refined for thee?
> I'm counted so, but count me o'er thyself,
>   Lest gold washed face, and brass in heart I be.
>   I fear my touchstone touches when I try
>   Me and my counted gold too overly.
>
> Am I new minted by thy stamp indeed?
>   Mine eyes are dim; I cannot clearly see.
> Be thou my spectacles that I may read
>   Thine image and inscription stamped on me.
>   If thy bright image do upon me stand,
>   I am a golden angel in thy hand.
>
> Lord, make my soul thy plate, thine image bright
>   Within the circle of the same enfile.
> And on its brims in golden letters write
>   Thy superscription in an holy style.
>   Then I shall be thy money, thou my horde:
>   Let me thy angel be, be thou my Lord.

Written in a style of extended metaphor known as the metaphysical conceit, this poem sets out to express spiritual value in terms of material value (gold). The most obvious figure for the conjunction between the spiritual and the material is the word "angel," which means both a heavenly being and an old English coin. Through this spiritual/material alloy, the poem attempts to make human value both derive from and coincide with divine value, to eliminate the space of difference or distance between the human and the divine.

The poem is composed of a series of questions and imperatives addressed to God. While these aim to alleviate doubt, difference, and distance, they seem only to widen the gap they attempt to close. Am I gold or purse? value-object or container? the poet asks. He then pursues the first possibility, only to stumble upon a new inside/outside opposition: "Lest gold washed face, and brass in heart I be." The gold begins to resemble a sign, with no guaranteed correlation between face (signifier) and heart (signified). The becoming-sign process continues in the second stanza, where the speaker is "stamped" with an image and an inscription. The speaker is now a reader, and what he reads is himself. God has become an image, and a corrective lens. In the final stanza, the text ("inscription") that was dimly decipherable in the second stanza turns out not yet to have been written. While the poem still yearns for a perfectly reciprocal container/contained relation ("I shall be thy money, thou my horde"), this relation now requires the active intervention of writing ("in golden letters write / Thy superscription"). In his increasingly aggressive submissiveness, the speaker tries to order God to take his place as the writer.

From metal to image to letters, from touching to reading to writing, from counted to almost-read to not-yet-written, the speaker seems to be farther away from coincidence with God at the end than he was at the beginning. The mediating elements only increase the *différance*. Yet this *différance* is also the space of the poem's existence. The speaker cannot *write* his way into an immediacy that would eliminate writing. Nor can he write himself into a submissiveness great enough to overtake the fact that it is he, not God, who writes. His conceit will never succeed in erasing the "conceit" of writing itself.

The logic of writing is thus a double logic: writing is called upon as a necessary remedy for *différance,* but at the same time it *is* the very *différance* for which a remedy must be sought. In Derrida's analyses of writing, this logic is called the logic of the *supplément*. In French, the word *supplément* means both an "addition" and a "substitute." To say that "A is a *supplément* to B" is thus to say something ambiguous. Addition and substitution are not exactly contradictory, but neither can they be combined in the traditional logic of identity. In the poem, the inscriptions, images, and even spectacles function as *supplément:* they are at once additions and substitutes simultaneously bridging and widening the gap between God and the speaker. Some sense of the way in which supplementary logic differs from the binary logic of identity (A = A) and noncontradiction (A ≠ not A) may be derived from the following list. In this list, all statements are to be taken as *simultaneously* equivalent to the statement "A is a *supplément* to B." (In terms of the Taylor poem, say B = the presence of, or coincidence with, God; and A = writing).

A is added to B.
A substitutes for B.
A is a superfluous addition to B.
A makes up for the absence of B.
A usurps the place of B.
A makes up for B's deficiency.
A corrupts the purity of B.
A is necessary so that B can be restored.
A is an accident alienating B from itself.
A is that without which B would be lost.
A is that through which B is lost.
A is a danger to B.
A is a remedy to B.
A's fallacious charm seduces one away from B.
A can never satisfy the desire for B.
A protects against direct encounter with B.

Supplementary logic is not only the logic of writing—it is also a logic that can only really exist *in* writing. That is, it is a nonintuitive logic that inheres (Lacan would say, "in-sists") in a text as a system of traces. Like an algebraic equation with more than one unknown, supplementary logic cannot be held in the head but must be worked out in external form. It is no accident that the word "differential" is central both to calculus and to Derrida's theory of writing.

Derrida's theory of writing turns out to have been, in fact, a theory of reading. The epigraph to his *Writing and Difference* is a quotation from Mallarmé: "Le tout sans nouveauté qu'un espacement de la lecture" ("All without innovation except for a certain spacing-out of reading"). What does it mean to introduce "space" into reading? For Mallarmé, it means two things. It means giving a signifying function to the materiality—the blanks, the typefaces, the placement on the page, the punctuation—of writing. And it also means tracking syntactic and semantic ambiguities in such a way as to generate multiple, often conflicting, meanings out of a single utterance. The "meaning" of a Mallarmé text, like that of a dream, cannot be grasped intuitively as a whole but must be worked out rigorously by following each strand in a network of relations. What Derrida generalizes and analyzes in other writings is this "spacing" that Mallarmé attempts to maximize. In his reading of Plato's *Phaedrus,* for instance, Derrida follows the ambiguity of the word *pharmakon,* which Plato uses to describe writing itself. *If pharmakon* can mean both "poison" and "remedy," what does it mean to call writing a *pharmakon*? As Derrida points out, translators of Plato have rendered this word by choosing to favor one side or the other of the ambiguity according to the context. They have subordinated its ambiguity to their notion of what makes the most sense. They have thus subordinated "writing" as spacing and ambiguity to "speech" as single intention. The ambiguity of the poison / remedy relation is tamed thereby into something far less unsettling. "Sense" is achieved, however, at a cost. To know the difference between poison and remedy may be reassuring, but that reassurance may well make it difficult to come to grips with the meaning of Socrates' death.

Thus "reading," for Derrida, involves following the "other" logics of structures of signification inscribed in writing that may or may not be in conformity with traditional logics of meaning, identity, consciousness, or intention. It involves taking seriously the elements that a standard reading disregards, overlooks, or edits out. Just as Freud rendered dreams and slips of the tongue *readable* rather than dismissing them as mere nonsense or error, so Derrida sees signifying force in the gaps, margins, figures, echoes, digressions, discontinuities, contradictions, and ambiguities of a text. When one writes, one writes more than (or less than, or other than) one thinks. The reader's task is to read what is written rather than simply attempt to intuit what might have been meant.

The possibility of reading materiality, silence, space, and conflict within texts has opened up extremely productive ways of studying the politics of language. If each text is seen as presenting a major claim that attempts to dominate, erase, or distort various "other" claims (whose traces nevertheless remain detectable to a reader who goes against the grain of the dominant claim), then "reading" in its extended sense is deeply involved in questions of authority and power. One field of conflict and domination in discourse that has been fruitfully studied in this sense is the field of sexual politics. Alice Jardine, in *Gynesis* (1985), points out that since logocentric logic has been coded as "male," the "other" logics of spacing, ambiguity, figuration, and indirection are often coded as "female," and that a critique of logocentrism can enable a critique of "phallocentrism" as well. A theory and practice of female writing *(écriture féminine)* has been developed in France by such writers as Hélène Cixous and Luce Irigaray,[3] who have attempted to write the specificity of female biological and ideological difference. While Cixous, Irigaray, and others work on the relations between writing and the body, many feminists on both sides of the Atlantic have been interested in the gender implications of the relations between writing and silence. In *The Madwoman in the Attic* (1979), Sandra Gilbert and Susan Gubar show how nineteenth-century women writers struggle for authorship against the silence that has already been prescribed for them by the patriarchal language they must both use and transform. Adrienne Rich also explores the traces of women's silence in a collection of essays entitled *On Lies, Secrets, and Silence* (1979). These and other works have as their project the attempt to read the suppressed, distorted, or disguised messages that women's writing has encoded. They require a reading strategy that goes beyond apparent intentions or surface meanings, a reading that takes full advantage of writing's capacity to preserve that which cannot yet, perhaps, be deciphered.

The writings of Western male authorities have often encoded the silence, denigration, or idealization not only of women but also of other "others." Edward Said, in *Orientalism* (1978), analyzes the discursive fields of scholarship, art, and politics in which the "Oriental" is projected as the "other" of the European. By reading against the grain of the writers' intentions, he shows how European men of reason and benevolence could inscribe a rationale for oppression and exploitation within their very discourse of Enlightenment.

While the critique of logocentrism undertaken by Derrida implies that Western patriarchal culture has always privileged the presence, immediacy, and ideality of speech over the distance and materiality of writing, this privilege has never, in fact, been unambiguous. An equal but more covert privileging of writing has also been operative. One of the ways in which colonial powers succeeded in imposing their domination over other peoples was precisely through writing. European civilization functioned with great effectiveness by remote control. And indeed, when comparing itself to other cultures, European culture has always seen its own form of literacy as a sign of superiority. The hidden but ineradicable importance of writing that Derrida uncovers in his readings of logocentric texts in fact reflects an unacknowledged, or "repressed," *grapho*centrism. It may well be that it is only in a text-centered culture that one can privilege speech in a logocentric way. The "speech" privileged in logocentrism is not literal but is a *figure* of speech: a figure, ultimately, of God.

Recent work by Henry Louis Gates, Jr., and others attempts to combine Derrida's critique of logocentrism with an equal critique of the way in which European graphocentrism has functioned historically to oppress and exploit non-European peoples. If European culture had ever unambiguously privileged speech and denigrated writing, there would have been no reason, for example, to forbid American slaves to read and write. The following passage from *The Narrative of the Life of Frederick Douglass, an American Slave, Written by Himself,* should be juxtaposed to Lévi-Strauss's suggestion in *Tristes Tropiques* that the function of writing is to enslave.[4] Douglass agrees, in a sense, but he does not stop there:

> Very soon after I went to live with Mr. and Mrs. Auld, she very kindly commenced to teach me the A,B,C. After I had learned this, she assisted me in learning to spell words of three or four letters. Just at this point of my progress, Mr. Auld found out what was going on, and at once forbade Mrs. Auld to instruct me further, telling her, among other things, that it was unlawful, as well as unsafe, to teach a slave to read. To use his own words, further, he said, "If you give a nigger an inch, he will take an ell. A nigger should know nothing but to obey his master—to do as he is told to do. Learning would *spoil* the best nigger in the world. Now," said he, "if you teach that nigger (speaking of myself) how to read, there would be no keeping him. It would forever unfit him to be a slave. He would at once become unmanageable, and of no value to his master. As to himself it could do him no good, but a great deal of harm. It would make him discontented and unhappy." These words sank deep into my heart, stirred up sentiments within that lay slumbering, and called into existence an entirely new train of thought. It was a new and special revelation, explaining dark and mysterious things, with which my youthful understanding had struggled, but struggled in vain. I now understood what had been to me a most perplexing difficulty—to wit, the white man's power to enslave the black man. It was a grand achievement, and I prized it highly. From that moment, I understood the pathway from slavery to freedom. (Douglass, 1845, 49)

What enslaves is not writing per se but *control* of writing, and writing as control. What is needed is not less writing but more consciousness of how it works. If, as Derrida claims, the importance of writing has been "repressed" by the dominant culture of the Western tradition, it is because writing can always pass into the hands of the "other." The "other" can always learn to read the mechanism of his or her own oppression. The desire to repress writing is thus a desire to repress the fact of the repression of the "other."

What is at stake in writing is the very structure of authority itself. Whether writing is seen as the instance of the law, the loss of immediacy, or the subversion of the master, whether it opens up a stance of domination, a space of exile, or the pathway to freedom, one thing, at least, is clear: the story of the role and nature of writing in Western culture is still in the process of being written. And the future of that story may be quite unforeseeable, as we pass from the age of the book to the age of the byte.

Notes

1. First published in *Critical Terms for Literary Study*, ed. Frank Lentricchia and Thomas McLaughlin (Chicago: University of Chicago Press, 1990), 39–49.

2. In May of 1968, a massive strike by ten million French workers, seeking better pay and working conditions, was joined by many university students, who closed down university campuses—the Sorbonne was turned into a commune—and agitated for reform of the French educational system. Order was restored after several months of turmoil, with only modest concessions from the government.

3. A novelist and playwright as well as a literary critic and theorist, Hélène Cixous founded Europe's first center for women's studies in the 1970s at the University of Paris VIII. She developed the concept of *écriture féminine* in such works as her pathbreaking 1975 essay "The Laugh of the Medusa." Luce Irigaray, philosopher, psychoanalyst, and cultural theorist, is best known for her books *Speculum of the Other Woman* (1974) and *This Sex Which Is Not One* (1977).

4. This is a recurrent theme in Claude Lévi-Strauss's *Tristes Tropiques*, a memoir of his early days traveling and doing anthropological research in Brazil; the book expands into a searching critique of the social inequalities underlying patterns of social organization. In *Of Grammatology*, Jacques Derrida gives an extended deconstructive analysis of the ambivalent discussions of writing and culture in *Tristes Tropiques*.

22

The Position of Translated Literature within the Literary Polysystem[1] (1978)

Itamar Even-Zohar

Since the early 1960s, Itamar Even-Zohar has been evolving a theory of sociocultural systems in which he sees each culture as composed of heterogeneous and dynamic networks that interrelate in a complex manner. Dissatisfied with what he saw as rigid interpretations of Ferdinand de Saussure's structural linguistics, Even-Zohar proposed the idea of "dynamic Functionalism" as a way to reckon with the interplay of historical and contemporary aspects of any cultural system, citing the Russian Formalists and the Prague structuralists as his main theoretical predecessors. His polysystem theory of literature postulates that literature functions as a system, with high and low, canonized and noncanonized works constantly informing and influencing each other, even though interference is usually exerted by canonized works. Over the years Even-Zohar has extended this postulate to cultures in general.

Born in Tel Aviv, Even-Zohar was educated at the Universities of Tel Aviv and Jerusalem. He has been a major contributor to the development of translation theory as part of his polysystem theory. Translated literature for Even-Zohar is its own system within a general literary polysystem, and can either become central or remain peripheral within a target culture through the domestication of foreign meanings. This is the argument developed in "The Position of Translated Literature in the Literary Polysystem" (1978), which appears here, an essay that had a great impact in helping shift translation studies from purely linguistic concerns toward a broader study of culture.

I

In spite of the broad recognition among historians of culture of the major role translation has played in the crystallization of national cultures, relatively little research has been carried out so far in this area. As a rule, histories of literatures mention translations when there is no way to avoid them, when dealing with the Middle Ages or the Renaissance, for instance. One might of course find sporadic references to individual literary translations in various other periods, but they are seldom incorporated into the historical account in any coherent way. As a consequence, one hardly gets any idea whatsoever of the function of translated literature for a literature as a whole or of its position within that literature. Moreover, there is no awareness of the possible existence of translated literature as a particular literary system. The prevailing concept is rather that of "translation" or just "translated works" treated on an individual basis. Is there any basis for a different assumption, that is for considering translated literature as a system? Is there the same sort of cultural and verbal network of relations within what seems to be an arbitrary group of translated texts as the one we willingly hypothesize for original literature? What kind of relations might there be among translated works, which are presented as completed facts, imported from other literatures, detached from their home contexts and consequently neutralized from the point of view of center-and-periphery struggles?

My argument is that translated works do correlate in at least two ways: (a) in the way their source texts are selected by the target literature, the principles of selection never being uncorrelatable with the home co-systems of the target literature (to put it in the most cautious way); and (b) in the way they adopt specific norms, behaviors, and policies—in short, in their use of the literary repertoire—which results from their relations with the other home co-systems. These are not confined to the linguistic level only, but are manifest on any selection level as well. Thus, translated literature may possess a repertoire of its own, which to a certain extent could even be exclusive to it.

It seems that these points make it not only justifiable to talk about translated literature, but rather imperative to do so. I cannot see how any scholarly effort to describe and explain the behavior of the literary poly-system in synchrony and diachrony can advance in an adequate way if that is not recognized. In other words, I conceive of translated literature not only as an integral system within any literary polysystem, but as a most active system within it. But what is its position within the polysystem and how is this position connected with the nature of its overall repertoire? One would be tempted to deduce from the peripheral position of trans-lated literature in the study of literature that it also permanently occupies a peripheral position in the literary polysystem, but this is by no means the case. Whether translated literature becomes central or peripheral, and whether this position is connected with innovatory ("primary") or conser-vatory ("secondary") repertoires, depends on the specific constellation of the polysystem under study.

II

To say that translated literature maintains a central position in the literary polysystem means that it participates actively in shaping the center of the polysystem. In such a situation it is by and large an integral part of innova-tory forces, and as such likely to be identified with major events in literary history while these are taking place. This implies that in this situation no clear-cut distinction is maintained between "original" and "translated" writings, and that often it is the leading writers (or members of the avant-garde who are about to become leading writers) who produce the most con-spicuous or appreciated translations. Moreover, in such a state when new literary models are emerging, translation is likely to become one of the means of elaborating the new repertoire. Through the foreign works, features (both principles and elements) are introduced into the home literature which did not exist there before. These include possibly not only new models of real-ity to replace the old and established ones that are no longer effective, but a whole range of other features as well, such as a new (poetic) language, or compositional patterns and techniques. It is clear that the very principles of selecting the works to be translated are determined by the situation gov-erning the (home) polysystem: the texts are chosen according to their com-patibility with the new approaches and the supposedly innovatory role they may assume within the target literature.

What then are the conditions which give rise to a situation of this kind? It seems to me that three major cases can be discerned, which are basically various manifestations of the same law: (a) when a polysystem has not yet been crystallized, that is to say, when a literature is "young," in the process of being established; (b) when a literature is either "peripheral" (within a large group of correlated literatures) or "weak," or both; and (c) when there are turning points, crises, or literary vacuums in a literature.

In the first case translated literature simply fulfills the need of a younger literature to put into use its newly founded (or renovated) tongue for as many literary types as possible in order to make it serviceable as a literary language and useful for its emerging public. Since a young literature cannot immediately create texts in all types known to its producers, it benefits from the experience of other literatures, and translated literature becomes in this way one of its most important systems. The same holds true for the second instance, that of relatively established literatures whose resources are limited and whose position within a larger literary hierarchy is generally peripheral. As a consequence of this situation, such literatures often do not develop the same full range of literary activities (organized in a variety of systems) observable in adjacent larger literatures (which in consequence may create a feeling that they are indispensable). They may also "lack" a repertoire which is felt to be badly needed vis-à-vis, and in terms of the presence of, that adjacent literature. This lack may then be filled, wholly or partly, by translated literature. For instance, all sorts of peripheral literature may in such cases consist of translated literature. But far more important is the consequence that the ability of such "weak" literatures to initiate innovations is often less than that of the larger and central literatures, with the result that a relation of dependency may be established not only in peripheral systems, but in the very center of these "weak" literatures. (To avoid misunderstanding, I would like to point out that these literatures may rise to a central position in a way analogous to the way this is carried out by peripheral systems within a certain polysystem, but this cannot be discussed here.)

Since peripheral literatures in the Western Hemisphere tend more often than not to be identical with the literatures of smaller nations, as unpalatable as this idea may seem to us, we have no choice but to admit that within a group of relatable national literatures, such as the literatures of Europe, hierarchical relations have been established since the very beginnings of these literatures. Within this (macro-)polysystem some literatures have taken peripheral positions, which is only to say that they were often modelled to a large extent upon an exterior literature. For such literatures, translated literature is not only a major channel through which fashionable repertoire is brought home, but also a source of reshuffling and supplying alternatives. Thus, whereas richer or stronger literatures may have the option to adopt novelties from some periphery within their indigenous borders, "weak" literatures in such situations often depend on import alone.

The dynamics within the polysystem creates turning points, that is to say, historical moments where established models are no longer tenable for a younger generation. At such moments, even in central literatures, translated literature may assume a central position. This is all the more true when at a turning point no item in the indigenous stock is taken to be acceptable, as a result of which a literary "vacuum" occurs. In such a vacuum, it is easy for foreign models to infiltrate, and translated literature may consequently assume a central position. Of course, in the case of "weak" literatures or literatures which are in a constant state of impoverishment (lack of literary items existing in a neighbor or accessible foreign literature), this situation is even more overwhelming.

III

Contending that translated literature may maintain a peripheral position means that it constitutes a peripheral system within the polysystem, generally employing secondary models. In such a situation it has no influence on major processes and is modelled according to norms already conventionally established by an already dominant type in the target literature. Translated literature in this case becomes a major factor of conservatism. While the contemporary original literature might go on developing new norms and models, translated literature adheres to norms which have been rejected either recently or long before by the (newly) established center. It no longer maintains positive correlations with original writing.

A highly interesting paradox manifests itself here: translation, by which new ideas, items, characteristics can be introduced into a literature, becomes a means to preserve traditional taste. This discrepancy between the original central literature and the translated literature may have evolved in a variety of ways, for instance, when translated literature, after having assumed a central position and inserted new items, soon lost contact with the original home literature which went on changing, and, thereby became a factor of preservation of unchanged repertoire. Thus, a literature that might have emerged as a revolutionary type may go on existing as an ossified *système d'antan*,[2] often fanatically guarded by the agents of secondary models against even minor changes.

The conditions which enable this second state are of course diametrically opposite to those which give rise to translated literature as a central system: either there are no major changes in the polysystem or these changes are not effected through the intervention of interliterary relations materialized in the form of translations.

IV

The hypothesis that translated literature may be either a central or peripheral system does not imply that it is always wholly one or the other. As a system, translated literature is itself stratified, and from the point of view of polysystemic analysis it is often from the vantage point of the central stratum that all relations within the system are observed. This means that while one section of translated literature may assume a central position, another may remain quite peripheral. In the foregoing analysis I pointed out the close relationship between literary contacts and the status of translated literature. This seems to me the major clue to this issue. When there is intense interference, it is the portion of translated literature deriving from a major source literature which is likely to assume a central position. For instance, in the Hebrew literary polysystem between the two world wars literature translated from the Russian assumed an unmistakably central position, while works translated from English, German, Polish, and other languages assumed an obviously peripheral one. Moreover, since the major and most innovatory translational norms were produced by translations from the Russian, other translated literature adhered to the models and norms elaborated by those translations.

The historical material analyzed so far in terms of polysystemic operations is too limited to provide any far-reaching conclusions about the chances of translated literature to assume a particular position. But work carried out in this field by various other scholars, as well as my own research, indicates that the "normal" position assumed by translated literature tends to be the peripheral one. This should in principle be compatible with theoretical speculation. It may be assumed that in the long run no system can remain in a constant state of weakness, "turning point," or crisis, although the possibility should not be excluded that some polysystems may maintain such states for quite a long time. Moreover, not all polysystems are structured in the same way, and cultures do differ significantly. For instance, it is clear that the French cultural system, French literature naturally included, is much more rigid than most other systems. This, combined with the long traditional central position of French literature within the European context (or within the European macro-polysystem), has caused French translated literature to assume an extremely peripheral position. The state of Anglo-American literature is comparable, while Russian, German, or Scandinavian would seem to show different patterns of behavior in this respect.

V

What consequences may the position taken by translated literature have on translational norms, behaviours, and policies? As I stated above, the distinction between a translated work and an original work in terms of literary behavior is a function of the position assumed by the translated literature at a given time. When it takes a central position, the borderlines are *diffuse*, so that the very category of "translated works" must be extended to semi- and quasi-translations as well. From the point of view of translation theory I think this is a more adequate way of dealing with such phenomena than to reject them on the basis of a static and a-historical conception of translation. Since translational activity participates, when it assumes a central position, in the process of creating new, primary models, the translator's main concern here is not just to look for ready-made models in his home repertoire into which the source texts would be transferable. Instead, he is prepared in such cases to violate the home conventions. Under such conditions the chances that the translation will be close to the original in terms of adequacy (in other words, a reproduction of the dominant textual relations of the original) are greater than otherwise. Of course, from the point of view of the target literature the adopted translational norms might for a while be too foreign and revolutionary, and if the new trend is defeated in the literary struggle, the translation made according to its conceptions and tastes will never really gain ground. But if the new trend is victorious, the repertoire (code) of translated literature may be enriched and become more flexible. Periods of great change in the home system are in fact the only ones when a translator is prepared to go far beyond the options offered to him by his established home repertoire and is willing to attempt a different treatment of text making. Let us remember that under stable conditions items lacking in a target literature may remain untransferable if the state of the polysystem does not allow innovations. But the process of opening the system gradually brings certain literatures closer and in the longer run enables a situation where the postulates of (translational) adequacy and the realities of equivalence may overlap to a relatively high degree. This is the case of the European literatures, though in some of them the mechanism of rejection has been so strong that the changes I am talking about have occurred on a rather limited scale.

Naturally, when translated literature occupies a peripheral position, it behaves totally differently. Here, the translator's main effort is to concentrate upon finding the best ready-made secondary models for the foreign text, and the result often turns out to be a non-adequate translation or (as I would prefer to put it) a greater discrepancy between the equivalence achieved and the adequacy postulated.

In other words, not only is the socio-literary status of translation dependent upon its position within the polysystem, but the very practice of translation is also strongly subordinated to that position. And even the question of what is a translated work cannot be answered *a priori* in terms of an a-historical out-of-context idealized state; it must be determined on the grounds of the operations governing the polysystem. Seen from this point of view, translation is no longer a phenomenon whose nature and borders are given once and for all, but an activity dependent on the relations within a certain cultural system.

Notes

1. From *Literature and Translation: New Perspectives in Literary Studies*, ed. James S. Holmes et al. (Leuven: Acco, 1978), 117–27.
2. "System of the old days."

23

Cross-Cultural Poetics: National Literatures[1] (1981)

Édouard Glissant

Pre-eminent French Caribbean writer and theorist, Édouard Glissant has contributed pathbreaking works to almost every genre (fiction, poetry, drama, criticism, theory) and is increasingly recognized as a pivotal figure in the field of anticolonial and postcolonial culture and criticism. Born in Martinique in 1928, Glissant was Frantz Fanon's junior by just a few years, and became active alongside him in the anticolonial ferment of the 1950s and 1960s in Paris. In the midsixties Glissant returned to Martinique, where he developed the analysis of Martinique's "successful colonization" described in *Caribbean Discourse* (1981). Unlike the vast majority of former colonial dependencies, Martinique entered the "post"-colonial era not through national independence but by being formally annexed to France in 1946 as an overseas department.

The dire cultural depersonalization that followed this assimilation to the French polity informs the last few pages of the following selection and defines the topical urgency of *Caribbean Discourse*, a text that ex-plicitly aims to contribute to the disalienation of Martinican culture. The waning of the great imperial structures calls for national cultures to inscribe themselves in a radically decentered cultural field in which claims to universality based on sameness give way to a decentered diversity, or "diversality" as he will name this condition in a subsequent text. Parody-ing Hegel, Glissant argues that, since they do not have the leisure to develop through successive stages, emergent literatures must "irrupt" into modernity and produce new forms for the expression of their historical being, forms that combine the oral and the written, literature's archaic function of sacralizing community and its modern function of desacralizing community.

Sameness and Diversity

I.

We recognize the changes of our present history as un-noticed moments of a great civilizational transformation: the passage from the transcendental universe of the Same, fruitfully imposed by the West, to a diffracted ensemble of the Diverse, conquered no less fruitfully by the peoples who have today seized their right of presence to the world.

The Same, which is neither uniformity nor sterility, punctuates the effort of the human spirit to transcend the universal humanism that sublimates all (national) particularities. The dialectical process of opposition and transcendence has, in Western history, *comprehended* the national as a privileged obstacle which had to be accomplished and overcome. In this situation, the individual, taken as the absolute vehicle of transcendence, has managed subversively to assert his right to contest the accident of particularity, even as he relies on it. But, in order to feed its pretension to universality, the Same required (had need of) the flesh of the world. The other is its temptation. Not yet the Other as a project of harmony, but the other as matter to sublimate. So the peoples of the world were prey to Western rapacity, before finding themselves the object of the affective or sublimating projections of the West.

The Diverse, which is neither chaos nor sterility, signifies the human spirit's struggle towards a transversal relation, without universalist transcendence. The Diverse needs the presence of peoples, no longer as objects to sublimate, but as a project to put into relation. Sameness requires Being, the Diverse established Relation. Just as the Same began with expansionist plunder in the West, so the Diverse came to light through the political violence and armed resistance of peoples. As the Same rises *within* the ecstasy of individuals, so Diversity disseminates itself *through* the impetus of communities. As the Other is the temptation of the Same, Totality is the exigency of the Diverse. You cannot become Trinidadian or Québecois, if you are not; but it is from now on true that if Trinidad and Québec did not exist as accepted components of the Diverse, something would be missing from the flesh of the world—and that today we would recognize that loss. In other words, if it was necessary for the Same to reveal itself in the solitude of Being, it is irresistibly imperative that the Diverse "pass" through the totality of peoples and communities. The Same is sublimated difference; the Diverse is consensual difference.[2]

If we do not consider the fundamental aspects of this passage (from Same to Diverse) that consist in political struggles, economic survival, and if we do not take count of the central episodes (annihilation of peoples, migrations, deportations, perhaps the most serious transformation that is assimilation), and if we insist on an encompassing viewpoint, we will see that the ideal of the Same, product of the Western imagination, has known a progressive enrichment, a place in harmony with the world, to the extent that it has managed to "slip by" almost without having to declare itself, from the Platonic idea to the lunar rocket. National conflicts have marked from within the West's impetus towards a single ambition: to impose on the world its particular values as universal values. Hence the very circumstantial slogan of the French bourgeoisie in 1789, "Liberty, Equality, Fraternity," has tended for a long time to be considered in an absolute sense as one of the cornerstones of universal humanism. Ironically, it did in fact signify this, but not by virtue of an inner necessity. It is thus that the positivism of Auguste Comte[3] actually became a kind of religion among an alienated elite in South America.

What is called almost everywhere the acceleration of history, a consequence of the saturation of Sameness, like a liquid overflowing its vessel, has everywhere released the pent-up exigency of the Diverse. This acceleration, swept along by political struggles, has suddenly allowed peoples who yesterday inhabited the hidden side of the earth (just as there was for a long time a hidden side of the moon) to assert themselves in the face of a totalized world. If they do not name themselves, they deprive the world of a part of itself. This naming can take a tragic form (Vietnam wars, crushing of the Palestinians, massacres in South Africa), but also manifests itself in politico-cultural expression: salvaging of traditional African tales, politically committed poetry, oral literature ("oraliture") from Haiti, difficult consensus of Caribbean intellectuals, quiet revolution in Québec. (Without taking into account the intolerable aberrations: African "empires," South American "regimes," self-inflicted genocide in Asia, which could be considered the—inevitable?—negative side of such a worldwide movement.) I define national literature as the urgency for each group to name itself: that is, the necessity not to disappear from the world scene and on the contrary to share in its enlargement.

Let us consider the literary work in its widest scope; we can agree that it serves two functions: the function of desacralization, the heretical function of intellectual analysis, whose purpose is to dismantle the internal mechanism of a given system, to expose the hidden workings, to demystify. It also has a function of sacralization, the function of re-assembling the community around its myths, its beliefs, its imaginary or its ideology. Let us say, in a parody of Hegel and his discussion of the epic and the conscience of the community, that the function of sacralization would be the product of a still-naive collective consciousness, and that the function of desacralization is the effect of a politicized consciousness. The problem facing national literatures today, as they are defined here, is that they must combine mythification and demystification, primal innocence with an acquired craftiness. And that, for example, in Québec the barbed sneers of Jacques Godbout are as necessary as the inspired flights of Gaston Miron.[4] The fact is that these literatures do not have the time to develop harmoniously from the collective lyricism of Homer to the mordant scrutiny of Beckett. They must include all at once struggle, militancy, rootedness, lucidity, distrust of self, absolute love, the form of the landscape, the emptiness of the cities, overcoming and obstinacy. That is what I call our irruption into modernity.

But another transition is taking place today, against which we can do nothing. The transition from the written to the oral.[5] I am not far from believing that the written is the universalizing influence of the Same, whereas the oral would be the organized manifestation of the Diverse. There is today a kind of revenge of so many oral societies that, because of their very orality—that is, their not being inscribed in the realm of transcendence— have suffered the assault of the Same without being able to defend themselves.[6] Today the oral can be preserved and be transmitted from one people to another. It appears that the written could increasingly perform the function of an archive and that writing would be reserved as an esoteric and magical art for a few. This is evident in the polluting proliferation of works in bookshops which are not products of writing, but of the cleverly oriented preserve of pseudoinformation.

The writer must not despair in the face of this phenomenon. For the only way, to my mind, of maintaining a function for writing (if this can be done)—that is, to release it from being an esoteric practice or a banal reserve of information—would be to irrigate it at the sources of the oral. If writing does not henceforth resist the temptation to transcendence, by, for instance, learning from oral practice and fashioning a theory from the latter if necessary, I think it will disappear as a cultural necessity from future societies. As the Same will be exhausted by the surprising dynamism of the Diverse, so writing will be confined to the closed and sacred world of the literary sign. There the dream of Mallarmé (which is therefore also that of M. Folch-Ribas[7]) will perfect itself, the old dream of the Same to open itself to the Book (with a capital *B*). But it will not be the book of the world.

A national literature poses all these questions. It must signal the self-assertion of new peoples, in what one calls their rootedness, and which is today their struggle. That is its sacralizing function, epic or tragic. It must express—and if it does not (and only if it does not) it remains regionalist, that is moribund and folkloric—the relationship of one culture to another in the Diverse, its contribution to totalization. Such is its analytical and political function which does not operate without calling into question its own existence.

We see that if Western literatures no longer need to solemnly formalize their presence to the world, a futile procedure after these serious charges against Western history, one by which these literatures would be qualified as a kind of mediocre nationalism, they have *on the other hand* to reflect on their new relationship with the world, by which they would signal no longer their preeminent place in the Same, but their shared task in the Diverse. This is what was understood by those French writers who, in the caricatured manner of Loti, the tragic manner of Segalen, the Catholic manner of Claudel, the esthetic manner of Malraux, sensed that after so much wandering through the West, it now finally was necessary to undertake the understanding of the East.[8] Today the Diverse brings new countries into the open. When I look at literary activity in France at present, I am struck by its inability to understand this impetus, this new basis for relationship in the world: that is to say, ultimately by its lack of generosity.[9] And I am not far from thinking that we find ourselves here (in France) in the presence of some kind of provisional suburb of the world.

But the Diverse is obstinate. It is surfacing everywhere. Western literatures will discover again the function of insertion and will become again sharers in the world, a sign of nations, that is to say, a dimension of that which is in Relation.

II.

I have argued elsewhere that a national language is the one in which a people produces. We can furthermore observe that the mother tongues of peoples recently discovering their place in the sun are, because of their historic situation, oral languages.

These two ideas allow us to throw light on the dense mass of new national literatures.

Where a cultural hinterland predated the intrusion of a transcendental Sameness, and where an independent process of production had been initiated, the problem is relatively "simple": it will be necessary to repossess the national language and culture by submitting them to the creative criticism of political thought. This is, I suppose, what can take place in Algeria. It is not necessary to create national solidarity; critical thought can demystify a social order, multilingualism (if it continues) is no longer a source of alienation.

Where a cultural hinterland did not predate the intrusion of transcendental Sameness, where a system of production allowed an "internalizing," without serious alienation, of the imported language, the cultural and political conflicts that arise are clear and straightforward. That is the case in Cuba, I think, where the Spanish language is truly the national language of Cuba. The solidarity of the nation is faced with no obstacle; monolingualism is not reductive.

Where alienation from the system of production works against a community that nevertheless can resort to a dense hinterland (whether this cultural density predated colonial intrusion, as in countries of black Africa, or was constituted after the fact, as in Haiti), the community does not disintegrate. Cultural contact is made (and perhaps its natural resources will dry up, thus creating the vulnerability of poor nations), but its language holds firm (even if multilingualism is present), and its struggle never ceases. It is capable of making its threatened language a weapon in the struggle, as the Puerto Ricans use Spanish against English. Where the absence of a preexisting cultural hinterland does not allow a people to take cover in a cultural underground and where an autonomous system of production has no longer been maintained, the tragedy begins. The maternal oral language is repressed or crushed by the official language, even and especially when the latter tends to become the natural language. That is a case of what I call a "cornered" community.[10]

No people tolerates for a very long time a brutal or insidious alienation from its cultural hinterland and a systematic reduction of its productive capacity. That is one of the basic axioms of Relation. National literature becomes in this case the exposure of this double adulteration. For, in the absence of national production and in a condition of cultural constraint, a people turns on itself; at this point it lives (submits to) its convulsions without being able to bring them to light on a collective basis. In such a situation the sacred is inconceivable; and sacrilege is degrading. Its collective spiritual energies turn, for instance, to superstitious practices and its critical capacity to an obsession with gossip. This is what can be observed, I know, in Martinique, where the process of being assimilated by an external (French) culture results in one of the most threatened instances, perhaps the most exemplary one, of insertion into the Diverse. On the margin of the political struggle, the writer tries to expose the inner mechanism of this insertion, even if his practice threatens to introduce temporarily a form of despair which is not resignation. Exhausting this despair, *of which no one is aware anymore in everyday life*, means reopening the wound and escaping the numbing power of Sameness. Therein does not lie pessimism, but the ultimate resource of whoever writes and wishes to fight on his own terrain.

Techniques

We say that a national literature emerges when a community whose collective existence is contested tries to put together the reasons for its existence.

The literary production that is part of such a collective consciousness in search of itself is not only a glorification of the community but also a reflection on (and concern with) the specificity of its expression. Discourse is not content merely to speak, but expresses at the same time why it speaks in this manner and not in another.

Just as a community can be constituted as an independent state and nevertheless suffer a fundamental cultural alienation, so an individual can cry that he wishes to regain his identity and yet suffer from a terminal inadequacy even in the way in which he articulates his cry.

Cultural alienation therefore can exist at a deeper level than conscious articulation. In this regard depersonalization affects the structures of "literary" production that are put into practice but not thought through.

One of the primary difficulties faced by a writer concerns the way in which he deals with reality. Now, realism, the theory and technique of literal or "total" representation, is not inscribed in the cultural reflex of African or American peoples. I am often irritated by reading books that give an account of the miserable reality of our countries, and it is because I then have the impression of being faced with a substitute, a wretched one, for Balzac or for Zola. Western realism is not a "flat" or shallow technique but becomes so when it is uncritically adopted by our writers. The misery of our lands is not only present, obvious. It contains a historical dimension (of a history that is not self-evident) that realism alone cannot account for. This is why the works I speak about often sink into a simplistic folklorization that undermines their investigative potential. Jacques Stephen Alexis[11] understood this need not to use without modification the techniques of

realism when he developed a theory of *marvelous realism* in Haitian literature, and García Márquez has illustrated this transcending of realism in the
baroque narrative of *One Hundred Years of Solitude*.

An immediate consequence of this approach can be found in the
function of landscape. The relationship with the land, one that is even more
threatened because the community is alienated from the land, becomes
so fundamental in this discourse that landscape in the work stops being
merely decorative or supportive and inscribes itself as constituent of being.
Describing the landscape is not enough. The individual, the community,
the land are indissociable in the constitutive episode of their history. Landscape is a character in this history. It must be understood in its depths.

These observations are linked to the problem of the rhythmic structure of the literary work. The pattern of the seasons has perhaps shaped, in
the works of Western literature, a balanced rhythm between neutral zones
of narrative that are periodically crossed by explosive flashes that arouse
the emotions and bring "revelation." A conclusive illustration of this technique is the European sonnet, with its final thrust that both summarizes
and transcends the clear meaning of the poem. It appears that the forms of
expression in black cultures do not follow this clever shifting from neutral
to strong moments in the structure of a work. The unvarying season (the
absence of a seasonal rhythm) leads to a monotony, a plainsong whose ob-
sessive rhythm creates a new economy of the expressive forms. To aim for
spectacular moments, or twists in the narrative, for "discoveries" is perhaps
for our writers to perpetrate at the technical level an unconscious and un-
justified submissiveness to literary traditions alien to their own. Technical
vigilance is here not a question of splitting hairs.

Also—and how often have I repeated this in my own discourse—
time in our poetry and novels[12] does not produce the impressive harmony
that Proust has, for instance, reconstituted. Many of us have never fully
understood our historical times; we have simply experienced them. That
is the case of Caribbean communities which only today have access to a
collective memory. Our quest for the dimension of time will therefore be
neither harmonious nor linear. Its advance will be marked by a polyphony
of dramatic shocks, at the level of the conscious as well as the unconscious,
between incongruous phenomena or "episodes" so disparate that no obvious link can be discerned. Majestic harmony does not prevail here, but (as
long as for us the history to be made will not have encountered the past
until now misunderstood) an anxious and often chaotic quest.

We realize that literature in these conditions cannot be an object
of pleasure or reassurance. Now this raises the question of *the one for whom*

the work is written. A generous tendency in our works tempts us to place ourselves from the outset "within reach" of those who suffer social or cultural alienation. A justifiable tendency insofar as we have a concrete effect on the symptoms of this alienation. But an almost elementary statement of our needs, if it is valuable in our daily struggle, can also prevent us from seeing the deeper structures of oppression which must nevertheless be brought to light. This act of exposure, paradoxically, is not performed each time in an open and clear way. Western thought has led us to believe that a work must always *give* itself without hiatus, and I know a number of our folktales whose powerful impact on their audience does not depend on the clarity of their meaning. It can happen that the work is not written *for someone*, but to dismantle the complex mechanism of frustration and the infinite forms of oppression.[13] Demanding that in such a situation they should be immediately understandable is the same as making the mistake of so many visitors who, after spending two days in Martinique, claim they can explain to Martinicans the problems in their country and the solutions that need to be implemented.[14]

Finally, we should perhaps not forget that we have a role to play in the complex reuniting of writing and speech; in so doing, make our contribution to the expression of a new man, liberated from the absolutes of writing and in touch with a new audience for the voice.

(But it is here that we must locate one of the "limitations" of literature. In a discussion in 1979 with the Haitian historian Leslie Manigat, we noticed the way in which the Rastafarian movement in the Caribbean [dirt and drugs, pride in refusing to work, the radical nature of their fierce rejection] corresponded to a moment when their "passage to action" sacralized or operationalized the work of Negritude. Leslie Manigat opposed what he called at this time the necessary "invasion of barbarians" to the intellectual dream of the lettered elite, who will always feel embarrassed—even hostile —in the face of these extremists, parallels of their own theory. The barbarian invasion is, however, necessary; it is through this that values can regain their equilibrium: the affirmation in the real of equal dignity for the components of a culture. But can the traditional intellectual who has theorized Negritude accept the Rasta who applies it in a concrete way? One can also see in this phenomenon one of the symptoms of the transition from the written to the oral. Reggae in the realm of the "audio-visual" corresponds to "poetry." Anglophone poets like Brathwaite [Barbados] or Walcott [St. Lucia] try, perhaps, to transcend [in drum-poetry] this opposition. Whereas I feel that Brathwaite revives thirty years later Aimé Césaire's discourse, he places it actually in a new context: the concrete and diverse realm of lived experience.[15] Brathwaite's link is not as much with Césaire's poetics as with the broken rhythms of Nicolás Guillén or Léon Gontran Damas.[16] The written becomes oral. Literature recuperates in this way a "reality" that seemed to restrain and limit it. A Caribbean discourse finds its expression as much in the explosion of the original cry, as in the patience of a recognized landscape, as in the imposition of lived rhythms.)

Notes

1. From Edouard Glissant, *Carribean Discourse: Selected Essays*, trans. J. Michael Dash (Charlottesville: University of Virginia Press, 1989). First published in the magazine *Liberté* in 1974, then in Glissant's *Le Discours antillais* (Paris: Seuil, 1981).

2. We reconsidered the issue in 1979 in the light of contemporary events: for instance, "the right to be different" could not be located in biological segregation—see M. Louis Pauwels and the "new right" in France—which would end up immediately in a hierarchy of cultural essences. The Diverse leads to Relation: that is the modern tendency among cultures, in their wanderings, their "structural" need for an unreserved equality. [Au.]

3. French philosopher (1798–1857), founder of positivism and a pioneering sociologist.

4. Jacques Godbout (b. 1933), novelist, filmmaker, and journalist; Gaston Miron (1928–96), poet. Both were active in efforts for Québec's independence from Canada.

5. At the time when we Martinicans experience the often alienating transition from orality to writing. [Au.]

6. This justified revenge cannot conceal the growing distance that, in fact, separates rich and poor countries. Any theory of this transition (from Sameness to Diversity, from written to oral) would be naive if it concealed in even a small way the terrible power of alienation and domination inflicted by the rich countries and their ultimate representative: the multinationals. It is silly to say this; it would be more so to forget it. [Au.]

7. Jacques Folch-Ribas (b. 1928), French Canadian novelist and art critic.

8. French novelist Pierre Loti (1850–1923) traveled widely and wrote melancholy, impressionistic novels set in a luxuriant East; Victor Segalen wrote a volume of poems, *Stèles* (1912), inspired by ancient Chinese grave markers. The poet and dramatist Paul Claudel served as French ambassador to Japan; his book *La Connaissance de l'est* was translated into English as *The East I Know* (1914). André Malraux (1901–76) wrote brooding adventure novels set in revolutionary China and in the Spanish Civil War.

9. The naiveté of the pronouncement of certain French representatives in international cultural conferences is staggering. Their ethnocentricity is not subtle and is impervious to even the probings of irony. [Au.]

10. Communities supported by their cultural hinterland and often by subsistence economies cannot be suppressed (the Kurds, in spite of being scattered through five countries), except by extermination and dispersion (the Armenians). Elsewhere, ancestral cultures have been eradicated by oblivion on the economic level, where survival (subsistence economy) has not been "organized" as a form of large-scale resistance (certain communities in Oceania). [Au.]

11. Haitian novelist, poet and activist; born in 1922, tortured and killed in 1961.

12. Again it must be admitted that these activities (the poem and the novel) are seen by us as exclusively intellectual (or for a few intellectuals) *in that they remain separate from the poetics of the collectivity*. These are simply signs of a possible orientation and which will no doubt be transformed when the collectivity comes into its own. Neither poem nor novel are for that matter our genres. Something else perhaps is still to come. [Au.]

13. In order to exorcise the chaos of a history that has been submitted to and not lived or created. There too the techniques of expression are not innocent. An exploration of the chaos of memory (obscured, alienated, or reduced to a range of natural references) cannot be done in the "clarity" of a linear narrative. The production of texts must also produce history, not in its capacity to facilitate some event, but in its ability to raise a concealed world to the level of consciousness. Exploration is not analytical but creative. The exposé is quivering with creativity, obscure because of its incongruous contents whose convergence is not immediately apparent. [Au.]

14. A work can go directly towards its objective, which in this situation is to clarify, at least to simplify *in order to be better understood*. This no doubt explains the impact of *Roots* by Alex Haley, whose aim was to bring to light an obliterated historical continuum. The simplicity of the technical means used, which are related to the enlarged televised version, is important to us. Whatever our reservations about this simplification (I think, for example, that the persuasive but overly calm picture of the journey by slave ship does not convey the anxious, diabolical nature of such an experience *where no individual remains himself*) or about the tendencies of the work that are too close to the author's ideology (the entire story ends with the emergence of a well-established conformist family that has succeeded), one could not deny here the worth of the simple techniques used and the objective sought after and attained. Bookshops have been broken into by black Americans in order to get copies of *Roots*. *Stealing as a means of cultural transfer*: the extraordinary historical consequence of a book in the world for which it is responsible. [Au.]

15. Aimé Césaire's long poem *Cahier d'un retour au pays natal* (*Notebook of a Return to the Native Land*, 1939) blends Caribbean rhythms and French Surrealist techniques. The contemporary Barbadan poet Edward Kamau Brathwaite is known for his transformation of techniques from popular music.

16. Nicholás Guillén (1902–89), Afro-Cuban poet who incorporated rhythms of drums and Cuban *son* in his verse; Léon Damas (1912–78), born in French Guiana, was an early champion of *négritude*, known for his agitated, syncopated verses.

24

The World, the Text, and the Critic[1] (1983)

Edward W. Said

Born in Jerusalem, brought up by Christian Palestinian parents in Egypt, and educated in a Massachusetts boarding school and at Princeton and Harvard, Edward Wadie Said (1935–2003) was an exile all his life. His early displacement from Palestine and the establishment of the State of Israel, which radicalized him, stimulated Said's lifelong journey of inquiry into the conjunction of aesthetics, text and politics. The results of Said's prolific work were a stream of essays and books, four decades of teaching at Columbia University, and close involvement in attempts to realize the peaceful coexistence of Palestine and Israel. He served as a member of the Palestinian National Council from 1977 to 1991, before resigning to protest the growing authoritarianism of its leader, Yasser Arafat, but he continued to press for Palestinian statehood and to dispute the limitations and distortions of Western representations of Arabs and the Arab-Israeli conflict, in such books as *The Question of Palestine* (1979) and *Covering Islam* (1997). Said's most influential book is *Orientalism* (1978), in which he traces the history of the Western construction of the Middle East as the inferior Other, ripe for European rule. *Orientalism* is considered a foundational text of Postcolonial Studies. It has been translated into almost forty languages, including Arabic, Hebrew and Vietnamese.

In the title essay of his important collection *The World, the Text, and the Critic* (1983), Said articulates a theory of the "worldliness" of a text in response to arguments for the hermetically sealed text in which meaning is only internal to that text. Said's elaboration of aesthetics begins with music, to which he also made a contribution as an influential music critic. He goes on to consider the social and political place of the literary critic, and makes a powerful case for the importance of critical endeavors to any text's impact in the world.

_____

Since he deserted the concert stage in 1964, the Canadian pianist Glenn Gould has confined his work to records, television, and radio. There is some disagreement among critics as to whether Gould is always, or only sometimes, a convincing interpreter of one or another piano piece, but there is no doubt that each of his performances now is at least special. One example of how Gould has been operating recently is suited for discussion here. In 1970 he issued a record of his performance of Beethoven's Fifth Symphony in the Liszt piano transcription. Quite aside from the surprise one felt at Gould's eccentric choice of the piece (which seemed more peculiar than usual even for the arch-eccentric Gould, whose controversial performances had formerly been associated either with classical or contemporary music), there were a number of oddities about this particular release. Liszt's Beethoven transcription was not only of the nineteenth century but of its most egregious aspect, pianistically speaking: not content with transforming the concert experience into a feast for the virtuoso's self-exhibition, it also raided the literature of other instruments, making of their music a flamboyant occasion for the pianist's skill. Most transcriptions tend on the whole to sound thick or muddy, since frequently the piano is attempting to copy the texture of an orchestral sound. Liszt's Fifth Symphony was less offensive than most transcriptions, mainly because it was so brilliantly reduced for the piano, but even at its most clear the sound was an unusual one for Gould to be producing. His sound previously had been the clearest and most unadorned of all pianists', which was why he had the uncanny ability to turn Bach's counterpoint almost into a visual experience. The Liszt transcription, in short, was an entirely different idiom, and yet Gould was very successful in it. He sounded as Lisztian now as he had sounded Bachian in the past.

Nor was this all. Accompanying the main disc was another one, a longish, informal interview between Gould and, as I recall, a record company executive. Gould told his interlocutor that one reason for his escape from "live" performance was that he had developed a bad performing habit, a kind of stylistic exaggeration. On his tours of the Soviet Union, for example, he would notice that the large halls in which he was performing caused him to distort the phrases in a Bach partita—here he demonstrated by playing the distorted phrases—so that he could more effectively "catch" and address his listeners in the third balcony. He then played the same phrases to illustrate how much more correctly, and less seductively, he was performing music when no audience was actually present.

It may seem a little heavy-handed to draw out the little ironies from this situation—transcription, interview, and illustrated performance styles all included. But it serves my main point: any occasion involving the aesthetic or literary document and experience, on the one hand, and the critic's role and his or her "worldliness," on the other, cannot be a simple one. Indeed Gould's strategy is something of a parody of all the directions we might take in trying to get at what occurs between the world and the aesthetic or textual object. Here was a pianist who had once represented the ascetic performer in the service of music, transformed now into unashamed virtuoso, whose principal aesthetic position is supposed to be little better than that of a musical whore. And this from a man who markets his record as a "first" and then adds to it, not more music, but the kind of attention-getting immediacy gained in a personal interview. And finally all this is fixed on a mechanically repeatable object, which controls the most obvious signs of immediacy (Gould's voice, the peacock style of the Liszt transcription, the brash informality of an interview packed along with a disembodied performance) beneath a dumb, anonymous, and disposable disc of black plastic.

If one thinks about Gould and his record, parallels will emerge with the circumstances of written performance. First of all, there is the reproducible material existence of a text, which in the most recent phases of Walter Benjamin's age of mechanical reproduction has multiplied and remultiplied so much as to exceed almost any imaginable limits. Both a recording and a printed object, however, are subject to certain legal, political, economic, and social constraints, so far as their sustained production and distribution are concerned; but why and how they are distributed are different matters. The main thing is that a written text of the sort we care about is originally the result of some immediate contact between author and medium. Thereafter it can be reproduced for the benefit of the world and according to conditions set by and in the world; however much the author demurs at the publicity he or she receives, once the text goes into more than one copy the author's work is in the world and beyond authorial control.

Second, a written and musical performance are both instances of style, in the simplest and least honorific sense of that very complex phenomenon. Once again I shall arbitrarily exclude a whole series of interesting complexities in order to insist on style as, from the standpoint of producer and receiver, the recognizable, repeatable, preservable sign of an author who reckons with an audience. Even if the audience is as restricted as oneself and as wide as the whole world, the author's style is partially a phenomenon of repetition and reception. But what makes style receivable as the signature of its author's manner is a collection of features variously called idiolect, voice, or irreducible individuality. The paradox is that something as impersonal as a text, or a record, can nevertheless deliver an imprint or a trace of something as lively, immediate, and transitory as a "voice." Glenn Gould's interview simply makes brutally explicit the frequent implicit need for reception or recognition that a text carries even in its most pristine, enshrined forms. A common form of this need is the staged (or recorded) convention of a talking voice addressing someone at a particular time and in a specific place. Considered as I have been considering it, then, style neutralizes the worldlessness, the silent, seemingly uncircumstanced existence of a solitary text. It is not only that any text, if it is not immediately destroyed, is a network of often colliding forces, but also that a text in its actually *being* a text is a being in the world; it therefore addresses anyone who reads, as Gould does throughout the very same record that is supposed to represent both his withdrawal from the world and his "new" silent style of playing without a live audience.

To be sure, texts do not speak in the ordinary sense of the word. Yet any simple diametric opposition asserted on the one hand between speech, bound by situation and reference, and on the other hand the text as an interception or suspension of speech's worldliness is, I think, misleading and largely simplified. Here is how Paul Ricoeur puts this opposition, which he says he has set up only for the sake of analytic clarification:

> In speech the function of reference is linked to the role of the
> *situation of discourse* within the exchange of language itself: in
> exchanging speech, the speakers are present to each other, but also
> to the circumstantial setting of discourse, not only the perceptual
> surroundings, but also the cultural background known by both
> speakers. It is in relation to this situation that discourse is fully
> meaningful: the reference to reality is in the last analysis reference
> to that reality which can be pointed out "around," so to speak, the
> instance of discourse itself. Language . . . and in general all the
> ostensive indicators of language serve to anchor discourse in the
> circumstantial reality which surrounds the instance of discourse.

Thus, in living speech, the *ideal* meaning of what one says bends towards a *real* reference, namely to that "about which" one speaks . . .

This is no longer the case when a text takes the place of speech . . . A text . . . is not without reference; it will be precisely the task of reading, as interpretation, to actualize the reference. At least, in this suspension wherein reference is deferred, in the sense that it is postponed, a text is somehow "in the air," outside of the world or without a world; by means of this obliteration of all relation to the world, every text is free to enter into relation with all the other texts which come to take the place of the circumstantial reality shown by living speech.[2]

According to Ricoeur, speech and circumstantial reality exist in a state of presence, whereas writing and texts exist in a state of suspension—that is, outside circumstantial reality—until they are "actualized" and made present by the reader-critic. Ricoeur makes it seem as if the text and circumstantial reality, or what I shall call *worldliness*, play a game of musical chairs, one intercepting and replacing the other according to fairly crude signals. But this game takes place in the interpreter's head, a locale presumably without worldliness or circumstantiality. The critic-interpreter has his position reduced to that of a central bourse on whose floor occurs the transaction by which the text is shown to be meaning x while saying y. And as for what Ricoeur calls "deferred reference," what becomes of it during the interpretation? Quite simply, on the basis of a model of direct exchange, it comes back, made whole and actual by the critic's reading.

The principal difficulty with all this is that without sufficient argument Ricoeur assumes circumstantial reality to be symmetrically and exclusively the property of speech, or the speech situation, or what writers would have wanted to say had they not instead chosen to write. My contention is that worldliness does not come and go; nor is it here and there in the apologetic and soupy way by which we often designate history, a euphemism in such cases for the impossibly vague notion that all things take place in time. Moreover, critics are not merely the alchemical translators of texts into circumstantial reality or worldliness; for they too are subject to and producers of circumstances, which are felt regardless of whatever objectivity the critic's methods possess. The point is that texts have ways of existing that even in their most rarefied form are always enmeshed in circumstance, time, place, and society—in short, they are in the world, and hence worldly.[3] Whether a text is preserved or put aside for a period, whether it is on a library shelf or not, whether it is considered dangerous or not: these matters have to do with a text's being in the world, which is a more complicated matter than the private process of reading. The same implications are undoubtedly true of critics in their capacities as readers and writers in the world.

If my use of Gould's recording of the Beethoven Fifth Symphony serves any really useful purpose, it is to provide an instance of a quasi-textual object whose ways of engaging the world are both numerous and complicated, more complicated than Ricoeur's demarcation drawn between text and speech. These are the engagements I have been calling worldliness. But my principal concern here is not with an aesthetic object in general, but with the text in particular. Most critics will subscribe to the notion that every literary text is in some way burdened with its occasion, with the plain empirical realities from which it emerged. Pressed too far, such a notion earns the justified criticism of a stylistician like Michael Riffaterre,[4] who, in "The Self-Sufficient Text," calls any reduction of a text to its circumstances a fallacy, biographical, genetic, psychological, or analogic.[5] Most critics would probably go along with Riffaterre in saying, yes, let's make sure that the text does not disappear under the weight of these fallacies. But, and here I speak mainly for myself, they are not entirely satisfied with the idea of a self-sufficient text. Is the alternative to the various fallacies *only* a hermetic textual cosmos, one whose significant dimension of meaning is, as Riffaterre says, a wholly inward or intellectual one? Is there no way of dealing with a text and its worldly circumstances fairly? No way to grapple with the problems of literary language except by cutting them off from the more plainly urgent ones of everyday, worldly language?

I have found a way of starting to deal with these questions in an unexpected place, which is perhaps why I shall now seem to digress. Consider the relatively unfamiliar field of medieval Arabic linguistic speculation. Many contemporary critics are interested in speculation about language in Europe, that is, in that special combination of theoretical imagination and empirical observation characterizing romantic philology, the rise of linguistics in the early nineteenth century, and the whole rich phenomenon of what Michel Foucault has called the discovery of language. Yet during the eleventh century in Andalusia, there existed a remarkably sophisticated and unexpectedly prophetic school of Islamic philosophic grammarians, whose polemics anticipate twentieth-century debates between structuralists and generative grammarians, between descriptivists and behaviorists. Nor is this all. One small group of these Andalusian linguists directed its energies against tendencies amongst rival linguists to turn the question of meaning in language into esoteric and allegorical exercises. Among the group were three linguists and theoretical grammarians, Ibn Hazm, Ibn Jinni, and Ibn Mada' al-Qurtobi, all of whom worked in Cordoba during the eleventh century, all belonging to the Zahirite school, all antagonists of the Batinist school. Batinists held that meaning in language is concealed within the words; meaning is therefore available only as the result of an inward-tending exegesis. The Zahirites—their name derives from the Arabic word for clear, apparent, and phenomenal; *Batin* connotes internal—argued that words had only a surface meaning, one that was anchored to a particular usage, circumstance, historical and religious situation.

The two opponents trace their origins back to readings of the sacred text, the Koran, and how that unique event—for, unlike the Bible, the Koran is an event—is to be read, understood, transmitted, and taught by later generations of believers. The Cordovan Zahirites attacked the excesses of the Batinists, arguing that the very profession of grammar (in Arabic *nahu*) was an invitation to spinning out private meanings in an otherwise divinely pronounced, and hence unchangeably stable, text. According to Ibn Mada' it was absurd even to associate grammar with a logic of understanding, since as a science grammar assumed, and often went so far as to create by retrospection, ideas about the use and meaning of words that implied a hidden level beneath words, available only to initiates.[6] Once you resort to such a level, anything becomes permissible by way of interpretation: there can be no strict meaning, no control over what words in fact say, no responsibility toward the words. The Zahirite effort was to restore by rationalization a system of reading a text in which attention was focused on the phenomenal words themselves, in what might be considered their once-and-for-all sense uttered for and during a specific occasion, not on hidden meanings they might later be supposed to contain. The Cordovan Zahirites in particular went very far in trying to provide a reading system that placed the tightest possible control over the reader and his circumstances. They did this principally by means of a theory of what a text is.

It is not necessary to describe this theory in detail. It is useful, however, to indicate how the controversy itself grew out of a sacred text whose authority derived from its being the uncreated word of God, directly and unilaterally transmitted to a Messenger at a particular moment in time. In contrast, texts within the Judeo-Christian tradition, at whose center is Revelation, cannot be reduced to a specific moment of divine intervention as a result of which the Word of God entered the world; rather the Word enters human history continually, during and as a part of that history. So a very important place is given to what Roger Arnaldez calls "human factors" in the reception, transmission, and understanding of such a text.[7] Since the Koran is the result of a unique event, the literal "descent" into world-liness of a text, as well as its language and form, are then to be viewed as stable and complete. Moreover, the language of the text is Arabic, which therefore becomes a privileged language, and its vessel is the Prophet (or Messenger), Mohammed, similarly privileged. Such a text can be regarded as having an absolutely defined origin and consequently cannot be referred back to any particular interpreter or interpretation, although this is clearly what the Batinites tried to do (perhaps, it has been suggested, under the influence of Judeo-Christian exegetical techniques).

In his study of Ibn Hazm, Arnaldez puts his description of the Koran in the following terms: the Koran speaks of historical events, yet is not it-self historical. It repeats past events, which it condenses and particularizes, yet is not itself an actually lived experience; it ruptures the human conti-nuity of life, yet God does not enter temporality by a sustained or concerted act. The Koran evokes the memory of actions whose content repeats itself eternally in ways identical with itself, as warnings, orders, imperatives, punishments, rewards.[8] In short, the Zahirite position adopts a view of the Koran that is absolutely circumstantial without at the same time making that worldliness dominate the actual sense of the text: all this is the ulti-mate avoidance of vulgar determinism in the Zahirite position.

Hence Ibn Hazm's linguistic theory is based upon an analysis of the imperative mode, since according to this the Koran at its most radical verbal level is a text controlled by two paradigmatic imperatives, *iqra* (read or recite) and *qul* (tell).[9] Since those imperatives obviously control the cir-cumstantial and historical appearance of the Koran (and its uniqueness as an event), and since they must also control uses (that is, readings) of the text thereafter, Ibn Hazm connects his analysis of the imperative mode with a juridical notion of *hadd*, a word meaning both a logico-grammatical definition and a limit. What transpires in the imperative mode, between the injunctions to read and write, is the delivery of an utterance (*khabar* in Arabic, translated by Arnaldez as *énoncé*), which is the verbal realization of a signifying intention, or *niyah*. Now the signifying intention is synony-mous not with a psychological intention but exclusively with a verbal inten-tion, itself something highly worldly—it takes place exclusively in the world, it is occasional and circumstantial in both a very precise and a wholly per-tinent way. To signify is only to use language, and to use language is to do so according to certain lexical and syntactic rules, by which language is in and of the world; the Zahirite sees language as being regulated by real usage, and neither by abstract prescription nor by speculative freedom. Above all, language stands between man and a vast indefiniteness: if the world is a gigantic system of correspondences between words and objects, then it is verbal form—language in actual grammatical use—that allows us to isolate the denominated objects from among these massively ordered correspondences. Thus, as Arnaldez puts it, fidelity to such "true" aspects of language is an ascesis of the imagination.[10] A word has a strict meaning understood as an imperative, and with that meaning there also goes a strictly ordained series of resemblances (correspondences) to other words and meanings, which, strictly speaking, play around the first word. Thus figurative language (as it occurs even in the Koran), otherwise elusive and at the mercy of the virtuosic interpreter, is part of the actual structure of language, and part therefore of the collectivity of language users.

What Ibn Hazm does, Arnaldez reminds us, is to view language as possessing two seemingly antithetical characteristics: that of a divinely ordained institution, unchanging, immutable, logical, rational, intelligible; and that of an instrument existing as pure contingency, as an institution signifying meanings anchored in specific utterances. It is exactly because the Zahirites see language in this double perspective that they reject reading techniques that reduce words and their meanings back to radicals from which (in Arabic at least) they may be seen grammatically to derive. Each utterance is its own occasion and as such is firmly anchored in the worldly context in which it is applied. And because the Koran, which is the paradigmatic case of divine-and-human language, is a text that incorporates speaking and writing, reading and telling, Zahirite interpretation itself accepts as inevitable not the separation between speech and writing, not the disjunction between a text and its circumstantiality, but rather their necessary interplay. It is the interplay, the constitutive interaction, that makes possible this severe Zahirite notion of meaning.

I have very quickly summarized an enormously complex theory, for which I cannot claim any particular influence in Western European literature since the Renaissance, and perhaps not even in Arabic literature since the Middle Ages. But what ought to strike us forcibly about the whole theory is that it represents a considerably articulated thesis for dealing with a text as significant form, in which—and I put this as carefully as I can—worldliness, circumstantiality, the text's status as an event having sensuous particularity as well as historical contingency, are considered as being incorporated in the text, an infrangible part of its capacity for conveying and producing meaning. This means that a text has a specific situation, placing restraints upon the interpreter and his interpretation not because the situation is hidden within the text as a mystery, but rather because the situation exists at the same level of surface particularity as the textual object itself. There are many ways for conveying such a situation, but what I want to draw particular attention to here is an ambition (which the Zahirites have to an intense degree) on the part of readers and writers to grasp texts as objects whose interpretation—by virtue of the exactness of their situation in the world—*has already commenced* and are objects already constrained by, and constraining, their interpretation. Such texts can thereafter be construed as having need at most of complementary, as opposed to supplementary, readings.

Now I want to discuss some of the ways by which texts impose constraints upon their interpretation or, to put it metaphorically, the way the closeness of the world's body to the text's body forces readers to take both into consideration. Recent critical theory has placed undue emphasis on the limitlessness of interpretation. It is argued that, since all reading is misreading, no one reading is better than any other, and hence all readings, potentially infinite in number, are in the final analysis equally misinterpretations. A part of this has been derived from a conception of the text as existing within a hermetic, Alexandrian textual universe, which has no connection with actuality. This is a view I do not agree with, not simply because texts in fact are in the world but also because as texts they place themselves—one of their functions as texts is to place themselves—and indeed are themselves, by soliciting the world's attention. Moreover, their manner of doing this is to place restraints upon what can be done with them interpretively.

Modern literary history gives us a number of examples of writers whose text seems self-consciously to incorporate the explicit circumstances of its concretely imagined, and even described, situation. One type of author—I shall be discussing three instances, Gerard Manley Hopkins,[11] Oscar Wilde, and Joseph Conrad—deliberately conceives the text as supported by a discursive situation involving speaker and audience; the designed interplay between speech and reception, between verbality and textuality, *is* the text's situation, its placing of itself in the world.

The three authors I mentioned did their major work between 1875 and 1915. The subject matter of their writing varies so widely among them that similarities have to be looked for elsewhere. Let me begin with a journal entry by Hopkins:

> The winter was called severe. There were three spells of frost with skating, the third beginning on Feb. 9. No snow to speak of till that day. Some days before Feb. 7 I saw catkins hanging. On the 9th there was snow but not lying on the heads of the blades. As we went down

a field near Caesar's Camp I noticed it before me *squalentem*, coat below coat, sketched in intersecting edges bearing 'idiom,' all down the slope:—I have no other word yet for that which takes the eye or mind in a bold hand or effective sketching or in marked features or again in graphic writing, which not being beauty nor true inscape yet gives interest and makes ugliness even better than meaninglessness.[12]

Hopkins' earliest writing attempts in this way to render scenes from nature as exactly as possible. Yet he is never a passive transcriber since for him "this world then is word, expression, news of God."[13] Every phenomenon in nature, he wrote in the sonnet "As Kingfishers Catch Fire," tells itself in the world as a sort of lexical unit: "Each mortal thing does one thing and the same: / Deals out that being indoors each one dwells;/ Selves—goes itself; *myself* it speaks and spells, / Crying *What I do is me: for that I came.*"[14] So in the notebook entry Hopkins' observation of nature is dynamic. He sees in the frost an intention to speak or mean, its layered coats *taking* one's attention because of the idiom it bears toward meaning or expression. The writer is as much a respondent as he is a describer. Similarly the reader is a full participant in the production of meaning, being obliged as a mortal thing to act, to produce some sense that even though ugly is still better than meaninglessness.

This dialectic of production is everywhere present in Hopkins' work. Writing is telling; nature is telling; reading is telling. He wrote to Robert Bridges on May 21, 1878, that in order to do a certain poem justice "you must not slovenly read it with the eyes but with your ears, as if the paper were declaiming it at you . . . Stress is the life of it."[15] Seven years later he specified more strictly that "poetry is the darling child of speech, of lips and spoken utterance: it must be spoken; *till it is spoken it is not performed*, it does not perform, it is not itself. Sprung rhythm gives back to poetry its true soul and self. As poetry is emphatically speech, speech purged of dross like gold in the furnace, so it must have emphatically the essential elements of speech."[16] So close is the identification in Hopkins' mind among world, word, and the utterance, the three coming alive together as a moment of performance, that he envisages little need for critical intervention. It is the written text that provides the immediate circumstantial reality for the poem's "play" (the word is Hopkins'). So far from being a document associated with other lifeless, worldless texts, Hopkins' own text was for him his child; when he destroyed his poems he spoke of the slaughter of the innocents, and everywhere he speaks of writing as the exercise of his male gift. At the moment of greatest desolation in his career, in the poem entitled simply "To R. B." the urgency of his feeling of poetic aridity is expressed biologically. When he comes to describe finally what it is he now writes, he says:

> O then if in my lagging lines you miss
> The roll, the rise, the carol, the creation,
> My winter world, that scarcely breathes that bliss
> Now, yields you, with some sighs, our explanation.[17]

Because his text has lost its ability to incorporate the stress of creation, and because it is no longer performance but what in another poem he calls "dead letters," he now can only write an explanation, which is lifeless speech "bending towards a real reference."

It was said of Oscar Wilde by one of his contemporaries that everything he spoke sounded as if it were enclosed in quotation marks. This is no less true of everything he wrote, for such was the consequence of having a pose, which Wilde defined as "a formal recognition of the importance of treating life from a definite reasoned standpoint."[18] Or as Algernon retorts to Jack's accusation that "you always want to argue about things" in *The Importance of Being Earnest*: "That's exactly what things were originally made for."[19] Always ready with a quotable comment, Wilde filled his manuscripts with epigrams on every conceivable subject. What he wrote was intended either for more comment or for quotation or, most important, for tracing back to him. There are obvious social reasons for some of this egoism, which he made no attempt to conceal in his quip "To love oneself is the beginning of a life-long romance," but they do not exhaust the speaking in Wilde's style. Having forsworn action, life, and nature for their incompleteness and diffusion, Wilde took as his province a theoretical, ideal world in which, as he told Alfred Douglas in *De Profundis*, conversation was the basis of all human relations.[20] Since conflict inhibited conversation as Wilde understood it from the Platonic dialogue, the mode of interchange was to be by epigram. This epigram, in Northrop Frye's terminology, is Wilde's radical of presentation: a compact utterance capable of the utmost range of subject matter, the greatest authority, and the least equivocation as to its author. When he invaded other forms of art, Wilde converted them into longer epigrams. As he said of drama: "I took the drama, the most objective form known to art, and made it as personal a mode of expression as the lyric or the sonnet, at the same time that I widened its range and enriched its characterization." No wonder he could say: "I summed up all systems in a phrase, and all existence in an epigram."[21]

De Profundis records the destruction of the Utopia whose individualism and unselfish selfishness Wilde had adumbrated in *The Soul of Man under Socialism*. From a free world to a prison and a circle of suffering: how is the change accomplished? Wilde's conception of freedom was to be found in *The Importance of Being Earnest*, where conflicting characters turn out to be brothers after all just because they say they are. What is written down (for example, the army lists consulted by Jack) merely confirms what all along has been capriciously, though elegantly, said. This transformation, from opponent into brother, is what Wilde had in mind in connecting the intensification of personality with its multiplication. When the communication between men no longer possesses the freedom of conversation, when it is confined to the merely legal liability of print, which is not ingeniously quotable but, because it has been signed, is now criminally actionable, the Utopia crumbles. As he reconsidered his life in *De Profundis* Wilde's imagination was transfixed by the effects of one text upon his life. But he uses it to show how in going from speech to print, which in a sense all of his other more fortunate texts had managed somehow to avoid by virtue of their epigrammatic individuality, he had been ruined. Wilde's lament in what follows is that a text has too much, not too little, circumstantial reality. Hence, with Wildean paradox, its vulnerability:

> You send me a very nice poem, of the undergraduate school of verse, for my approval: I reply by a letter of fantastic literary conceits . . . Look at the history of that letter! It passes from you into the hands of a loathsome companion: from him to a gang of blackmailers: copies of it are sent about London to my friends, and to the manager of the theatre where my work is being performed: every construction but the right one is put on it: Society is thrilled with the absurd rumours that I have had to pay a huge sum of money for having written an infamous letter to you: this forms the basis of your father's worst attack: I produce the original letter myself in Court to show what it really is: it is denounced by your father's counsel as a revolting and insidious attempt to corrupt Innocence: ultimately it forms part of a criminal charge: the Crown takes it up: the Judge sums up on it with little learning and much morality: I go to prison for it at last. That is the result of writing you a charming letter.[22]

For in a world described by George Eliot as a "huge whispering gallery," the effects of writing can be grave indeed: "As the stone which has been kicked by generations of clowns may come by curious little links of effect under the eyes of a scholar, through whose labours it may at last fix the date of invasions and unlock religions, so a bit of ink and paper which has long been an innocent wrapping or stop-gap may at last be laid open under the one pair of eyes which have knowledge enough to turn it into the opening of a catastrophe."[23] If Dr. Casaubon's caution has any purpose at all, it is by rigid secrecy and an endlessly postponing scriptive will to forestall the opening of a catastrophe. Yet he cannot succeed since Eliot is at pains to show that even Casaubon's tremendously nursed *Key* is a text, and therefore in the world. Unlike Wilde's, Casaubon's disgrace is posthumous, but their implication in a sort of worldly textuality takes place for the same reason, which is their commitment to what Eliot calls an "embroiled medium."

Lastly, consider Conrad. Elsewhere in this book I shall be describing the extraordinary presentational mode of his narratives, how each of them dramatizes, motivates, and circumstances the occasion of its telling, how all of Conrad's work is really made out of secondary, reported speech, and how the interplay between appeals to the eye and the ear in his work is highly organized and subtle, and is that work's meaning. The Conradian encounter is not simply between a man and his destiny embodied in a moment of extremity, but just as persistently, the encounter between speaker and hearer. Marlow is Conrad's chief invention for this encounter, a man who is haunted by the knowledge that a person such as Kurtz or Jim "existed for me, and after all it is only through me that he exists for you."[24] The chain of humanity—"we exist only in so far as we hang together"—is the transmission of actual speech, and existence, from one mouth and then from one eye to another. Every text that Conrad wrote presents itself as unfinished and still in the making. "And besides, the last word is not said, —probably shall never be said. Are not our lives too short for that full utterance which through all our stammerings is of course our only and abiding intention?"[25] Texts convey the stammerings that never ever achieve that full utterance, the statement of wholly satisfactory presence, which remains distant, attenuated somewhat by a grand gesture like Jim's self-sacrifice. Yet even though the gesture closes off a text circumstantially, in no way does it empty it of its actual urgency.

This is a good time to remark that the Western novelistic tradition is full of examples of texts insisting not only upon their circumstantial reality but also upon their status as *already* fulfilling a function, a reference, or a meaning in the world. Cervantes and Cide Hamete come immediately to mind.[26] More impressive is Richardson playing the role of "mere" editor for *Clarissa*, simply placing those letters in successive order after they have done what they have done, arranging to fill the text with printer's devices, reader's aids, analytic contents, retrospective meditations, commentary, so that a collection of letters grows to fill the world and occupy all space, to become a circumstance as large and as engrossing as the reader's very understanding. Surely the novelistic imagination has always included this unwillingness to cede control over the text in the world, or to release it from the discursive and human obligations of all human presence; hence the desire (almost a principal action of many novels) to turn the text back, if not directly into speech, then at least into circumstantial, as opposed to meditative, duration.

No novelist, however, can be quite as explicit about circumstances as Marx is in *The Eighteenth Brumaire of Louis Bonaparte*. To my mind no work is as brilliant and as compelling in the exactness with which circumstances (the German word is *Umstände*) are shown to have made the nephew possible, not as an innovator, but as a farcical repetition of the great uncle. What Marx attacks are the atextual theses that history is made up of free events and that history is guided by superior individuals.[27] By inserting Louis Bonaparte in a whole intricate system of repetitions, by which first Hegel, then the ancient Romans, the 1789 revolutionaries, Napoleon I, the bourgeois interpreters, and finally the fiascos of 1848-1851 are all seen in a pseudo-analogical order of descending worth, increasing derivativeness, and deceptively harmless masquerading, Marx effectively textualizes the random appearance of a new Caesar. Here we have the case of a text itself providing a world-historical situation with circumstances otherwise hidden in the deception of a *roi des drôles*.[28] What is ironic—and in need of the analysis I shall be giving in subsequent parts of this book—is how a text, by being a text, by insisting upon and employing all the devices of textuality, preeminent among them *repetition*, historicizes and problematizes all the fugitive significance that has chosen Louis Bonaparte as its representative.

There is another aspect to what I have just been saying. In producing texts with either a firm claim on or an explicit will to worldliness, these writers and genres have valorized speech, making it the tentacle by which an otherwise silent text ties itself to the world of discourse. By the valorization of speech I mean that the discursive, circumstantially dense interchange of speaker facing hearer is made to stand—sometimes misleadingly—for a democratic equality and copresence in actuality between speaker and hearer. Not only is the discursive relation far from equal in actuality, but the text's attempt to dissemble by seeming to be open democratically to anyone who might read it is also an act of bad faith. (Incidentally, one of the strengths of Zahirite theory is that it dispels the illusion that a surface reading, which is the Zahirite ambition, is anything but difficult.) Texts of such a length as *Tom Jones* aim to occupy leisure time of a quality not available to just anyone. Moreover, all texts essentially dislodge other texts or, more frequently, take the place of something else. As Nietzsche had the perspicacity to see, texts are fundamentally facts of power, not of democratic exchange.[29] They compel attention away from the world even as their beginning intention as texts, coupled with the inherent authoritarianism of the authorial authority (the repetition in this phrase is a deliberate emphasis on the tautology within all texts, since all texts are in some way self-confirmatory), makes for sustained power.

Yet in the genealogy of texts there is a first text, a sacred prototype, a scripture, which readers always approach through the text before them, either as petitioning suppliants or as initiates amongst many in a sacred chorus supporting the central patriarchal text. Northrop Frye's theory of literature makes it apparent that the displacing power in all texts finally derives from the displacing power of the Bible, whose centrality, potency, and dominating anteriority inform all Western literature. The same is no less true, in the different modes I discussed earlier, of the Koran. Both in the Judeo-Christian and in the Islamic traditions these hierarchies repose upon a solidly divine, or quasi-divine, language, a language whose uniqueness, however, is that it is theologically and humanly circumstantial.

We often forget that modern Western philology, which begins in the early nineteenth century, undertook to revise commonly accepted ideas about language and its divine origins. That revision tried first to determine which was the first language and then, failing in that ambition, proceeded to reduce language to specific circumstances: language groups, historical and racial theories, geographical and anthropological theses. A particularly interesting example of how such investigations went is Ernest Renan's[30] career as a philologist; that was his real profession, not that of the boring sage. His first serious work was his 1848 analysis of Semitic languages, revised and published in 1855 as *Histoire générale et système comparé des langues sémitiques*. Without this study the *Vie de Jésus* could not have been written. The accomplishment of the *Histoire générale* was scientifically to describe the inferiority of Semitic languages, principally Hebrew, Aramaic, and Arabic, the medium of three purportedly sacred texts that had been spoken or at least informed by God—the Torah, the Koran, and, later, the derivative Gospels. Thus in the *Vie de Jésus* Renan would be able to insinuate that the so-called sacred texts, delivered by Moses, Jesus, or Mohammed, could not have anything divine in them if the very medium of their supposed divinity, as well as the body of their message to and in the world, was made up of such comparatively poor worldly stuff. Renan argued that, even if these texts were prior to all others in the West, they held no theologically dominant position.

Renan first reduced texts from objects of divine intervention in the world's business to objects of historical materiality. God as author-authority had little value after Renan's philological and textual revisionism. Yet in dispensing with divine authority Renan put philological power in its place. What comes to replace divine authority is the textual authority of the philological critic who has the skill to separate Semitic languages from the languages of Indo-European culture. Not only did Renan kill off the extratextual validity of the great Semitic sacred texts; he confined them as objects of European study to a scholarly field thereafter to be known as Oriental.[31] The Orientalist is a Renan or a Gobineau, Renan's contemporary quoted here and there in the 1855 edition of the *Histoire générale*, for whom the old hierarchy of sacred Semitic texts has been destroyed as if by an act of parricide; the passing of divine authority enables the appearance of European ethnocentrism, by which the methods and the discourse of Western scholarship confine inferior non-European cultures to a position of subordination. Oriental texts come to inhabit a realm without development or power, one that exactly corresponds to the position of a colony for European texts and culture. All this takes place at the same time that the great European colonial empires in the east are beginning or, in some cases, flourishing.

I have introduced this brief account of the twin origin of the Higher Criticism and of Orientalism as a European scholarly discipline in order to be able to speak about the fallacy of imagining the life of texts as being pleasantly ideal and without force or conflict and, conversely, the fallacy of imagining the discursive relations in actual speech to be as Ricoeur would have it, a relation of equality between hearer and speaker.

Texts incorporate discourse, sometimes violently. There are other ways, too. Michel Foucault's archeological analyses of systems of discourse are premised on the thesis, adumbrated by Marx and Engels in *The German Ideology*, that "in every society the production of discourse is at once controlled, selected, organized and redistributed according to a certain number of procedures, whose role is to avert its powers and dangers, to cope with chance events, to evade its ponderous, awesome materiality." Discourse in this passage means what is written and spoken. Foucault's contention is that the fact of writing itself is a systematic conversion of the power relationship between controller and controlled into "mere" written words—but writing is a way of disguising the awesome materiality of so tightly controlled and managed a production. Foucault continues:

> In a society such as our own we all know the rules of *exclusion*. The most obvious and familiar of these concerns what is *prohibited*. We know perfectly well that we are not free to say just anything. We have three types of prohibition, covering objects, ritual with its surrounding circumstances, and the privileged or exclusive right to speak of a particular subject; these prohibitions interrelate, reinforce and complement each other, forming a complex web, continually subject to modification. I will note simply that the areas where this web is most tightly woven today, where the danger spots are most numerous, are those dealing with politics and sexuality . . . In appearance, speech may well be of little account, but the prohibitions surrounding it soon reveal its links with desire and power . . . Speech is no mere verbalization of conflicts and systems of domination . . . it is the very object of man's conflicts.[32]

Despite Ricoeur's simplified idealization, and far from being a type of conversation between equals, the discursive situation is more usually like the unequal relation between colonizer and colonized, oppressor and oppressed. Some of the great modernists, Proust and Joyce prominent among them, had an acute understanding of this asymmetry; their representations of the discursive situation always show it in this power-political light. Words and texts are so much of the world that their effectiveness, in some cases even their use, are matters having to do with ownership, authority, power, and the imposition of force. A formative moment in Stephen Dedalus' rebellious consciousness occurs as he converses with the English dean of studies:

> What is that beauty which the artist struggles to express from lumps of earth, said Stephen coldly.

> The little word seemed to have turned a rapier point of his sensitiveness against this courteous and vigilant foe. He felt with a smart of dejection that the man to whom he was speaking was a countryman of Ben Jonson. He thought:—The language in which we are speaking is his before it is mine. How different are the words *home, Christ, ale, master*, on his lips and on mine! I cannot speak or write these words without unrest of spirit. His language, so familiar and so foreign, will always be for me an acquired speech. I have not

made or accepted its words. My voice holds them at bay. My soul frets in the shadow of his language.[33]

Joyce's work is a recapitulation of those political and racial separations, exclusions, prohibitions instituted ethnocentrically by the ascendant European culture throughout the nineteenth century. The situation of discourse, Stephen Dedalus knows, hardly puts equals face to face. Rather, discourse often puts one interlocutor above another or, as Frantz Fanon brilliantly described the extreme to which it could be taken in *The Wretched of the Earth*, discourse reenacts the geography of the colonial city:

> The zone where the natives live is not complementary to the zone inhabited by the settlers. The two zones are opposed, but not in the service of a higher unity. Obedient to the rules of pure Aristotelian logic, they both follow the principle of reciprocal exclusivity. No conciliation is possible, for of the two terms, one is superfluous. The settlers' town is a strongly-built town, all made of stone and steel. It is a brightly-lit town; the streets are covered with asphalt, and the garbage-cans swallow all the leavings, unseen, unknown and hardly thought about. The settler's feet are never visible, except perhaps in the sea; but there you're never close enough to see them. His feet are protected by strong shoes although the streets of his town are clean and even, with no holes or stones. The settler's town is a well-fed town, an easygoing town; its belly is always full of good things. The settler's town is a town of white people, of foreigners.
>
> The town belonging to the colonized people, or at least the native town, the negro village, the medina, the reservation, is a place of ill fame, peopled by men of evil repute. They are born there, it matters little where or how; they die there, it matters not where, nor how. It is a world without spaciousness; men live there on top of each other, and their huts are built on top of the other. The native town is a hungry town, starved of bread, of meat, of shoes, of coal, of light. The native town is a crouching village, a town on its knees, a town wallowing in the mire. It is a town of niggers and dirty arabs. The look that the native turns on the settler's town is a look of lust, a look of envy; it expresses his dreams of possession—all manner of possession: to sit at the settler's table, to sleep in the settler's bed, with his wife if possible. The colonized man is an envious man. And this the settler knows very well; when their glances meet he ascertains bitterly, always on the defensive, "They want to take our place."

It is true, for there is no native who does not dream at least once a day of setting himself up in the settler's place.[34]

No wonder that the Fanonist solution to such discourse is violence. Such examples make untenable the opposition between texts and the world, or between texts and speech. Too many exceptions, too many historical, ideological, and formal circumstances, implicate the text in actuality, even if a text may also be considered a silent printed object with its own unheard melodies. The concert of forces by which a text is engendered and maintained as a fact not of mute ideality but of *production* dispels the symmetry of even rhetorical oppositions. Moreover, the textual Utopia envisioned each in his own way by T. S. Eliot and Northrop Frye, whose nightmarish converse is Borges' library, is at complete odds with form in texts. My thesis is that any centrist, exclusivist conception of the text, or for that matter of the discursive situation as defined by Ricoeur, ignores the self-confirming will to power from which many texts can spring. The minimalist impulse in Beckett's work is, I think, a counterversion of this will, a way of refusing the opportunity offered to him by modernist writing.

But where in all this is the critic and criticism? Scholarship, commentary, exegesis, *explication de texte*, history of ideas, rhetorical or semiological analyses: all these are modes of pertinence and of disciplined attention to the textual matter usually presented to the critic as already at hand. I shall concentrate now on the essay, which is the traditional form by which criticism has expressed itself. The central problematic of the essay as a form is its *place*, by which I mean a series of three ways the essay has of being the form critics take, and locate themselves in, to do their work. Place therefore involves relations, affiliations, the critics fashion with the texts and audiences they address; it also involves the dynamic taking place of a critic's own text as it is produced.

The first mode of affiliation is the essay's relation to the text or occasion it attempts to approach. How does it come to the text of its choice? How does it enter that text? What is the concluding definition of its relation to the text and the occasion it has dealt with? The second mode of affiliation is the essay's intention (and the intention, presumed or perhaps created by the essay, that its audience has) for attempting an approach. Is the critical essay an attempt to identify or to identify with the text of its choice? Does it stand between the text and the reader, or to one side of one of them? How great or how little is the ironic disparity between its essential formal incompleteness (because after all it is an essay) and the formal completion of the text it treats? The third mode of affiliation concerns the essay as a zone in which certain kinds of occurrences happen as an aspect of the essay's production. What is the essay's consciousness of its marginality to the text it discusses? What is the method by which the essay permits history a role during the making of its own history, that is, as the essay moves from beginning to development to conclusion? What is the quality of the essay's speech, toward, away from, into the *actuality*, the arena of nontextual historical vitality and presence that is taking place simultaneously with the essay itself? Finally, is the essay a text, an intervention between texts, an intensification of the notion of textuality, or a dispersion of language away from a contingent page to occasions, tendencies, currents, or movements in and for history?

A just response to these questions is a realization of how unfamiliar they are in the general discussion of contemporary literary criticism. It is not that the problems of criticism are undiscussed, but rather that criticism is considered essentially as defined once and for all by its secondariness, by its temporal misfortune in having come after the texts and occasions it is supposed to be treating. Just as it is all too often true that texts are thought of as monolithic objects of the past to which criticism despondently appends itself in the present, then the very conception of criticism symbolizes being outdated, being dated from the past rather than by the present. Everything I tried earlier to say about a text—its dialectic of engagement in time and the senses, the paradoxes in a text by which discourse is shown to be immutable and yet contingent, as fraught and politically intransigent as the struggle between dominant and dominated—all this was an implicit rejection of the secondary role usually assigned to criticism. For if we assume instead that texts make up what Foucault calls archival facts, the archive being defined as the text's social discursive presence in the world, then criticism too is another aspect of that present. In other words, rather than being defined by the silent past, commanded by it to speak in the present, criticism, no less than any text, is the present in the course of its articulation, its struggles for definition.

We must not forget that the critic cannot speak without the mediation of writing, that ambivalent *pharmakon*[35] so suggestively portrayed by Derrida as the constituted milieu where the oppositions are opposed: this is where the interplay occurs that brings the oppositions into direct contact with each other, that overturns oppositions and transforms one pole into another, soul and body, good and evil, inside and outside, memory and oblivion, speech and writing.[36] In particular the critic is committed to the essay, whose metaphysics were sketched by Lukács in the first chapter of his *Die Seele und die Formen*. There Lukács said that by virtue of its form the essay allows, and indeed is, the coincidence of inchoate soul with exigent material form. Essays are concerned with the relations between things, with values and concepts, in fine, with significance. Whereas poetry deals in images, the essay is the abandonment of images; this abandonment the essay ideally shares with Platonism and mysticism. If, Lukács continues, the various forms of literature are compared with sunlight refracted in a prism, then the essay is ultraviolet light. What the essay expresses is a yearning for conceptually and intellectuality, as well as a resolution to the ultimate questions of life. (Throughout his analysis Lukács refers to Socrates as the typical essayistic figure, always talking of immediate mundane matters while at the same time through his life there sounds the purest, the most profound, and the most concealed yearning—*Die tiefste, die verborgenste Sehnsucht ertönt aus diesem Leben.*)[37]

Thus the essay's mode is ironic, which means first that the form is patently insufficient in its intellectuality with regard to living experience and, second, that the very form of the essay, its being an essay, is an ironic destiny with regard to the great questions of life. In its arbitrariness and irrelevance to the questions he debates, Socrates' death perfectly symbolizes essayistic destiny, which is the absence of a real tragic destiny. Thus, unlike tragedy, there is no internal conclusion to an essay, for only something outside it can interrupt or end it, as Socrates' death is decreed offstage and abruptly ends his life of questioning. Form fills the function in an essay that images do in poetry: form is the reality of the essay, and form gives the essayist a voice with which to ask questions of life, even if that form must always make use of art—a book, a painting, a piece of music—as what seems to be the purely occasional subject matter of its investigations.

Lukács' analysis of the essay has it in common with Wilde that criticism in general is rarely what it seems, not least in its form. Criticism adopts the mode of commentary on and evaluation of art; yet in reality criticism matters more as a necessarily incomplete and preparatory process toward judgment and evaluation. What the critical essay does is *to begin* to create the values by which art is judged. I said earlier that a major inhibition on critics is that their function as critics is often dated and circumscribed for them by the past, that is, by an already created work of art or a discrete occasion. Lukács acknowledges the inhibition, but he shows how in fact critics appropriate for themselves the function of starting to make values for the work they are judging. Wilde said it more flamboyantly: criticism "treats the work of art as a starting point for a new creation."[38] Lukács put it more cautiously: "the essayist is a pure instance of the precursor."[39]

I prefer the latter description, for as Lukács develops it the critic's position is a vulnerable one because he or she prepares for a great aesthetic revolution whose result, ironically enough, will render criticism marginal. Later, this very idea will be converted by Lukács into a description of the overthrow of reification by class consciousness, which in turn will make class itself a marginal thing.[40] Yet what I wish to emphasize here is that critics create, not only the values by which art is judged and understood, but they embody in writing those processes and actual conditions in the present by means of which art and writing bear significance. This means what R. P. Blackmur, following Hopkins, called the bringing of literature to performance. More explicitly, the critic is responsible to a degree for articulating those voices dominated, displaced, or silenced by the textuality of texts. Texts are a system of forces institutionalized by the reigning culture at some human cost to its various components.[41] For texts after all are not an ideal cosmos of ideally equal monuments. Looking at the Grecian urn Keats *sees* graceful figures adorning its exterior, and also he actualizes in language (and perhaps nowhere else) the little town "emptied of this folk, this pious morn." The critic's attitude to some extent is sensitive in a similar way; it should in addition and more often be frankly inventive, in the traditional rhetorical sense of *inventio* so fruitfully employed by Vico, which means finding and exposing things that otherwise lie hidden beneath piety, heedlessness, or routine.

Most of all, criticism is worldly and in the world so long as it opposes monocentrism, a concept I understand as working in conjunction with ethnocentrism, which licenses a culture to cloak itself in the particular authority of certain values over others. Even for Arnold, this comes about as the result of a contest that gives culture a dominion that almost always hides its dark side: in this respect *Culture and Anarchy* and *The Birth of Tragedy* are not very far apart.

Notes

1. From Edward W. Said, *The World, the Text, and the Critic* (Cambridge: Harvard University Press, 1983). First published in *Bulletin of the Midwest Modern Language Association* 8:2 (1975), 1–23. Except as indicated, notes are by Said.
2. Paul Ricoeur, "What Is a Text? Explanation and Interpretation," in David Rasmussen, *Mythic-Symbolic Language and Philosophical Anthropology: A Constructive Interpretation of the Thought of Paul Ricoeur* (The Hague: Nijhoff, 1971), 138. For

a more interesting distinction between oeuvre and text, see Roland Barthes, "De l'Oeuvre au texte," *Revue d'esthéthique*, 3 (1971), 225–232.

3. I have discussed this in chap. 4 of *Beginnings: Intention and Method* (New York: Basic Books, 1975).

4. French literary critic (1924–2006) who was influential in the development of structuralist criticism and taught in the United States. [Ed.]

5. Riffaterre, "The Self-Sufficient Text," *Diacritics* (Fall 1973), 40.

6. This is the main polemical point in his tract *Ar-rad'ala'l nuhat*, ed. Shawki Daif (Cairo, 1947). The text dates from 1180.

7. Roger Arnaldez, *Grammaire et théologies chez Ibn Hazm de Cordoue* (Paris: J. Vrin, 1956), pp. 12 and passim. There is a clear, somewhat schematic account of Ibn Ginni, Ibn Mada, and others in Anis Fraiha, *Nathariyat fil Lugha* (Beirut: Al-Maktaba al Jam'iya, 1973).

8. Arnaldez, *Grammaire et théologie,* 12.

9. Ibid., 69.

10. Ibid., 77.

11. Jesuit priest and English poet (1844–89) who was virtually unknown in his time and whose twentieth-century celebrity established him among the finest Victorian poets. [Ed.]

12. *The Journals and Papers of Gerard Manley Hopkins*, ed. Humphry House and Graham Storey (London: Oxford University Press, 1959), 195.

13. Ibid., 129.

14. *The Poems of Gerard Manley Hopkins*, ed. W.H. Gardner and N.H. Mackenzie (London: Oxford University Press, 1967), 90.

15. *The Letters of Gerard Manley Hopkins to Robert Bridges*, ed. Claude Colleer Abbott (Oxford: Oxford University Press, 1955), 51–52.

16. Quoted in Anthony Bisshof, S.J., "Hopkins' Letters to his Brother," *Times Literary Supplement*, December 8, 1972, 1511.

17. *Poems of Hopkins,* 108.

18. *The Artist as Critic: Critical Writings of Oscar Wilde*, ed. Richard Ellmann (New York: Vintage, 1970), 386.

19. *Complete Works of Oscar Wilde*, ed. J. B. Foreman (London: Collins, 1971), 335.

20. Oscar Wilde, *De Profundis* (New York: Vintage, 1964), 18.

21. Ibid., 80, 61.

22. Ibid., 34–35.

23. *Middlemarch*, ed. Gordon S. Haight (Boston: Houghton Mifflin, 1956), 302.

24. *Lord Jim* (Boston: Houghton Mifflin, 1958), 161.

25. Ibid., 161.

26. Cervantes presented his *Don Quixote* as a translation from the Arabic of a Moorish historian, Cide Hamete Benengeli. [Ed.]

27. Karl Marx, *Der Achtzehnte Brumaire des Louis Bonaparte* (1852; Berlin: Dietz Verlag, 1947), 8.

28. King of the rogues. [Ed.]

29. Nietzsche's analyses of texts in this light are to be found everywhere in his work, but especially in *The Genealogy of Morals* and in *The Will to Power*.

30. French philosopher and writer (1823–92) best known best known for his work on early Christianity and his political theories, especially on questions of nationalism. [Ed.]

31. See in particular Ernst Renan, *Histoire générale et système comparé des langues sémitiques*, in *Oeuvres complètes*, ed. Henriette Psichari (Paris: Calmann-Lévy, 1947–1961), 8:147–157.

32. Michel Foucault, "The Discourse on Language," in *The Archeology of Knowledge*, tr. A. M. Sheridan Smith (New York: Pantheon, 1972), 216.

33. *A Portrait of the Artist as a Young Man* (New York: Viking Press, 1964), 189.

34. Fanon, *The Wretched of the Earth*, tr. Constance Farrington (New York: Grove Press, 1964), 31–32.

35. Greek for both "poison" and "remedy." [Ed.]

36. Jacques Derrida, "La Pharmacie de Platon" in *La Dissémination* (Paris: Seuil, 1972), pp. 145 and passim.

37. Georg Lukács, *Die Seele und die Formen* (1911; repr. Berlin: Luchterhand, 1971), 25.

38. Wilde, *The Artist as Critic*, 367.

39. Lukács, *Die Seele und die Formen*, 29.

40. See Lukács, *History and Class Consciousness: Studies in Marxist Dialectics*, tr. Rodney Livingstone (London: Merlin Press, 1971), 178–209.

41. See the discussion of this point in Richard Poirier, *The Performing Self: Compositions and Decompositions in the Languages of Everyday Life* (New York: Oxford University Press, 1971).

25

The Quest for Relevance[1] (1986)

Ngũgĩ wa Thiong'o

Distinguished professor of English and Comparative Literature and director of the International Center for Writing and Translation at the University of California at Irvine, Ngũgĩ has been exiled from Kenya since 1982. He was a prime enemy of the state under Daniel arap Moi's repressive government: his theater work with residents of Limuru near Nairobi led to his detention without trial for a year in 1978. Before his detention Ngũgĩ had been an influential public intellectual in Kenya, critical of state violence and corruption. He became known internationally through his novels, including *Weep Not, Child* (1964) and *A Grain of Wheat* (1967), in which characters attempt to orient themselves in the postcolony.

In order to speak to the marginalized of Kenyan society, once in detention Ngũgĩ composed the first novel ever written in his native language of Gikuyu, *Caitaani Mutharabaini* (*Devil on the Cross*, 1980). The issue of language has been Ngũgĩ's central concern ever since; he has repeatedly returned to the subject in books of essays, from *Detained: A Writer's Prison Diary* (1981) to *Penpoints, Gunpoints, and Dreams* (1998). He co-founded *Mũtiiri*, the first Gikuyu-language journal of cultural criticism, and he continues to write fiction in Gikuyu and translate it into English. His work has been translated into many languages including Telugu, Chinese, Russian, and German.

His central contention is that "colonial" languages such as English and French have had a distorting influence on the self-perceptions of

Africans. In his most influential critical work, *Decolonising the Mind* (1986), Ngũgĩ saw global capital as the main structuring system for the continued dominance of "European" languages as vehicles for the propagation of global culture. He even signaled that *Decolonising the Mind* was his farewell to English as his language of criticism, to be replaced by Gikuyu, a move that did not last long. In "The Quest for Relevance," reprinted here, he concludes the book by arguing that marginal languages and cultures achieve relevance when they are centrally understood in their own contexts.

I

So far I have talked about language in creative literature generally and in theatre and fiction in particular. I should have gone on to talk about "The language of African poetry" but the same arguments apply even more poignantly in the area of poetry. The existence and the continuing growth of poetry in African languages, clearly and unequivocally so in orature (oral literature), make it manifestly absurd to talk of African poetry in English, French or Portuguese. Afro-European poetry, yes; but not to be confused with African poetry which is the poetry composed by Africans in African languages. For instance, written poetry in Swahili goes back to many centuries. While the poetic political compositions of the great anti-imperialist Somali fighter, Hassan, will be known by heart by every Somali-speaking herdsman, not a line by even the best of African poets in foreign languages will be known by any peasant anywhere in Africa. As for a discussion of the other language of poetry—where poetry, like theatre and fiction, is considered as a language in itself with its own structures of beats, metres, rhymes, half-rhymes, internal rhymes, lines and images—it calls for different resources including a knowledge of the particular African languages of its expression, which I cannot, at present, even pretend to possess.

Instead, I shall attempt to sum up what we have so far been discussing by looking at what immediately underlies the politics of language in African literature; that is the search for a liberating perspective within which to see ourselves clearly in relationship to ourselves and to other selves in the universe. I shall call this "a quest for relevance" and I want to look at it as far as it relates, not to just the writing of literature, but to the teaching of that literature in schools and universities and to the critical approaches. In other words, given that there is literature in Africa and in the world, in what order should it be presented to the child and how? This involves two processes: the choice of material and the attitude to, or inter-pretation of, that material. These two processes will themselves affect and be affected by the national and the class bases of the choice and the attitude to the material chosen. Finally the national and even the class bases of our choice and perspective will affect and be affected by the philosophic base from which we look at reality, a matter over which there can never be any legislation. Already as you can see we are entangled in a kind of vicious circle with everything affecting and being affected by everything else. But let me explain the question of base.

How we see a thing—even with our eyes—is very much dependent on where we stand in relationship to it. For instance we are all in this lec-ture theatre. But what we see of the room and how much of it we see is de-pendent on where we are now sitting as we listen to this talk. For instance you all can see the wall behind me: and I can see the wall behind you. Some of you are seated in such places as physically allow you to see much more of this room than others. What is clear is that were we to leave this room and describe it, we would end up with as many descriptions of this room as there are people here tonight. Do you know the story of the seven blind men who went to see an elephant? They used to have so many conflicting specu-lations as to the physical make-up of an elephant. Now at last they had a chance to touch and feel it. But each touched a different part of the animal: leg, ear, tusk, tail, side, trunk, belly and so they went home even more divided as to the physical nature, shape and size of an elephant. They ob-viously stood in different positions or physical bases in their exploration of the elephant. Now, the base need not be physical but could also be philo-sophical, class or national.

In this book I have pointed out that how we view ourselves, our en-vironment even, is very much dependent on where we stand in relationship to imperialism in its colonial and neo-colonial stages; that if we are to do anything about our individual and collective being today, then we have to coldly and consciously look at what imperialism has been doing to us and to our view of ourselves in the universe. Certainly the quest for relevance and for a correct perspective can only be understood and be meaningfully resolved within the context of the general struggle against imperialism.

It is not always easy to see this in literature. But precisely because of that, I want to use the example of the struggle over what is to be taught, and in what order, with what attitudes or critical approaches, to illustrate the anti-imperialist context of the quest for relevance in Africa today. I want to start with a brief description of what has been called "the great Nairobi literature debate" on the teaching of literature in universities and schools.

The debate started innocuously when on 20 September 1968 the then head of the English Department, Dr James Stewart, presented proposals to the Arts Faculty Board on the development of the English Department. The proposals were in many ways pertinent. But they were all preceded by two crucial sentences:

> The English department has had a long history at this college and has built up a strong syllabus which *by its study of the historic continuity of a single culture throughout the period of emergence of the modern west* makes it an important companion to History and to Philosophy and Religious Studies. However, it is bound to become less *British,* more open to other writing in English (American, Caribbean, African, Commonwealth) and also to continental writing, for comparative purposes.[2]

A month later on 24 October 1968 three African lecturers and researchers at the University responded to Dr Stewart's proposals by calling for the abolition of the English Department as then constituted. They questioned the underlying assumption that the English tradition and the emergence of the modern west were the central root of Kenya's and Africa's consciousness and cultural heritage. They rejected the underlying notion that Africa was an extension of the West. Then followed the crucial rejoinder:

> Here then, is our main question: if there is a need for a "study of the historic continuity of a single culture," why can't this be African? Why can't African literature be at the centre so that we can view other cultures in relationship to it? (146)

Hell was let loose. For the rest of 1968 and spilling over into 1969 the debate raged on, engulfing the entire faculty and the university. Thus within four sentences the stage was set for what has become the most crucial debate on the politics of literature and culture even in Kenya of today. What was interesting was that the details of the debate were the same: all sides were agreed on the need to include African, European and other literatures. But what would be the centre? And what would be the periphery, so to speak? How would the centre relate to the periphery? Thus the question of the base of the take-off, the whole question of perspective and relevance, altered the weight and relationship of the various parts and details to each other.

In order to see the significance of the debate and why it raised so much temper we have to put it in a historical context of the rise of English studies in Africa, of the kind of literature an African student was likely to encounter and of the role of culture in the imperialist domination of Africa.

III

English studies in schools and higher institutions of learning became systematised after the Second World War with the setting up of the overseas extensions of the University of London in Uganda, Nigeria, Ghana, Sierra Leone, Kenya and Tanzania; and with very few variations they offered what also obtained in London. The syllabus of the English Department for instance meant a study of the history of English literature from Shakespeare, Spencer and Milton to James Joyce and T. S. Eliot, I. A. Richards and the inevitable F. R. Leavis. Matthew Arnold's quest for the sweetness and light of a hellenized English middle class; T. S. Eliot's high culture of an Anglo-Catholic feudal tradition, suspiciously close to the culture of the "high table" and to the racial doctrines of those born to rule; the Leavisite selected "Great Tradition of English Literature" and his insistence on the moral significance of literature; these great three dominated our daily essays. How many seminars we spent on detecting this moral significance in every paragraph, in every word, even in Shakespeare's commas and fullstops? For some reason the two most outstanding critical minds that might have made my study of English Literature really meaningful even in a colonial setting—Arnold Kettle and Raymond Williams—were studied, if at all, only remotely and fleetingly even in the time from 1959 to 1964. But here I am not looking at which writer or critic was more suitable to our situation or even the difference in their world outlook. What was more important was that they all fell within English tradition except in the study of drama where names like those of Aeschylus, Sophocles and Aristotle or Ibsen, Chekhov, Strindberg and Synge would appear quaint and strange in their very un-Englishness. The centrality and the universality of the English tradition was summed up in the title of an inaugural lecture by Professor Warner of Makerere, *Shakespeare in Africa,* in which he grew almost ecstatic about the fact that some of his students had been able to recognise some characters of Jane Austen's novels in their own African villages. So, English literature was applicable to Africa too: the defence of English studies in an African situation was now complete. In schools the English language and English literature syllabuses were tailored to prepare the lucky few for an English degree at university. So the syllabuses had the same pattern. Shakespeare, Milton, Wordsworth, Shelley, Keats and Kipling were familiar names long before I knew I would even make it to Makerere.

In my book, *Writers in Politics*—particularly in the essay "Literature and Society"—I have tried to sum up the kind of literature available to African children in the classrooms and libraries for their school and university education, by placing it into three broad categories.

First was the great humanist and democratic tradition of European literature: Aeschylus, Sophocles, Shakespeare, Balzac, Dickens, Dostoevsky, Tolstoy, Gorky and Brecht to mention just a few names. But their literature, even at its most humane and universal, necessarily reflected the European experience of history. The world of its setting and the world it evoked would be more familiar to a child brought up in the same landscape than to one brought up outside, no matter how the latter might try to see Jane Austen's characters in the gossiping women of his rural African setting. This was not helped by a critical tradition that often presented these writers, Shakespeare included, as if they were mindless geniuses whose only consistent quality was a sense of compassion. These writers, who had the sharpest and most penetrating observations on the European bourgeois culture, were often taught as if their only concern was with the universal themes of love, fear, birth and death. Sometimes their greatness was presented as one more English gift to the world alongside the bible and the needle. William Shakespeare and Jesus Christ had brought light to darkest Africa. There was a teacher in our school who used to say that Shakespeare and Jesus used very simple English, until someone pointed out that Jesus spoke Hebrew. The "Great Tradition" of English literature was the great tradition of "literature"!

Then there was the literature of liberal Europeans who often had Africa as the subject of their imaginative explorations. The best example is Alan Paton's *Cry the Beloved Country.* Here an African eschewing violence, despite the racist violence around him, is the perfect hero. The Reverend Stephen Kumalo is presented in such a way that all our sympathies are with him. He is the embodiment of the biblical man who offers the enemy the left cheek to strike, after the right cheek has already been bashed in by the same enemy. Kumalo is the earlier literary version in an African setting of those Americans in the sixties who thought they could stop the Vietnam war by blowing bubbles and offering flowers to club and gun wielding policemen. Joyce Cary in *Mister Johnson* had gone a stage further in his liberalism. In this novel he offered an idiotic African as the hero. Mister Johnson is the dancing, fun-loving African full of emotional vitality and the endearing human warmth of a child. In the novel he is condemned to death. What was his dearest wish? To be shot dead by the European District Officer. The District Officer grants him that wish. Don't we do the same for our horses and cats? The point is that in the novel the reader is supposed to admire both the District Officer and Mister Johnson: they have established a human contact—that of the rider and the horse, the master and his servant. Karen Blixen's book *Out of Africa* falls within the same liberal mould: to her Africans are a special species of human beings endowed with a great spirituality and a mystical apprehension of reality or else with the instinct and vitality of animals, qualities which "we in Europe" have lost.

The third category was the downright racist literature of writers like Rider Haggard, Elspeth Huxley, Robert Ruark, and Nicholas Monsarrat. In such a literature there were only two types of Africans: the good and the bad. The good African was the one who co-operated with the European coloniser; particularly the African who helped the European coloniser in the occupation and subjugation of his own people and country. Such a character was portrayed as possessing qualities of strength, intelligence and beauty. But it was the strength and the intelligence and the beauty of a sell-out. The bad African character was the one who offered resistance to the foreign conquest and occupation of his country. Such a character was portrayed as being ugly, weak, cowardly and scheming. The reader's sympathies are guided in such a way as to make him identify with Africans collaborating with colonialism and to make him distance himself from those offering political and military resistance to colonialism. One can see the same schema at work today in the portrayal of the various African regimes in the Western media. Those regimes, as in Kenya and Ivory Coast, which have virtually mortgaged the future of their countries to Euro-American imperialism, are portrayed as being pragmatic, realistic, stable, democratic and they are often shown as having achieved unparalleled economic growth for their countries. But other regimes like those of Nkrumah's Ghana or Nasser's Egypt which strove for a measure of national self-reliance are portrayed as being simplistic, unrealistic, doctrinaire, authoritarian and are often shown as having brought only economic chaos to their countries. Thus imaginative literature had created the necessary racist vocabulary and symbols long before the T.V. and the popular media had come to dominate the scene.

African children who encountered literature in colonial schools and universities were thus experiencing the world as defined and reflected in the European experience of history. Their entire way of looking at the world, even the world of the immediate environment, was Eurocentric. Europe was the centre of the universe. The earth moved around the European intellectual scholarly axis. The images children encountered in literature were reinforced by their study of geography and history, and science and technology where Europe was, once again, the centre. This in turn fitted well with the cultural imperatives of British imperialism. In this book I have in fact tried to show how the economic control of the African people was effected through politics and culture. Economic and political control of a people can never be complete without cultural control, and here literary scholarly practice, irrespective of any individual interpretation and handling of the practice, fitted well the aim and the logic of the system as a whole. After all, the universities and colleges set up in the colonies after the war were meant to produce a native elite which would later help prop up the Empire. The cool, level-headed servant of the Empire celebrated in Kipling's poem "If"; the gentleman who could keep his head against the rising storms of resistance; the gentleman who would meet with triumph and disaster and treat those two imposters just the same; the gentleman who had not the slightest doubt about the rightness of colonialism despite the chorus of doubt around; this gentleman was now being given African robes in the post-war schools and universities of an ageing imperialism.

The structures of the literary studies evolved in the colonial schools and universities had continued well into independence era completely unaffected by any winds of cultural change. The irony of all this was that these departments were being run in countries where the oral tradition, the basis of all genres of written literature be it a poem, a play, or a story, was beating with life and energy, and yet they were unaffected by the surging creative storm all around them. The study of the historic continuity of a single culture throughout the period of emergence of the modern west was still the organising principle of literature teaching in schools and colleges.

Seen against this background, the rejection of that principle in 1968 was therefore more than a rejection of a principle in a literary academic debate. It was questioning the underlying assumptions behind the entire system that we had inherited and had continued to run without basic questions about national perspective and relevance. The question is this: from what base do we look at the world?

IV

Three lecturers, Owuor Anyumba, Taban Lo Liyong and myself, were emphatic in our rejection and affirmation: our statement said,

We reject the primacy of English literature and cultures. The aim, in short, should be to orientate ourselves towards placing Kenya, East Africa and then Africa in the centre. All other things are to be considered in their relevance to our situation and their contribution towards understanding ourselves . . . In suggesting this we are not rejecting other streams, especially the western stream. We are only clearly mapping out the directions and perspectives the study of culture and literature will inevitably take in an African university. (146)

We proposed a new organising principle which would mean a study of Kenyan and East African literature, African literature, third world literature and literature from the rest of the world. We concluded:

We want to establish the centrality of Africa in the department. This, we have argued, is justifiable on various grounds, the most important one being that education is a means of knowledge about ourselves. Therefore, after we have examined ourselves, we radiate outwards and discover peoples and worlds around us. With Africa at the centre of things, not existing as an appendix or a satellite of other countries and literatures, things must be seen from the African perspective. (150)

But our boldest call was for the placing, within the national perspective, of oral literature (orature) at the centre of the syllabus:

The oral tradition is rich and many-sided . . . the art did not end yesterday; it is a living tradition . . . familiarity with oral literature could suggest new structures and techniques; and could foster attitudes of mind characterized by the willingness to experiment with new forms . . . The study of the Oral Tradition would therefore supplement (not replace) courses in Modern African Literature. By discovering and proclaiming loyalty to indigenous values, the new literature would on the one hand be set in the stream of history to which it belongs and so be better appreciated; and on the other be better able to embrace and assimilate other thoughts without losing its roots. (148)

Orature has its roots in the lives of the peasantry. It is primarily their compositions, their songs, their art, which forms the basis of the national and resistance culture during the colonial and neo-colonial times. We three lecturers were therefore calling for the centrality of peasant and worker heritage in the study of literature and culture.

The new organising principle was accepted after a long debate which engulfed the entire University and which, at one time, also included all the participants at the 1969 Nairobi Conference of English and Literature Departments of the Universities of East and Central Africa. African Orature; literature by Africans from the Continent, the Caribbean, and Afro-America; literature of "third" world peoples from Asia and Latin America; literature from the rest of the world including Europe and North America; roughly in that order of relevance, relationship and perspective, would form the basis of a new literature syllabus with English as the mediating language. The actual syllabus resulting from the 1968–9 debate was necessarily a compromise. For instance East African poetry was to be taught in *its European context*. It was not until 1973, when the majority of the staff in the department were Africans, that the syllabus was streamlined to reflect the new perspectives without a qualifying apologia.The growth of the Literature Department at the University of Nairobi, a department which has produced students who can, by starting from their environment, freely link the rural and urban experiences of Kenyan and African literature to that of García Márquez, Richard Wright, George Lamming, Balzac, Dickens, Shakespeare and Brecht is a far cry from those days in the fifties and sixties when they used to try and detect Jane Austen's characters in their villages.

V

But that was not the end of the Nairobi Literature Debate. In September 1974 a crucial conference on "The Teaching of African Literature in Kenyan Schools" was held at Nairobi School. The conference was jointly organised by the Department of Literature, University of Nairobi and the Inspectorate of English in the Ministry of Education. It was attended by two hundred secondary school teachers of literature and English; the staff of the departments of literature and of the faculties of education, University of Nairobi and Kenyatta University College; delegates from departments of literatures of Dar es Salaam, Makerere and Malawi Universities; representatives of the Inspectorate of English, Ministry of Education and of the Kenya Institute of Education; observers from the Ministry of Education in Tanzania and Uganda; representatives from the then East African Community; East Africa Examination Council; East Africa Literature Bureau; trade union delegates from the Kenya National Union of Teachers (KNUT);

and four publishers: Jomo Kenyatta Foundation, East African Literature Bureau, East Africa Publishing House and Oxford University Press. As if to give it an even more truly international character, there were visiting delegates from the University of West Indies at Mona, Jamaica, the University of Ife, Nigeria and from Auckland University, New Zealand. This impressive gathering was the result of hard organisational efforts of the steering committee chaired by Eddah Gachukia and S. A. Akivaga.

The conference was clearly motivated by the same quest for relevance which earlier had led to the reconstitution of the Department of Literature. In the recommendations of a working committee elected by the conference, it is argued that:

> Prior to independence, education in Kenya was an instrument of colonial policy designed to educate the people of Kenya into acceptance of their role as the colonized. The education system at independence was therefore an inheritance of colonialism so that literature syllabuses were centred on the study of an English literary tradition taught by English teachers. Such a situation meant that Kenyan children were alienated from their own experience [and] identity in an independent African country. (Recommendations of the Working Committee, p. 7)

Addressing itself to questions of language and literature, a resolution passed at the end of the conference stated:

> The present language and literature syllabuses are inadequate and irrelevant to the needs of the country. They are so organised that a Kenyan child knows himself through London and New York. Both should therefore be completely overhauled at all levels of our education system and particularly in schools. (8)

The conference, which was charged with examining the role of literature in society and the nature of literature taught in secondary schools and its relevance to Kenya's present day needs, called for the centrality of oral literature as a take-off base to contemporary literature. They argued that a sound educational policy was one which enabled students to study the culture and the environment of their society first, then set it in relation to the culture and environment of other societies: "African literature, literature of the African diaspora, and all other literatures of related experiences must be at the core of the syllabuses" (8). A working committee set up by the conference with Dougal Blackburn as Chairman and R. Gacheche as the Secretary came up with detailed recommendations on policy and on syllabuses along the principles outlined in the conference resolution. The seventy-three page document was titled: *Teaching of Literature in Kenya Secondary Schools —Recommendations of the Working Committee* and was clearly the result of months of hard work and commitment.

Looking at the document ten years later, one is struck, not so much by their critique of the existing syllabuses or by their detailed proposals for change—though both are impressive and still relevant to the similar debates and issues today—but by the consciousness that guided the critique and the proposals.

The pan-African consciousness is strong. The authors see Africa as one and they reject the division of Africa into sub-Saharan (Black Africa; Real Africa) and Northern (Arabic; Foreign; Mediterranean Africa). They want a Kenyan child to be exposed to the literature from north, south, west and east Africa:

> The centuries old Arab civilization has exerted tremendous influence on the literature of modern North Africa and also many parts of the continent. To date their influence has been denied by our educators and the literature of North Africa and the Arab world has largely been ignored. (59)

The authors want to pursue the African connection to the four corners of the earth, so to speak, and they want Kenyan children to be exposed to those historical links of biology, culture and struggle, particularly in Afro-American and Caribbean literature:

> It is often asked, why study Caribbean and Afro-American literature? What is the connection between African and the West Indian and Afro-American?
>
> (a) We have the same bio-geographic roots: the people of the West Indies and Afro-America are Africans who, a few hundred years ago, were brutally uprooted from the African continent.
>
> (b) We have shared the same past of humiliation and exploitation under slavery, and colonialism; we have also shared the glorious past of struggle, and fight against the same force.
>
> (c) Equally important, we have the same aspirations for the total liberation of all the black people, in the world. Their literature, like our literature embodies all the above aspects of *our struggle for a cultural identity*.
>
> Apart from that, African peoples of the Diaspora have contributed much to Africa's cultural and political growth. Blyden, C.L. R. James, George Padmore, W. E. Dubois, Marcus Garvey and many others were part and parcel of Africa's struggle for independence. The

literary movements from the West Indies and from Afro-America have creatively interacted with those in Africa. Aimé Césaire, Frantz Fanon, Claude McKay, Langston Hughes, Léon Damas, René Depestre, Paul Robeson—all these giants of culture and the arts have positively contributed to the growth of African Literature.

Most of these comments would apply equally well to the literature of the third world especially that of Asia and Latin America (61–2).

Africa; African connections; third world; indeed, the authors of the report are very conscious of the internationalist setting and context of the national experience. Like the university Literature Department, which was conscious of the immense value of world literature, they too refused to substitute national chauvinism for the British colonial chauvinism of the existing syllabuses. A Kenyan child would be exposed to world literature and the democratic tradition in world literature.

In accordance with the principle of teaching beginning with the students' immediate environment and moving out towards the world, the teaching of non-African literature in schools should aim to introduce the Kenyan student to *the world context of the black experience.* Such study should therefore include European and American literature, with their historical and present influences on the societies and literatures of black peoples, and a study of literature from other parts of the third world such as Latin America and Asia. Criteria for selection should attempt to balance: literary excellence, social relevance, and narrative interest. *The aim is to instill in the student a critical love of literature, which will both encourage its pursuit in later years and ensure that such a pursuit is engaged in fruitfully . . .* Given the nature of Kenyan society, we recommend that attention be paid to literature expressing the experience of a changing society, and that it be ensured that the variety of experience of different classes in society be covered. (70–1)

Their recommendations for the teaching of world literature come face to face with the issue of language; and they have authors which include Tolstoy, Gogol, Gorky, Dostoevsky (Russian); Zola, Balzac, Flaubert (French); Ibsen (Norwegian); Faulkner, Arthur Miller, Upton Sinclair, Hemingway (American); Dickens, Shakespeare, Conrad, Yeats, Synge (British and Irish); Mann and Brecht (German). They see the necessity or inevitability of continued use of English, but they strongly call for Swahili to be made compulsory in all schools but particularly for those students of English and literature and drama:

A clear programme of Swahili literature be introduced and be made compulsory in schools.

Every language has its own social and cultural basis, and these are instrumental in the formation of mental processes and value judgements. Whereas it is accepted that we use English and will continue to do so for a long time to come, the strength and depth of our cultural grounding will ultimately depend on our ability to invoke the idiom of African Culture in a language that is closer to it. Swahili has a major and an increasing role to play in Kenya, and needs to be given greater emphasis than it has hitherto been accorded.

An immediate step that should be taken to fulfill this aim is that adequate numbers of Swahili teachers should be trained. (21)

All in all, the report is shot through and through with a consciousness that literature is a powerful instrument in evolving the cultural ethos of a people. They see literature as part of the whole ideological mechanism for integrating a people into the values of a dominant class, race, or nation. Imperialism, particularly during colonialism, provides the best example of how literature as an element of culture was used in the domination of Africa. The report notes:

That Africa as a continent has been a victim of forces of colonial exploitation, oppression and human degradation. In the field of culture she was taught to look on Europe as her teacher and the centre of man's civilization, and herself as the pupil. In this event Western culture became the centre of Africa's process of learning, and Africa was relegated to the background. Africa uncritically imbibed values that were alien and had no immediate relevance to her people. Thus was the richness of Africa's cultural heritage degraded, and her people labelled as primitive and savage. The colonizer's values were placed in the limelight, and in the process, evolved a new African who denied his original image, and exhibited a considerable lack of confidence in his creative potential. (7)

The writers are therefore shocked that syllabuses designed to meet the needs of colonialism should continue well into the independence era.

It was noted with shock and concern that even ten years after Independence, in practically every school in the republic our students were still being *subjected to alien cultural values which are meaningless especially to our present needs.* Almost all books used in our schools are written by foreign authors; out of 57 texts of drama studied at EAACE level in our schools between 1968 and 1972 only one was African. It became obvious that very little is being done in schools to expose our students to their cultural and physical environment. (7–8)

They are therefore conscious of the fact that an actual literature syllabus, no matter how far reaching in its scope and composition of texts and authors, is limited unless literature is seen and taught as an ideological component of the continuing national liberation process. In one of their conclusions they write:

Three major principles that emerged from the conference have guided the discussions of the working committee and the preparation of this final report.

(i) *A people's culture is an essential component in defining and revealing their world outlook. Through it, mental processes can be conditioned, as was the case with the formal education provided by the colonial governments in Africa.*

(ii) A sound educational policy is one which enables students to *study the culture and environment of their own society first, then* in relation to the culture and environment of other societies.

(iii) *For the education offered today to be positive and to have creative potential for Kenya's future it must be seen as an essential part of the continuing national liberation process.* (19–20)

The hell let loose by the conference and by its subsequent recommendations was almost a repeat of the 1968–9 University-based debate. But now the debate became national. Some newspapers opened their pages to the literature debate revealing in the process a wide range of views on the issue from extreme hostility to passionate commitment. Believe it or not, in the early seventies academics and teachers could hold such a debate and assert the primacy of the Kenyan people and their experience of the history of struggle without fear of being labelled Marxist, Communist or radical and being hauled into prisons and detention camps. Even so the proposals and the model syllabus worked out to reflect the new perspective of Kenya, East Africa, Africa, Third World and the rest of the world, were not readily accepted by the Ministry of Education. They became the subject of a continuing debate and struggle in the educational corridors of power. The proposals were strengthened and argued about in yet other follow-up conferences and in 1981 were still a matter of controversy. In 1982 a syllabus like that of the

Literature Department was labeled by some political elements as Marxist. Kenya-centrism or Afro-centrism was now equated with Marxism.

I am not sure if today the proposals have been accepted or not. I think some elements, like the oral literature components, have been introduced in the school literature curriculum. But I expect the controversy continues. For the quest for relevance and the entire literature debate was not really about the admissibility of this or that text, this or that author, though it often expressed itself as such. It was really about the direction, the teaching of literature, as well as of history, politics, and all the other arts and social sciences, ought to take in Africa today. The debate, in other words, was about the inherited colonial education system and the consciousness it necessarily inculcated in the African mind. What directions should an education system take in an Africa wishing to break with neo-colonialism? What should be the philosophy guiding it? How does it want the "New Africans" to view themselves and their universe? From what base: Afrocentric or Eurocentric? What then are the materials they should be exposed to: and in what order and perspective? Who should be interpreting that material to them: an African or non-African? If African, what kind of African? One who has internalized the colonial world outlook or one attempting to break free from the inherited slave consciousness? And what were the implications of such an education system for the political and economic set up or status quo? In a neo-colonialist context, would such an education system be possible? Would it not in fact come into conflict with political and economic neo-colonialism?

Whether recommendations in the quest for relevance are successful or not ultimately depends on the entire government policy towards culture, education and language, and on where and how it stands in the anti-imperialist process in Africa today.

Whatever the destiny of the 1974 proposals on literature in schools, the values, assumptions and the attitudes underlying the entire "Nairobi Literature Debate" are today at the heart of the contending social forces in Kenya, in Africa and in the third world and they all boil down to the question of relevance, in philosophical, class and national terms.

____

VI

At the level of the national base for relevance, two conflicting lines have emerged in Kenyan intellectual circles and particularly in the interpretation of history, politics and economic development.

One line identifies with the imperialist heritage, colonial and neo-colonial, and it sees in imperialism the motive force of Kenya's development. The more rapidly Kenya loses her identity in the West and leaves her fate in imperialist interests, the faster will be her development and her movement to the modernity of the twentieth century. This line is particularly clear in the interpretation of history where a corpus of state intellectuals has emerged who now openly write manuals in praise of colonialism. These state intellectuals scoff at the heroic and patriotic struggles of Kenyan people of all the nationalities to free Kenya from the stranglehold of imperialistic capitalism. For them the tradition of collaboration with British imperialism is what brought about independence and not the resistance tradition of Waiyaki, Koitalel, Me Katilili, Mahkan Singh and Gama Pinto, a tradition carried to new heights by Dedan Kimathi and the Kenya Land and Freedom Army (Mau Mau). For these state intellectuals imperialist Europe is the beginning of Kenya's history and progress. Imperialism created Kenya. Therefore, for these intellectuals, the neo-colonial state is the model instrument for Africa's rapid development.

The other line identifies with the tradition of resistance in all the nationalities. It sees in the activities and actions of ordinary men and women of Kenya, the basis of Kenya's history and progress. The line, best exemplified by the Kenyan intellectuals now in jails, detention camps or in exile—these are clearly *not* state functionaries—insists that Kenya and the needs of Kenya come first. For them, the national perspective in economy (even capitalism if the national capital and enterprise were dominant), politics and culture is of paramount importance. To get the correct national perspective, democracy—where a whole range of opinions, views and voices can freely be raised—is an absolute minimum. For them the starting point is a democratic Kenya—the Kenya of peasants and workers of all the nationalities with their heritage of languages, cultures, glorious histories of struggle, vast natural and human resources. From this starting point they can radiate outwards to link with the heritage and struggles of other peoples in Africa, the third world peoples, Europe and the Americas; with the struggles of the people the world over, the vast democratic and socialistic forces daily inflicting mortal blows to imperialist capitalism. A study of African literature, culture and history, starting from a national base, would therefore be linked with progressive and democratic trends in world literature, culture and history. For them the quest for relevance is not a call for isolationism but a recognition that national liberation is the basis of an internationalism of all the democratic and social struggles for human equality, justice, peace and progress. For them, the neo-colonial state is the negation of Africa's progress and development. The defeat of imperialism and neo-colonialism and hence the liberation of natural and human resources and the entire productive forces of the nation, would be the beginning of Africa's real progress and development. The national, viewed from the needs and activities of the majority—peasant and workers—is the necessary base for a take-off into the world of the twentieth and twenty-first centuries, the international democratic and socialist community of tomorrow.

The Nairobi Literature Debate and the enormous reactions it generated *for* and *against* reflected the fierce struggle of the two lines in Kenya today. In answering the question—are the sources of our inspiration foreign or national?—the proposed changes implied an unequivocal rejection of the imperialist and foreign and an affirmation of the democratic and national. For the first time since Independence in 1963, the defenders of imperialist and neo-colonial culture were put on the defensive.

VII

While the Nairobi Literature Debate has clearly been able to isolate the national democratic basis of relevance, it has not always been as successful in isolating the philosophic and class bases of relevance—although they are implied.

The philosophic and the class bases of relevance are even more crucial when it comes to the area of critical approaches and interpretations. For the critic, whether teacher, lecturer, interpreter or analyst, is a product of a class society. Each child by birth, family or parents' occupation is brought up in a given class. By education children are brought up in the culture, values and world outlook of the dominant class which may or may not be the same as the class of their birth and family. By choice they may opt for one or the other side in the class struggles of their day. Therefore their interpretation of literature and culture and history will be influenced by their philosophical standpoint, or intellectual base, and their conscious or unconscious class sympathies.

First the philosophical base. Is a person's standpoint that of idealist or materialist? Is their mode of thinking and reasoning dialectical or metaphysical? Does the critic see values, ideas and the spiritual as superior to material reality? Does the critic see reality as static for all time or reality as changing all the time? Does the critic see things, processes, phenomena as linked or as separate mutually exclusive entities? Since literature, like religion and other areas of culture, is a reflection of the world of nature and human community, the outlook of a critic in real life will profoundly affect their interpretation of the-reflected reality.

This is even more true of class sympathies and identification.

A critic who in real life is suspicious of people fighting for liberation will suspect characters who, though only in a novel, are fighting for liberation. A critic who in real life is impatient with all the talk about classes, class struggle, resistance to imperialism, racism and struggles against racism, of reactionary versus revolutionary violence, will be equally impatient when he or she finds the same themes dominant in a work of art. In criticism, as in creative writing, there is an ideological struggle. A critic's world outlook, his or her class sympathies and values will affect evaluations of Chinua Achebe, Sembene Ousmane, Brecht, Balzac, Shakespeare, Lu Hsun, García Márquez or Alex La Guma.

The quest for relevance calls for more than choice of material. The attitude to the material is also important. Of course, over this, there can never be any legislation. But it is crucial to be alert to the class ideological assumptions behind choices, utterances and evaluations. The choice of what is relevant and the evaluation of a quality is conditioned by the national, class and philosophical base. These factors underlay the controversy attending the whole quest for relevance in the teaching of literature in Kenyan schools and universities.

VIII

For the Nairobi Literature Debate and the quest for relevance were basically challenges as to where people stand in the big social issues of the world today. In the era of imperialism where do we really stand? In a society built on a structure of inequality, where do we stand? Can we remain neutral, cocooned in our libraries and scholarly disciplines, muttering to ourselves: I am only a surgeon; I am a scientist; I am an economist; or I am simply a critic, a teacher, a lecturer? As Brecht says in a poem addressed to the students of the Workers' and Peasants' Faculty:

> Your science will be valueless, you'll find
> And learning will be sterile, if inviting
> Unless you pledge your intellect to fighting
> Against all enemies of mankind.[3]

Or his poem addressed to Danish working-class actors:

> And that is where you
> The workers' actors, as you learn and teach
> Can play your part creatively in all the struggles
> Of men of your time, thereby
> Helping, with your seriousness of study and the cheerfulness of
> knowledge
> To turn the struggles into common experience and
> Justice into a passion.[4]

When one day the simple men and women of all our countries will, as foreseen in the poem addressed to apolitical intellectuals by the late Guatemalan poet Otto René Castillo, rise and ask us what we did when our nations died out slowly, "like a sweet fire, small and alone," yes when they will ask us—

> What did you do when the poor
> suffered, when tenderness
> and life
> burned out in them?[5]

—we, who teach literature, history, the arts, culture, religions, should be able to answer proudly, like the Brechtian intellectual, we helped turn the struggles into the spheres of common knowledge and, above all, justice into a passion.

IX

The Nairobi Literature Debate is a continuing debate. It is there in East, West, South and North Africa. It is there in the Caribbean. It is there in Asia and Latin America. The relevance of literature. The relevance of art. The relevance of culture. What literature, what art, what culture, what values? For whom, for what? The debate, even for Kenyans, has not for instance settled the issue of multi-national languages in the same country. English is still the linguistic medium of the debate; and of the temporary solutions of the 1968–9 and 1974 conferences. The language question cannot be solved outside the larger arena of economics and politics, or outside the answer to the question of what society we want.

But the search for new directions in language, literature, theatre, poetry, fiction and scholarly studies in Africa is part and parcel of the overall struggles of African people against imperialism in its neo-colonial stage. It is part of that struggle for that world in which my health is not dependent on another's leprosy; my cleanliness not on another's maggot-ridden body; and my humanity not on the buried humanity of others.

A hundred and fifty years ago, that is forty years before the Berlin Conference, a German visionary saw how money taken from the worker and the poor had come to dominate human relations:

> It transforms fidelity into infidelity, love into hate, hate into love, virtue into vice, vice into virtue, servant into master, idiocy into intelligence, and intelligence into idiocy . . . He who can buy bravery is brave though he be a coward.[6]

He foresaw a new world based on a relationship, not of stolen property, but of human qualities calling forth even more human qualities in all of us:

> Assume man to be man and his relationship to be a human one: then you can exchange love for only love, trust for trust, etc. If you want to enjoy art, you must be an artistically cultivated person; if you want to exercise influence over other people, you must be a person with a stimulating and encouraging effect on other people. Every one of your relations to man and to nature must be a *specific expression,* corresponding to the object of your will, of your *real individual* life. If you love without evoking love in return—that is, if your loving as loving does not produce reciprocal love; if through a *living expression* of yourself as a loving person you do not make yourself a *beloved one,* then your love is impotent—a misfortune. (ibid.)

That was not a German Pope in the Vatican but Karl Marx in the British Museum library. And it was he who threw another challenge to all scholars, all philosophers, all the men and women of letters, all those who in their different disciplines are trying to explain the world. Hitherto, he wrote:

> The philosophers have only *interpreted* the world in various ways; the point, however, is to *change* it.[7]

Change it? This sentiment is in keeping with the vision of all "The Wretched of the Earth" in Africa, Asia and Latin America who are struggling for a new economic, political and cultural order free from imperialism in its colonial or in its more subtle but more vicious neo-colonial form. It is the sentiment of all the democratic and socialistic forces for change in the world today, forces once addressed by Brecht in the poem, "Speech to Danish Working Class Actors on the Art of Observation":

> Today everywhere, from the hundred-storeyed cities
> Over the seas, cross-ploughed by teeming liners
> To the loneliest villages, the word has spread
> That mankind's fate is man alone. Therefore
> We now ask you, the actors
> Of our time—a time of overthrow and of boundless mastery
> Of all nature, even men's own—at last
> To change yourselves and show us mankind's world
> As it really is: made by men and open to alteration.[8]

This is what this book on the politics of language in African literature has really been about: national, democratic and human liberation. The call for the rediscovery and the resumption of our language is a call for a regenerative reconnection with the millions of revolutionary tongues in Africa and the world over demanding liberation. It is a call for the rediscovery of the real language of humankind: the language of struggle. It is the universal language underlying all speech and words of our history. Struggle. Struggle makes history. Struggle makes us. In struggle is our history, our language and our being. That struggle begins wherever we are; in whatever we do: then we become part of those millions whom Martin Carter[9] once saw sleeping not to dream but dreaming to change the world.

Notes

1. From *Decolonising the Mind: The Politics of Language in African Literature* (Portsmouth, N.H.: Heinemann, and London: James Currey, 1986).

2. Ngũgĩ wa Thiong'o, *Homecoming,*London 1969, 145.

3. Brecht, *Collected Poems,* Methuen Edition, 450, lines 5–8.

4. Ibid., lines 160–66.

5. The whole poem is in Robert Marquez, ed. *Latin American Revolutionary Poetry* (New York and London, 1974).

6. Karl Marx, *Economic and Philosophic Manuscripts of 1844.*

7. Karl Marx, *Theses on Feuerbach,* no. XI.

8. Brecht, *Collected Poems,* Methuen Edition, 234, lines 35–43.

9. Martin Clyde Carter (1927–97), Guyanese poet and politician whose major themes were protest and resistance. [Ed.]

PART FOUR

Contemporary Explorations

26

Comparative Cosmopolitanism[1] (1992)

Bruce Robbins

One of the most active contributors to debates on cosmopolitanism, on the vocation of intellectuals, and on the role of the Left in contemporary cultural practice and study, Bruce Robbins is a scholar of nineteenth- and twentieth-century fiction, literary and cultural theory, and postcolonial studies. Robbins was educated at Harvard University and currently teaches at Columbia. In essays such as "The Sweatshop Sublime" (2002), he has interrogated the critical procedures by which activism is effected both inside and outside universities. His books include *Secular Vocations: Intellectuals, Professionalism, Culture* (1993), in which he challenges the much-lamented death of the intellectual due to professionalization, and *Upward Mobility and the Common Good: Toward a Literary History of the Welfare State* (2007), which explores an archive of upward mobility stories in narratives from the nineteenth century into the twenty-first. He also contributes the occasional blog to online discussions of current scholarly issues.

In "Comparative Cosmopolitanism" (1992), Robbins sets in a comparative frame a range of prevalent definitions of "cosmopolitanism" in order to respond to the backlash against pluralism that had entered American education in the preceding two decades. In the late 1980s conservative critics had launched vociferous attacks on the expansion of educational curricula to include the voices of women, and of ethnic and sexual minorities. Robbins argues for a culturally grounded cosmopolitanism, one that can mediate between global and local perspectives and values.

In the recent, much-publicized backlash against the left's influence in the academy, which is hard to disengage from journalistic cheerleading for the Gulf War, there has been a strange coincidence. On the one hand, literature departments are accused by the right of abandoning "Culture" capital C in favor of *multiculturalism,* defined by *The New York Times Magazine* as "the drive to include non-Western materials in every possible course."[2] On the other hand, in variants of a ubiquitous master-narrative of academicization-as-decline, literature departments are also accused of falling from the commonness of "Culture" into the privacy of *professionalism*—self-enclosed, jargon-ridden, hyper-theoretical, ignoring the common reader and lacking any general human concern. Academics as a professional "conspiracy against the laity"; minority constituencies who insist on having their numbers and cultural differences recognized in the curriculum, without concern for the value of their cultural exhibits as judged by some more general standard—in both cases the target is the same: the particular as opposed to the universal, the "special interest" pressing for its own advantage at the expense of the common good.

There is some reason to be skeptical about any version of the common good that can ally against it two such unlike terms as "non-Western cultures" and "American professionals." But this is just the alliance I want to examine. My premise here will be that the Right is right: not in its opposition of the universal and the particular, about which more later, but in the (perhaps unconscious) implication that the unprecedented global reach of the Anglo-American humanities, our[3] recent reaching out to diverse world written and oral traditions and to colonial, post-colonial, and minority discourse, is somehow related to the local self-interest, the social or institutional being of critics, scholars, and other cultural workers as a group. To this premise must be added, however, the question of whether relating local self-interest and global vision necessarily constitutes, as both right and left often assume, an accusation. I will answer that it is not. Cultural criticism in the United States has often claimed to be oppositional by virtue of its unworldliness—its joint appeal to a restricted, elevated canon and to Arnoldian or Weberian disinterestedness. Both appeals have been largely discredited in recent years. (Perhaps because it became increasingly difficult to believe, with the increasing academicization of intellectual life, that institutions servicing so many thousands of people a year could be entirely staffed by, and engaged in producing, mavericks and outsiders.) But the

brouhaha in the press over multiculturalism and the continuing vulnerability of "tenured radicals" to attack, not least from themselves, suggest that
no alternative description of where intellectuals think they stand (especially when they are not being Eurocentrists) or what intellectual activities
they engage in (especially when they are speaking about other cultures) has
successfully taken the place of the former ideal. This essay is an attempt
to sketch out such an alternative description. Now, perhaps, it is time to
consider the new brand of intellectual oppositionality that might be emerging from what I call our new worldliness—worldliness in the two senses of
1) planetary expansiveness of subject-matter, on the one hand, and 2) un-
embarrassed acceptance of professional self-interest, on the other.

The right is clearly wrong—indeed, it is contradicting itself—when it suggests
that multiculturalism and professionalism are related as parallel versions
of particularism. Applied to these two objects, the charge of particularism
indicates not a parallel but an intersection. For if professional critics *were*
hermetically sealed in an ivory tower, then why *would* they respond to "pressure" from "minorities"? If academics were as self-enclosed as we are told
(and as some of us appear on occasion to believe), then why would they
support multiculturalism? Between these two cases of supposed particularism, there would in fact seem to be some sort of communication, some
common language, common interest, common ground. But what ground
could that be?

When we speak today of "world literature" or "global culture," we
are not naming an optional extension of the canon; we are speaking of a
new framing of the whole which revalues both unfamiliar and long-accepted
genres, produces new concepts and criteria of judgment, and affects even
those critics who never "do" world literature or colonial discourse at all—
affects all critics, that is, by shifting criticism's whole sense of intellectual
enterprise. In an unprecedented and somewhat mysterious way, what it
means to be an intellectual or a critic seems to have become worldly or
transnational or—to use a willfully provocative word—cosmopolitan.
But this worldliness or cosmopolitanism does not yet seem to have moved
forward to the stage of conscious self-definition, self-legitimation, or self-
defense. If the neo-conservatives have been quick to attack the emergent or
perhaps already dominant sensibility which supports multicultural inclusiveness, they have kept the term cosmopolitanism for themselves. Contrasting it to particularism or "cultural egocentricity," Dinesh D'Souza's
Illiberal Education, for example, cites it with full approval.[4] The left meanwhile, groping for a line of defense stronger than "diversity for diversity's

sake," has almost completely shunned the term. And this is in large part, I think, *because* it connects international or global subject-matter with the embarrassingly local placement of intellectuals in relatively privileged institutions.

Beyond the adjectival sense of "belonging to all parts of the world; not restricted to any one country or its inhabitants," the word cosmopolitan immediately evokes the image of a privileged person: someone who can claim to be a "citizen of the world" by virtue of independent means, high-tech tastes, and globe-trotting mobility. The association of cosmopolitan globality with privilege is so deeply unattractive to us, I think, because deep down we tend to agree with the right that, especially when employed as academics, intellectuals *are* a "special interest" group representing nothing but themselves. Why else, I wonder, would we put ourselves through such extraordinarily ostentatious and unproductive self-torment over the issue of "representation," that is, the metropolitan right or privilege of "representing" non-metropolitan others? We have not thereby done anything to remedy the great historical injustices of colonialism and neo-colonialism. What we have done is helped to produce the great public relations disaster called "political correctness." And, as Edward Said recently suggested, we have *not* done even the little we could do to correct the simple, brutal "ignorance" of Middle Eastern culture which permitted the personification of Iraq as Saddam Hussein and the destruction from the air whose casualties are still being counted. Rather than accepting the inescapability of "representation" and making the best use we can of its powers, we have preferred to take it as an unwarranted or questionable privilege, an occasion for repetitive self-questioning.

This is not to say that the privileges associated with cosmopolitanism can be, as the saying goes, "left unexamined." The first entry under "cosmopolitan" in the *Oxford English Dictionary,* from John Stuart Mill's *Political Economy,* suggests one reason why left-wing critics have recoiled from it: "Capital," Mill writes in 1848, "is becoming more and more cosmopolitan." Cosmopolitanism would seem to mimic capital in seizing for itself the privilege (to paraphrase Wall Street) of "knowing no boundaries." Which is also the gendered privilege of knowing no bodies: of being, in Donna Haraway's words, "a conquering gaze from nowhere," a gaze that claims "the power to see and not be seen, to represent while escaping representation."[5] We may also remember that the gendered and classed privilege of mobile observation in a world of tight borders and limited visibility corresponds to a traditional self-image of criticism itself—criticism as disinterestedness, neutrality, objectivity—that the Left rightfully shies away from. The very act of comparison, as in "comparative literature," can seem to signal a liberation from insularity and national prejudice into the one true judgment. And when the international range of comparison suddenly and dramatically expands to include the world outside Europe, there is the danger that, under cover of the most democratic intentions, what will be re-invented is the old "free-floating intellectual" and/or an even older version of privileged impartiality. The most visibly ineligible example is perhaps V. S. Naipaul, who has recently been singing the praises of what he calls "our universal civilization."[6] Naipaul presents himself (in Rob Nixon's words) as "the ultimate literary *apatride,* the most comprehensively uprooted of twentieth-century writers and most bereft of national traditions" (1). And he does so in order to lay claim to Arnoldian objectivity, to a "secure, reputable tradition of extratraditionalism" (11)—that is, to "detachment" in the geographical, empirical, and political senses of the word (3).[7]

As an image of criticism, "detachment" is deservedly obsolete. It is an article of our contemporary faith that, like Naipaul, intellectuals and academics are not "detached" but *situated*—situated, for instance, as metropolitans and/or as professionals. To say this, however, is already to feel some impious stirrings of doubt. What precisely do we mean by the "situatedness" we devoutly claim to believe in? What excess baggage does it carry? How tightly does it restrict access to the other places we may come from, the other places we communicate with? How far can this metaphor of locality be reconciled with the expansive awareness or worldliness that we also aspire to?

In an effort to begin thinking through this piece of piety, let us consider, for example, Tim Brennan's application of the term "cosmopolitan" to Salman Rushdie. Brennan speaks of the "almost boastful cosmopolitanism" (134) of "third world metropolitan celebrities," including Rushdie, who are celebrated at the expense of "the domestic or indigenous artist in the process of an actual anticolonial struggle" (135).[8] In another article, he places Rushdie in a group of "cosmopolitan commentators on the Third World, who offer an *inside view* of formerly submerged peoples for target reading publics in Europe and North America in novels that comply with metropolitan tastes." [9] The message of such cosmopolitans—a critique of Third World nationalism and Third World elites—"is very familiar to us," Brennan concludes, "because it has been easier to embrace in our metropolitan circles than the explicit challenges of, say, the Salvadoran protest-author Manlio Argueta. . . ." Thus the metropolis understands the Third

World in terms of a "disengagement" and a "rootlessness" that are "not at all characteristic of the 'counter-hegemonic aesthetics' of much Third World writing" (64).

This argument can be classified as strongly reader- or reception-determined. According to Brennan, the decisive, definitive reality behind Rushdie's writing, a social reality pinpointed with the authority of a lexicon borrowed from market research, is the "target reading publics" of Europe and North America: the "tastes" of the metropolitan consumer. Now the category of the "metropolitan" is clearly necessary here, as it is necessary to Rob Nixon's project of dispelling "the myth of Naipaul's homelessness" (27). But simply to catch an author in the act of belonging to the metropolis, even one who claims to belong nowhere, is a two-finger exercise, given that we believe in advance that everyone belongs somewhere, that there is no alternative to belonging. The exercise becomes complicated, unpredictable, and worth doing only when we ask what it *means* to belong, or how many different ways of belonging there may be. Absolute homelessness is indeed a myth, and so is cosmopolitanism in its strictly negative sense of "free[dom] from national limitations or attachments"—as in the doctrine, in George Boas's words, "that nationality is insignificant from every point of view."[10] But this negative sense of "cosmopolitan" coexists from the outset in tension with more positive ones: with the scientific sense of "world-wide distribution," and with the more general sense of "belonging" to parts of the world other than one's nation. In any given case, it seems reasonable to try to sustain this tension, valuing the negative relation to nationality (which has its attractions these days, especially since the United Nations voted its support to U.S. war in the Gulf) without giving up an insistence on belonging—an insistence that includes the possibility of presence in other places, dispersed but real forms of membership, a density of overlapping allegiances rather than the abstract emptiness of non-allegiance.

After all, we know in other contexts that "grounding," "placement," and "location" are tricky metaphors. Whether mediated by the Marxist global division of labor or the psychoanalytic model of selfhood, the notion that we are where we are not is an equal and opposite constituent of the new common sense. If our supposed distances are really localities, as we piously repeat, it is also true that there are distances *within* what we thought were *merely* localities. No localization can be assumed to determine absolutely. If it could, then the charge of "metropolitanism" that falls on "celebrities" like Naipaul and Rushdie would also have to fall crushingly on the metropolitan critic who *makes* that charge, whatever his or her own political intentions and degree of celebrity.[11] Situatedness would indeed be our "faith," in the most dogmatic sense, if we allowed it to suggest the surrogate divinity of a single, absolutely determining cause and if we did so, moreover, largely as a masochistic means of punishing and paralyzing ourselves.

Not enough imagination has gone into the different modalities of situatedness-in-displacement. And one of the places where we must learn to see a more complex function or "office" of placement is the university. It says something about the humanities as institutionalized in the university, for example, that they can both over-appreciate the rootlessness of the world's Naipauls *and, for reasons that are no less institutional,* feed off what Brennan calls "protest-authors" as well. It says—and this is the beginning of an answer to the Right's charge that professional scholars esoterically ignore the general welfare—it says that critics have to legitimate themselves to the public, that they do so as transmitters of cultural artifacts whose value to the public is a site of interpretive contest, as the size and limits of that public are also sites of contest, and that those who criticize Naipaul as a metropolitan are simply engaging in that contest, which is to say behaving in no less "professional" a manner, obeying no less "professional" a logic, than those who delight to see their prejudices confirmed by Naipaul's trashing of the postcolonial nations. The political differences that count are not differences about professionalism as such.[12]

Professional self-legitimation can of course proceed by universalizing those values ("Western culture") of which the critic is custodian and transmitter. But professional self-legitimation can also base itself on the premise that all universals are merely particulars in disguise. The anticosmopolitan jargon of the authentically particular and the authentically local provides no escape from or political alternative to the realm of the professional. It simply conceals the exemplification, representation, and generalization in which any intellectual work, professional or not, is inescapably involved, its own included.

Consider, for example, how the piety of the particular functions within the most basic and apparently neutral of scholarly concepts: that of specificity. In her seminal essay "Under Western Eyes: Feminist Scholarship and Colonial Discourses," Chandra Talpade Mohanty objected that first-world feminist scholarship has often used the category "woman" in a universalizing way "with little regard for historical specificities" (340).[13] Her objection to "ethnocentric universalism" (336) in the name of specific situations was extremely useful then, and it remains indispensable now.[14] Nevertheless, it entitles one to inquire into the specific situation in which it itself is formulated and received. What about the (presumably "western"?) logic which values and rewards this insistence on ("eastern"?) specificity? Why should the professional discourse of metropolitan critics greet the call for specificity with such suspiciously unanimous enthusiasm?

One answer to these questions appears in Mohanty's counter-example of scholarship that is *not* "ethnocentric universalism," the example of a "careful, politically focussed local analysis" of lacemakers in Narsapur, India. This analysis leads to the conclusion, Mohanty says, that "There is no easy generalization in the direction of 'women' in India, or 'women in the third world'; nor is there a reduction of . . . the exploitation of the lace-makers to cultural explanations about the passivity or obedience that might characterize these women and their situation. . . . These Narsapur women are not mere victims of the production process. . . ." I am in full sympathy with what I take to be Mohanty's intent here, but I am troubled by the possible consequences of her phrasing. If we agree that there is "no easy generalization," don't we want to retain the right to *difficult* general-ization? Critics other than Mohanty might easily conclude, otherwise, that generalization *as such* was politically undesirable. Whereas generalizing is precisely what Mohanty is doing. What she uncovers among the Nar-sapur women is not so much a set of particulars as an instance of a rather general rule: the rule that exploitation will always be met with resistance. As Mohanty herself notes, the finding of active agency among the Narsapur women registers nothing but that specific generalization which symmetri-cally opposes Orientalist generalizations about women's "passivity" and "obedience." "Specificity," in other words, functions here as an innocuous mask which hides not only a claim to epistemological authority, but also, more significantly, the unnecessarily camouflaged transmission of *counter-*universals, *alternative* generalizations.[15]

I am trying to suggest three things. First, that the act of finding "agency" in text after text corresponds to a logic which is as much a part of our "professional" or "metropolitan" situatedness as the act of neglecting or denying it would be. Second, that a critic's transmission of the cultural value called "agency" should not disguise itself as a defense of the particu-lar, the local, and the specific, since it involves generalizations that are no less dramatically synthetic—the people united will never be defeated, or the unconquerable human spirit—than the Orientalist stereotypes they are marshalled against. And third, that if we do not need "easy generalizations," we do need difficult ones—for example, the more difficult though less pious procedure of *not* assuming agency to be everywhere present, but try-ing to explain why it is where it is and why it isn't where it isn't.

It is arguable that, as a critical procedure or paradigm, the formulaic recovery of inspirational agency may foster political quiescence, while a more politicized criticism might in fact result from a focus on vaster, less anthropomorphic, less hortatory structures. After all, why *do* we all value "agency" so highly? As an abstraction that lends itself equally well to the Marxism of Lukács and the humanism of Matthew Arnold, agency legitimates the specific politics of neither one. What it does legitimate is the public representativeness of criticism as such, its responsiveness to the active voice or will of the people. When the academic humanist pulls this particular rabbit from his or her text, the point is both that the people make their own history and also, however implicitly, that the academic who is representing them as so doing, by transmitting this tidbit of the cultural heritage, is himself or herself acting in the interests of the people thereby, including the people who make that academic's own immediate history—the public legislators and private funders who pass judgment on academic legitimacy.

However desirable agency may be, there is at any rate no inherent connection between it and the particular, the specific, the local. Here an edifyingly unliterary parallel presents itself: the so-called "localities" debate which has raged over the past few years among radical geographers. The move in geography to study the smaller, sub-regional units known as localities came at a time when the worldwide restructuring of the capitalist economy seemed at once to be increasing the scale of global interconnectedness and, in direct proportion, to be decreasing the power of the human agents concerned to grasp or resist its operations. In scaling down the size of the units studied, geographers were hoping to draw on the empirical authority of the particular, or rather were hoping *through* that authority to sustain a waning illusion of agency. Hidden away in the miniaturizing precision of "locality," with its associations of presence and uniqueness, empirical concreteness, complete experience, accessible subjectivity, has been the nostalgia for a collective subject-in-action that is no longer so easy to localize. As one essay in the debate concluded, *"We do not have some privileged access to understanding patterns of human agency simply by studying localities"* (187).[16] Thinking small is not enough; agency is not to be had so predictably. The unit of coherence where transformative energies have the best chance of seizing hold is not predictable in advance; it might well be larger, not smaller. As Neil Smith writes: "it is not clear in the current restructuring that, in economic terms at least, coherent regions continue to exist as subdivisions of the national rather than international economy."[17]

This suggests the case for a certain cosmopolitanism—not one obsessed with embodying a preconceived totality, but one which does not judge in advance the macro-political scale of its units, which sees "worlding" as a process, to quote Gayatri Spivak, and a process in which more than one "world" may be realized, where "worlds" may be contested.[18] "Cosmos" (world) in "cosmopolitan" originally meant simply "order" or "adornment" —as in cosmetics—and was only later extended metaphorically to refer to "the world." Cosmetics preceeded totality. Worlding, then, might be seen as "making up" the face of the planet—something that can be done in diverse ways. At the same time, the case for this more modest cosmopolitanism is also a case for a certain professionalism—a professionalism which, without presumption of ultimate totalizing certainty, believes in its own intellectual powers of generalization, abstraction, synthesis, and representation at a distance, and in the process of putting them to use. Which believes, one might say, in its own *work*.

Here, then, is a task: to drop the conversation-stopping, always-reversible charge of "privilege" and instead to discriminate degrees of complacency, degrees of service to the general welfare, within an overarching acknowledgment that the professional producers and transmitters of knowledge are *of course* not motivated solely (if at all) by pure disinterested altruism. This effort can begin where the cosmopolitan's privileges are most grossly accepted. In the new volume *Global Culture,* there is an essay called "Cosmopolitans and Locals in World Culture," written by Ulf Hannerz, which defines the figure of the cosmopolitan by a series of exclusions. "Anybody who moves about in the world" (238), the author writes, is not a cosmopolitan.[19] Nor is it sufficient to have "a willingness to engage with the Other" (239). Cosmopolitans are not tourists, for whom they are likely to be mistaken, since "tourists are not participants" (242). They are not exiles, since the exile's involvement with another culture has been "*forced*" (242). "Most ordinary labour migrants are not cosmopolitans either. For them going away may be, ideally, home plus higher income; often the involvement with another culture is not a fringe benefit but a necessary cost, to be kept as low as possible" (243). "The perspective of the cosmopolitan must entail relationships to a plurality of cultures understood as distinct entities" (239).

At this point, if not before, one becomes aware of how self-serving the process of definition is. Imagining cultures as "distinct entities" makes them into objects of artistic appreciation for the passing connoisseur; it is a way of imagining that all privileges of mobility and comparison inhere in the cosmopolitan observer. As the definition narrows further, it accumulates still more privileges. Cosmopolitans, like expatriates and ex-expatriates, "are people who have *chosen* to live abroad" (my italics). They know "that they can go home when it suits them." Today, this knowledge is less often guaranteed by independent means than by their occupations. "Transnational cultures today tend to be more or less clearcut occupational cultures" (243). What occupations? The climactic example of transnational occupational culture is—to no one's surprise—the intellectuals.

This more or less shameless use of the new "global culture" to reinvent or re-legitimate Mannheim's "free-floating" intellectuals seems to corroborate, once again, the fear that cosmopolitanism is only a tool of privilege and self-aggrandizement. But this is not the precise moral I draw from it. The essay's criteria for true cosmopolitanism share a good deal with traditional aesthetics: in its view, cosmopolitanism becomes an autonomous, unforced appreciation of coherence and novelty among distinct cultural entities. The editor of the volume in which this essay appears, Mike Featherstone, stresses the same point when he describes "transnational intellectuals" as those who "seek out and adopt a reflexive, metacultural or *aesthetic* stance to divergent cultural experiences" (9—my italics). In my own view, it is this aestheticism, with its presumption of inequality and its spectatorial absence of commitment to change that inequality, which disqualifies the essay from representing the new transnationality of intellectual work. What we have to object to, in other words, is the particular position that the essay tries to legitimate, and not the effort of self-legitimation itself.

By producing a new, international pedigree for the old idea of the intellectual as autonomous critic, this essay joins the genre of the allegory of vocation. Allegories of vocation are critical works which, while doing whatever other interpretive tasks they set themselves, also perform a second, most often implicit function: they invent and arrange their concepts and characters so as to narrativize and argue for the general value and significance of the intellectual vocation they exemplify. Examples include Raymond Williams's *Culture and Society,* which tells the story of how leftist critics like Williams himself arose from Romanticism to write works like *Culture and Society,* or Gilbert and Gubar's *The Madwoman in the Attic,* which turns *Jane Eyre* into a paradigm for the rise of the twentieth-century feminist critic. (Or, for that matter, Gayatri Spivak's "Three Women's Texts and a Critique of Imperialism," which revises the *Jane Eyre* paradigm into an allegory of post-colonial criticism.) My point here is that I have not *criticized* any of these works by identifying the genre they belong to. If we accept the premise that we *want* to do significant work—that we want the privilege, if you like, of doing work that is more significant than merely earning a living—then we must desire and value texts which help explain, to ourselves and to others, why a particular sort of work is meaningful and valuable. We can criticize the aestheticism of this cosmopolitan, in other words, but not the fact that the essay makes a case for intellectuals. What should be set against it is another case for intellectuals that mobilizes cosmopolitanism differently.

As an alternative within the same genre, then, I will take up in conclusion the rich and influential work of historian of anthropology James Clifford, work which has been so inspiring to students seeking a sense of intellectual vocation in the confusingly transnational space of contemporary knowledge, I think, in part because it has struggled with our ambivalence both about cosmopolitanism and about professionalism. Clifford's position on cosmopolitanism seems to be expressed unequivocally in his influential review of Edward Said's *Orientalism*. There the term "cosmopolitan" is unmistakably derogatory. "Said's basic values," Clifford says, "are cosmopolitan." This statement concludes Clifford"s case that "humanist common denominators . . . are meaningless, since they bypass the local cultural codes that make personal experience articulate." "The privilege of standing above cultural particularism, of aspiring to the universalist power that speaks for humanity . . . is a privilege invented by a totalizing Western liberalism" (263). What must always be avoided, Clifford declares, even if the concept of culture itself is eventually abandoned, is "the positing of cosmopolitan essences" (274–75).

In this context, "totalizing Western liberalism" seems to name what is wrong both with cosmopolitanism and with professionalism. Clifford's essay "On Ethnographic Self-Fashioning: Conrad and Malinowski," first published in 1985, has thus been taken as an undermining of the scientific model of ethnographic authority that Malinowski did so much to make the professional standard, an undermining carried out in large part by invidious juxtaposition with the messily literary, unsystematic, unprofessional figure of Conrad.[20] "By professionalizing fieldwork," Clifford writes, "anthropology transformed a widespread predicament into a scientific method" (95). Conrad, who acknowledges the same (cosmopolitan) predicament without escaping into scientific method, thus seems to embody the literary as an alternative to the professional.

If this were all, it would be manifestly insufficient. For, as Paul Rabinow pointed out in his contribution to *Writing Culture,* it would leave Clifford no way of acknowledging the fact that, however "literary" his style, in relation to the anthropologists who are his subjects, he too is playing a professional role. "There is only one 'professional,' so to speak, in the crowd," Rabinow comments. "For, whereas all the others mentioned are practicing anthropologists, James Clifford has created and occupied the role of ex officio scribe to our scribblings. . . . Clifford takes us as his natives" (242). A "new specialty is currently in the process of self-definition," Rabinow says (242). But Clifford's "own writing and situation," which define this specialty, "are left unexamined" (244).[21]

This sort of tit-for-tat, in which injurious epithets like "specialist," "professional," and "metropolitan" are asked to stand in for substantive political judgment, must always be the result as long as it is assumed that to go ahead and *examine* one's professional "writing and situation," to open one's eyes finally and painfully to the "situatedness" of a metropolitan or a cosmopolitan, is ipso facto to judge oneself intolerably contaminated and self-contradictory. One of the extraordinary strengths of Clifford's work is that this is an assumption he has come increasingly to question. If one looks more closely at the Conrad/Malinowski essay, one sees that in fact neither "professional" nor "cosmopolitan" functions there as a term of opprobrium. A struggle with "cosmopolitanism" (95), we are told, is something Conrad and Malinowski have in common. And the essay is about a "difficult accession to innovative *professional* expression" (96—my italics) that they also have in common.

And that Clifford himself has in common with them as well. The last line of this extremely moving essay is an ambiguous quotation from Conrad's Marlow: "You see me, whom you know." The point of the ambiguity seems clear: the essay can itself be read as an allegory of vocation describing a "difficult accession to innovative professional expression" shared not only by Conrad and Malinowski, but by Clifford too, along with many of his readers. One might think of the essay, then, as just that act of professional self-examination that Rabinow found lacking in *Writing Culture*. Much of its power comes from the extra work it does to redescribe and legitimate the work of the *historian* of anthropology along with that of the anthropologist, the professional, second-order work of criticism as well as the "primary," "unprofessional" work of the novelist.

In Clifford's allegorical reading of Conrad, "Heart of Darkness" becomes an alternative model of writing that is no less professional than Malinowski's professional ethnography. The decisive difference between them is that Conrad includes the experience of fashioning and self-fashioning, the activity of selecting and discarding, that goes into any ethnographic writing. His fiction includes the exclusions—the Lie to the Intended, the tearing off of Kurtz's "Exterminate the brutes!" from the official report—

exclusions that are inevitable in all professional discourse. Professional discourse, the moral would seem to go, cannot be purified; it can only be saved by its ironic self-consciousness of its impurity.

We may or may not feel that this solution "works"—that it rises above, say, irony as a mode or style of living with exclusion too comfortably. But in fact this is only one of two resolutions to the dilemma of professional exclusiveness that the essay explores. After all, why *is* exclusion inevitable? On the one hand, Clifford suggests that, like fiction, even the most scientific discourse selects and fashions and invents. Here only self-consciousness will help. On the other hand, however, he also suggests that the Lie to the Intended and the tearing off of "Exterminate the brutes!" are exclusions produced not by representation in general, but more precisely by the writer's or professional's deliberate act of loyalty to the arbitrary limits of his chosen culture. Marlow, Clifford says, "learns to lie—that is, to communicate within the collective partial fictions of cultural life" (99). Clifford tries to restrict the damage this will do as a paradigm of professional ethnography: the "ethnographic standpoint" is better represented, he adds, not by Marlow but by the second narrator, silently listening to him, who "salvages, compares, and (ironically) believes these staged truths." But this distinguishing of narrators does not seriously affect the result: professional writing seen as "local, partial knowledge," or more strongly (but relegated to a footnote), as "a positive choice for the 'lie of culture'" (99). "[L]ike Marlow's account aboard the *Nellie,* the truths of cultural descriptions are meaningful to specific interpretive communities in limiting historical circumstances" (112). The arbitrary, exclusive cultural wholeness that Malinowski imposes upon the Trobriands results from an arbitrary, even absurd act of self-defining allegiance to the professional community of English anthropologists. The ethnographer lies about his cultural objects, presenting them as more "local" than they are, in order to make himself a member of the "local" culture of his fellow professionals.

This is a dead end of professional self-definition from which ironic self-consciousness offers no hope of rescue. But Clifford does find a way out of it. The logic of self-rescue goes from "culture" to the "post-cultural" and finally back to the "cosmopolitan." If it is no longer feasible to think of the cultures studied by ethnography as distinct entities, as Clifford repeatedly suggests, then why assume that the professional culture *of ethnographers* is a distinct entity? If we must learn to see other cultures not as distinct, different wholes, but as mobile, fluid, hybrid, and inclusive, then why insist on a necessary and absolute exclusiveness in studying the culture that studies those cultures? In writing himself out of "culture" as an absurd but necessary (and necessarily exclusive) order, Clifford also writes himself out of "the profession" as a similarly necessary (and exclusive) absurdity. Instead of a dichotomy of professional describers of culture, on the one hand, and their non-professional objects of description, on the other, Clifford now assumes a "post-cultural" space where the subjects and objects of description are at least potentially reversible, where the mobility required for observation and comparison is not monopolized by one side, where the word "local" has lost much of its contrastive force. His name for this space—a space that is not exclusively professional—is "cosmopolitanism."

In the work that has followed *The Predicament of Culture*, Clifford has radically revised his opinion of cosmopolitanism.[22] Rather than speaking in the name of the local, as in the review of *Orientalism*, he has been pointing out the manifold abuses of "thinking local," the distortions involved in taking "the field" and "the village" as localizations of culture. He has been calling on anthropologists to bring back into their ethnographies the "cosmopolitan intermediaries" who intervene in and help constitute them, and "to focus on hybrid, cosmopolitan experiences as much as on rooted, native ones." Clifford can approve of cosmopolitanism because he has been seeing it, and teaching others to see it, as neither the consequence nor the prerogative of "totalizing Western liberalism"; he has been seeing it as something he himself shares with his subjects. It is not only gentlemen travellers, but the people of color who were the servants of those travellers, who have "specific cosmopolitan viewpoints." Even the organized coercion of migrant labor produces "cosmopolitan workers." "The notion that certain classes of people are cosmopolitan (travellers) while the rest are local (natives)" is only "the ideology of one (very powerful) travelling culture." Questions of power aside, "they" and "we" can no longer be divided as "local" and "cosmopolitan."

Thus the latter term becomes available again for general use. Instead of renouncing cosmopolitanism as a false universal, one can embrace it as an impulse to knowledge that is shared with others, a striving to transcend partiality that is itself partial, but no more so than the similar cognitive strivings of many diverse peoples. The world's particulars can now be recoded, in part at least, as the world's *"discrepant cosmopolitanisms."*

A final few words about how comparative attention to "discrepant cosmopolitanisms" can and cannot help us respond to the current backlash. In an article in *The New Yorker* which does its bit for this backlash, Cynthia Ozick comes to her conclusion on multiculturalism: "I would not wish to drop Homer or Jane Austen or Kafka to make room for an Aleutian Islander of lesser gifts, unrepresented though her group may be on the college reading list."[23] I take Clifford's reversal on cosmopolitanism as a hint that one of the various moves we might make against this use of the Aleutian Islander as an empty figure for pure particularity, and against the label of cultural particularism in general, is to fill the figure in, not just *as* a particular (worthy of the same respect as every other particular), but also, perhaps, as the carrier and embodiment of a certain cosmopolitanism. One might for example bring forward an essay by Claude Lévi-Strauss on the "cosmopolitanism" of native Americans along the Pacific Northwest coast. Apropos of the putative Westernness of the Great Ideas, one might emphasize the word "Egypt" on the first page—unfortunately, *only* on the first page—of an article called "The Greek Origins of the Idea of Cosmopolitanism," which reads as follows: "The earliest recorded formulation of this idea is supplied by modern archaeological discovery at Tell el-Amarna, in Egypt. Inscriptions have been found there, written by Akhnaton (pharaoh of Egypt from 1375 to 1358 BC)."[24] Or one might counter ethnocentrisms both right and left with cosmopolitanism like that of the last page of *I, Rigoberta Menchu:* "[M]y commitment to our struggle knows no boundaries nor limits. That's why I've travelled to many places. . . ."[25]

The scholarly project of accumulating instances of cosmopolitanism from around the globe could help us make the point that the concept is neither a Western invention nor a Western privilege. When the Right suggests that after all, there is ethnocentrism everywhere, that is, in the Third World too, the inevitable prelude to the suggestion that, after all, only in "the West" has there been any move away from it, we can then say not just that unequal power has made Eurocentrism qualitatively different in its effects from other ethnocentrisms. We can also say that we *value* the move away from ethnocentrism—in all the many places, Western and non-Western, where it has occurred. To take an empirical route out of the oversimple binary of universal and particular, rather than performing a merely logical or deconstructive exercise on it, would put the matter across to a broader audience, and it would also have the advantage of distinguishing cosmopolitanism from an abstract, ahistorical universalism. For it would bring out many diverse and overlapping syncretisms and secularisms[26] for which the term is an umbrella. (The opposition between religion and secularism itself might be one casualty of such a project.)

The limits of the term "cosmopolitanism" are also its conjunctural virtues. No one actually is or ever can be a cosmopolitan in the full sense of belonging everywhere. If such a thing were conceivable, it would not be desirable, for as Donna Haraway has pointed out, it could only exist in the form of complete cultural relativism.[27] The interest of the term cosmopolitanism is located, then, not in its full theoretical extension, where it becomes a paranoid fantasy of ubiquity and omniscience, but rather (paradoxically) in its local applications, where the unrealizable ideal produces normative pressure against such alternatives as, say, the fashionable "hybridization." Its provocative association with privilege is perhaps better understood, in this context, as the normative edge that cosmopolitanism tries to add to the inclusiveness and diversity of multiculturalism—as an attempt to name a necessary but difficult normativeness. The term is not as philosophically ambitious as the word "universalism," though it does some of the same work. (It makes room for moments of generalizing, one might say, without offering license for uninhibited universalizing.) Nor is it as politically ambitious as the word "internationalism." But it does start us asking what form such an internationalism might best take. The academy-bashing journalists have been suggesting that multiculturalism is nothing but an attempt to revive the naive Third Worldism of the 1960s, with its automatic division between Imperialist Bad Guys and Newly Independent Good Guys. It seems to me that the term cosmopolitanism better describes the sensibility of our moment. Now, as opposed perhaps to two or three decades ago, anti-imperialism has been and must be newly careful, skeptical, measured in its support of any nation. Recently and paradigmatically, it has had to learn to oppose Bush's war without defending Saddam Hussein. More generally, it has been to school with movements in the name of gender, class, and sexual orientation which, in Jean Franco's words, "have sprung up on the margins of the nation state" and "no longer couch cultural or political projects in national terms" (205).[28] Our moment, one might say, is that of the globalizing of such movements—a moment to which there would correspond, ideally, some new, de-nationalized internationalism.

If cosmopolitanism cannot deliver an explicitly and directly political program, it is at least a step toward this sort of internationalist political education. By suggesting that there is no uniquely correct place to stand, it can take some of the moralism out of our politics. Better still, by doing so it can liberate us to pursue a long-term process of trans-local connecting that is both political and educational at once. And in the midst of the short-term politico-educational crisis where we now find ourselves, it can designate a teaching of culture capable of mobilizing the energy and enthusiasm of a broad front of people who are not all or even predominantly leftists, whatever the right may think. As a practice of comparison, a range of tolerances and secularisms, an international competence or mode of citizenship that is the monopoly of no one class or civilization, it answers the charges of "particularism" and "loss of standards," insisting confidently that multiculturalism is a common program, a critical program, a positive ideal of interconnected knowledge and pedagogy, that elevates rather than lowers existing educational standards.[29] If you doubt its power, listen to Sylvia Wynter's critique of California's new, insufficiently multicultural history texts. Wynter calls for a new framework which "seeks to go beyond the model of a nation-state coterminus only with Euro-immigrant America, to one coterminus as a 'world' civilization, with all its peoples; and therefore, for the first time in recorded history, coterminus (as a land that's not been yet but must be) with humankind."[30]

The word "cosmopolitan" comes from the Greek for "citizen of the world." In an international context, the model of citizenship is extremely problematic. In the absence of a world state—which at present seems unimaginable, or imaginable only as nightmare—the cosmopolitan cannot be to the globe as the citizen is to the nation, and to suggest the contrary is to create dangerous illusions of global equality, responsibility, and voter-like control. To associate a citizen's rights and obligations with a cosmopolitan's knowledge is also to risk a new slide toward elitism. I'm moved to put it forward anyway, or at least to use it in pointing toward a site that some other term may fill better, largely because of the Gulf War, because of the failure of internationalism that the Gulf War illustrated, and because of my sense that the central task for intellectuals in this particular corner of North America is to do something about the desperate pretensions of this failing, flailing nation to act as world policeman. It seems to me that the knowledge that might have helped stop this war, and that might help stop American citizens from making or approving other wars like it, has a strong claim to be considered, in our own day, "the best that is known and thought." At any rate, to preserve and transmit such knowledge, trying to educate future citizens of the world rather than future world policemen, seems to me a task worthy of any humanist's intellectual curiosity and sympathetic imagination.

Notes

1. From *Social Text* 31/32 (1992), 169–86. Notes (some omitted here) are the author's.

2. Anne Matthews, "Deciphering Victorian Underwear and Other Seminars," *The New York Times Magazine,* February 10, 1991, 57.

3. As the word "our" suggests, I am primarily interested here in addressing people who, like myself, earn an uneasy living from cultural work in professions and institutions that sometimes seem aimed against the political and ethical principles which give that work such meaning as it has. Those who work elsewhere, or who escape such contradictions between work and politics by sustaining their radicalism without the help of tenure, will I hope pardon what may look like the self-indulgent narcissism of this exercise. Others will hopefully excuse what they may see as my evasion of personal detail.

4. Dinesh d'Souza, "Illiberal Education," *The Atlantic Monthly* (March 1991), 51–79.

5. Donna Haraway, "Situated Knowledge," *Simians, Cyborgs, and Women* (London: Free Association Books, 1990), 188.

6. V. S. Naipaul, "Our Universal Civilization," *New York Review of Books* (January 31, 1991), 22–25.

7. Rob Nixon, "London Calling: V. S. Naipaul and the License of Exile," *South Atlantic Quarterly,* 87:1 (1988), 1–37.

8. Tim Brennan, "India, Nationalism, and Other Failures," *South Atlantic Quarterly* 87:1 (1988), 131–146, 134–35.

9. Tim Brennan, "The National Longing for Form," Homi K. Bhabha, ed., *Nation and Narration* (London: Routledge, 1990), 44–70, 63.

10. George Boas, "Types of Internationalism in Early Nineteenth-Century France," *International Journal of Ethics* 38:1 (1927), 152.

11. It seems possible that the vocabulary of "celebrity" functions in cases like this to tarnish a given writer obliquely, that is, to do so without invoking the vocabulary of *class,* which is more seriously contaminating, on the one hand, but also too visibly contaminating for one's allies as well as one's enemies, hence often unusable.

12. This point has been forcefully articulated by Stanley Fish in "Anti-Professionalism," *Doing What Comes Naturally* (Durham: Duke University Press, 1989), 215–46.

13. Chandra Mohanty, "Under Western Eyes: Feminist Scholarship and Colonial Discourses," *boundary 2* (12:3/ 13:1, Spring/Fall 1984), pp. 333–58.

14. One thinks of the extraordinary universalizing of Lyotard's use of the Cashinahua Indians as figures for all of non-Western humanity in *The Postmodern Condition.*

15. Agency occupies much the same place in another equally classic polemic on behalf of Third World specificity, Kumkum Sangari's "The Politics of the Possible," *Cultural Critique* 6 (Fall 1987), 157–86.

16. Simon Duncan and Mike Savage, "Space, Scale, and Locality," *Antipode* 21:3 (1989), 179–206.

17. Neil Smith, "Dangers of the Empirical Turn," *Antipode* 19 (1987), 59–68.

18. Spivak, "Three Women's Texts and a Critique of Imperialism," *Critical Inquiry* 12 (1985), 243–62.

19. Ulf Hannerz, "Cosmopolitans and Locals in World Culture," Mike Featherstone, ed., *Global Culture, Theory, Culture and Society* 7 (London: Sage, 1990), 237–51.

20. Repr. in *The Predicament of Culture* (Cambridge: Harvard UP, 1988), 255–76.

21. Paul Rabinow, "Representations are Social Facts," *Writing Culture*, ed. James Clifford and George E. Marcus (Berkeley and Los Angeles: University of California Press, 1986), 258.

22. James Clifford, "Travelling Cultures," in Lawrence Grossberg, Cary Nelson, Paula Treichler, eds., *Cultural Studies* (New York: Routledge, 1992).

23. Cynthia Ozick, "A Critic At Large: T. S. Eliot at 101," *The New Yorker,* Nov. 20, 1989, 125. I discuss this passage at greater length in "Othering the Academy: Professionalism and Multiculturalism," *Social Research* (June 1991).

24. Hugh Harris, "The Greek Origins of the Idea of Cosmopolitanism," *The International Journal of Ethics* 38:1 (1927), 1.

25. Elisabeth Burgos-Debray, ed., *I, Rigoberta Menchú: An Indian Woman in Guatemala,* tr. Ann Wright. (London: Verso, 1984), 247.

26. This term would probably be a matter of dispute.

27. Haraway, "Situated Knowledges," 191.

28. Jean Franco, "The Nation as Imagined Community," H. Aram Veeser, ed., *The New Historicism* (New York: Routledge, 1989), 204–12.

29. For a forceful exposition of "critical multiculturalism," see the article of this title by the Chicago Cultural Studies Group, *Critical Inquiry* 18:3 (1992), 530–55.

30. Sylvia Wynter, quoted in Robert Reinhold, "Class Struggle," *The New York Times Magazine,* Sept 29, 1991, 47.

27

Literature, Nation, and Politics[1] (1999)

Pascale Casanova

Pascale Casanova's *La République mondiale des lettres* (*The World Republic of Letters*, 1999) has attracted attention around the world for its innovative discussion of world literature. Her book is the fruit of some two decades' work on twentieth-century literature, following a prize-winning book on the transnational author Samuel Beckett (*Beckett the Abstractor*, 1977). In a career as a literary critic and journalist and a researcher at the Center for Research in Arts and Language in Paris, Casanova developed an encyclopedic knowledge of contemporary literature and a keen interest in the politics of literary culture. Drawing on the work of historian Fernand Braudel and sociologist Pierre Bourdieu, Casanova undertakes a systematic historical and sociological analysis of the production and circulation of literature in the world. She argues that, starting in the sixteenth century and with Paris as its center, a world republic of letters—a semiautonomous field of literature—began to emerge in which literature gained and produced a distinct kind of value or cultural capital. While fundamentally bound up in the development of the modern nation-state, the field of literature is not uniquely determined by political history, but establishes its own distinct system of power relations.

The World Republic of Letters is particularly valuable for the powerful analysis it provides of the basic inequality of the literary field of world literature, an inequality which comes into particularly sharp focus when writers from the periphery (Kafka, Ramuz, Yacine, Chamoiseau among others) seek to gain admittance to a world centered on metropolitan

spaces such as Paris. At the same time, however, canonical French literature has increasingly drawn its energy from writers and works coming
into Parisian literary space. In the following selection of her book, Casanova describes the historical emergence of the world republic of letters
and reflects on the implications of adopting a hard-edged sociological
perspective on the global dimensions of literature.

The particular case of Paris, denationalized and universal capital of the literary world, must not make us forget that literary capital is inherently national. Through its essential link with language—itself always national, since
invariably appropriated by national authorities as a symbol of identity—
literary heritage is a matter of foremost national interest.[2] Because language
is at once an affair of state and the material out of which literature is made,
literary resources are inevitably concentrated, at least initially, within the
boundaries of the nation itself. Thus it is that language and literature
jointly provide political foundations for a nation and, in the process, ennoble each other.

The National Foundations of Literature

The link between the state and literature depends on the fact that, through
language, the one serves to establish and reinforce the other. Historians
have demonstrated a direct connection between the emergence of the first
European states and the formation of "common languages" (which then
later became "national languages").[3] Benedict Anderson, for example, sees
the expansion of vernaculars, which supplied administrative, diplomatic,
and intellectual support for the emerging European states of the late fif-
teenth and early sixteenth centuries, as the central phenomenon underlying the appearance of these states.[4] From the existence of an organic
bond, or interdependence, between the appearance of national states, the
expansion of vernaculars into common languages, and the corresponding
development of new literatures written in these vernaculars, it follows that
the accumulation of literary resources is necessarily rooted in the political
history of states.

More precisely, both the formation of states and the emergence of literatures in new languages derive from a single principle of differentiation. For it was in distinguishing themselves from each other, which is to say in asserting their differences through successive rivalries and struggles, that states in Europe gradually took shape from the sixteenth century onward, thereby giving rise to the international political field in its earliest form. In this embryonic system, which may be described as a system of differences (in the same sense in which phoneticists speak of language as a system of differences), language evidently played a central role as a "marker" of difference. But it also represented what was at stake in the contests that took place at the intersection of this nascent political space and the literary space that was coming into existence at the same time,[5] with the paradoxical result that the birth of literature grew out of the early political history of nation-states.

The specifically literary defense of vernaculars by the great figures of the world of letters during the Renaissance, which very quickly assumed the form of a rivalry among these "new" languages (new in the literary market), was to be advanced equally by literary and political means.[6] In this sense the various intellectual rivalries that grew up during the Renaissance in Europe may be said to have been founded and legitimized through political struggles. Similarly, with the spread of nationalist ideas in the nineteenth century and the creation of new nations, political authority served as a foundation for emerging literary spaces. Owing to the structural dependence of these new spaces, the construction of world literary space proceeded once more through national rivalries that were inseparably literary and political.

From the earliest stages of the unification of this space, national literary wealth, far from being the private possession of nations whose natural "genius" it was supposed to express, became the weapon and the prize that both permitted and encouraged new claimants to enter international literary competition. In order to compete more effectively, countries in the center sought to define literature in relation to "national character" in ways that in large measure were themselves the result of structural opposition and differentiation. Their dominant traits can quite often be understood—as in the cases of Germany and England, rising powers seeking to challenge French hegemony—in deliberate contrast with the recognized characteristics of the predominant nation. Literatures are therefore not a pure emanation of national identity; they are constructed through literary rivalries, which are always denied, and struggles, which are always international.

Given, then, that literary capital is national, and that there exists a relation of dependence with regard first to the state, then to the nation, it becomes possible to connect the idea of an economy peculiar to the literary world with the notion of a literary geopolitics. No national entity exists in and of itself. In a sense, nothing is more international than a national state: it is constructed solely in relation to other states, and often in opposition to them. In other words, no state—neither the ones that Charles Tilly calls "segmented" (or embryonic) nor, after 1750, "consolidated" (or national) states, which is to say the state in its modern sense—can be described as a separate and autonomous entity, the source of its own existence and coherence.[7] To the contrary, each state is constituted by its relations with other states, by its rivalry and competition with them. Just as the state is a relational entity, so the nation is inter-national.

The construction (and reconstruction) of national identity and the political definition of the nation that developed later, notably during the course of the nineteenth century, were not the product of isolated experience, of private events unfolding behind the ramparts of an incomparable and incommensurate history. What nationalist mythologies attempt to reconstitute (after the fact, in the case of the oldest nations) as autarkic singularities arise in reality only from contact between neighboring peoples. Thus Michael Jeismann has been able to demonstrate that Franco-German antagonism—a veritable "dialogue des ennemis"—permitted nationalism to flourish in each country in reaction against a perceived "natural" enemy.[8] Similarly, Linda Colley has shown that the English nation was constructed through and through in opposition to France.[9]

The analysis of the emergence of nationalism needs to go beyond the assumption of a binary and belligerent relation between nations to take into account a much more complex space of rivalries that proceed both for and through a variety of forms of capital, which may be literary, political, or economic. The totality of world political space is the product of a vast range of national competition, where the clash between two historical enemies—such as the one described by Danilo Kiš between Serbs and Croats—represents only the simplest and most archaic form.[10]

Depoliticization

Little by little, however, literature succeeded in freeing itself from the hold of the political and national authorities that originally it helped to establish and legitimize. The accumulation of specifically literary resources, which involved the invention and development of a set of aesthetic possibilities, of forms, narrative techniques, and formal solutions (what the Russian formalists were to call "procedures")—in short, the creation of a specific history (more or less distinct from national history, from which it could no longer be deduced)—allowed literary space gradually to achieve independence and determine its own laws of operation. Freed from its former condition of political dependency, literature found itself at last in a position to assert its own autonomy.

Writers, or at least some of them, could thus refuse both collectively and individually to submit to the national and political definition of literature. The paradigm of this refusal is undoubtedly Zola's "J'accuse."[11] At the same time, international literary competition, now also detached from strictly national and political rivalries, acquired a life of its own. The spread of freedom throughout world literary space occurred through the autonomization of its constituent spaces, with the result that literary struggles, freed from political constraints, were now bound to obey no other law than the law of literature.

Thus, to take an example that is apparently most unfavorable to the argument I am making, the German literary renaissance at the end of the eighteenth century was associated in part with national issues, being the literary counterpart to the founding of the German nation as a political entity. The rise of the idea of a national literature in Germany is explained first by political antagonism with France, then the culturally dominant power in Europe. Isaiah Berlin in particular has argued that German nationalism had its roots in a sense of humiliation:

The French dominated the western world, politically, culturally, militarily. The humiliated and defeated Germans . . . responded, like the bent twig of the poet Schiller's theory, by lashing back and refusing to accept their alleged inferiority. They discovered in themselves qualities far superior to those of their tormentors. They contrasted their own deep, inner life of the spirit, their own profound humility, their selfless pursuit of true values—simple, noble, sublime—with the rich, worldly, successful, superficial, smooth, heartless, morally empty French. This mood rose to fever pitch during the national resistance to Napoleon, and was indeed the original exemplar of the reaction of many a backward, exploited, or at any rate patronized society, which, resentful of the apparent inferiority of its status, reacted by turning to real or imaginary triumphs and glories in its past, or enviable attributes of its own national or cultural character.[12]

The prodigious development of German literary culture, beginning in the second half of the eighteenth century, was therefore initially connected with matters of immediate political import: to insist on cultural grandeur was also a way of affirming the unity of the German people beyond the fact of its political disunion. But the arguments that were employed, the principles that were at issue in the debates of the period and the very form that these debates assumed, the stature of the greatest German poets and intellectuals, their poetical and philosophical works, which were to have revolutionary consequences for all of Europe, and for French literature in particular—all these things gradually gave German romanticism an exceptional degree of independence and a power all its own. In the German case, romanticism was, and at the same time was not, national; or, rather, it was national to start with and then subsequently detached itself from national authority. As a consequence, the challenge to French dominance in literature in the nineteenth century needs to be analyzed on the basis of the literary, rather than the political, history of the two countries.

Similarly, notwithstanding differences of time and place, Latin American writers managed in the twentieth century to achieve an international existence and reputation that conferred on their national literary spaces (and, more generally, the Latin American space as a whole) a standing and an influence in the larger literary world that were incommensurate with those of their native countries in the international world of politics. Here, as in the German case, literature enjoys a relative autonomy when the accumulation of a literary heritage—which is to say the international recognition that attaches to writers who are designated by critics in the center as "great" writers—enabled national literary cultures to escape the hold of national politics. As Valery Larbaud pointed out, the literary and intellectual map cannot be superimposed upon the political map, since neither literary history nor literary geography can be reduced to political history. Nonetheless, literature remains relatively dependent on politics, above all in countries that are relatively unendowed with literary resources.

World literary space has therefore developed and achieved unity in accordance with a parallel movement that, as we shall see, is ordered in relation to two antagonistic poles. On the one hand, there is a progressive enlargement of literary space that accompanies the spread of national independence in the various parts of the world. And, on the other, there is a tendency toward autonomy, which is to say literary emancipation in the face of political (and national) claims to authority.

The original dependence of literature on the nation is at the heart of the inequality that structures the literary world. Rivalry among nations arises from the fact that their political, economic, military, diplomatic, and geographical histories are not only different but also unequal. Literary resources, which are always stamped with the seal of the nation, are therefore unequal as well, and unequally distributed among nations. Because the effects of this structure weigh on all national literatures and on all writers, the practices and traditions, the forms and aesthetics that have currency in a given national literary space can be properly understood only if they are related to the precise position of this space in the world system. It is the hierarchy of the literary world, then, that gives literature its very form. This curious edifice, which joins together writers from different spaces whose mutual rivalry is very often the only thing they have in common—a rivalry whose existence, as I say, is always denied—was constructed over time by a succession of national conflicts and challenges to formal and critical authority. Unification of the literary world therefore depends on the entry of new contestants intent upon adding to their stock of literary capital, which is both the instrument and the prize of their competition: each new player, in bringing to bear the weight of his national heritage—the only weapon considered legitimate in this type of struggle—helps to unify international literary space, which is to say to extend the domain of literary rivalry. In order to take part in the competition in the first place, it is necessary to believe in the value of what is at stake, to know and to recognize it. It is this belief that creates literary space and allows it to operate, despite (and also by virtue of) the hierarchies on which it tacitly rests.

The internationalization that I propose to describe here therefore signifies more or less the opposite of what is ordinarily understood by the neutralizing term "globalization," which suggests that the world political and economic system can be conceived as the generalization of a single and universally applicable model. In the literary world, by contrast, it is the competition among its members that defines and unifies the system while at the same time marking its limits. Not every writer proceeds in the same way, but all writers attempt to enter the same race, and all of them struggle, albeit with unequal advantages, to attain the same goal: literary legitimacy.

It is not surprising, then, that Goethe elaborated the notion of *Weltliteratur* precisely at the moment of Germany's entry into the international literary space. As a member of a nation that was a newcomer to the game, challenging French literary and intellectual hegemony, Goethe had a vital interest in understanding the reality of the situation in which his nation now found itself. Displaying the perceptiveness commonly found among newcomers from dominated communities, not only did he grasp the international character of literature, which is to say its deployment outside national limits; he also understood at once its competitive nature and the paradoxical unity that results from it.

A New Method of Interpretation

These resources—at once concrete and abstract, national and international, collective and subjective, political, linguistic, and literary—make up the specific heritage that is shared by all the writers of the world. Each writer enters into international competition armed (or unarmed) with his entire literary "past": by virtue solely of his membership in a linguistic area and a national grouping, he embodies and reactivates a whole literary history, carrying this "literary time" with him without even being fully conscious of it. He is therefore heir to the entire national and international history that has "made" him what he is. The cardinal importance of this heritage, which amounts to a kind of "destiny" or "fate," explains why even the most international authors, such as the Spaniard Juan Benet or the Serb Danilo Kiš, conceive of themselves, if only by way of reaction against it, in terms of the national space from which they have come. And the same thing must be said of Samuel Beckett, despite the fact that few writers seem further removed from the reach of history, for the course of his career, which led him from Dublin to Paris, can be understood only in terms of the history of Irish literary space.

None of this amounts to invoking the "influence" of national culture on the development of a literary work, or to reviving national literary history in its traditional form. Quite the contrary: understanding the way in which writers invent their own freedom—which is to say perpetuate, or alter, or reject, or add to, or deny, or forget, or betray their national literary (and linguistic) heritage—makes it possible to chart the course of their work and discover its very purpose. National literary and linguistic patrimony supplies a sort of a priori definition of the writer, one that he will transform (if need be, by rejecting it or, as in the case of Beckett, by conceiving himself in opposition to it) throughout his career. In other words, the writer stands in a particular relation to world literary space by virtue of the place occupied in it by the national space into which he has been born. But his position also depends on the way in which he deals with this unavoidable inheritance; on the aesthetic, linguistic, and formal choices he is led to make, which determine his position in this larger space. He may reject his national heritage, forsaking his homeland for a country that is more richly endowed in literary resources than his own, as Beckett and Michaux did; he may acknowledge his patrimony while trying at the same time to transform it and, in this way, to give it greater autonomy, like Joyce (who, though he left his native land and rejected its literary practices and aesthetic norms, sought to found an Irish literature freed from nationalist constraints); or he may affirm the difference and importance of a national literature, like Kafka, as we shall see, but also like Yeats and Kateb Yacine. All these examples show that, in trying to characterize a writer's work, one must situate it with respect to two things: the place occupied by his native literary space within world literature and his own position within this space.

Determining the position of a writer in this way has nothing to do with the usual sort of national contextualization favored by literary critics. On the one hand, national (and linguistic) origin is now related to the hierarchical structure of world literature as a whole; and, on the other hand, it is recognized that no two writers inherit their literary past in exactly the same fashion. Most critics, however, are led by a belief in the singularity and originality of individual writers to privilege some aspect of their biography that hides this structural relation. Thus, for example, the feminist critic who studies the case of Gertrude Stein concentrates on one of its aspects—the fact that she was a woman and a lesbian—while forgetting, as though it were something obvious not needing to be examined, that she was American.[13] Yet the United States in the 1920s was literarily a dominated country that looked to Paris in order to try to accumulate resources it lacked. Any analysis that fails to take into account the world literary structure of the period and of the place occupied in this structure by Paris and the United States, respectively, will be incapable of explaining Stein's permanent concern to develop a modern American national literature (through the creation of an avant-garde) and her interest in both American history and the literary representation of the American people (of which her gigantic enterprise *The Making of Americans* is no doubt the most outstanding proof).[14] The fact that she was a woman in the community of American intellectuals in exile in Paris is, of course, of crucial importance for understanding her subversive impulses and the nature of her aesthetic ambitions. But the deeper structural relationship, obscured by critical tradition, remains paramount. Generally speaking, one can point to some feature of every writer's career—important, to be sure, but nonetheless secondary—that conceals the structural pattern of literary domination.

The dual historicization proposed here makes it possible not only to find a way out from the inevitable impasse of literary history, which finds itself relegated to a subordinate role and accused of being powerless to grasp the essence of literature; it also allows us to describe the hierarchical structure of the literary world and the constraints that operate within it. The inequality of the transactions that take place in this world goes unperceived, or is otherwise denied or euphemistically referred to, because the ecumenical picture it presents of itself as a peaceful world, untroubled by rivalry or struggle, strengthens received beliefs and assures the continued existence of a quite different reality that is never admitted. The simple idea that dominates the literary world still today, of literature as something pure and harmonious, works to eliminate all traces of the invisible violence that reigns over it and denies the power relations that are specific to this world and the battles that are fought in it. According to the standard view, the world of letters is one of peaceful internationalism, a world of free and equal access in which literary recognition is available to all writers, an enchanted world that exists outside time and space and so escapes the mundane conflicts of human history. This fiction, of a literature emancipated from all historical and political attachments, was invented in the most autonomous countries of world literary space. It is in these countries, which for the most part have managed to free themselves from political constraints, that the belief in a pure definition of literature is strongest, of literature as something entirely cut off from history, from the world of nations, political and military competition, economic dependence, linguistic domination—the idea of a universal literature that is nonnational, nonpartisan, and unmarked by political or linguistic divisions. It is perhaps not surprising, then, that very few writers at the center of world literature have any idea of its actual structure. Though they are familiar with the constraints and norms of the center, they fail to recognize them as such since they have come to regard them as natural. They are blind almost by definition: their very point of view on the world hides it from them, for they believe that it coincides with the small part of it they know.

The irremediable and violent discontinuity between the metropolitan literary world and its suburban outskirts is perceptible only to writers on the periphery, who, having to struggle in very tangible ways in order simply to find "the gateway to the present" (as Octavio Paz put it), and then to gain admission to its central precincts, are more clearsighted than others about the nature and the form of the literary balance of power.[15] Despite these obstacles, which are never acknowledged—so great is the power of denial that accompanies the extraordinary belief in literature—they nonetheless manage to invent their own freedom as artists. It is by no means a paradox, then, that authors living today on the edges of the literary world, who long ago learned to confront the laws and forces that sustain the unequal structure of this world and who are keenly aware that they must be recognized in their respective centers in order to have any chance of surviving as writers, should be the most sensitive to the newest aesthetic inventions of international literature, from the recent attempts of Anglo-Saxon writers to devise a worldwide cross-fertilization of styles to the latest narrative techniques of Latin American novelists, among others. This lucidity, and the impulse to rebel against the existing literary order, are at the very heart of their identity as writers.

For all these reasons, ever since French hegemony reached its height at the end of the eighteenth century, radical challenges to the existing literary order have appeared in the most impoverished territories of the international republic of letters, shaping and lastingly modifying its structure, which is to say the very forms of literature. Particularly with Herder, the challenge to the French monopoly on literary legitimacy succeeded so well in establishing itself that an alternative pole was able to be created. But it is nonetheless true that dominated men and women of letters have often been incapable of grasping the reasons for their special lucidity. Even if they are clearsighted with regard to their particular position and to the specific forms of dependency in which they are caught up, their perception of the global structure of which they are a part remains incomplete.

Notes

1. From *The World Republic of Letters*, trans. M. B. DeBevoise (Cambridge: Harvard University Press, 2004), 34–44. First published as *La République mondiale des lettres* (Paris: Seuil, 1999). Notes are the author's.

2. The terms "nation" and "national" are used here for the sake of convenience, while taking care to guard against the risk of anachronism.

3. See particularly Daniel Baggioni, *Langues et nations en Europe* (Paris: Payot, 1997), 74–77. Baggioni distinguishes between "common" and "national" languages in order to avoid confusion and anachronism.

4. See Benedict Anderson, *Imagined Communities: Reflections on the Origin and Spread of Nationalism* (London: Verso, 1983).

5. Thus Jacques Revel has been able to show how languages were very gradually associated (through maps) with spaces delimited by "linguistic boundaries." See Daniel Nordman and Jacques Revel, "La formation de l'espace français," in *Histoire de la France*, ed. André Burguière and Jacques Revel, 4 vols. (Paris: Seuil, 1989–1993), I: 155–162.

6. The Italian poet Bembo, du Bellay and Ronsard in France, Thomas More in England, Sebastian Brant in Germany all took part in the humanist movement, advocating a return to ancient literatures while defending their own "illustrious vulgar tongue" (in Dante's phrase).

7. See Charles Tilly, *European Revolutions, 1492–1992* (Oxford: Blackwell, 1993), 29–36.

8. See Michael Jeismann, *Das Vaterland der Feinde: Studien zum nationalen Feindbegriff und Selbstverständnis in Deutschland und Frankreich, 1792–1918* (Stuttgart: Klett-Cotta, 1992).

9. See Linda Folley, *Britons: Forging the Nation, 1707–1837* (New Haven: Yale University Press, 1992).

10. Danilo Kiš, *La Leçon d'anatomie*, trans. Pascale Delpech (Paris: Fayard, 1993), 29–31.

11. In the Dreyfus Affair, Zola abruptly broke with everything that until then had linked the writer with the nation, national honor, and nationalist discourse, and, by betraying the nationalist right, proclaimed his own autonomy. He thereby put himself in a position, in the very name of his own autonomy and freedom, to proclaim Dreyfus' innocence. This amounted to inventing a totally new relation to politics: a sort of denationalized politicization of literature.

12. Isaiah Berlin, "The Bent Twig: On the Rise of Nationalism," in *The Crooked Timber of Humanity: Chapters in the History of Ideas*, ed. Henry Hardy (New York: Knopf, 1991), 246.

13. This neglect is due also the primacy always accorded in literary criticism to the "psychology" of the writer.

14. Originally published in an edition of 500 copies, printed in Dijon in 1925 by Maurice Darantière for Contact Éditions of Paris.

15. Octavio Paz, *In Search of the Present: 1990 Nobel Lecture*, bilingual ed., trans. Anthony Stanton (San Diego: Harcourt Brace Jovanovich, 1990), 17.

28

Comparative Literature in China[1] (2000)

Zhou Xiaoyi and Q. S. Tong

The past several decades have seen a steady growth worldwide in the establishment of programs and national associations of comparative literature. Nowhere has this growth been more pronounced than in mainland China, where programs and courses have been established at some sixty institutions since the end of the Cultural Revolution. The following article is by two Chinese scholars closely engaged with new developments in comparative and East/West studies. Zhou Xiaoyi works in English literature at Beijing University. He received his Doctor of Philosophy degree from Lancaster University in 1993 and was Research Fellow at the University of Hong Kong between 1997 and 2000. Zhou has published widely on English and comparative literature, literary theory, and cultural studies, and is the author of *Beyond Aestheticism: Oscar Wilde and Consumer Society* (Beijing University Press, 1996). Q. S. Tong works in English literature at the University of Hong Kong. His publications include "Reinventing China: The Use of Orientalist Views on the Chinese Language" in *Interventions: International Journal of Post-Colonial Studies* 2.1 (2000). He has also co-edited *Critical Zone: A Forum of Chinese and Western Knowledge* (2004, 2006).

In their essay, Zhou and Tong outline the history of comparative literature in China, analyzing the uses of non-Western literature in the construction of Chinese modernity. They then undertake a searching critique of the current wave of comparative study as caught up in following

Western theoretical fads, and they argue for the need to move beyond the old alternatives of stark binarisms on the one hand, and vague universalism on the other.

On the landscape of modern Chinese literary scholarship, comparative literature is perhaps one of the most versatile and active fields of study. As an academic discipline and a mode of intellectual inquiry and scholarly production, comparative literature was imported to China from the West, via Japan, in the early twentieth century. At a time of major intellectual and social shifts of the country and when many Chinese writers, artists, as well as scholars took upon themselves to reform traditional values and practices, radical intellectuals such as Hu Shi, Chen Duxiu, Lu Xun, and Zhou Zuoren, among others, advocated the importation and acceptance of Western thought. Parallel to this and as a natural result of the said interest, the translation of Western works became a national enterprise and the domains of literature experienced an unprecedented influx of new concepts, formulations, approaches, and practices. In the scholarship of literature new areas of study were established and comparative literature was one of them.

The term comparative literature was first used by the poet and critic Huang Ren (1866–1913), professor of literature at Suzhou University, in his lecture notes where he refers to Posnett's 1886 *Comparative Literature* (see Xu 109). Next, Lu Xun (1881–1936), father of modern Chinese literature, encountered Western writings on comparative literature while he was a student in Japan. In a letter he wrote in 1911 to Xu Shoushang, Lu mentions the Japanese translation of Frédéric Loliée's 1906 *Histoire des littératures comparées des origines au XXe siècle* (see Lu Vol. 11, 331) and he has used the comparative method in his work as early as 1907 (see Lu Vol. 1, 63–115). In the early twentieth century, when in China Western culture and thought gained much currency, in literary scholarship a discipline that explores Chinese and Western literatures would have its natural appeal.

The general interest in the subject and approach resulted in a series of translations of Western works. For example, Fu Donghua, a translator of considerable repute, translated and published in 1930 Loliée's *Histoire des littératures comparées,* and Paul Van Tieghem's *La Littérature comparée* was brought out in Chinese in 1936 by the poet Dai Wangshu (1905–50), only five years after its publication in Paris in 1931. Further, poets Zhang Xishen and Wang Fuquan, respectively, translated from Japanese and French works on comparative literature: Zhang's translations appeared in the journal *New China* in the 1920s, later reprinted by the Commercial Press, and Wang's translations were published as a series in *Awakening: The Supplement of Republican Daily* (1924).

These texts not only popularized comparative literature but also made it possible to formally institute it as an academic subject in university education. The establishing of comparative literature as a field of study at National Tsinghua University (Beijing) in the 1920s is probably one of the most important events in the early history of comparative literature in China. At Tsinghua, courses on or closely related to comparative literature included Wu Mi's "Zhongxishi zhi bijiao" ("Comparative Studies of Chinese and Western Poetics") in 1926 and Chen Yinke's "Xiren zhi dongfangxue muluxue" ("Bibliography of Sinology") in 1927. And I. A. Richards, who was a visiting professor at Tsinghua University from 1929 to 1931, also taught comparative literature while at Tsinghua (see Xu 111). By the mid-1930s, comparative literature as an academic subject and a mode of cross-cultural inquiry was firmly established and was to further develop into a prominent discipline in the history of modern Chinese literary scholarship. The period from the 1930s to the 1950s is the most formative time for the discipline in China. Then, after a period of twenty years of silence,[2] came another active period, from the late 1970s to the early 1990s.

In these two main periods, series of books in the field appeared, either authored by Chinese scholars or translated into Chinese from various Western languages. In our brief survey it is not possible to record in detail all the major developments of comparative literature in China. However, here we sketch some significant moments. Our purpose is to consider the intellectual and historical conditions under which comparative literature has obtained such remarkable popularity and prominence in Chinese scholarship and to show that the development and currency of comparative literature is closely related to the formation of China's literary modernity.

Comparative Literature in China, 1920s to the 1950s

In the early decades of the twentieth century, comparative literature in China was preoccupied with literary and cultural encounters between China and three major cultural sites: India, Russia, and Europe. As is well-known, Indian religious culture has had enormous influence on Chinese culture and literature since Buddhism entered China. For instance Buddhist fables were quickly appropriated and transformed into some of the most famous Chinese narratives in fiction. Later, Buddhist thought constituted an important source of inspiration for Tang poetry,[3] manifested often in the poet's epiphanic understanding of the essence of nature and life in seemingly detached descriptions of landscapes or natural objects. Wang Wei, for example, typically in some of his best-known poems, fuses Zen Buddhist understanding with natural surroundings, in such an empathetic mode that the poetic self and the natural other become a totality. Although Buddhism has been a very significant source of inspiration for Chinese literary production, it is not until the first half of the twentieth century that Chinese scholars, by then equipped with Western concepts and methodologies from of comparative literary studies, begin to examine the influence of Buddhism on Chinese literature and for that matter on Chinese culture as a whole. In literary studies, work by Hu Shi, Chen Yinke, and Ji Xianlin represent outstanding achievements in the field.

Hu Shi (1891–1962) studied with John Dewey and after his return to China became, together with Chen Duxiu and Lu Xun, a prominent leader of the new cultural movement. He advocated the importance of textual exegesis and achieved a great deal himself in his own practice of textual criticism. In his seminal article, "Xi you ji kaozheng" ("Studies of *Journey to the West*"), he identifies Indian sources in this classic Chinese novel. As a leader of the new cultural movement and an admirer of Western scholarship and knowledge, Hu Shi, in directing his readers' attention to the influence of Buddhism on Chinese culture, suggests an underlying political agenda. For him, it is of vital importance for China to look beyond its boundaries and to adopt modern Western knowledge in order to reinvigorate Chinese literature and Chinese culture as a whole. Similar to Hu Shi, Ji Xianlin (1911–), who spent about ten years in Germany between 1925 and 1945, has an abiding interest in Indian culture and has devoted almost all his life to the study of its influences on Chinese tradition.

Although he has been much less involved politically, his research methodology manifests an understanding of modern scholarship that is not totally ideologically innocent. Modern Chinese literature is to a great extent influenced by Russian and Soviet literature, respectively. Since the publication of Lu Xun's "Kuangren riji" ("The Diary of a Madman"), the first text of Chinese modernity, Russian and Soviet literature have been instrumental in the development of modern Chinese literature. A whole generation of Chinese writers such as Mao Dun, Jiang Guangci, Guo Moruo, Shen Congwen, Ai Wu, Xia Yan, Ba Jin, and Sha Ting at some stage showed great interest in Russian and Soviet literature and all were influenced by them to various degrees. Thus, given this importance of Russian and Soviet literature in modern Chinese literature, the study of their reception in China has been a prominent theme of Chinese comparative literary studies. An early example is Zhou Zuoren's "Wenxue shang de erguo yu zhongguo" ("Russia and China in Literature," 1920), in which Zhou, although offering no case studies comparing Russian and Chinese writers, suggests that the two literary traditions share some similarities in terms of their analogous social and political conditions (see Zhou 5–8). Zhou's analysis in fact suggests the immediate relevance of Russian literature to Chinese literary production and anticipates the centrality of Russian-Soviet literary influence in modern Chinese literature.

Admittedly, the discourse of Chinese revolutionary literature after the 1930s is pervasively tinctured with a Russo-Soviet literary ethos. In responding to this unique aspect of modern Chinese literature, critical studies of Chinese reception of Russian-Soviet literature became a major strand of comparative literary studies in China between the 1940s and 1950s. For example, Ge Baoquan has published between 1956 and 1962 a series of essays on Russian writers and their influence on Chinese authors and their texts, Han Changjing and Feng Xuefeng published on Lu Xun and Russian literature, and others such as Ye Shuifu, Feng Zhi, and Ge Yihong wrote on Russian-Soviet literature in China. Of course, that Russian-Soviet literature acquired such high visibility in modern Chinese literature and, consequently, received a large amount of critical attention is by no means extraordinary considering the close political ties between China and the Soviet Union in the 1950s (see, e.g., Xu 241–48).

In Chinese comparative literature concerning Indian and Chinese literature and Russian and Chinese literature, it is noticeable that much of the scholarly attention is focused on how Chinese literature and Chinese culture have been influenced by inspirations drawn from India and Russia, respectively, and comparatively. In contrast, critical inquires into the encounters between Chinese literature and European literature have been largely centered on China's influence on Europe, in particular on English-language literature. In the case of the latter, scholars such as Chen Shouyi, Fang Zhong, and Fan Cunzhong contributed significantly to our historical knowledge of early cultural encounters between England and China in the seventeenth and eighteenth centuries. Chen Shouyi was probably the first one who systematically studied the reception of Chinese literature in Europe. As early as in the 1920s he published a number of studies on the circulation of Chinese literary works in Europe.

Among his other studies, Chen studied the process in which the Chinese play "Zhaoshi Guer" ("The Orphan of the Zhaos") was translated into English, French, German, and Russian, and examined how it was received and parodied in the West. This play is arguably the single most influential Chinese literary work before the nineteenth century in Europe, and a whole group of European authors including Voltaire and Goethe on the continent and Richard Hurd, William Hatchett, and Arthur Murphy in England showed intensive interest in this "exotic" story.

Fang Zhong (1902–91), who studied in Britain and the United States, continued to research in this extraordinarily rich field: In his essay "Shiba shiji yingguo wenxue yu zhong guo" ("Eighteenth-Century English Literature and China") (1931), he discusses English imagination and exoticism as revealed in its discursive formulations about the remote and mysterious "Cathay." Fang divides the English reception of China in the eighteenth century into three stages: From the early eighteenth century to 1740, from 1740 to 1770, and the remaining decades after 1770. According to Fang, in the first stage, China begins to increase its visibility in British consciousness as seen in Addison and Steele's writings. In the second stage, a number of writers such as Oliver Goldsmith and Horace Walpole use extensively cultural resources from China. In the last phase, interest in China generally wanes in England, although John Scott, for example, employs Chinese materials in his poetry. Fang argues that in the eighteenth century China is considered a fascinating culture in a positive context while it is only in the nineteenth century that this image of China changes. Like many Chinese scholars of comparative literature, Fang Zhong attempts to present a narrative of the formation of English literary knowledge about China and explains the formations of rationalized historical processes in which changes in the English idea or image of China maybe fully explained.

However, history is far richer than our theoretical imagination. While China is viewed as a model of human civilization in the eighteenth century, China is at the same time regarded as an example of corruption and degeneration. For instance Robinson Crusoe's account of China from a negative point of view or James Beattie's views on the Chinese language are other representations of matters Chinese in the late eighteenth century. Fan Cunzhong's studies of Chinese literature in England are built on a massive amount of primary sources and the scope of the topics covered in these articles shows that Fan, in a systematic way, attempts to examine the formation of the English idea of China by offering detailed case studies.

Fan Cunzhong's and Fang Zhong's studies represent major steps in the study of English literary knowledge of China in the eighteenth century. At the same time, we note that so far no major studies exist of Chinese literature in nineteenth-century England although we know that English knowledge of China in the nineteenth century continued to expand. Even after the Opium War (1840–42),[4] for instance, there were several exhibitions of Chinese culture organized in England and some nineteenth-century English authors including Thomas de Quincey produced a substantial amount of writing on China. This gap in comparative literary scholarship is significant. For one, scholars in Chinese comparative literature appear to be curiously selective in the choice of their topics. In the eighteenth century when China as a country and a cultural phenomenon was generally held or imagined as an alternative model of civilization for the West, the European reception of the Chinese political system, the Chinese way of life, and Chinese attitudes and ideas would seem to be more gratifying topics for Chinese scholars. Although Western discursive formations of the idea and image of China are mostly manifestations of the Western fancy for the exotic Other, China, presented as such, would help build a sense of national pride (see Fan 1984).

In the 1950s, although scholars in comparative literature such as Ji Xianlin and Fan Cunzhong continue to be productive in their areas, it is generally agreed that their research was largely a continuation of their earlier work without being able to offer new insights or present new materials. From the 1960s to the 1970s, comparative literature is silent: One obvious explanation for this is that the political situation in China during the time permitted no studies of Western literature, and comparative literature, by definition, is concerned with foreign literature, and thus the interregnum. Obviously, the political exclusion of comparative literature was a consequence of Mao's cultural policy and an extension of the establishment of political uniformity in the domain of literary studies.

Comparative Literature in China, 1970s to the 1990s

In the West, with the adoption of literary and culture theory beginning with the late 1960s by English and other single-language studies, comparative literature—the discipline where literary and culture theory occupied a prominent position since its inception—has been attracting increasingly less interest and more and more students of literature have turned away from it for a number of reasons. As an academic discipline, comparative literature increasingly has lost its vigor and radicalism seen in the 1950s and the 1960s and now it appears a discipline waiting to be replaced by cultural studies or translation studies not necessarily taught and worked on in departments of comparative literature. Intellectually, the option to redirect comparative literature into cultural studies and/or translation studies has been suggested, for example, by Susan Bassnett in her widely quoted *Comparative Literature: A Critical Introduction* (1993) and she suggests that comparative literature as a discipline is "dead" (47).

While all this may indeed be the situation of the discipline, to various degrees, in the West, in the non-Western world including China, comparative literature has enjoyed an amazing and sustained popularity. Specifically in China, since the late 1970s comparative literature has been one of the most prominent areas of research, attracting a large number of scholars and students. This extraordinary popularity of comparative literature after the 1970s has been construed as a continuity of its establishment in the 1930s and 1940s, and Chinese scholars in comparative literature tend to disagree with Bassnett's pronouncements. Instead, they prefer, in general, to turn to the classics of Western comparative literature such as Wellek and Warren's *Theory of Literature* for a theoretical defense and legitimization of the practice of comparative literature, one that is built on the assumption of the existence of commonalities of cultures.[5]

Indeed, one of the main concerns of Chinese comparative literature in the new period is to legitimize itself as a discipline and to reestablish its centrality in the Chinese system of literary scholarship. Again, one useful way to reinforce the discipline's importance is to make available Western works on comparative literature in Chinese. Thus, in the period in question most seminal texts in English, French, and German have been translated into Chinese. In addition, a number of anthologies of critical essays on comparative literature have been published. Following this intellectual revival, the Chinese renaissance of comparative literature is now solidified in its institutionalization as well, to the point that after 1987 even public interest in comparative literature is manifest in the media. A spate of articles, essays, reviews, etc., appeared in Chinese newspapers, thus forming a public forum on comparative literature. Scholars from the older generation such as Ji Xianlin, Ge Baoquan, Fang Zhong, Yang Zhouhan, Li Funing, Fan Cunzhong, Qian Zhongshu, and Jia Zhifang all participated in this extraordinary public discussion of the uses of comparative literature in China. Soon comparative literature found its way into the university classroom on a massive scale. Since Shi Zhecun offered in 1987 his course of comparative literature, the first of its kind after 1949, more than sixty institutions in China have established comparative literature as an academic subject before the end of the 1990s (see Liu and Wang 107–10).

In retrospect, admittedly, translations of Western works on literary theory revitalized and perhaps reinvented comparative literature as one of the most liberal areas of study and research in China. During the period to the 1990s, the remarkable nationwide enthusiasm for comparative literature brought out a large number of publications in the field, most of which are visibly concerned with either new critical methodologies in the discipline or the historiography of comparative literature. Arguably, Chinese scholars of comparative literature are generally well informed of the latest critical developments in the West and have an unfailing interest in quickly turning more influential theoretical publications into Chinese. Translation in China has been a national enterprise and has played an instrumental part in the making of China's literary modernity. However, the choice of Western texts for translation often reveals the needs of China's self-fashioning rather than recognition of their inherent values. In the field of comparative literature, René Wellek and Austin Warren and Henry H.H. Remak (e.g., 1961) are the most translated Western scholars because some of their formulations can be readily appropriated for legitimating and strengthening comparative literature, not just as an academic discipline but as an agency enabling a dialogical relationship between Chinese and Western literary traditions and thereby allowing Chinese literature to be integrated into a world system of literature. Embedded in this desire to have a direct and equal dialogue with other literary traditions is the conviction of the existence of a common system of valuation in culture akin to Goethe's much debated notion of *Weltliteratur*.

In the 1980s, a central theme of comparative literature in China was constructed on the belief in an innate aesthetic value of literary production that was not determined by time and space but is universally shared. The notion of literariness in American New Criticism was understood as a textual quality that defines what literature is and this was rapidly transformed into a principle of critical practice. This focus on literariness in the 1980s represents a major shift from the practice of comparative literature in the 1930s, which, as suggested above, was primarily concerned with archeological discoveries of major foreign cultural sources that found their way into Chinese literature.

The Function of Comparative Literature in China

The renaissance and rise of comparative literature in China in the period up to the 1990s are both a result and a source of energy for China's literary modernity. As a discursive literary and critical practice, as a mode and a subject of literary studies, its development mirrors China's social developments in the twentieth century. Although imported and adapted from the West, Chinese comparative literature has gone through a different passage of evolution. In the 1930s and 1940s what attracted most scholarly attention in the field was the intellectual excitement derived from discoveries of early histories of China's encounters with the West and India, for example, similar to the French school of comparative literature. However, in the 1980s Chinese comparative literature, inspired by formulations of American New Criticism, found its own path of progress and process. The large number of Western critical works translated into Chinese during this period were either works by the New Critics or by those associated with them. The resurrection of New Criticism in Chinese comparative literature, both methodological and theoretical, and its notion of literariness have been appropriated into a critical dogma that refuses to consider literature as a social, historical, and political discourse. This approach in Chinese comparative literature in practice refuses to allow the discipline to be incorporated into cultural studies. Thus, generally speaking, Chinese comparative literature in the 1980s has been exclusively interested in its own self-fashioning and showed a visible indifference to the rise of critical discourse with regard to postmodernism in the Euro-American world, a discourse and critical practice that challenges forms of essentialism including the essentialist notion of literariness.

Ganesh Devy argues that the rise of comparative literature in India is closely tied to the rise of Indian nationalism and that as such has much to do with the politics of identity. In turn, Bassnett considers Devy's view applicable to the rise of comparative literature in the West: The term comparative literature in "Europe . . . first appeared in an age of national struggles, when new boundaries were being erected and the whole question of national culture and national identity was under discussion throughout Europe and the expanding United States of America" (Bassnett 8–9). To consider the historical origin of comparative literature as a discipline is at the same time to specify its political and ideological provenance. Not just in India and the Euro-American world, but also in China, the advent of comparative literature is, historically speaking, interwoven with the narration of nation as a strategy of forming national identity.

In the 1930s and 1940s, a large amount of comparative literary studies were primarily concerned with the possibilities of comparison between Chinese literary productions and those elsewhere, interested in searching for common themes and motifs among them or similarities among writers. Arbitrary comparisons were widely practiced and imposed upon authors or texts that have no relationships whatsoever. For example, Zhao Jingshen, in his study of Chinese Yuan drama, compares Shakespeare with Tang Xianzu, simply on the basis of the closeness of the dates of birth of the two. And his comparison of Li Yu and Molière is triggered by his observation that "they both wrote comedies" (Zhao 278–83). Zhao Jingshen was a playwright and might be excused for the crudeness of his studies, but comparisons of this kind have been a very popular approach among prominent scholars in Chinese comparative literature. Comparative studies of Li Po and Goethe by Liang Zongdai, Chinese and Western dramaturgy by Bin Xin, and Chinese and Western poetics by Zhu Guangqian tend to be conducted on the basis of observed similarities and are generally devoid of genuine insights and interesting observations (see *Zhongguo bijiao wenxue yanjiu ziliao* [Research materials on Chinese comparative literature] 1989, 226–31, 244–65, 240–43, 208–19).

The lack of intellectual rigour of comparative studies of this kind is attributable to a misinformed notion of comparative literature as nothing but "comparison" that, in practice, encourages comparative studies for the sake of comparison. However, the great amount of enthusiasm for this approach among scholars of comparative literature is indicative of a hidden agenda of Chinese comparative literature. In Zhu Guangqian's study, for example, Western and Chinese views on love and nature are compared. And some of the differences between them, according to Zhu, can be only fully appreciated with recognition of the differences between Chinese national characteristics and their Western counterparts. National characteristics are indeed often understood as the causes of differences or similarities between cultural traditions. What is manifest in this type of comparative studies is then an attempt to foreground, by comparing China and the West in terms of their generalized national traits, the uniqueness of Chinese national temperament as if it were a real category that could be grasped and comprehended.

Chinese comparative literature therefore is heavily self-referential, and other literary traditions brought in for comparison serve as a Lacanian mirror image in which the self might be understood and constructed, as it were. It is precisely through such comparisons that Fan Cunzhong, for example, has experienced the feeling of national pride in Goldsmith's or Johnson's encomia of China, and it is also through comparisons of this kind that the value and worth of Chinese culture are reconfirmed. It is, then, obvious that the advocacy of the importance of "literariness" as a theme of comparative literary studies in China has an underlying ideological agenda, for the very notion of "literariness" legitimates comparisons between authors, texts, and literary practices regardless of their historical and social specificities and encompasses them in a world system of literature. It is then no surprise that the American New Criticism and Russian Formalism constituted the most important sources of theoretical authority for the practice of comparative literature in China, and some of the most distinguished practitioners of comparative literature in China have either translated works by the New Critics and Formalists or written about them. The influence of New Criticism is still visible today, as manifested in the scholarly tenacity of holding the text as the only legitimate object of study and regarding culture as only providing a context in which "literariness" of the text can be grasped.

In relation to this notion of comparative literature is the desire to build a Chinese school of comparative literature. John Deeney argues, for example, that it is necessary to look seriously into the possibility of a "Third World" comparative literature by employing the mode of Chinese thinking in comparative studies. The Chinese school of comparative literature, according to him, must start with the firm establishment of the sense of China's cultural identity, which will evolve gradually into the stage of self-consciousness (see Deeney 266).

The call for a Chinese school of comparative literature met with enthusiastic responses on the Mainland. In our opinion, however, a careful examination of this proposal for a Chinese school of comparative literature shows a lack of substance as well as impracticality. What underscores this proposal is a politics of recognition that aims to establish Chinese comparative literature as an equal partner on the international stage of comparative literature. In this sense, this movement toward a Chinese school of comparative literature is a strategic one rather than one that is motivated by serious theoretical considerations. The rise and development of Chinese comparative literature in the twentieth century are closely bound up with China's national project of modernization, inspired and supported by Western Enlightenment values. Its renaissance in the late 1970s after the Cultural Revolution further testifies to its close intellectual relation to Enlightenment values and humanism. Since the mid-nineteenth century, the idea or ideal of modernity has been haunting Chinese consciousness. Faced with the real danger of China being dismembered by Western powers and Japan in the early twentieth century, Chinese intellectuals embraced Enlightenment values and practices and were convinced that rationalism, equality, and technological improvement were solutions to what Bertrand Russell once called "the problem of China."

But this total acceptance of Enlightenment values and practices has been very costly, as it inevitably means a total acceptance, as a starting point, of such binaries as the traditional and the modern and China and the West as reality. It is known that binarism of this kind has been used as a familiar strategy to configure global economy, centralizing and marginalizing at the same time cultures in an imagined map of world civilizations. Those cultures placed marginally in this global configuration are thus caught in the crisis generated from their own uncertainty about their sense of identity. This is, for example, why Hu Shi, in his comparative studies of Chinese and Indian literature, came to the conclusion that China should learn from the West. The desire to dislocate China from its marginal position and to reposition it in relation to the centrality of Western culture has been a cause of the developments of comparative literature in China. Some of the most frequently asked questions include: Why is there no epic in Chinese literature and why is there no tragedy in China? (e.g., Zhu 220–25). But why should there be such genres in Chinese literature?

Looking back at some of the concerns of Chinese scholars of comparative literature, one is necessarily struck by the lack of sophistication and naiveté with which their critical inquiries have been conducted. But those imagined issues, those perceived differences between Chinese and Western literature have unfortunately trapped some of the most distinguished Chinese scholars owing to the said binary mode of thinking. To identify gaps, incongruities, and differences between Chinese and Western literary traditions and practices, in the ultimate analysis, is to reconfirm the existence of the universality of certain literary qualities, values and practices, by which those very gaps, incongruities and differences might be examined. This belief of the universal applicability of literary values is nowhere more manifest than in the pursuit of textual "literariness" and in the call for the establishing of a Chinese school of comparative literature. The former is to extend the New Critics' critical practice into the study of Chinese literary production and the latter is largely for the purpose of popularizing indigenous literary practices and presenting them as indispensable not only for the Chinese but for all cultures.

Chinese comparative literature as a critical practice may thus be considered a product of China's pursuit of modernity in the twentieth century. The crisis of comparative literature that has been a cause of concern for scholars in China in recent years registers, in fact, a deeper level of crisis that is also the crisis of the ideological and political foundation of comparative literature—its conviction in the existence of the universality of literary values. In recent years, the Enlightenment project with all its paradoxes has been brought under close critical scrutiny in the West; and the deconstruction of Eurocentrism has serious ramifications. Under this new intellectual condition, the ideology of comparative literature has been accordingly questioned, and it is no longer possible, intellectually at least, to conduct comparative studies on the basis of binarism without serious and careful modifications. The crisis of comparative literature is the crisis of the ideological understanding of the function of comparative literature, but it may constitute an opportunity to reinvent comparative studies in response to the challenges of recent critical developments.

There is now increasing awareness in China of the invalidity of structuring comparative studies on the principle of binarism. For example, Lydia Liu's *Translingual Practice: Literature, National Culture, and Translated Modernity—China, 1900–1937* (1995) represents much needed new development in cross-cultural studies and thus comparative literature. What is particularly relevant in terms of Liu's work in its critical methodology is her careful discussion of how power relationships are embodied in some of the concepts and keywords that have traveled to China and how these power relationships generate(d) social realities through translingual practice. Liu's study reaches far beyond the scope of orthodox comparative literary studies concerned only with cross-cultural influence and reception or with questions like why and how cross-cultural influence is exercised and what determines cross-cultural reception. If comparative literature wishes to overcome its own perpetual crises, it has to get rid of the rigidity of its self-definition, it has to reach beyond the level of literature and must direct its attention to other forms of cultural production, including literature. And in this sense, it perhaps matters very little how it should be called: Comparative literature or (cross-)cultural studies. And we propose that this notion is applicable to both Chinese comparative literature and comparative literature in the West and elsewhere.

Works Cited

Bassnett, Susan. *Comparative Literature: A Critical Introduction*. Oxford: Blackwell, 1993.
Brunel, Pierre, Claude Pichois, and André Rousseau. *Shenmo shi bijiao wenxue?* (What is comparative literature?). Tr. Ge Lei. Beijing: Peking UP, 1989.

Chen Shouyi. "Shiba shiji ouzhou wenxue li de Zhaoshi guer" ("The Orphan of the Zhaos in Eighteenth-Century European Literature"). *Lingnan xuebao* (*The Journal of Lingnan College*) 1.1 (1929): 114–46.

Deeney, John. "Bijiao wenxue zhongguo xuepai" ("The Chinese School of Comparative Literature"). *Bijiao wenxue yanjiu zhi xinfaangxiang* (New orientations for comparative literature). By John Deeney. Taipei: Lianjing, 1986. 265–70.

Devy, Ganesh N. "The Commonwealth 'Period' and Comparative Literature." *Aspects of Comparative Literature: Current Approaches*. Ed. Chandra Mohan. New Delhi: India Publishers, 1989, 144–53.

Fan Cunzhong. "Shiqiba shiji yingguo liuxing de zhongguo xi" ("Popular Chinese Dramatic Works in England in the Seventeenth and Eighteenth Centuries"). *Qingnian zhongguo* (Youthful China) 2.2 (1940): 172–86.

———. "Shiqiba shiji yingguo liuxing de zhongguo sixiang" ("Popular Chinese Thoughts in England in the Seventeenth and Eighteenth Centuries"). *Wenshizhe jikan* (Literature, history and philosophy quarterly) 1.2–3 (1943).

———. "Qiongsi jueshi yu zhongguo wenhua." 1947. ("Sir William Jones and Chinese Culture"). *Zhongguo bijiao wenxue yanjiu ziliao* (Research materials on Chinese comparative literature). Beijing: Peking University Press, 1989. 168–84.

———. "Zhaoshi guer zaju zai qimeng shiqi de yingguo" ("The Chinese Orphan in the England of the Age of Enlightenment." 1957. *Bijiao wenxue lunwenji* (Comparative literature studies: A collection). Ed. Zhang Longxi and Wen Rumin. Beijing: Peking UP, 1984. 83–120.

Fang Zhong. "Shiba shiji yingguo wenxue yu zhong guo." 1931. ("Eighteenth-Century English literature and China"). *Zhongguo bijiao wenxue yanjiu ziliao* (Research materials on Chinese comparative literature). Beijing: Peking University Press, 1989, 137–67.

Guyard, Marius-François. *Bijiao wenxue* (*La Littérature comparée*). Trans. Yan Bao. Beijing: Peking University Press, 1983.

Hu Shi. "Xi you ji kaozheng" ("Studies of *A Journey to the West*"). *Hu Shi Gudian Wenxue Yanjiu Lunji* (Studies in classical literature). Shanghai: Shanghai guji chubanshe, 1988, 886–923.

Jost, François. *Bijiao wenxue daolun* (Introduction to comparative literature). Trans. Liao Bingjun. Changsha: Huanan wenyi chubanshe, 1988.

Liu, Lydia. *Translingual Practice: Literature, National Culture, and Translated Modernity—China, 1900–1937*. Stanford: Stanford University Press, 1995.

Liu Xianbiao and Wang Zhenmin. *Bijiao wenxue yu xiandaiwenxue* (Comparative literature and modern literature). Hangzhou: Zhongguo meishu chubanshe, 1994.

Loliée, Frédéric A. *Bijiao wenxueshi* (*Histoire des littératures comparées des origines au XXe siècle*). Trans. Fu Donghua. Shanghai: The Commercial Press, 1930.

Lu Xun. *Lun Xun quanji* (Collected works of Lu Xun). 16 Vols. Beijing: Renmin wenxue chubanshe, 1981.

Miner, Earl. *Bijiao shixue* (*Comparative Poetics*). Trans. Wang Yugeng and Song Weijie. Beijing: Zhongyang bianyi chubanshe, 1998.

Posnett, Hutcheson Macaulay. *Comparative Literature*. 1886. New York: Johnson, 1970.

Remak, Henry H. H. "Bijiao wenxue de dingyi yu gongyong" ("Comparative Literature: Its Definition and Function"). 1961. *Bijiao wenxue yangjiu ziliao* (Materials in comparative literature studies). Ed. Research Group in Comparative Literature, Beijing Normal University. Beijing: Beijing Normal University Press, 1986.

Van Tieghem, Paul. *Bijiao wenxue lun* (*La Littérature comparée*). Trans. Dai Wangshu. 1936. Taipei: Commercial Press, 1995.

Wellek, René, and Austin Warren. *Wenxue lilun* (*Theory of Literature*). 1949. Trans. Liu Xiangyu, Xing Peiming, Chen shengsheng, and Li Zheming. Beijing: Sanlian shudian, 1984.

Xu Yangshang. *Zhongguo bijiao wenxue yuanliu* (Origins and developments of comparative literature in China). Zhengzhou: Zhongzhou guji chubanshe, 1998.

Zhao Jingshen. "Tang xianzu yu shashibiya" ("Tang Xianzu and Shakespeare"). *Zhongguo bijiao wenxue yanjiu ziliao* (Research materials on Chinese comparative literature). Beijing: Peking University Press, 1989. 278–83.

Zhongguo bijiao wenxue yanjiu ziliao (Research materials on Chinese comparative literature). Beijing: Peking University Press, 1989.

Zhou Zuoren. "Wenxue shang de erguo yu zhongguo" ("Russia and China in Literature." 1920. *Zhongguo bijiao wenxue yanjiu ziliao* (Research materials on Chinese comparative literature). Beijing: Peking University Press, 1989. 5–12.

Zhu Guangqian. "Changpianshi zai zhongguo heyi bufada" ("Why Is there No Epic in Chinese Literature"). *Zhongguo bijiao wenxue yanjiu ziliao* (Research materials on Chinese comparative literature). Beijing: Peking University Press, 1989. 220–25.

Notes

1. From the electronic journal *Comparative Literature and Culture* 2:4 (2000); http://clcwebjournal.lib.purdue.edu/clcweb00-4/zhou&tong00.html. Reprinted in *Comparative Literature and Comparative Cultural Studies*, ed. Steven Tötösy de Zepetnek (West Lafayette, Ind.: Purdue University Press, 2003), 268–83.

2. A reference to the period of the Cultural Revolution under Mao Zedong during the 1960s and 1970s, when many intellectuals were sent to work in fields and factories, and study of foreign cultures was sharply curtailed.

3. Classical poetry written during the Tang Dynasty (618–907).

4. The war waged by England in China in support of the lucrative opium trade, following efforts by the Chinese government to ban the sale and use of opium.

5. René Wellek and Austin Warren published their widely cited and often translated *Theory of Literature* in 1949.

29

From *Translation, Community, Utopia* (2000)

Lawrence Venuti

One of the world's leading theorists of translation, Lawrence Venuti is also
an accomplished practicing translator; he has published vivid translations
of a range of nineteenth- and twentieth-century Italian works, including
Dino Buzzati's experimental short story collection *Restless Nights*, the
sexually charged lyrics of Antonia Pozzi's *Breath*, and Iginio Torchetti's
gothic novel *Passion*. Professor of English at Temple University, Venuti has
written widely on translation, most notably in *The Scandals of Translation:
Towards an Ethics of Difference* (1992) and *The Translator's Invisibility: A
History of Translation* (1995). In his books, Venuti argues for the importance of recognizing the translator's role as a crucial mediator between
cultures and eras, and he advances a theory of "foreignizing" translation
as an alternative to the common tendency of translations to assimilate
foreign works to host-country values. His essay "Translation, Community,
Utopia" serves as the conclusion to his encyclopedic anthology, the
Routledge *Translation Studies Reader* (2d ed., 2004). In this essay, Venuti
develops an argument for translation as a vehicle for creating a utopian
space of intercultural connection and communication.

> Language is a repository of ancient errors and a treasury of potential truths.
> —Jean-Jacques Lecercle

An Antinomy in Theory

Even though no one seems likely to deny that communication is the primary aim and function of a translated text, today we are far from thinking that translating is a simple communicative act. In contemporary translation theory informed by Continental philosophical traditions such as existential phenomenology and poststructuralism, language is constitutive of thought, and meaning a site of multiple determinations, so that translation is readily seen as investing the foreign-language text with a domestic significance (see, for example, Heidegger 1975, Lewis 2004, Benjamin 1989). Translation never communicates in an untroubled fashion because the translator negotiates the linguistic and cultural differences of the foreign text by reducing them and supplying another set of differences, basically domestic, drawn from the receiving language and culture to enable the foreign to be received there. The foreign text, then, is not so much communicated as inscribed with domestic intelligibilities and interests. The inscription begins with the very choice of a text for translation, always a very selective, densely motivated choice, and continues in the development of discursive strategies to translate it, always a choice of certain domestic discourses over others. Hence, the domesticating process is totalizing, even if never total, never seamless or final. It can be said to operate in every word of the translation long before the translated text is further processed by readers, made to bear other domestic meanings and to serve other domestic interests.

Seen as domestic inscription, never quite cross-cultural communication, translation has moved theorists towards an ethical reflection wherein remedies are formulated to restore or preserve the foreignness of the foreign text (see, for example, Berman 2004, and Venuti 1995, 1998). Yet an ethics that counters the domesticating effects of the inscription can only be formulated and practiced primarily in *domestic* terms, in domestic dialects, registers, discourses, and styles. And this means that the linguistic and cultural differences of the foreign text can only be signaled indirectly, by their displacement in the translation, through a domestic difference introduced into values and institutions at home. This ethical attitude is therefore simultaneous with a political agenda: the domestic terms of the inscription become the focus of rewriting in the translation, discursive strategies where the hierarchies that rank the values in the domestic culture are disarranged to set going processes of defamiliarization, canon reformation, ideological critique, and institutional change. A translator may find that the very concept of the domestic merits interrogation for its concealment of heterogeneity and hybridity which can complicate existing stereotypes, canons, and standards applied in translation.

When motivated by this ethical politics of difference, the translator seeks to build a community with foreign cultures, to share an understanding with and of them and to collaborate on projects founded on that understanding, going so far as to allow it to revise and develop domestic values and institutions. The very impulse to seek a community abroad suggests that the translator wishes to extend or complete a particular domestic situation, to compensate for a defect in the translating language and literature, in the translating culture. As Maurice Blanchot argues, the very notion of community arises when an insufficiency puts individual agency into question (Blanchot 1988: 56). The ethically and politically motivated translator cannot fail to see the lack of an equal footing in the translation process, stimulated by an interest in the foreign, but inescapably leaning towards the receptor. This translator knows that translations never simply communicate foreign texts because they make possible only a domesticated understanding, however much defamiliarized, however much subversive or supportive of the domestic.

In the absence of cross-cultural communication unaffected by domestic intelligibilities and interests, what kinds of communities can translation possibly foster? What communities can be based on the domestic inscription of the foreign that limits and redirects the communicative aim of translation?

Communication in Translation

In the 1970s, the formalist theorist Gideon Toury tried to define translation as a communicative act while acknowledging the domestic values that come into play, the target norms that constrain communication. Translation, he wrote,

> is communication in translated messages within a certain cultural-linguistic system, with all relevant consequences for the decomposition of the source message, the establishment of the invariant, its transfer across the cultural-linguistic border and the recomposition of the target message. (Toury 1980: 17; his emphasis)

"The establishment of the invariant": if communication in translation is defined as the transmission of an invariant, doesn't the very need to establish the invariant mean that translating does something more and perhaps other than communicate? The source message is always interpreted and reinvented, especially in cultural forms open to interpretation, such as literary texts, philosophical treatises, film subtitling, advertising copy, conference papers, legal testimony. How can the source message ever be invariant if it undergoes a process of "establishment" in a "certain" target language and culture? It is always reconstructed according to a different set of values and always variable according to different languages and cultures. Toury ultimately reckoned with the problem of communication by sidestepping it altogether: he shifted the emphasis away from exploring an equivalence between the translation and the foreign text and instead focused on the acceptability of the translation in the target culture. Thinking about the foreign is thus preempted in favor of research that describes domestic cultural norms.

But let's pursue this preempted line of enquiry. What formal and thematic features of a foreign novel, for instance, can be described as invariant in the translation process? Since canons of accuracy vary according to culture and historical moment, definitions of what constitutes the invariant will likewise vary. Let's ask the question of current translation practices. Today, translators of novels into most languages seek to maintain unchanged the basic elements of narrative form. The plot isn't rewritten to alter events or their sequence. And none of the characters' actions is deleted or revised. Dates, historical and geographical markers, the characters' names—even when the names are rather complicated and foreign-sounding—these are generally not altered or only in rare cases (e.g. Russian names). Contemporary canons of accuracy are based on an adequacy to the foreign text: an accurate translation of a novel must not only reproduce the basic elements of narrative form, but should do so in roughly the same number of pages.

In 1760, however, Abbé Prévost claimed that accuracy governed his French version of Samuel Richardson's *Pamela* even though he reduced the seven English volumes to four in French. "I have not changed anything pertaining to the author's intention," the Abbé asserted, "nor have I changed much in the manner in which he put that intention into words" (Lefevere 1992: 39). To us, such statements don't merely substitute a different canon of accuracy (founded on notions of authorial intention and style); they also seem to exceed the very genre of translation. Prévost's text involved abridgement and adaptation as well.

In current practices, a translation of a novel can and must communicate the basic elements of narrative form that structure the foreign-language text. But it is still not true that these elements are free from variation. Any language use is likely to vary the standard dialect by sampling a diversity of substandard or minor formations: regional or group dialects, jargons, clichés and slogans, stylistic innovations, archaisms, neologisms. Jean-Jacques Lecercle calls these variations the "remainder" because they exceed communication of a univocal meaning and instead draw attention to the conditions of the communicative act, conditions that are in the first instance linguistic and cultural, but that ultimately embrace social and political factors (Lecercle 1990). The remainder in literary texts is much more complicated, of course, usually a sedimentation of formal elements and generic discourses, past as well as present (Jameson 1981: 140–1).

Any communication through translating, then, will involve the release of a domestic remainder, especially in the case of literature. The foreign text is rewritten in domestic dialects and discourses, registers and styles, and this results in the production of textual effects that signify only in the history of the receiving language and culture. The translator may produce these effects to communicate the foreign text, trying to invent domestic analogues for foreign forms and themes. But the result will always go beyond any communication to release target-oriented possibilities of meaning.

Consider a recent English translation of an Italian novel, *Declares Pereira,* Patrick Creagh's 1995 version of Antonio Tabucchi's *Sostiene Pereira* (1994). Creagh's English consists mostly of the current standard dialect. But he cultivated a noticeable strain of colloquialism that sometimes veers into underworld argot. He rendered "taceva" ("silent") as "gagged," "quattro uomini dall'aria sinistra" ("four men with a sinister air") as "four shady-looking characters," "stare con gli occhi aperti" ("stay with your eyes open") as "keep your eyes peeled," "un personaggio del regime" ("a figure in the regime") as "bigwig," "senza pigiama" ("without pajamas") as "in his birthday-suit," and "va a dormire" ("go to sleep") as "beddy-byes" (Tabucchi 1994: 13, 19, 43, 73, 108, 196; Creagh 1995: 5, 9, 25, 45, 67, 127). Creagh also mixed in some distinctively British words and phrases. He rendered "orrendo" ("horrible") as "bloody awful," "una critica molto negativa" ("a very negative criticism") as "slating," "pensioncina" ("little boarding house") as "little doss-house," "sono nei guai" ("I'm in trouble") as "I'm in a pickle," "parlano" ("they talk") as "natter," and "a vedere" ("to look") as "to take a dekko" (Tabucchi 1994: 80, 81, 84, 104, 176; Creagh 1995: 50, 51, 54, 64, 115).

Within parentheses I have inserted alternative renderings to highlight the range and inventiveness of Creagh's translating. The alternatives should not be regarded as somehow more accurate than his choices. In each case, both renderings establish a lexicographical equivalence, a similarity to the Italian text consistent with dictionary definitions. Creagh's choices communicate meanings that can be called "invariant" only insofar as they are reduced to a basic meaning shared by both the Italian and the English.

Creagh's translation, however, varies this meaning. The variation might be called a "shift" as that concept has been developed in translation studies since the 1960s (see, for example, Catford 1965; Blum-Kulka 2004; Toury 1995). If Creagh's English is juxtaposed to Tabucchi's Italian, lexical shifts can indeed be detected, shifts in register from the current standard dialect of Italian to various colloquial dialects in British and American English. In response to my queries, Creagh admitted that "some phrases are more colloquial in English than in Italian," making clear that his shifts are not required by structural differences between the two languages, but rather motivated by literary and cultural aims: "I even tried," Creagh stated, "to use only idioms that would have been current in 1938," the period of the novel, "and to hand them to the right speaker, to make slight linguistic differences between the characters" (personal correspondence: 8 December 1998).

Yet the notion of a shift does not entirely describe the textual effects set going by Creagh's choices. His translation signifies beyond his literary and cultural intentions by releasing a peculiarly English remainder: the different dialects and registers establish a relation to English literary styles, genres, and traditions. In terms of generic distinctions, Tabucchi's novel is a political thriller. Set under the Portuguese dictator António de Oliveira Salazar, it recounts how one Pereira, the aging cultural editor of a Lisbon newspaper, is slowly radicalized over a few weeks which climax when he prints an attack on the fascist regime. Creagh's polylingual mixture of standard and colloquial, British and American, gives his prose an extremely conversational quality that is consistent with Tabucchi's presentation of the thriller plot: Pereira's narrative takes an oral form, an official testimony to an unnamed authority (hence the curious title). Yet the slangy English also alters the characterization of Pereira by suggesting that he is less staid and perhaps younger than the elderly journalist presented in the Italian text.

At the same time, the British and American slang refers to moments in the history of English-language fiction. It recalls thrillers that address similar political themes, notably such novels of Graham Greene as *The Confidential Agent* (1939), which, like Tabucchi's, is set during the Spanish Civil War and involves an attempt to aid the Republican side against Franco. By virtue of this literary reference, Creagh's translation in effect invites the reader to distinguish between Tabucchi's leftwing opposition to fascism and Greene's more cautious liberalism (Diemert 1996: 180–1). Greene saw his thrillers as "entertainments" engaged in social and political issues, designed "not to change things but to give them expression" (Allain 1983: 81). The linguistic resemblances between Creagh's translation and Greene's novel highlight the ideological differences that distinguish Tabucchi's and Greene's treatments of the same historical event.

Thus, although Creagh's translation can be said to communicate the form and theme of Tabucchi's novel, neither of these features escapes the variations introduced by the inscription of an English-language remainder. The remainder does not just inscribe a domestic set of linguistic and cultural differences in the foreign text, but supplies the loss of the foreign-language differences which constituted that text. The loss occurs, as Alasdair MacIntyre has observed, because in any "tradition-bearing community" the "language-in-use is closely tied to the expression of the shared beliefs of that tradition," and this gives a "historical dimension" to languages which often fails to survive the translating process (MacIntyre 1988: 384). MacIntyre argued that this problem of untranslatability is most acute with "the internationalized languages-in-use in late twentieth-century modernity," like English, which "have minimal presuppositions in respect of possibly rival belief systems" and so will "neutralize" the historical dimension of the foreign text (ibid.). In English translation, therefore,

> a kind of text which cannot be read as *the text it is* out of context is nevertheless rendered contextless. But in so rendering it, it is turned into a text which is no longer the author's, nor such as would be recognized by the audience to whom it was addressed. (385)

Creagh's translation at once inscribed an English-language cultural history in Tabucchi's novel and displaced the historical dimension of the Italian text. This text occupies a place in a narrative tradition that includes resistance novels during and after the Second World War, as well as novels about life under fascism, Alberto Moravia's *Il conformista* (1951; The Conformist), for instance, and Giorgio Bassani's *Il giardino dei Finzi-Contini* (1962; The Garden of the Finzi-Continis). The very fact that Italian history contains a fascist tradition ensured that Tabucchi's readers would understand the Salazarist regime in distinctively Italian terms, not merely as an allusion to Mussolini's dictatorship, but as an allegory of current events. *Sostiene Pereira* was written in 1993 and published the following year, when a center-right coalition gained power in Italy with the election victory of Silvio Berlusconi's Forza Italia movement. As Tabucchi himself said of his novel, "those who didn't love the Italian political situation took it as a symbol of resistance from within" (Cotroneo 1995: 105, my translation). Invested with this peculiarly Italian significance, *Sostiene Pereira* sold 300,000 copies within a year of publication.

Although favorably received by British and American reviewers, Creagh's translation hardly became a bestseller. Within two years of publication the American edition published by New Directions sold 5,000 copies. Creagh maintained a lexicographical equivalence, but the remainder in his translation was insufficient to restore the cultural and political history that made the novel so resonant for Italian readers, as well as readers in other European countries with similar histories, such as Spain.

Communication through Inscription

Can a translation ever communicate to its readers the understanding of the foreign text that foreign readers have? Yes, I want to argue, but this communication will always be partial, both incomplete and inevitably slanted towards the domestic scene. It occurs only when the domestic remainder released by the translation includes an inscription of the foreign context in which the text first emerged.

The form of communication at work here is second-order, built upon but signifying beyond a lexicographical equivalence, encompassing but exceeding what Walter Benjamin called "information" or "subject matter." "Translations that are more than transmissions of subject matter," Benjamin wrote, "come into being when in the course of its survival a work has reached the age of its fame" (Benjamin 1968: 72). I understand the term "fame" to mean the overall reception of a literary text, not only in its own language and culture, but in the languages of the cultures that have translated it, and not only the judgments of reviewers at home and abroad, but the interpretations of literary historians and critics and the images that an internationally famous text may come to bear in other cultural forms and practices, both elite and mass. A translation of a foreign novel can communicate not simply dictionary meanings, not simply the basic elements of narrative form, but an interpretation that participates in its "potentially eternal afterlife in succeeding generations." And this interpretation can be one that is shared by the foreign-language readers for whom the text was written. The translation will then foster a common understanding with and of the foreign culture, an understanding that in part restores the historical context of the foreign text—although for domestic readers.

[Venuti gives a further example, omitted here, of two translations of Albert Camus's *L'Etranger* that find American equivalences for the colloquial register of the original, with varying relations to the work's original existentialist context.]

Heterogeneous Communities

The domestic inscription in translating constitutes a unique communicative act, however indirect or wayward. It creates a domestic community of interest around the translated text, an audience to whom it is intelligible and who put it to various uses. This shared interest may arise spontaneously when the translation is published, attracting readers from different cultural constituencies that already exist in the translating language. It may also be housed in an institution where the translation is made to perform different functions, academic or religious, cultural or political, commercial or municipal. Any community that arises around a translation is far from homogeneous in language, identity, or social position. Its heterogeneity might best be understood in terms of what Mary Louise Pratt calls a "linguistics of contact," in which language-based communities are seen as decentered across "lines of social differentiation" (Pratt 1987: 60). A translation is a linguistic "zone of contact" between the foreign and translating cultures, but also within the latter.

The interests that bind the community through a translation are not simply focused on the foreign text, but reflected in the domestic values, beliefs, and representations that the translator inscribes in it. And these interests are further determined by the ways the translation is used. In the case of foreign texts that have achieved canonical status in an institution, a translation becomes the site of interpretive communities that may support or challenge current canons and interpretations, prevailing standards and ideologies (cf. Fish 1980 and the criticisms in Pratt 1986: 46–52). In the case of foreign texts that have achieved mass circulation, a translation becomes the site of unexpected groupings, fostering communities of readers who would otherwise be separated by cultural differences and social divisions yet are now joined by a common fascination. A translation can answer to the interests of a diverse range of domestic audiences, so that the forms of reception will not be entirely commensurable. Because translating traffics in the foreign, in the introduction of linguistic and cultural differences, it is equally capable of crossing or reinforcing the boundaries between domestic audiences and the hierarchies in which they are positioned. If the domestic inscription includes part of the social or historical context in which the foreign text first emerged, then a translation can also create a community that includes foreign intelligibilities and interests, an understanding in common with another culture, another tradition.

Consider the readerships that gather around a poetry translation. In 1958 the American translator Allen Mandelbaum published the first book-length English version of the modern Italian poet Giuseppe Ungaretti. It was warmly welcomed by Italian academic specialists at American universities, some of whom were themselves Italian natives. The reviewer for the journal *Comparative Literature*, Giovanni Cecchetti, wrote his review in Italian and concluded that Mandelbaum's translation "does honor to Italian studies in America and can be recommended to anyone who wishes to familiarize himself with the work of one of the major poets of our time" (Cecchetti 1959: 268, my translation). The "our" suggests the extent of Cecchetti's esteem for Ungaretti's poetry, an assertion of universal value. But since he was reviewing in Italian the first English translation of that poetry, the "our" couldn't be universal because it didn't yet include British and American readers lacking Italian. Cecchetti imagined a community that was partly actual, professional, and partly potential.

The Ungaretti project also applied a standard of accuracy consistent with the interpretation that prevailed in the Italian academic community. Mandelbaum maintained a fairly strict lexicographical equivalence and even imitated Ungaretti's syntax and line breaks. He read Ungaretti's achievement, like the Italian scholars, as an effort "to bury the cadaver of literary Italian" by developing a spare, precise poetic language devoid of "all that was but ornament" (Mandelbaum 1958: xi). It was in these terms that the reviewers judged Mandelbaum's versions successful. "If one is tempted to observe that in many places the translation is too literal," wrote Carlo Golino, "further reflection will show that it would have been impossible to do otherwise and still retain the rich allusiveness of Ungaretti's words" (Golino 1959: 76).

Mandelbaum's translation was thus the site of an academic community's interest in Ungaretti's poetry, an American readership that nonetheless shared an Italian understanding of the text and in fact included Italian natives. In this context the translation ultimately achieved canonical status. In 1975, almost two decades after its first publication, it was reissued in a revised and expanded edition from Cornell University Press.

All the same, it is possible to perceive an appeal to another community in Mandelbaum's translation, a domestic readership that is incommensurable with the interests of the Italian academics and the prevailing interpretation of Ungaretti. While Mandelbaum adhered closely to the terse fragmentation of Ungaretti's Italian texts, he also introduced a poetical register, a noticeable strain of Victorian poeticism. Mandelbaum rendered "morire" ("die") as "perish," "buttato" ("thrown") as "cast," "ti basta un'illusione" ("an illusion is enough for you") as "you need but an illusion," "sonno" ("sleep") as "slumber," "riposato" ("rested") as "reposed," "potrò guardarla" ("I can watch her") as "I can gaze upon her" (Mandelbaum 1958: 7, 13, 25, 37, 145). He used syntactical inversions: some were added, while others were the results of literal translating, calques of the Italian.

[Following further analysis of Mandelbaum's translation choices in relation to the poetics of his day, Venuti continues:]

Mandelbaum's version bridged the cultural gap between Ungaretti's actual Italian readership and his potential American audience. Translating a modern Italian poet into the discourse that dominated American poetry translation was effectively a canonizing gesture, a poetic way of linking him—for American readers—to canonical poets like Homer and Dante (not to mention the echoes of Tennyson, Shakespeare, Marlowe). Yet this domestic inscription deviated from Ungaretti's significance in the Italian poetic tradition, the view, as Mandelbaum put it, that Ungaretti "purged the language of all ornament" (Mandelbaum 1958: xi). The ornate English version was addressing another audience, distinctly American, poetry readers familiar with British and American poetic traditions as well as recent translations that were immensely popular.

Indeed, Mandelbaum's translation discourse was so familiar as to be invisible to the reviewer for *Poetry* magazine, Ned O'Gorman, an American poet who published his first collection of poems in the same year. O'Gorman found Ungaretti's poetry "truly magnificent," while quoting and commenting on the translation as if it were the Italian text (O'Gorman 1959a: 330). What O'Gorman liked about (Mandelbaum's) Ungaretti was the fact that it was poetical: he praised the Italian poet for writing "of a world transformed into poetry" and proclaimed "the *Recitative*" as "his finest poem" (ibid.: 331). The poems in O'Gorman's first book reflected this judgment. They included "An Art of Poetry," where he wrote: "Poetry begins where rhetoric does" (O'Gorman 1959b: 26).

Mandelbaum's readerships were fundamentally incommensurable. Even though written in English, the translation was intelligible to each of them in different linguistic and cultural terms. The Italian academic community also did not recognize the Victorian poeticism. For them, however, this stylistic feature was invisible because English was not their native language and because, as foreign-language academics, they were most concerned with the relation between the English version and the Italian text: lexicographical equivalence. Cecchetti noticed one of Mandelbaum's poetical turns, his rendering of "smemora" ("to lose one's memory," "to forget") with the archaism "disremembers" (ibid.: 51; cf. *OED)*. Yet this choice was seen as appropriate to "the rare and suggestive flavor" of the Italian and indicative of the translator's "poetic sensibility" (Cecchetti 1959: 267).

The fact that in English this sensibility might be alien to Ungaretti's modernist poetics seems to have been recognized—in print—only by a British reader, interestingly enough. A reviewer for the London *Times,* who agreed with Cecchetti that Ungaretti was "one of the most distinguished poets alive," felt that "Mr. Mandelbaum translates with a quite exceptional insensitivity" *(The Times* 1958: 13C). There can be no doubt that the reviewer had Mandelbaum's poeticisms in mind, since he preferred to recommend a "good crib," the very close French version that Jean Lescure published in 1953 (where "D'altri diluvi una colomba ascolto" was turned into "J'écoute une colombe venue d'autres déluges" [Lescure 1953: 159]). Only a native reader of English poetry who also knew the Italian texts and their position in the Italian poetic tradition was able to perceive the English-language remainder in Mandelbaum's version.

The readerships that gathered around this poetry translation were limited, professionally or institutionally defined, and determined by their cultural knowledge, whether of the foreign language and literature or the literary traditions in the translating language. The translation became the focus of divergent communities, foreign and domestic, scholarly and literary. And in its ability to support their linguistic and cultural differences, to be intelligible and interesting to them in their own terms, the translation fostered its own community, one that was *imagined* in Benedict Anderson's sense: the members "will never know most of their fellow-members, meet them, or even hear of them, yet in the minds of each lives the image of their communion" (Anderson 1991: 6). In the case of a translation, this image is derived from the representation of the foreign text constructed by the translator, a communication domestically inscribed. To translate is to invent for the foreign text new readerships who are aware that their interest in the translation is shared by other readers, foreign and domestic—even when those interests are incommensurable.

The imagined communities that concerned Anderson were nationalistic, based on the sense of belonging to a particular nation. Translations have undoubtedly formed such communities by importing foreign ideas that stimulated the rise of large-scale political movements at home. At the turn of the twentieth century, the Chinese translator Yan Fu chose works on evolutionary theory by T. H. Huxley and Herbert Spencer precisely to build a national Chinese culture. He translated the Western concepts of aggression embodied in social Darwinism to form an aggressive Chinese identity that would withstand Western colonial projects, notably British (Schwartz 1964; Pusey 1983). Hu Shih, a contemporary observer, later recalled the impact of Huxley's *Evolution and Ethics* in Yan Fu's version: "after China's frequent military reversals, particularly after the humiliation of the Boxer years, the slogan 'Survival of the Fittest' (lit., 'superior victorious, inferior defeated, the fit survive') became a kind of clarion call" (translated and quoted in Schwartz 1964: 259, n. 14).

The imagined communities fostered by translation produce effects that are commercial, as well as cultural and political. Consider, for example, the mass audience that gathers around a translated bestseller. Because of its sheer size, this community is an ensemble of the most diverse domestic constituencies, defined by their specific interests in the foreign text, yet aware of belonging to a collective movement, a national market for a foreign literary fascination. These constituencies will inevitably read the translation differently, and in some cases the differences will be incommensurable. Yet the greatest communication gap here may be between the foreign and domestic cultures. The domestic inscription in the translation extends the appeal of the foreign text to a mass audience in another culture. But widening the domestic range of that appeal means that the inscription cannot include much of the foreign context. A translated bestseller risks reducing the foreign text to what domestic constituencies have in common, a dialect, a cultural discourse, an ideology.

This can be seen in the reception that greeted Irene Ash's English version of *Bonjour Tristesse* (1955), Françoise Sagan's bestselling novel. In France, the French text had been acclaimed as an accomplished work of art: it won the Prix des Critiques and sold 200,000 copies. In England and the United States, the translation drew favorable comments on its style and likewise stayed on the bestseller lists for many months. But no reviewer failed to abandon considerations of aesthetic form for more functional standards, expressing amazement at the youthful age of the author (19) and distaste for the amorality of its theme: a 17-year-old girl schemes to prevent her widowed father from remarrying, so that he can continue to engage in a succession of affairs. The *Chicago Tribune* was typical: "I admired the craftsmanship, but I was repelled by the carnality" (Hass 1955: 6).

This general response varied according to the values of the particular constituency addressed by the reviewer. The Catholic weekly *Commonweal* sternly pronounced the novel "childish and tiresome in its single-minded dedication to decadence" (Nagid 1955: 164), whereas the sophisticated *New Yorker* referred simply to the "father's hedonistic image," subtly suggesting that at 40 he deserves "pity" (Gill 1955: 114-15). In post-Second World War America, where the patriarchal family assumed new importance and "husbands, especially fathers, wore the badge of 'family man' as a sign of virility and patriotism" (May 1988: 98), Sagan's pleasure-seeking father and daughter were certain to make her novel an object of both moral panic and titillation. The reviewer for the *New Statesman and Nation* was unique in trying to understand it in distinctively French terms, describing the youthful heroine as "a child of the *bebop,* the night clubs, the existentialist cafés," comparing her and her father to "M. Camus's amoral Outsider" (Raymond 1955: 727-8).

Ash's English version was of course the decisive factor that enabled Sagan's novel to support a spectrum of very different responses in Anglo-American cultures. The translation was immediately intelligible to a wide English-language readership: it was cast in the most familiar dialect of current English, the standard, but it also contained some lively colloquialisms that matched similar forms in the French text. Ash rendered "le dernier des salauds" ("the last of the sluts") as "the most awful cad," "loupé" ("failed") as "flunked," and "ce fut la fin" ("that was the end") as "things came to a head" (Sagan 1954: 32, 34, 45; Ash 1955: 25, 27, 35). She aimed for a high degree of fluency by translating freely, making deletions and additions to the French to create more precise formulations in English:

> Au café, Elsa se leva et, arrivée a la porte, se retourna vers nous d'un air langoureux, très inspiré, à ce qu'il me sembla, du cinéma américain et mettant dans son intonation dix ans de galanterie française: "Vous venez, Raymond?"

> (After coffee, Elsa stood up and, on reaching the door, turned back towards us with a languorous air, very inspired—so it seemed to me—by American cinema, and investing her tone with ten years of French flirtation: "Are you coming, Raymond?") (Sagan 1954: 38, my translation)

> After coffee, Elsa walked over to the door, turned around, and struck a languorous, movie-star pose. In her voice was ten years of French coquetry: "Are you coming, Raymond?" (Ash 1955: 30)

Here the translator cut down forty words of French to twenty-nine in English. The use of the popular "movie-star pose" (for "du cinéma américain") is symptomatic of the drive toward readability.

By increasing the readability of the English text, such freedoms endowed the narrative with verisimilitude, producing the illusion of transparency that permitted the English-language reader to take the translation for the foreign text (Venuti 1995: 12). The reviewer for the *Atlantic,* impressed that "the novel has such a solid air of reality about it," commented on Ash's writing as if it were Sagan's: "Simple, crystalline, and concise, her prose flows along swiftly, creating scene and character with striking immediacy and assurance" (Rolo 1955: 84, 85).

Ash's freedoms may have been invisible, but they inevitably released a domestic remainder, textual effects that varied according to the specific passage where they occurred, but that were generally engaging, even provocative. The reviewer for the *New Statesman and Nation* was also unique in noticing her freedoms ("she has not been afraid to pare and clip the text to suit the English reader"), and he discussed an example where the "distinct gain in English" consisted of "an added, elegiac dimension" (Raymond 1955: 728). With a different passage, Ash's rewriting might be not just sentimental or melodramatic, but steamy, exaggerating the erotic overtones of the French:

> il avait pour elle des regards, des gestes qui s'adressaient à la femme qu'on ne connaît pas et que l'on désire connaître—dans le plaisir.

> (for her he had looks [and] gestures that are addressed to the woman whom one does not know yet desires to know—in pleasure.) (Sagan 1954: 378, my translation)

> I noticed that his every look and gesture betrayed a secret desire for her, a woman whom he had not possessed and whom he longed to enjoy. (Ash 1955:29)

Ash's translation, however free in places, maintained a sufficient degree of lexicographical equivalence to communicate the basic narrative elements of the French text. Yet the addition of words like "betrayed" and "secret" in this passage shows that she made the narrative available to an English-language audience with rather different moral values from its French counterpart, a morality that would restrict sexuality to marriage or otherwise conceal it. This is a rather odd effect in a novel where a father does not conceal his sexual promiscuity from his adolescent daughter. Ash inscribed Sagan's novel with a domestic intelligibility and interest, addressing a community that shared little of the foreign context where the novel first emerged.

The Utopian Dimension in Translation

The communities fostered by translating are initially potential, signaled in the text, in the discursive strategy deployed by the translator, but not yet possessing a social existence. They depend for their realization on the ensemble of domestic cultural constituencies among which the translation will circulate. To engage these constituencies, however, the translator involves the foreign text in an asymmetrical act of communication, weighted ideologically towards the translating culture. Translating is always ideological because it releases a domestic remainder, an inscription of values, beliefs, and representations linked to historical moments and social positions in the receiving culture. In serving domestic interests, a translation provides an ideological resolution for the linguistic and cultural differences of the foreign text.

Yet translating is also Utopian. The domestic inscription is made with the very intention to communicate the foreign text, and so it is filled with the anticipation that a community will be created around that text— although in translation. In the remainder lies the hope that the translation will establish a domestic readership, an imagined community that shares an interest in the foreign, possibly a market from the publisher's point of view. And it is only through the remainder, when inscribed with part of the foreign context, that the translation can establish a common understanding between domestic and foreign readers. In supplying an ideological resolution, a translation projects a utopian community that is not yet realized.

Behind this line of thinking lies Ernst Bloch's theory of the Utopian function of culture, although revised to fit an application to translation. Bloch's is a Marxist utopia. He saw cultural forms and practices releasing a "surplus" that not only exceeds the ideologies of the dominant classes, the "status quo," but anticipates a future "consensus," a classless society, usually by transforming the "cultural heritage" of a particular class, whether dominant or dominated (Bloch 1988: 46–50).

I construe Bloch's Utopian surplus as the domestic remainder inscribed in the foreign text during the translation process. Translating releases a surplus of meanings which refer to domestic cultural traditions through deviations from the current standard dialect or otherwise standardized languages—through archaisms for example, or colloquialisms. Implicit in any translation is the hope for a consensus, a communication and recognition of the foreign text through a domestic inscription.

Yet the inscription can never be so comprehensive, so total in relation to domestic constituencies, as to create a community of interest without exclusion of hierarchy. It is unlikely that a foreign text in translation will be intelligible or interesting (or both simultaneously) to every readership in the receiving situation. And the asymmetry between the foreign and domestic cultures persists, even when the foreign context is partly inscribed in the translation. Utopias are based on ideologies, Bloch argued, on interested representations of social divisions, representations that take sides in those divisions. In the case of translating, the interests are ineradicably domestic, always the interests of certain domestic constituencies over others.

Bloch also pointed out that the various social groups at any historical moment are non-contemporaneous or non-synchronous in their cultural and ideological development, with some containing a "remnant of earlier times in the present" (Bloch 1991: 108). Cultural forms and practices are heterogeneous, composed of different elements with different temporalities and affiliated with different groups. In language, the dialects and discourses, registers and styles that coexist in a particular period can be glimpsed in the remainder released by every communicative act. The remainder is a "diachrony-within-synchrony" that stages "the return within language of the contradictions and struggles that make up the social; it is the persistence within language of past contradictions and struggles, and the anticipation of future ones" (Lecercle 1990: 182, 215). Hence, the domestic inscription in any translation is what Bloch calls an "anticipatory illumination" *(Vor-Schein)*, a way of imagining a future reconciliation of linguistic and cultural differences, whether those that exist among domestic groups or those that divide the foreign and domestic cultures.

In Mandelbaum's version of Ungaretti's poetry, the utopian surplus is the Victorian poeticism. This English-language remainder didn't just exceed the communication of the Italian texts; it also ran counter to the modernist experiment they cultivated in the context of Italian poetic traditions. During the 1950s, however, Mandelbaum's poeticism projected an ideal community of interest in Ungaretti by reconciling the differences between two readerships, Italian and American, scholarly and literary. Today, we may be more inclined to notice, not the ideal, but the ideologies of this community: Mandelbaum's translation was an asymmetrical act of communication that at once admitted and excluded the Italian context, while supporting incommensurable responses among American constituencies. Yet the ideological force of the translation made it utopian in its own time, hopeful of communicating the foreign significance of the foreign text through a domestic inscription. And this utopian projection eventually produced real effects. The American readership latent in Mandelbaum's poetical remainder reflected a dominant tendency in American poetry translation, helping his version acquire cultural authority in and out of the academy.

Translating that harbors the Utopian dream of a common understanding between foreign and domestic cultures may involve literary texts, whether elite or mass. But usually it takes much more mundane forms, serving technical or pragmatic purposes. Consider community or liaison interpreting, the oral, two-way translating done for refugees and immigrants who must deal with the social agencies and institutions of the host country. Community interpreters perform in a variety of legal, medical, and educational situations, including requests for political asylum, court appearances, hospital admissions, and applications for welfare. Codes of ethics, whether formulated by professional associations or by the agencies and institutions themselves, tend to insist that interpreters be "panes of glass" which "allow for the communication of ideas, once again, without modification, adjustment or misrepresentation" (Schweda Nicholson 1994: 82; see also Gentile, Ozolins and Vasilakakos 1996). But such codes don't take into account the cultural and political hierarchies in the interpreting situation, the fact that—in the words of a British interpreting manual—"the client is part of a powerless ethnic minority group whose needs and wishes are often ignored or regarded as not legitimate by the majority group" (Shackman 1984: 18; see also Sanders 1992). And of course the "pane of glass" analogy represses the domestic inscription in any translating, the remainder that prevents the interpreting from being transparent communication even when the interpreter is limited to exact renderings of foreign words.

In practice, many community interpreters seem to recognize the asymmetries in the interpreting situation and make an effort to compensate for them through various strategies (Wadensjö 1998: 36). Robert Barsky's study of refugee hearings in Canada demonstrates that the interpreter can put the refugee on an equal footing with the adjudicating body only by releasing a distinctively domestic remainder. The foreign-language testimony must be inscribed with Canadian values, beliefs, and representations, producing textual effects that work only in English or French. Legal institutions value linear, transparent discourse, but the experiences that refugees must describe—exile, financial hardship, imprisonment, torture— are more than likely to shake their expressive abilities, even in their own languages. "Restricting the interpreter's role to rendering an 'accurate' translation of the refugee's utterances—which may contain hesitations, grammatical errors and various infelicities—inevitably jeopardizes the claimant's chances of obtaining refugee status, irrespective of the validity of the claim" (Barsky 1996: 52). Similarly, the interpreter must reconcile the cultural differences between Canada and the refugee's country by adding information about the foreign context, historical, geographical, political, or sociological details that may be omitted in testimony and unknown to Canadian judges and lawyers. "Insisting upon an interpretation limited exclusively to words uttered evacuates the cultural data which could be essential to the refugee's claim" (Barsky 1994: 49).

Barksy provides a telling example of a Pakistani claimant who spoke French during the hearing, apparently in an effort to lend weight to his case with the Québec authorities. But his French was weak, and his claim was previously denied because of interpreting problems, as he tried to explain:

> Moi demander, moi demander Madame, s'il vous plaît, cette translation lui parle français. Vous demander, parle français. Parce qu'elle m'a compris, vous qu'est ce qu'elle a dit. Moi compris. Madame m'a dit, désolé Monsieur, seul anglais.

> (Literally: Me ask, me ask Madame, please this translation speak to him French. You ask, speak French. Because she understood me, you that is what she said. Me understand. Madam said to me, sorry sir, only English.) (Barsky 1996: 53, his translation)

The claimant was testifying with a Pakistani interpreter who rendered the broken French into intelligible and compelling English:

> He has a complaint with the interpreter there. He speaks better French than English, but the interpreter was interpreting from Urdu to English. He is not too good in English, better in French, which he could understand. An interpreter was provided to interpret the hearing into English, which he did not agree to. So he was having a hard time expressing himself or understanding the CPO, lawyers, himself, and the interpreter. There is no satisfaction in the hearing. And that is one reason why I lost the case.

When effective, community interpreting provides a complicated ideological resolution for the linguistic and cultural differences of the refugee's or immigrant's speech. The interpreting inevitably communicates the foreign text in domestic terms, in the terms of the host country, but the domestic inscription also needs to include a significant part of the foreign context that gives meaning to the claim. This sort of interpreting, although seemingly partial to the client, is not in fact ideologically one-sided: it serves both foreign and domestic interests. The ideology of the resolution is fundamentally democratic insofar as the aim is to overcome the asymmetries that exist between the client and the representatives of the social agency within and outside of the interpreting situation. According to the British manual, the community interpreter permits "professional and client, with very different backgrounds and perceptions and in an unequal relationship of power and knowledge, to communicate to their mutual satisfaction" (Shackman 1984: 18). An important requirement for this mutual satisfaction, clearly, is the idea that a consensus as to the validity of the claim, shared by the two parties, has emerged in rational communication. Yet the communication can be seen as rational only when the interpreter so intervenes as to enable both the client to participate fully and the agency representatives to arrive at an informed understanding of the claim.

Community interpreting that takes an interventionist approach thus presupposes what Jürgen Habermas calls an "ideal speech situation," distinguished by conditions that are normally "counterfactual" because "improbable": they include "openness to the public, inclusiveness, equal rights to participation, immunization against external or internal compulsion, as well as the participants' orientation toward reaching understanding (that is, the sincere expression of utterances)" (Habermas 1998: 367). In presupposing such conditions, the community interpreter works ultimately to foster a domestic community that is receptive to foreign constituencies, but that is not yet realized—or at least its realization will not be advanced until the client is given political asylum, due process, medical care, or welfare benefits, as the case may be. Even then, of course, the receptive domestic community is primarily a Utopian projection that does not eliminate the social hierarchies in which the refugee or immigrant is actually positioned. Still, it does express the hope that linguistic and cultural differences will not result in the exclusion of foreign constituencies from the domestic scene. Translating might be motivated by much more questionable things.

―――――――

Works Cited

Allain, M.-F. (1983) *The Other Man: Conversations with Graham Greene*, tr. G. Waldman, London: Bodley Head.

Anderson, B. (1991) *Imagined Communities*, rev. ed., London: Verso.

Ash, I. (trans.) (1955) F. Sagan, *Bonjour Tristesse*, New York: Dutton.

Barsky, R. F. (1994) *Constructing a Productive Other: Discourse Theory and the Convention Refugee Hearing*, Amsterdam: Benjamins.

———. (1996) "The Interpreter as Intercultural Agent in Convention Refugee Hearings," *The Translator* 2:45–64.

Benjamin, A. (1989) *Translation and the Nature of Philosophy*, London: Routledge.

Benjamin, W. (1968) "The Task of the Translator," in *Illuminations*, ed. H. Arendt, tr. Harry Zohn, New York: Schocken, 69–82.

Berman, A. (2004) "Translation and the Trials of the Foreign," in Venuti (2004), 276-89.

Blanchot, M. (1988) *The Unavowable Community*, tr. P Joris, Barrytown, New York: Station Hill Press.

Bloch, E. (1988) *The Utopian Function of Art and Literature*, ed. and tr. J Zipes and F. Mecklenburg, Cambridge, MA: MIT Press.

———. (1991) *Heritage of Our Times*, tr. N. Plaice and S. Plaice, Oxford: Polity.

Blum-Kulka, S. (2004) "Shifts of Cohesion and Coherence in Translation," in Venuti (2004), 291–305.

Catford, J.C. (1965) *A Linguistic Theory of Translation*. London: Oxford U. P.

Cecchetti, G. (1959) Review of Mandelbaum (1958), *Comparative Literature* 11: 262–68.

Cotroneo, R. (1995) "Sostiene Tabucchi," *L'Espresso*, 2 June, 104–8.

Creagh, Patrick, tr. (1995) *Declares Pereira: A Testimony* (London: Harvill).

Diemert, B. (1996) *Graham Greene's Thrillers and the 1930s*, Montreal: McGill-Queen's U. P.

Fish, S. (1980) *Is There a Text in This Class?*, Cambidge, MA: Harvard U. P.

Gentile, A., U. Ozolins, and M. Vasilakakos (1996) *Liaison Interpreting: A Handbook*, Melbourne: Melbourne U. P.

Gill, B. (1955) "The Uses of Love," *New Yorker*, 5 March, 114–15.

Golino, C. (1959) Review of Mandelbaum (1958), *Italian Quarterly* 3: 76.

Habermas, J. (1998) *On the Pragmatics of Communication*, ed. M. Cooke, Cambridge: MIT Press.

Hass, V.P. (1955) Review of Ash (1955), *Chicago Sunday Tribune*, 24 April, 6.

Heidegger, M. (1975) *Early Greek Thinking*, ed. and tr. D.F. Krell and F.A. Capuzzi, New York: Harper and Row.

Jameson, F. (1981) *The Political Unconscious*, Ithaca: Cornell U. P.

Lecercle, J-J. (1990) *The Violence of Language*, London: Routledge.

Lefevere, A. (1992) *Translation/History/Culture: A Sourcebook* London: Routledge.

Lescure, J. (tr.) (1953) Giuseppe Ungaretti, *Les cinq livres*, Paris: Editions de Minuit.

Lewis, P.E. (2004) "The Measure of Translation Effects," in Venuti (2004), 256–75.

MacIntyre, A. (1988) *Whose Justice? Which Rationality?*, Notre Dame: U. of Notre Dame P.

Mandelbaum, A. (ed. and tr.) (1958) G. Ungaretti, *Life of a Man*, Milan: Scheiwiller, London: Hamish Hamilton, and New York: New Directions.

May, E.T. (1988) *Homeward Bound*, New York: Basic Books.

Nagid, N. L. (1955) "The Decadent Life," *Commonweal*, 13 May, 163–6.

O'Gorman, N. (1959a) "Language and Vision," *Poetry* 93: 329–32.

———. (1959b) *The Night of the Hammer*, New York: Harcourt Brace.

Pratt, M. L. (1986) "Interpretive Strategies/Strategic Interpretations," in J. Arac (ed.) *Postmodernism and Politics*, Minneapolis: U. of Minnesota P., 26–54.

———. (1987) "Linguistic Utopias," in N. Fabb et al. (eds.) *The Linguistics of Writing*, Manchester: Manchester U. P.

Pusey, J. R. (1983) *China and Charles Darwin*. Cambridge, MA: Harvard U. P.

Raymond, J. (1955) "Two First Novels," *New Statesman and Nation*, 21 May, 727–8.

Rolo, C. J. (1955) Review of Ash (1955), *Atlantic*, April, 84–6.

Sagan, F. (1954) *Bonjour Tristesse*, Paris: Julliard.

Sanders, M. (1992) "Training for Community Interpreters," in C. Piken (ed.) *ITI Conference 6 Proceedings*. London: Aslib.

Schwartz, B. (1964) *In Search of Wealth and Power: Yan Fu and the West*, Cambridge: Harvard U. P.

Schweda Nicholson, N. (1994) "Professional Ethics for Court and Community Interpreters," in D. L. Hammond (ed.) *Professional Issues for Translators and Interpreters*, Amsterdam: Benjamins.

Shackman, J. (1984) *The Right to Be Understood: A Handbook on Working with, Employing and Training Community Interpreters*, Cambridge: National Extension College.

Tabucchi, A. (1994) *Sostiene Pereira: Una testimonianza*, Milan: Feltrinelli.

Times of London (1958) "Perplexities and Poetry," 6 November, 13C.

Toury, Gideon. (1980) *In Search of a Theory of Translation*, Tel Aviv: Porter Institute for Poetics and Semiotics.

———. (1995) *Descriptive Translation Studies—and Beyond*, Amsterdam and Philadelphia: Benjamins.

Venuti, Lawrence. (1995) *The Translator's Invisibility: A History of Translation*, London and New York: Routledge.

———. (1998) *The Scandals of Translation: Towards an Ethics of Difference*, London and New York: Routledge.

———. (2004) *The Translation Studies Reader*, 2nd Ed., London and New York: Routledge.

Wadensjö, C. (1998) "Community Interpreting," in M. Baker (ed.) *Encyclopedia of Translation Studies*, London: Routledge, 33–7.

30

Crossing Borders[1] (2003)

Gayatri Chakravorty Spivak

Born to middle-class parents in Calcutta in 1942, Spivak was educated in a mission school, then took an honors degree at the University of Calcutta before coming to the United States, where she received a doctorate at Cornell University with a dissertation on Yeats written under the supervision of Paul de Man. She then taught at the Universities of Iowa and Pittsburgh before coming to Columbia, where she has directed Columbia's Institute for Comparative Literature and Society and is a university professor.

Spivak captured the attention of literary scholars with her 1976 translation into English of Jacques Derrida's *De la grammatologie*. She soon became a major contributor to debates on post-structuralism, and has since been a key figure in the elaboration of postcolonial theory, although she remains hard to define because of the breadth of her intellectual engagements. In her important essay "Can the Subaltern Speak?" (1985) she critiqued, among other things, the retention of the West as subject in French cultural theory and the positioning of *sati* (widows' self-immolation) in British and Hindu law. She has been concerned with the situation of meanings of migrancy in metropolitan countries in relation to citizenship in previously colonized countries.

Spivak has referred to herself as a "para-disciplinary, ethical philosopher." To this end, her work has encompassed the deconstruction of feminism (in particular the French feminist theory of Cixous, Irigaray, and Kristeva), Marxism, literary criticism, and Postcolonialism itself as well as probing discussions of human rights and the institution of Comparative Literature, themes developed in *Outside in the Teaching Machine* (1993) and *A Critique of Postcolonial Reason: Toward a History of the Vanishing Present* (1999). Parallel to her intellectual work on these topics has been her involvement since the late 1980s in teacher training in Bangladesh and India.

Spivak's multifaceted and transnational work has included the theory and practice of translation. She has translated Mahasweta Devi's stories from Bengali into English, and she has written extensively on problems of linguistic and cultural translation. In her 2003 book *Death of a Discipline*, whose opening chapter is given here, Spivak sees comparative literature as a discipline that can train the imagination to listen to the voice of the Other. She calls for comparatists to learn from area studies in maintaining a commitment to rigorous language learning and to local idiom though close reading in the age of globalization.

Since 1992, three years after the fall of the Berlin Wall, the discipline of comparative literature has been looking to renovate itself. This is presumably in response to the rising tide of multiculturalism and cultural studies. The first pages of Charles Bernheimer's *Comparative Literature in the Age of Multiculturalism* tell a story that those with experience of national-level professional organizations at work can flesh out in the imagination into a version of the Quarrel of the Ancients and the Moderns:

> In the summer of 1992 . . . [the] president of the American Comparative Literature Association (ACLA) asked me to appoint and chair a committee charged to write a so-called Report on Standards for submission to the association. The bylaws of the ACLA . . . mandated that such a report be prepared every ten years. The first report was submitted in 1965 by a committee chaired by my thesis director, Harry Levin; the second was submitted in 1975 by a committee chaired by Tom Greene. A third report was written ten years thereafter, but . . . the chair of that committee was so dissatisfied with the document that he exercised a pocket veto and never submitted it. . . . The first two reports . . . are impressively strong articulations of a view of comparative literature which, in my view, no longer applies to actual practices in the field. . . . A diverse group of top scholars

from diverse institutions . . . felt uneasy about being asked to establish "standards" and decided to give more importance to our ideas about the intellectual mission of the discipline than to spelling out requirements (. . . the report [was renamed] the Report on the State of the Discipline).[2]

This is an account of the transformation of comparative literary studies. Comparative social studies, as represented by Area Studies, were undergoing their own transformation. This is well represented by a recent influential pamphlet by Toby Volkman, written while she was Program Officer at the Ford Foundation, from which I have taken my chapter title: "Crossing Borders":

> Recent developments have challenged some of the premises of area studies itself. The notion, for example, that the world can be divided into knowable, self-contained "areas" has come into question as more attention has been paid to movements between areas. Demographic shifts, diasporas, labor migrations, the movements of global capital and media, and processes of cultural circulation and hybridization have encouraged a more subtle and sensitive reading of areas' identity and composition.[3]

The rest of Volkman's pamphlet contains actual descriptions of institutional projects under six headings: Reconceptualization of "Area"; Borders and Diasporas; Border-Crossing Seminars and Workshops; Curricular Transformation and Integration; Collaborations with Nongovernmental Organizations, Activists, and the Media; and Rethinking Scientific Areas. There are a few examples of Ethnic Studies and Area Studies pulling together, but the only one that may touch traditional comparative literature is the project at Middlebury College, building on its already considerable resources of European language teaching. Indeed, although "popular culture" is an item often included, literature does not seem particularly important in this venture of, as Volkman's subtitle suggests, "Revitalizing Area Studies."[4]

If this is what may be called the current situation, the recent past of these two institutional enterprises can perhaps be recounted as follows. Area Studies were established to secure U.S. power in the Cold War. Comparative Literature was a result of European intellectuals fleeing "totalitarian" regimes. Cultural and Postcolonial Studies relate to the 500 percent increase in Asian immigration in the wake of Lyndon Johnson's reform of the Immigration Act of 1965. Whatever our view of what we do, we are made by the forces of people moving about the world.

How can we respond to the changes brought about by the end of the Cold War, as both the Bernheimer report and the Volkman pamphlet implicitly ask? A simple splicing of Comp. Lit. and Cultural studies/multiculturalism will not work or will work only too well; same difference. A combination of Ethnic Studies and Area Studies bypasses the literary and the linguistic. What I am proposing is not a politicization of the discipline. We are *in* politics. I am proposing an attempt to depoliticize in order to move away from a politics of hostility, fear, and half solutions. Why, for example, as in the fairly representative passage below, appropriate Brecht to trash Ethnic Studies and Cultural Studies in order to praise a friend's book in the pages of a journal that was established in 1949, in the full flush of Area Studies development, "at a time when the strengthening of good international relations [was] of paramount importance"?

> In the face of the wholesale selling-off of the German intellectual tradition by current "German Studies" and the shallowing of philosophically-informed literary theory by the conversion of comparative literature into cultural studies, *Premises* brings to mind Brecht's 1941 comment on Benjamin's "Theses on the Philosophy of History": "one thinks with horror of how small the number is of those who are ready even to misunderstand something like this."[5]

Compared to such an outburst, my ideas for an inclusive comparative literature are so depoliticized as to have, unlike the Bernheimer report or the Volkman pamphlet, little to do with the times. I thought Comparative Literature should be world embracing at the beginning of my career. And I continue to believe that the politics of the production of knowledge in area studies (and also anthropology and the other "human sciences") can be touched by a new Comparative Literature, whose hallmark remains a care for language and idiom.

In 1973, when I was an associate professor, I invited Claudio Guillén to the University of Iowa to give a minicourse. Guillén was moved by my idealism about a global Comparative Literature. He put me on the Executive Committee of the International Comparative Literature Association. I went to Visegrad the following year. I wish I could regale the reader with the symptomatology of that meeting, but must confine myself to one detail.

The association was putting together new scholarly volumes on the periods of European literary history. We discussed the production details of the volume on the Renaissance, if memory serves. I offered to get contacts for scholars in the Indian languages so that we could enlarge the scope of the series. I offered to be active in setting up committees for such investigations in the other comparative clusters of the world: Korean-

Chinese-Japanese; Arabic-Persian; the languages of Southeast Asia; African languages. A foolish notion, no doubt. M. Voisine of the Sorbonne, a senior member of the committee, quelled me with a glance: "My friend René Etiemble tells me," he said, "that there is a perfectly acceptable scholarly history of literatures in Chinese."

Memory has no doubt sharpened the exchange. And one person's caustic remark cannot represent an entire discipline. What the exchange does vouch for, however, is my longstanding sense that the logical consequences of our loosely defined discipline were, surely, to include the open-ended possibility of studying all literatures, with linguistic rigor and historical savvy. A level playing field, so to speak.

As it happened, I had also been speaking of what was not yet called Cultural Studies teaming up with Area Studies for some time. Selecting one example among many, I quote myself, admonishing, in 1988: "As we in the margins try to shore up our defenses, we tend to leave untouched the politics of the specialists of the margin—area studies, anthropology, and the like."[6]

Even from a restricted U.S. perspective, it seems obvious that the sources of literary agency have expanded beyond the old European national literatures. For the *discipline,* the way out seems to be to acknowledge a definitive future anteriority, a "to come"-ness, a "will have happened" quality. This is a protection from self-destructive competition for dwindling resources. It is also a protection from losing the best of the old Comparative Literature: the skill of reading closely in the original. Such a philosophy of planning welcomes nonexhaustive taxonomies, provisional system making, but discourages map-making literary criticism as an end in itself because diagnostic cartography does not keep the door open to the "to come." It is in the acknowledgment of such an open future that we need to consider the resources of Area Studies, specifically geared for what lies beyond the Euro-U.S.

In spite of all the noise about "these times," if the 145 departments or programs listed in the bulletin of the ACLA form a representative sample, the general model in Comparative Literature seemed still, in 2000 when these lectures were delivered, to be Europe and the extracurricular Orient. Ten Comp. Lit. units in the United States seem to have some arrangement with either the social sciences or multiculturalism, and only two of these mention Area Studies. I have no doubt that this is now changing, but cannot keep up with the pace of that change.

Area Studies were founded in the wake of the Cold War and funded by federal grants, backed up by the great foundations, especially Ford.

To meet the demands of war, scholars of diverse disciplines *were forced* to pool their knowledge in frantic attempts to advise administrators and policy makers . . . The war also showed the need for trained personnel for most foreign areas. . . .In these Army Specialized Training Programs and Civil Affairs Training Schools many professors had their first experience with curricula organized by area rather than by discipline, and many students made a real beginning in the study of foreign areas and in their languages,

says the introduction to the "national conference on the study of world areas, which was held in New York on November 28–30, 1947."[7] Language and Area Centers between 1959 and 1968 were authorized by Public Law 85-864, the National Defense Education Act of 1958 (as amended), Title VI.

Without the support of the humanities, Area Studies can still only transgress frontiers, in the name of crossing borders; and, without a transformed Area Studies, Comparative Literature remains imprisoned within the borders it will not cross. Area studies have resources but also built-in, restricted, but real interdisciplinarity. If one goes down the list of Comparative Literature programs and departments, the interdisciplinarity with music, philosophy, art history, and media remains less persuasive and exceptional. And, whatever we think about the relationship between Comparative Literature and Area Studies, the polarity between Area Studies and Cultural Studies is clear.

Area Studies exhibit quality and rigor (those elusive traits), combined with openly conservative or "no" politics. They are tied to the politics of power, and their connections to the power elite in the countries studied are still strong; the quality of the language learning is generally excellent, though just as generally confined to the needs of social science fieldwork; and the data processing is sophisticated, extensive, and intensive. Academic "Cultural Studies," as a metropolitan phenomenon originating on the radical fringes of national language departments, opposes this with no more than metropolitan language-based presentist and personalist political convictions, often with visibly foregone conclusions that cannot match the implicit political cunning of Area Studies at their best; and earns itself a reputation for "lack of rigor" as well as for politicizing the academy.[8] The languages of the cultures of origin are invoked at best as delexicalized and fun mother tongues. The real "other" of Cultural Studies is not Area Studies but the civilization courses offered by the European national language departments, generally scorned by Comparative Literature. It is therefore a real sign of change that the Ford initiative, as reflected in the Volkman pamphlet, seems to bring together Ethnic/Cultural Studies and Area Studies. It remains to be seen if the extraordinary metropolitan enthusiasm in the former will undermine the linguistic rigor of the latter. I will discuss that question in the last chapter. Let us return to Comparative Literature.

Area Studies related to foreign "areas." Comparative Literature was made up of Western European "nations." This distinction, between "areas" and "nations," infected Comparative Literature from the start.[9]

If the "origin" of Area Studies was the aftermath of the Cold War, the "origin" of U.S. Comparative Literature had something of a relationship with the events that secured it: the flights of European intellectuals, including such distinguished men as Erich Auerbach, Leo Spitzer, René Wellek, Renato Poggioli, and Claudio Guillén, from "totalitarian" regimes in Europe. One might say that U.S. Comparative Literature was founded on inter-European hospitality, even as Area Studies had been spawned by interregional vigilance.

One way that the nation-region divide is already being negotiated in comparative literature is by destabilizing the "nation"(s)—introducing Francophony, Teutophony, Lusophony, Anglophony, Hispanophony within the old "national" boundaries; the biggest winner in the United States is "Global English." The effort, recalling the initial Birmingham model of Cultural Studies, is to put some black on the Union Jack or, to put a spin on Jesse Jackson's slogan, to paint the red, white, and blue in the colors of the rainbow.[10] This destabilization follows the lines of the old imperialisms and competes with the diversified metropolitan nationalism of Ethnic/Cultural Studies.

The new step that I am proposing would go beyond this acknowledgment and this competition. It would work to make the traditional linguistic sophistication of Comparative Literature supplement Area Studies (and history, anthropology, political theory, and sociology) by approaching the language of the other not only as a "field" language. In the field of literature, we need to move from Anglophony, Lusophony, Teutophony, Francophony, et cetera. We must take the languages of the Southern Hemisphere as active cultural media rather than as objects of cultural study by the sanctioned ignorance of the metropolitan migrant. We cannot dictate a model for this from the offices of the American Comparative Literature Association. We can, however, qualify ourselves and our students to attend upon this as it happens elsewhere. Here and now, I can only caution against some stereotypes: that such an interest is antihybridist, culturally conservative, "ontopologist," "parochial."[11] Indeed, I am inviting the kind of language training that would disclose the irreducible hybridity of all languages. As I have said elsewhere: "The verbal text is jealous of its linguistic signature but impatient of national identity. Translation flourishes by virtue of that paradox."[12] Other stereotypes are correct but irrelevant: namely, that attention to the languages of the Southern Hemisphere is inconvenient and impractical.[13]

Inconvenient. There are a few hegemonic European languages and innumerable Southern Hemisphere languages. The only principled answer to that is: "Too bad." The old Comparative Literature did not ask the student to learn every hegemonic language; nor will the new ask her or him to learn all the subaltern ones! Can the "native informant" ever become the subject of a "cultural study" that does not resemble metropolitan language-based work? If one asks this question, one sees that the destabilization offered by a merely metropolitan Cultural Studies must exclude much for its own convenience, for the cultural claims of the metropolitan migrant.

Jacques Derrida is the rare philosopher who thinks that philosophical "concepts [cannot] transcend idiomatic differences."[14] Such insights do not apply only to French and German or Greek and Latin. Engagement with the idiom of the global other(s) in the Southern Hemisphere, uninstitutionalized in the Euro-U.S. university structure except via the objectifying, discontinuous, transcoding tourist gaze of anthropology and oral history, is our lesson on displacing the discipline. This is not brought about by the reterritorialized desire of the metropolitan migrant to collaborate with the South, generally through the United Nations by way of nongovernmental organizations (NGOs). As I have argued elsewhere, such collaboration is generally possible only with the class, physically "based" in the global South, increasingly produced by globalization, that is sufficiently out of touch with the idiomaticity of nonhegemonic languages.[15]

What I am suggesting may sound discouraging. I hate to use this word, but perhaps it gives us a certain kind of honesty. It should not paralyze us. We cannot not try to open up, from the inside, the colonialism of European national language-based Comparative Literature and the Cold War format of Area Studies, and infect history and anthropology with the "other" as producer of knowledge. From the inside, acknowledging complicity. No accusations. No excuses. Rather, learning the protocol of those disciplines, turning them around, laboriously, not only by building institutional bridges but also by persistent curricular interventions. The most difficult thing here is to resist mere appropriation by the dominant.[16]

Indeed, the question of the old imperialisms and the new empire is itself different if uncoupled from high-culture radicalism. While I was working on this manuscript, I was also looking at the *Report of the Mayor's*

Task Force on the City University of New York, undertaken in 1998.[17] The question before us was "What is English? Literary Studies in a Public Urban University." The City University of New York was faulted because 87 percent of its incoming undergraduate class was in remedial English. The report separated the old minorities—giving them the code name of New York City public school graduates—from the new—emergent since Lyndon Johnson lifted the quota system in 1965: "During the 1990's, the white population of New York City declined by 19.3%, while the black, Hispanic, and Asian population have risen by 5.2%, 19.3%, and 53.5%, respectively."

If you sit in on these so-called remedial classes, you perceive the institutional incapacity to cope with the crossroads of race, gender and class—even when the teacher has the best will in the world—to come to grips "with the actual play of the choice of English as tongue in the imagination of these working-class new immigrant survival artists. *Le Thé Au Harem d'Archi Ahmed.*[18] As a comparativist I would like to suggest that, just as no "literary studies" in New York City and no doubt in Los Angeles should forget that the answer to the question "What is English?" is that it is more than half the ingredient for producing human capital (the other half being mathematics), so also, literary studies will have to acknowledge that the European outlines of its premise and one of its tasks—positing the idea of the universality of each of the European national languages (the jealously guarded particular domain of the old Comparative Literature)—have, in globality and in subaltern U.S. multiculturalism, altogether disappeared. There are Haitians and West Africans in those CUNY remedial classes whose imaginations are crossing and being crossed by a double aporia—the cusp of two imperialisms. I have learned something from listening to their talk about and in Creole/French/so-called pidgin and English-as-a-second-language-crossing-into-first—the chosen tongue. I have silently compared their imaginative flexibility, so remarkably and necessarily much stronger, because constantly in use for social survival and mobility, than that of the Columbia undergraduate, held up by the life-support system of a commercializing anglophone culture that trivializes the humanities. It is time, in globality, in New York, and no doubt elsewhere in the metropolis, to put the history of Francophony, Teutophony, Lusophony, Anglophony, Hispanophony *also*—not *only* (please mark the difference)—in a comparative focus.

To pursue this line of thinking further would be to address the question of the thickening of class analysis itself and would take us away from the question of Comparative Literature. I place this parenthesis here so that the reader will take this postponement into account.

Outside of "Gender and Development," the question of human rights is most often confined within trade-related political paradigms leading to military intervention, ostensibly based on game theory and rational choice as unacknowledged theoretical models. If a responsible comparativism can be of the remotest possible use in the training of the imagination, it must approach culturally diversified ethical systems diachronically, through the history of multicultural empires, without foregone conclusions. This is the material that is used to fashion violence in the multiform global imaginary. Pedagogically speaking, such studies are much more successful through language-based literary investigation than through evidence from interested cultural informants, like East Asian capitalist men or South or West Asian fundamentalists.

Again, I am not advocating the politicization of the discipline. I am advocating a depoliticization of the politics of hostility toward a politics of friendship to come, and thinking of the role of Comparative Literature in such a responsible effort.

If we seek to supplement gender training and human rights intervention by expanding the scope of Comparative Literature, the proper study of literature may give us entry to the performativity of cultures as instantiated in narrative. Here we stand outside, but not as anthropologist; we stand rather as reader with imagination ready for the effort of othering, however imperfectly, as an end in itself. It is a peculiar end, for "It cannot be motivated . . . except in the requirement for an increase or a supplement of justice [here to the text], and so in the experience of an inadequation or an incalculable disproportion."[19] This is preparation for a patient and provisional and forever deferred arrival into the performative of the other, in order not to transcode but to draw a response. Believe me, there is a world of difference between the two positions. In order to reclaim the role of teaching literature as training the imagination—the great inbuilt instrument of othering—we may, if we work as hard as old-fashioned Comp. Lit. is known to be capable of doing, come close to the irreducible work of translation, not from language to language but from body to ethical semiosis, that incessant shuttle that is a "life."

This last sentence draws on the work of Melanie Klein, which I have elsewhere summarized as follows:[20]

The human infant grabs on to some one thing and then things. This grabbing (begreifen as in das Begriff or concept) of an outside indistinguishable from an inside constitutes an inside, going back and forth and coding everything into a sign-system by the thing(s) grasped. One can call this crude coding a "translation." In this never-ending shuttle, violence translates into conscience and vice versa. From birth to death this "natural" machine, programming the mind perhaps as genetic instructions program the body (where does body stop and mind begin?) is partly metapsychological and therefore outside the grasp of the mind. Thus "nature" passes and repasses into "culture," in a work or shuttling site of violence (deprivation—evil—shocks the infant system-in-the-making more than satisfaction —some say *Paradiso* is the dullest of *The Divine Comedy*—but the passage from mind to body is also violent as such): the violent production of the precarious subject of reparation and responsibility. To plot this weave, the reader—in my estimation, Klein was more a reader than an analyst in the strict Freudian sense—, translating the incessant translating shuttle into that which is read, must have the most intimate access to the rules of representation and permissible narratives which make up the substance of a culture, and must also become responsible and accountable to the writing/translating of the presupposed original.[21]

It is in this painstaking supplementation of the impatient bounty of human rights that we encounter the limit of that moving frontier of Area Studies/ Comparative Literature that is always a "discipline to come," through a type of language learning that fosters access to textuality. Part of this uncertain future is the growing virtualization of frontiers. What we are witnessing in the postcolonial and globalizing world is a return of the demographic, rather than territorial, frontiers that predate and are larger than capitalism. These demographic frontiers, responding to large-scale migration, are now appropriating the contemporary version of virtual reality and creating the kind of parastate collectivities that belonged to the shifting multicultural empires that preceded monopoly capitalism. The problem with the Bernheimer report was that it responded only to the unexamined culturalism of such symptomatic collectivities, the stereotyped producers and consumers of Cultural/Ethnic Studies.

But these are matters for the next two chapters. For now I want to repeat my concern for the literary specificity of the autochthone, which, lost in the shuffle between Cultural Studies and Comparative Literature, could not appear at all in *Comparative Literature in the Age of Multiculturalism*. Comparative Literature and Area Studies *can* work together in the fostering not only of national literatures of the global South but also of the writing of countless indigenous languages in the world that were programmed to vanish when the maps were made. The literatures in English produced by the former British colonies in Africa and Asia should be studied and supported. And who can deny the Spanish and Portuguese literatures of Latin America? Yet the languages that were historically prevented from having a constituted readership or are now losing readership might be allowed to prosper as well, even as the writers contribute to our need for languages. We do not need to map them. Together we can offer them the solidarity of borders that are easily crossed, again and again, as a permanent from-below interruption of a Comparative Literature to come, the irony of globalization.[22]

As far as I am concerned, then, there is nothing necessarily new about the new Comparative Literature. Nonetheless, I must acknowledge that the times determine how the necessary vision of "comparativity" will play out. Comparative Literature must always cross borders. And crossing borders, as Derrida never ceases reminding us via Kant, is a problematic affair.[23]

I have remarked above that borders are easily crossed from metropolitan countries, whereas attempts to enter from the so-called peripheral countries encounter bureaucratic and policed frontiers, altogether more difficult to penetrate. In spite of the fact that the effects of globalization can be felt all over the world, that there are satellite dishes in Nepalese villages, the opposite is never true. The everyday cultural detail, condition and effect of sedimented cultural idiom, does not come up into satellite country. Putting it this way should make it immediately obvious that the solution is not clear-cut. Let us postpone solution talk and consider a staging of such restricted permeability in Maryse Condé's first novel.

An important infrastructural problem of the restricted permeability of global culture is the lack of communication within and among the immense heterogeneity of the subaltern cultures of the world. In Maryse Condé's *Heremakhonon*, there is a moment when an undisclosed West African subaltern speaker, possibly feminine, says to the French-speaking upper-class young woman from Guadaloupe, who will later compliment herself on knowing Creole, "What strangeness that country [*quelle étrangeté ce pays*] which produced [*qui ne produisait*] neither Mandingo, nor Fulani, nor Toucouleur, nor Serer, nor Woloff, nor Toma, nor Guerze, nor Fang, nor Fon, nor Bété, nor Ewe, nor Dagbani, nor Yoruba, nor Mina, nor Ibo. And it was still Blacks who lived there [*Et c'étaient tout de même des Noirs qui vivaient là!*]."[24] The young woman passes this by, noting only her pleasure at being complimented on her appearance: "'Are all the women of that country as pretty as Mademoiselle?' I got a silly pleasure out of hearing

this." Is this characterization or political comment? How far should literature be read as sociological evidence? We should at least note that Condé
herself remarks, in the preface to the much later second French edition, "I
had the idea of putting the narrative in the mouth of a negative heroine."[25]
Where on this grid of reading literature as text and/or evidence of uneven
permeability shall we put a graduate student's comment that the subaltern's
remark is improbable, because only an academically educated person would
know such a comprehensive list of African languages? The least sense of
the shifting demographies of Africa would correct this.

Commenting after the fact on the lines of communication among
countries colonized by the same power in the previous centuries, it is possible to speak of an "enabling violation." Perhaps these languages died, but
they got French.[26] Can one make such an uninvolved judgment about
changes happening in one's own time?

In Richard Philcox's brilliant translation of the passage from Condé I have
cited above we read "Fulani and Toucouleur" for the French "Peul and
Toucouleur" in the list of languages. Let us pause a moment on this detail
of translation, which the metropolitan reader of the translation will undoubtedly pass over.

> The Fulbe are a distinct people who apparently originated [text for
> unpacking there] just above the Sahel between Mauritania and Mali
> and over the centuries migrated through the savannah of West Africa
> as far as the Lake Chad area. One of the areas they settled was the
> mid-Senegal valley. The mid-valley people referred to themselves as
> Haalpulaar'en (singular Haalpulaar, speaker of pulaar), whether they
> were pastoralists or cultivators. It was the nineteenth century French
> ethnographers who divided these people into distinct groups: the
> largely non-Muslim pastoralists were called peuls while the mostly
> Muslim agriculturalists were called toucouleurs. English travelers
> to the Sokoto Palisades (in present day Nigeria) adopted the Hausa
> word for the Fulbe there—Fulani.[27]

These proper names of languages carry the sedimentation of the
history of the movement of peoples. Strictly speaking, Fulani includes both
Peul and Toucouleur, and so is not an appropriate alternative for the latter.
But the implied reader of the translation is not expected to have this information. The idea of shifting demographic frontiers caught in the virtuality
of the Internet and telecommunication is generally assigned to postmodern
globalization. The best among the globalizers know that there may be a

history here. The eminent globality theorist, Professor Saskia Sassen, for example, invokes shifting demographic frontiers and admits that she needs a historical fix.[28] I had quoted this passage from Condé in answer when she expressed that need, but could not complete the reading. Today, in this more appropriate context, I finish the task.

The new Comparative Literature makes visible the import of the translator's choice. In the translation from *French* to *English* lies the disappeared history of distinctions in another space—made by the French and withdrawn by the English—full of the movement of languages and peoples still in historical sedimentation at the bottom, waiting for the real virtuality of our imagination. If we remain confined to English language U.S. Cultural Studies, we will not be instructed either by the staging of restricted permeability or by the disappeared text of the translation from and into the European national languages that form the basis of what we know as Comparative Literature. Cultural Studies, tied to plot summary masquerading as analysis of representation, and character analysis by a precritical model of motivation or an unearned psychoanalytic vocabulary would reduce *Heremakhonon* to a *Bildungsroman* about Veronica. The old country—an undifferentiated "Africa"—exists as a backdrop for the New World African. And for Comparative Literature it does not exist at all.

I return, then, to my general argument in this opening chapter: collaborate with and transform Area Studies. A reading of *Heremakhonon* would, for example, be strengthened by a sense of Africa that might emerge from such collaboration, for the text stages the folly of imagining an undifferentiated "Africa" as a backdrop for the New World African.

There are, of course, many institutional obstacles to such collaboration. Among them is institutional fear on both sides. Disciplinary fear. The social sciences fear the radical impulse in literary studies, and over the decades, we in the humanities have trivialized the social sciences into their rational expectation straitjackets, not recognizing that, whatever the state of the social sciences in our own institution, strong tendencies toward acknowledging the silent but central role of the humanities in the area studies paradigm are now around. Sustained and focused discussion is all the more necessary as the boundaries of disciplinary knowledge are being redrawn.

If the distaste for the social sciences and Area Studies can be overcome, there is, as we have already seen, the fear of Cultural Studies. We are afraid to let the permeability be unrestricted by our own moves. Suppose through the approved channel of Francophony, Teutophony, Lusophony, Anglophony, Hispanophony, they should begin to want to "rediscover their 'heritage' languages and cultures?"[29] Since, in this scenario, Area Studies are odious, we will be back in Cultural Studies, monolingual, presentist, narcissistic, not practiced enough in close reading even to understand that the mother tongue is actively divided.

In such a scenario it is hard not to read literature, sometimes, as a didactic aid. Let me invite you to compare the fear of Cultural Studies to this picture painted by the Magistrate, a benevolent imperialist, for the fearful young imperialist officer in J. M. Coetzee's *Waiting for the Barbarians*:

> [The barbarians] do not doubt that one of these days we [the colonizers] will pack our carts and depart to wherever it was we came from, that our buildings will become homes for mice and lizards, that their beasts will graze on these rich fields we have planted. You smile? Shall I tell you something? Every year the lake-water grows a little more salty. There is a simple explanation—never mind what it is. The barbarians know this fact. At this very moment they are saying to themselves, "Be patient, one of these days their crops will start withering from the salt, they will not be able to feed themselves, they will go." That is what they are thinking. That they will outlast us.[30]

Throughout this chapter, I have, in a rather Utopian manner, been repeatedly urging a joining of forces between Comparative Literature and Area Studies, because the times seem to have come up to meet me halfway. I have confessed that I am aware of the strong forces at work against the possibility of such a coalition. At first glance, I have suggested that it is disciplinary fear that seems to keep out Area Studies. But there is also the fear, I have added, that at this point, the "new" Area Studies might lead us back to the fear of the loss of quality control seething under the surface of the original Bernheimer report. The ominous humor of Mary Louise Pratt's invocation of George Orwell's *Animal Farm* reflects that general unease:

> Let us imagine . . . that we CompLit types are the animals in the coops and pens. The farmer no longer exists. He has retired to Florida, and before he left, he opened all the doors and gates. What do we want to do? The foxes now have access to the henhouse; the hens, however, are free to go somewhere else. Animals will move from pasture to pasture and pen to pen; strange matings will occur and new creatures [be] born. The manure pile will be invaded and its winter warmth enjoyed by all. It will be a while till new order and new leadership emerge. But the farmer won't be back.[31]

In fact, the farmer did not go far. Today the backlash is on the rise. There is a demand for humanism, with a nod toward Asia; for universalism, however ambiguous; for quality control; to fight terrorism.

For a way out, in the new Comparative Literature, I turn again to Coetzee's novel. *Waiting for the Barbarians* is, perhaps like all qualitative rather than quantitative texts, also a staging of what may be called logic and rhetoric—assuming that they can be so neatly distinguished. There are passages that resemble the one I have quoted above, where the protocol may be called "logical" when placed in distinction from what I am going to call "rhetorical." These logical passages are often accounts of the fruits of imperial experience, as above, with some historical generalizability within the loose outlines of the narrative. Over against these are the many passages where the Magistrate tries to grasp the barbarian in an embrace that is both singular and responsible. The exemplary singularity is "the girl," a young barbarian woman whose name we never learn, whose name perhaps neither the Magistrate nor the writer figure knows. The staging of rhetoricity in the novel is the Magistrate's attempt to decipher her. This is quite different from the staging of the logical Magistrate, a capable and experienced senior official who is able to summarize the characteristics of empire. A series of dreams may be one account of this deciphering effort. To have sex with the girl is another.

The Magistrate, usually a promiscuous man, is generally unable to perform what would be recognizable as an act of sex with this young barbarian woman. What comes through in his efforts to do so is his repeated generalization that the meaning of his own acts is not clear if he tries to imagine her perspective: "I feed her, shelter her, use her body, if that is what I am doing, in this foreign way."[32] I cannot forget that Freud urges us to investigate the uncanny because we are ourselves *Fremd-sprächig*, "foreign speakers."[33] What can it mean but seeing the other as placed, native?

The girl is returned to her people. In a surprising example of characterological asyndeton or *recusatio,* the Magistrate intervenes on behalf of tortured barbarian prisoners and is himself tortured brutally and systematically. His imprisonment, which comes before this, reduces him to nothing. Coetzee describes him describing his deciphering effort thus: "So I continue to swoop and circle around the irreducible figure of the girl, casting one net of meaning after another over her. . . . What does she see? The protecting wings of a guardian albatross or the black shape of a coward crow afraid to strike while its prey yet breathes?"

The passage begins with a paradox. The logic of noncontradiction requires that what is irreducible is truth, not figure. The passage continues with a figuring of the undecidability of meaning. Web after web is thrown. But the meaning that is sought is the meaning of the Magistrate as subject, as perceived by the barbarian as other. This meaning is undecidable in at least two ways. First, there is no stable declaration of meaning. And second, the alternative possibilities of the meaning of the dominant self in the eyes of the barbarian other are given as questions. It is possible to suggest that two alternatives are standing in for an indefinite structure of possibilities here.

Of course, the literary is not a blueprint to be followed in unmediated social action. But if as teachers of literature we teach reading, literature can be our teacher as well as our object of investigation. And, since we are imprisoned in the vicious circle of our stakes in institutional power, the Magistrate's researches in extremis can perhaps rearrange our desires. With team teaching and institutional goodwill, we can continue to supplement Area Studies with this lesson in view. Our own undecidable meaning is in the irreducible figure that stands in for the eyes of the other. This is the effortful task: to displace the fear of our faceless students, behind whom are the eyes of the global others.

Otherwise, who crawls into the place of the "human" of "humanism" at the end of the day, even in the name of diversity? We must consider "Collectivities."

Notes

1. From *Death of a Discipline* (New York: Columbia University Press, 2003), 1–23. Notes are the author's.

2. "Preface," in Charles Bernheimer, ed., *Comparative Literature in the Age of Multiculturalism* (Baltimore: Johns Hopkins University Press, 1995), ix–x.

3. Toby Alice Volkman, *Crossing Borders: Revitalizing Area Studies* (New York: Ford Foundation, 1999), ix. This attempt—to rethink Area Studies after the Cold War—is now somewhat outdated. The watchword now is "Area Studies after 9/11," and the configuration resembles the earlier Area Studies initiative, which I discuss in my text. [A page-long quotation, omitted here, follows from a congressional report advocating language funding as strategically useful for American interests abroad, especially in the Middle East. Spivak comments:] At this point, to withdraw in-depth language learning and close reading from Comparative Literature when it moves to the global South is to decide that the only relationship the United States can have with those areas is based on considerations of security, that the critical intimacy of literary learning must remain isolationist in the Euro-U.S.

4. The statistics may have changed slightly in the intervening years, but the general picture remains the same.

5. George E. Rowe, "50th Anniversary of *Comparative Literature*" and Timothy Bahti, "Impossibility, Free," *Comparative Literature* 51:1 (1999): 1, 62. Bahti is right, *Premises* is a fine book, and the times are near Fascist, more so than in 1999.

The solution is not to go back to an exclusivist Eurocentric comparative literature spawned in the late forties.

6. "Versions of the Margin: J. M. Coetzee's *Foe* Reading Defoe's *Crusoe/Roxana*" in Jonathan Arac and Barbara Johnson, eds., *Consequences of Theory: Selected Papers of the English Institute, 1987–88* (Baltimore: Johns Hopkins University Press, 1990), 154; the lecture was delivered two years earlier.

7. Charles Wagley, *Area Research and Training: A Conference Report on the Study of World Areas* (New York: Columbia University, n.d.), 1; emphasis mine.

8. These sentiments are expressed in Margaret Talbot, "The Way We Live Now: 11-18-01; Other Woes" *New York Times Magazine,* November 18, 2001, 23, in the wake of September 11.

9. The groundbreaking energy of *Orientalism,* by Edward W. Said (New York: Pantheon, 1978) tends to conflate Oriental Studies, Area Studies, and Comparative Literature. Enabled by its initiating impulse, we now make these distinctions.

10. The Birmingham metaphor is taken from the title of a book by one of the most brilliant students at the first Cultural Studies group: Paul Gilroy, *There Ain't No Black in the Union Jack: The Cultural Politics of Race and Nation* (New York: Routledge, 1992 [1987]). There are more differences than similarities here. These differences have been charted by Lawrence Grossberg in *Dancing in Spite of Myself: Essays on Popular Culture* (Durham: Duke University Press, 1997), 191–218.

11. For "ontopologist," see Jacques Derrida, *Specters of Marx: the State of the Debt, the Work of Mourning, and the New International,* tr. Peggy Kamuf (New York: Routledge, 1994), 82. In a back issue of *The New Yorker* (June 23 & 30, 1997), Salman Rushdie refers to all the literatures of India not in English as "parochial."

12. Gayatri Chakravorty Spivak, "Translation as Culture," *parallax* 6:1 (2000): 21.

13. When I make this point, I often hear "But everyone can't learn all the languages!" Just as the old Comparative Literature did not require learning "all the European languages," so also does this new version of Comparative Literature not ask you to learn all the world's languages. The only requirement is that, when you work with literatures of the global South, you learn the pertinent languages with the same degree of care. As you go toward the already available resources of Area Studies, learn the language with literary depth rather than only social scientific fluency.

14. Jacques Derrida, *Given Time: 1. Counterfeit Money,* tr. Peggy Kamuf (Chicago: University of Chicago Press, 1992), 54; the next reference is to 67.

15. "Righting Wrongs." In Nicholas Owen, ed., *Human Rights and Human Wrongs* (Oxford: Oxford University Press, 2003).

16. As usual, Raymond Williams's system of residual-dominant-emergent-archaic-preemergent gives me the best handle on mapping culture as process (Raymond Williams, *Marxism and Literature* [Oxford: Oxford University Press, 1977], 121–127). This is why I began with an account of academic memos, a mundane record of the dominant appropriating a social emergent.

17. 1999 Report of the Mayor's Task Force on CUNY, chaired by Benno C. Schmidt Jr., entitled, "The City University of New York: An Institution Adrift." The passage quoted is from p. 13.

18. Mehdi Charef, *Le Thé Au Harem d'Archi Ahmed* (Paris: Mercure de France, 1983). The phrase is an Arabic transformation of the theorem of Archimedes worked out by a young North African immigrant boy in the low-income housing projects in the outskirts of Paris. This is a typical example of how the underclass imagination swims in the deep waters of metropolitan survival.

19. Derrida, "Force of Law," in *Acts of Religion*, tr. Gil Anidjar (New York: Routledge, 2002), 249: translation modified.

20. What follows is my own interpretative digest of Melanie Klein, *Works* (New York: Free Press, 1984), vols. 1–4. Giving specific footnotes is therefore impossible. The details may also not resemble orthodox Kleinian psychoanalysis.

21. Spivak, "Translation as Culture," 13.

22. For the definition of irony I am using here, see Paul de Man, *Allegories of Reading: Figural Language in Rousseau, Nietzsche, Rilke and Proust* (New Haven: Yale University Press, 1979), 301.

23. Jacques Derrida, *The Monolingualism of the Other*, tr. Patrick Mensah (Stanford: Stanford University Press, 1998), 57–58.

24. Maryse Condé, *Heremakhonon* (Boulder: Three Continents, 1985), 24.

25. Maryse Condé, *En attendant le bonheur (Heremakhonon)* (Paris: Seghers, 1988), 12.

26. Derrida has an uncharacteristically hardheaded comment about the poor souls who must cross to Europe to seek refuge or escape from poverty: "Today, on this earth of humans, certain people must yield to the homo-hegemony of dominant languages. They must learn the language of the masters, of capital and machines; they must lose their idiom in order to survive or live better" (Derrida, *Monolingualism*, 30).

27. Michael Gomez, *Pragmatism in the Age of Jihad: The Precolonial State of Bundu* (Cambridge: Cambridge University Press, 1992), 22–23.

28. Saskia Sassen, discussion after Keynote, Conference on Comparative Literature in Transnational Times, Princeton University, March 23–24, 2000.

29. Volkman, *Crossing Borders*, ix.

30. J. M. Coetzee, *Waiting for the Barbarians* (New York: Penguin, 1982), 51.

31. Mary Louise Pratt, "Comparative Literature and Global Citizenship," in Bernheimer, ed., *Comparative Literature in the Age of Multiculturalism* (Baltimore: Johns Hopkins University. Press, 1995), 58.

32. Coetzee, *Waiting*, 30; the next quoted passage is from 81.

33. Sigmund Freud, "The Uncanny," in *The Standard Edition of the Psychological Works*, tr. Alix Strachey et al. (New York: Norton, 1961–), 17:221.

31

Evolution, World-Systems, *Weltliteratur*[1] (2006)

Franco Moretti

Professor of English and Comparative Literature at Stanford University and founder of Stanford's Center for the Study of the Novel, Franco Moretti continues to stir controversy for his advocacy of "distant reading." Through this approach to literary history, he eschews close reading, preferring to develop maps as a tool for understanding the use of space in literature and to use statistical data for understanding the diffusion of literature and literary influences. He has discussed his methods in "Conjectures on World Literature" (2000) and in a subsequent book, *Graphs, Maps, Trees: Abstract Models for a Literary History* (2005), of which the article given here is an outgrowth.

  Moretti was educated at the University of Rome and taught first in Italy and then at Columbia University before moving to Stanford. Working mainly on nineteenth- and early-twentieth-century European literature, he achieved early prominence for his essay collection *Signs Taken for Wonders* (1983), which investigated the politics of aesthetics in an incisive and lively style, analyzing, among other subjects, Restoration tragedy, Balzac's fiction, and James Joyce's *Ulysses*. He subsequently began to concentrate particularly on narrative and genre theory, the central emphasis of his book *The Modern Epic: The World-System from Goethe to García Márquez* (1998). He then served as general editor of a major collaborative study of the novel throughout history and in all its forms, published in five volumes in Italy; a two-volume selection has been published by Princeton under the title *The Novel* (2006). To date, his books have been translated into fifteen languages.

The following essay weaves together several of Moretti's major interests, as he proposes developing a new theory of *Weltliteratur* adequate for a globalizing age by combining lessons from evolution and world-systems theory.

―――――――

Although the term 'world literature' has been around for almost two centuries, we do not yet have a genuine theory of the object—however loosely defined—to which it refers. We have no set of concepts, no hypotheses to organize the immense quantity of data that constitute world literature. We do not *know* what world literature is.

This paper will not fill the void. But it will sketch a comparison of two theories that have often struck me as excellent models for the task: evolutionary theory, and world-system analysis. I will begin by outlining their potential contribution to literary history; then I will discuss their compatibility; and finally, outline the new image of *Weltliteratur* that emerges from their encounter.[2]

―――――――

I

It is easy to see why evolution is a good model for literary history: it is a theory that explains the extraordinary variety and complexity of existing forms on the basis of a historical process. In a refreshing contrast to literary study—where theories of form are usually blind to history, and historical work blind to form—for evolution form and history are really the two sides of the same coin; or perhaps, one should say, adopting a more evolutionary metaphor, they are the two dimensions of the same tree.

Take the only image in the entire *Origin of Species*: the tree that appears in the fourth chapter, 'Natural Selection,' in the section on 'Divergence of Character.' A tree, or a 'diagram,' as Darwin calls it in the text, as if to emphasize that is designed to visualize the interplay of two variables: history along the vertical axis, which charts the regular passage of time (every interval, 'one thousand generations')—and form along the horizontal axis, which follows for its part the morphological diversification that will eventually lead to 'well-marked varieties,' or to entirely new species.

The horizontal axis follows formal diversification. . . . But Darwin's words are stronger: he speaks of 'this rather perplexing subject,' whereby forms do not just 'change,' but do so by always *diverging* from each other (remember, we are in the section on 'Divergence of Character'). Whether as a result of geo-historical accidents, or under the action of a specific 'principle'—as far as I can tell, the question is still open—divergence pervades the history of life, defining its morphospace as an intrinsically expanding one. 'A tree can be viewed as a simplified description of a matrix of *distances*' write Cavalli-Sforza, Menozzi and Piazza in the methodological prelude to their *History and Geography of Human Genes*; and their work with genetic groups and linguistic families, that branch away from each other in geography and morphology at once, makes clear what they mean: a tree is a way of sketching *how far* a given form has moved from another one, or from their common point of origin.

A theory that takes as its central problem the *multiplicity of forms* existing in the world; that explains them as the result of *divergence and branching*; and that bases divergence on a process of *spatial separation*: here is what evolutionary theory has to offer to literary history. Many different forms, in a discontinuous space: not a bad starting point, for the study of world literature.

II

In world-systems analysis the coordinates change, as the onset of capitalism brusquely reduces the many independent spaces needed for the origin of species (or of languages) to just three positions: core, periphery, semi-periphery. The world becomes *one*, and *unequal*: one, because capitalism constrains production everywhere on the planet; and unequal, because its network of exchanges requires, and reinforces, a marked unevenness between the three areas.

Here, too, it is easy to understand the theory's appeal for literary study. On its basis, we can finally grasp the *unity* of world literature, as in Goethe's and Marx's *Weltliteratur*. And then, the theory illuminates the *internal articulations* of the literary system: like capitalism, *Weltliteratur* is itself one and unequal, and its various components—the world's many national and local literatures—are often thwarted in their development by their position within the system as a whole. Itamar Even-Zohar (whose 'polysystem theory' is quite similar to world-systems analysis) puts it very well when he observes that, within the international literary system, 'there is no symmetry': powerful literatures from the core constantly 'interfere' with the trajectory of peripheral ones (whereas the reverse almost never happens), thus constantly increasing the inequality of the system.[3]

While studying the international market for eighteenth–nineteenth-century novels, I reached very similar conclusions to Even-Zohar's. Here, the crucial mechanism by which the market operated was that of *diffusion*: books from the core were incessantly exported into the semi-periphery and the periphery, where they were read, admired, imitated, turned into models—thus drawing those literatures into the orbit of core ones, and indeed 'interfering' with their autonomous development. And then, this asymmetric diffusion imposed a stunning *sameness* to the literary system: wave after wave of epistolary fiction, or historical novels, or *mystères*, dominated the scene everywhere—often, like American action movies today, more thoroughly in the smaller markets of peripheral cultures than in their country of origin.

World literature as one and unequal: this was the contribution of the world-systems approach. The *international constraints* under which literature is written: the limits that the world market imposes on the imagination. 'Diffusion is the great conservative force in human history,' wrote A. L. Kroeber[4]—and he was absolutely right.

III

One can hardly imagine a more clearcut antithesis. Evolution foregrounds the *diversification* of existing forms produced by speciation; world-system analysis, the *sameness* (or at any rate, the limits on diversity) enforced by diffusion. I am simplifying of course, evolution includes mutation *and* selection (i.e. both the production and the elimination of diversity), just as world-system analysis specifies *different* positions within the international division of labour. But still, think of those titles: *The Origin of* species, plural, and *The modern world*-system, singular: grammar is a good index of the opposite research projects. And the geographical substratum of the two theories duplicates the antithesis: Darwin's breakthrough famously occurred in an *archipelago*, because the origin of species (Ernst Mayr's 'allopatric speciation') needs a world made of separate spaces; but the long-distance trade of modern capitalism *bridges* the greatest of oceans, and subjects all societies to a single, continuous geography.

A theory of diversification; a theory of sameness. Clearly, the two are incompatible. Just as clearly, they both explain important aspects of world literature. They are both true: but they *cannot* both be true.[5] Or perhaps, better, they cannot be true—*unless literature itself functions in two completely incompatible ways.*

This sounds like an absurd idea; but it does have a historical and morphological rationale. The historical argument is simple: diversification and sameness are both present in literary history because they arise in different epochs, and from different social mechanisms. Diversification is the result of the (relative) isolation of human cultures from their origins until a few centuries ago; sameness appears much later, sometime around the eighteenth century, when the international literary market becomes strong enough to (begin to) subjugate those separate cultures. Here I am simplifying again, there have been earlier episodes of widespread diffusion (like the petrarchist epidemics of late medieval Europe), just as there have been *later* episodes of diversification; but the point is that each of the two principles has an elective affinity with a different socio-historical configuration; and that, by and large, we have moved from the one to the other.

This, in broad strokes, is the historical argument. The morphological one is different. So far, I have implicitly accepted the evolutionary assumption that in literature, just as in nature, *diversity equals divergence*: that new forms only arise by branching out from pre-existing ones via some kind of mutation. Now, if this were the case, then diffusion (and with it the world-systems approach) would have very little to say on literary innovation: great at explaining how forms *move*, a theory of diffusion cannot account for how they *change*, for the simple reason that diffusion is not meant to multiply forms, but to *reduce* their number by maximizing the space occupied by just one of them. Diffusion is the great conservative—not creative—force of human history.

In literature, just as in nature, diversity equals divergence . . . But what if the *convergence* of distinct lineages could also produce new forms?

IV

This question will strike many readers as almost a rhetorical one. 'Darwinian evolution,' writes Stephen Jay Gould, 'is a process of constant separation and distinction. Cultural change, on the other hand, receives a powerful boost from amalgamation and anastomosis of different traditions. A clever traveler may take one look at a foreign wheel, import the invention back home, and change his local culture fundamentally and forever.'[6] The clever traveler is a poor example (it is a case of diffusion, not of amalgamation), but the general point is clear, and well expressed by the historian of technology George Basalla: 'different biological species usually do not interbreed,' he writes: 'artifactual types, on the other hand, are routinely combined to produce new and fruitful entities.'[7]

Routinely combined . . . That's it: for most scholars, convergence is the basic, if not the *only* mode of cultural history. I have criticized elsewhere this position, countering it with a sort of cyclical division of labour between divergence and convergence in the shaping of the literary morphospace.[8] Here, I will only add that the decisive historical watershed is again the establishment of an international market: divergence being the main path of literary change before its advent, and convergence afterwards. Thomas Pavel's morphological reflections in *La Pensée du roman*—based on a very different conceptual framework from the present paper—offers excellent (because independent) corroboration for this thesis: divergence is for him the driving force in the first fifteen centuries of the novel's existence, and convergence from the eighteenth century onwards.[9]

From the eighteenth century onwards . . . Or in other words: convergence becomes active in literary life *at exactly the same time as diffusion*. And one wonders: is it merely a temporal coincidence, or is there a functional relationship between them?

V

Let me begin with a concrete example. Years ago, one of the greatest critics of our time, Antonio Candido, wrote a tryptich of essays (on Zola's *Assommoir* [1877], Verga's *Malavoglia* [1881], and Azevedo's *Cortiço* [1890]), in which he followed the diffusion of the naturalist novel from the core (France), through the semi-periphery (Italy) and into the periphery (Brazil) of the world literary system. And he discovered, among many other things, a sort of *internal asymmetry* in the diffusion of naturalism: whereas the structure of Zola's plot is largely retained by Verga and Azevedo, his *style* tends to be heavily transformed: in Verga, by his Sicilian-Tuscan orchestration of collective speech, and by the use of proverbs; in Azevedo, by the recourse to allegory, and the narrator's frequent ethical intrusions (especially in sexual matters).[10]

Now, Verga and Azevedo are far from being unique. In the late nineteenth century, as the diffusion of modern novels reaches with increasing regularity peripheral cultures, their greatest writers all subject western European models to a similar process of *stylistic overdetermination*: the analytico-impersonal style of nineteenth-century France is replaced by judgmental, loud, sarcastic, emotional voices, always somewhat at odds with the story they are narrating. In slightly different forms, we find the same arrangement in Multatuli's anti-imperialist classic, *Max Havelaar, or The Coffee Sales of the Netherlands Trading Company* (1860), and in Rizal's Filipino masterpiece *Noli me tangere* (1886–87); in Futabatei's *Drifting Clouds* (1887), the 'first modern Japanese novel,' and in Tagore's Rashomon-like political parable, *Home and the World* (1916).

Italy, Brazil, Indonesia, Philippines, Japan, Bengal . . . The specifics obviously differ from case to case, but the formal logic is always the same: these novels are all 'amalgamations of different traditions'—and all of the same kind: they combine *a plot from the core*, and *a style from the periphery*.[11] The realist-naturalist plot of lost illusions and social defeat reaches more or less intact the periphery of the literary system; but in the course of the journey, it becomes somehow detached from the 'serious' tone that used to accompany it, and is joined to a new stylistic register.

But how is it possible for plot and style to become 'detached'?

VI

It is possible, because the novel is a *composite* form, made of the two distinct layers of 'story' and 'discourse'—or, in my slight simplification, of plot and style: plot presiding over the internal concatenation of the events, and style over their verbal presentation. Analytically, the distinction is clear; textually a little less so, because plot and style are usually so tightly interwoven that their separation is hard to imagine. And yet, *if diffusion intervenes, 'moving' novels across the literary system*, they do indeed separate: plot travels well, remaining fairly stable from context to context, whereas style disappears, or changes.

Why this difference? Two reasons. First, plot is usually the main point of a novel, and hence it must be as solid as possible. To highlight how inextricable this narrative concatenation ought to be, Boris Tomasevskij coined in 1925 the metaphor of the 'bound motifs,' that 'cannot be omitted [...] without disturbing the whole causal-chronological course of events.'[12] But if bound motifs 'cannot be omitted,' neither can they really be changed: and so, concludes Tomashevskij, 'they are usually distinguished by their 'vitality': that is, 'they appear unchanged in the works of the most various schools'—and just as unchanged, we may add, in the works of the most various countries.[13]

The second reason for the different destinies of plot and style is not structural, but linguistic. Diffusion usually means translation, and hence reformulation from one language into another. Now, plot is largely *independent* from language: it remains more or less the same, not only from language to language, but even from one sign system to another (from novel to illustration, film, ballet . . .). Style is however nothing *but* language, and its translation—*traduttore traditore*—is almost always an act of betrayal: the more complex a style is, in fact, the greater the chance that its traits will be lost in the process.

So. As novelistic forms travel through the literary system, their plots are (largely) preserved, while their styles are (partly) lost—and are replaced by 'local' ones, as in Azevedo and the other novelists mentioned above.

The result is a hybrid form that does indeed 'amalgamate different traditions,' as Gould would have it. But for many of these texts, *dissonance* would be more precise than amalgamation: dissonance, disagreement, at times a lack of integration between what happens in the plot, and how the style evaluates the story, and presents it to the reader. *Form as a struggle*: this is what we have here: a struggle between the story that comes from the core, and the viewpoint that 'receives' it in the periphery. That the two are not seamlessly fused is not just an aesthetic given, then, but the crystallization of an underlying *political* tension. In this respect, the morphology of hybrid texts is an invaluable vantage point from which to observe the endless spiral of hegemony and resistance created by world literature.

VII

The term 'world literature' has been around for almost two centuries, but we still do not know what world literature is . . . Perhaps, because we keep collapsing under a single term *two distinct world literatures*: one that precedes the eighteenth century—and one that follows it. The 'first' *Weltliteratur*, a mosaic of separate, 'local' cultures; it is characterized by strong internal diversity; it produces new forms mostly by divergence; and is best explained by (some version of) evolutionary theory.[14] The 'second' *Weltliteratur* (which I would prefer to call world literary system) is unified by the international literary market; it shows a growing, and at times stunning amount of sameness; its main mechanism of change is convergence; and is best explained by (some version of) world-systems analysis.

What are we to make of these two world literatures? I think they offer us a great chance to rethink the place of history in literary studies. A generation ago, the literature of the past used to be the only 'great' literature; today, the only 'relevant' literature is that of the present. In a sense, everything has changed. In another, nothing has, because both positions are profoundly *normative* ones, much more concerned with value judgments than with actual knowledge. Instead, the lesson of the two world literatures is that the past and the present of literature should be seen, not as 'better' or 'worse' epochs, but as *structurally so unlike each other* that they require completely different theoretical approaches. Learning to study *the past as past*, then, and *the present as present:* such is the intellectual challenge posed by *Weltliteratur* in the twenty-first century. But this is a very large topic that deserves a study of its own.

Notes

1. An earlier version of this essay was previously published in *Review* 3 (2005). This version appeared in *Studying Transcultural Literary History*, ed. Gunilla Lindberg-Wada (Berlin: de Gruyter, 2006), 113–21. Notes are the author's.

2. Embarrassingly enough, I have used evolution and world-systems analysis for over ten years—even in the same book!—without ever considering their compatibility. Evolution was crucial for the morphological argument of *Modern Epic* (London, 1996), whose thematic aspect was in turn strongly shaped by world-systems analysis. A few years later, world-systems analysis played a major role in *Atlas of the European Novel: 1800–1900* (London: Verso, 1998), and in the articles 'Conjectures on World Literature' and 'More Conjectures,' *New Left Review* (2000, 2003); while evolution was the basis for 'The Slaughterhouse of Literature,' *Modern Language Quarterly* (2000) and 'Graphs, Maps, Trees: Abstract Models for Literary History, 3,' *New Left Review* (2004); a few passages from this article are more or less repeated in the present text.

3. Itamar Even-Zohar, 'Laws of Literary Interference,' *Poetics Today* 11:1 (1990), 62.

4. A. L. Kroeber, 'Diffusionism,' in Etzioni and Etzioni (eds), *Social Change* (New York, 1964), 144.

5. Obviously enough, I am here speaking of their truth *when applied to literature*; in their original fields (biology and economic history) the two theories are simply incomparable.

6. Stephen Jay Gould, *Full House: The Spread of Excellence from Plato to Darwin* (New York: Harmony, 1996), 220–21.

7. George Basalla, *The Evolution of Technology* (Cambridge: Cambridge University Press, 1988), 137–38.

8. See *Graphs, Maps, Trees* (London, 2005).

9. Thomas Pavel, *La Pensée du roman* (Paris, 2003).

10. Antonio Candido, *O discurso e a cidade* (São Paulo, 1993).

11. It can hardly be a coincidence that the greatest problematizer of narrative voice in western European literature—Joseph Conrad—had himself worked in the colonies, and owed his formal breakthrough (Marlow's laborious, defensive irony) to his wish to represent the periphery to a metropolitan audience. In his case, of course, the ingredients of the amalgamation are reversed: a plot from the periphery—and a style from the core

12. Boris Tomashevsky, "Thematics" (1925), in Lee T. Lemon and Marion J. Reis (eds), *Russian Formalist Criticism: Four Essays* (Nebraska University Press, 1965), 68.

13. Here, the analogy with biological mutation is arresting. 'In DNA and protein regions of vital importance for function, one finds perfect—or almost perfect—conservation,' write Cavalli-Sforza, Menozzi, and Piazza in *The History and Geography of Human Genes* (Princeton: Princeton University Press, 1994, 15): 'this indicates strong selective control against changes that would be deleterious; it also shows that evolutionary improvement in this region is rare or absent. However, variation is quite frequent in chromosome regions that are not of vital importance.' Within narrative structure, bound motifs are the equivalent of those 'protein regions of vital importance for function,' where one finds 'near perfect conservation,' whereas the 'chromosome regions that are not of vital importance,' and where variation is therefore quite frequent, have their parallel in the 'free motifs' of Tomashevsky's model, which 'may be omitted without destroying the coherence of the narrative,' and which are as a consequence quite variable ('each literary school has its characteristic stock [of free motifs]').

14. Speaking of 'local' cultures does not exclude the existence of large regional systems (Indo-European, East Asian, Mediterranean, Meso-American, Scandinavian . . .), which may even overlap with each other, like the eight thirteenth-century 'circuits' of Janet Abu-Lughod's *Before European Hegemony* (Oxford, 1989). But these geographical units are not yet stably subordinated to a single center like the one that emerged in eighteenth century France and Britain.

32

A New Comparative Literature[1] (2006)

Emily Apter

Professor of French and Comparative Literature at New York University, Emily Apter was educated at Harvard and Princeton Universities. She works in literatures of France, North Africa, the Caribbean, Germany, Britain, and North America in the nineteenth and twentieth centuries. Her recent essays have focused on paradigms of "oneworldedness" especially as conceived by Édouard Glissant, on literary world-systems, and on translation as a form of intellectual labor. Her books include *Feminizing the Fetish: Psychoanalysis and Narrative Obsession in Turn-of-the-Century France* (1991), and *Continental Drift* (1999), an important study of the interplay of writing in France and in France's former colonies.

In *The Translation Zone: A New Comparative Literature* (2006), Apter rethinks translation in light of the September 11, 2001, attacks on the World Trade Center in New York. In particular, she considers the expansion of the field of translation studies from its traditional concern with linguistic fidelity to original texts to include both real-world issues such as war and conceptual issues such as the use of creoles and pidgins in literature, and she discusses the place of language and literature in debates about canon formation. In the book's concluding essay, included here, Apter seeks to break the identification of language with nation. What she proposes is "a new Comparative Literature" based on translation, which she sees variously initiated in the work of Leo Spitzer, Jacques Derrida, Edward Said, and Gayatri Spivak.

In attempting to rethink critical paradigms in the humanities after 9/11, with special emphasis on language and war, the problem of creolization and the mapping of languages "in-translation," shifts in the world canon and literary markets, and the impact of enhanced technologies of information translation, I have tried to imagine a program for a new comparative literature using translation as a fulcrum. I began with an attempt to rethink the disciplinary "invention" of comparative literature in Istanbul in the 1930s, using the work of Leo Spitzer and Erich Auerbach as figures whose names became synonymous with defining early iterations of global humanism in exile. I end with some reflections on what happens to philology when it is used to forge a literary comparatism that has no national predicate, and that, in naming itself *translatio* names the action of linguistic self-cognizing, the attempt to bring-to-intelligibility that which lies beyond language ("God," Utopia, Nature, DNA, a Unified Field Theory of Expressionism).

In naming a translational process constitutive of its disciplinary nomination comparative literature breaks the isomorphic fit between the name of a nation and the name of a language. As Giorgio Agamben has observed (with reference to Alice Becker-Ho's determination that Gypsy *argot* failed to qualify as a language since Gypsies as a people were deemed to be without nation or fixed abode), "we do not have, in fact, the slightest idea of what either a people or a language is" (*Means without Ends*, 64).[2] The Gypsy case, for Agamben, reveals the shaky ground on which language nomination rests. In affirming that "Gypsies are to a people what *argot* is to language," Agamben unmasks standard language names as specious attempts to conceal the fact that "all peoples are gangs and *coquilles,* all languages are jargons and *argots*" (65, 66). For Agamben, languages that defy containment by structures of the state (as in Catalan, Basque, Gaelic), or the blood and soil mythologies of peoples, might conceivably prompt the ethical "experience of the pure existence of language" (68). "It is only by breaking at any point the nexus between the existence of language, grammar, people, and state that thought and praxis will be equal to the tasks at hand," Agamben concludes (69).

Samuel Weber performs a similar dissection of national/nominal language fallacies with more direct pertinence to translation, noting that,

> [T]he linguistic systems between which translations move are designated as "natural" or "national" languages. However, these

terms are anything but precise or satisfactory. . . . The imprecision of these terms is in direct proportion to the linguistic diversity they seek to subsume. . . . The difficulty of finding a generic term that would accurately designate the class to which individual languages belong is indicative of the larger problem of determining the principles that give those languages their relative unity or coherence— assuming, that is, that such principles really exist.[3]

Comparative literature answers Weber's call for the generic term to which individual languages belong. As such, it functions as an abstract generality or universal sign on the order of Wittgenstein's *Urzeichen* [elemental sign], which sounds out the *forçage*[4] of nation-subject and language-subject in the process of nomination. We hear this *forçage* in an expression like *traduit de l'américain* ("translated from the American"), which captures a non-existent language coming into being through the act of rendering it coincident with the name of a nation or people. There is, of course, no standard language with discrete grammatical rules and protocols called "American." "American" may be the name of a language referring (in nominalist terms) to a possible world of language, but it is neither a term used by North American speakers of English to refer to their idiolect, nor a legitimate nation-marker. (As Jean-Luc Godard said recently, "I would really like to find another word for 'American.' When someone says 'American' they mean someone who lives between New York and Los Angeles, and not someone who lives between Montevideo and Santiago.")[5] As the name of a language, "American" implicitly consigns Spanish to "foreign"-language status even though millions of hemispheric subjects of the Americas claim Spanish as their native tongue. A new comparative literature would acknowledge this jockeying for power and respect in the field of language. A new comparative literature seeks to be the name of language worlds characterized by linguistic multiplicity and phantom inter-nations.

In *Poétique de la relation* Edouard Glissant authorizes the move toward linguistic inter-nationalism when he subordinates instabilities of nomination to geopoetics, replacing the old center-periphery model with a world system comprised of multiple linguistic singularities or interlocking small worlds, each a locus of poetic opacity. Glissant's paradigm of the *tout-monde,* building on the nondialectical ontological immanence of Deleuze and Guattari, offers a model of aporetic community in which small worlds (modeled perhaps after a deterritorialized Caribbean) connect laterally through bonds of Creole and a politics of mutualism centered on resistance to debt. Looking ahead to a day when *toutmondisme* will surpass *tiermondisme,* that is to say, when the nation form gives way to the immanent, planetary totality of Creole, Glissant imagines Creole "transfigured into word of the world."[6] Building on Glissant, the authors of *Éloge de la créolité* envision *créolité* as "*the world diffracted but recomposed,* a maelstrom of signifieds in a single signifier: a Totality . . . . *full knowledge of Creoleness,* they argue, *will be reserved for Art,* for art absolutely."[7] As Peter Hallward has remarked: "The nation's loss is . . . Creole's gain."[8]

Insofar as Creole heralds a condition of linguistic postnationalism and denaturalizes monolingualization (showing it to be an artificial arrest of language transit and exchange), it may be said to emblematize a new comparative literature based on translation. Though, as I have argued in this book, Creole has emerged as an omnibus rubric, loosely applied to hybridity, *métissage,* platforms of cross-cultural encounter, or to language as a critical category of literary history; it has also emerged as a synonym for traumatic lack. Marked by the Middle Passage, and the coarse commands of human traffickers and plantation owners, Creole carries a history of stigma comparable to that of pidgin translation in nineteenth-century Chinese. In Haun Saussy's estimation, Chinese pidgin translation was, for the grammarians, an exhibition of "incompleteness . . . an unequal relationship between normal speech in the target language and the halting, misarticulated, or excessive speech of the source language it represents." In Saussy's reading, Walter Benjamin's sacred, interlinear ideal of translation offers the possibility of revaluing pidgin because interlinear's word-for-word literalism authorizes a translation full of holes: "Pidgin stands for—it makes audible and visible—the incommensurability of languages. The discussion of Chinese, that 'grammarless' language, gives pidgin its greatest representational license."[9] Recuperated in the guise of sacred translation, Creole, like pidgin, may be cast as a language "blessed" with the fullness of aporia.

For Derrida, the aporia names the conceptual impasse of death lodged in the body of language. Beginning with a phrase "*Il y va d'un certain pas* [It involves a certain step/not; he goes along at a certain pace]," Derrida associates the *pas* with a "recumbant corpse" or limit-condition between language and that which is other to itself:[10]

> a Babel "*from* and *within* itself . . . the stranger at home, the invited or the one who is called. . . . This border of translation does not pass among various languages. It separates translation from itself, it separates translatability within one and the same language. A certain pragmatics thus inscribes this border *in the very inside of the so-called French language.*" (*Aporias,* 10)

Derrida's concept of aporia—heard in the "*no, not, nicht, kein*" of alterity —is linked to the politics of monolingualism in *Monolingualism of the Other: Or the Prosthesis of Origin* (1996).[11] The book's epigraphs from Glissant and Abdelkebir Khatibi attest to a rare engagement with *francophonie* as theoretical terrain. Derrida, with tongue in cheek, competes with Khatibi for title to the stateless status of the *Franco-Magrébin* subject. The hyphen signifies all the problems of national/linguistic unbelonging characteristic of post-Independence Algerians, including the way in which Jews, Arabs, and French were neighbored, yet separated, by the French language. "This language will never be mine," says Derrida of French, drawing from his own experience of national disenfranchisement the lesson that language is loaned to communities of speakers. "The untranslatable remains (as my law tells me) the poetic economy of the idiom" (56). Contrary to what one might expect, the prosthetic "other" in Derrida's title "monolingulism of the other," is not polyglottism, but an aporia within ipseity, an estrangement in language as such. For Derrida, untranslatability is the universal predicate of language names.

Derrida's aporia deconstructs the nationalist nominalism of language names by locating an always-prior other within monolingual diction. The aporia loosens the national anchor from the language name, wedging a politics of the subject between the name of a nation and the name of a language. Blocking the automatic association of specified language properties with the universal set of a given nation, Derrida's aporia approximates the logician's "X" in the modern nominalist formula "For any X, if X is a man, it is mortal," which disables the universal qualifier "all men are mortal" and relativizes the human status of the subject in question. X may or may not be a man in the same way that Francophone speaker X may or may not be French. The contingency of the subject suggests here that French speakers who are French nationals constitute one possible world of French speakers among many. Once the national predicate is dislodged, no speaker maintains exclusive ownership of language properties; the right to language is distributed more freely as language is classed as the property of X-many lease-holders.

Abolishing the divides of inside/outside, guest/host, owner/tenant, "the monolinguism of the other" names a comparatism that neighbors languages, nations, literatures, and communities of speakers. This idea of "neighboring" is borrowed from Kenneth Reinhard, specifically his Levinasian understanding of a "comparative literature otherwise than comparison . . . a mode of reading logically and ethically prior to similitude, a reading in which texts are not so much grouped into 'families' defined by similarity and difference, as into 'neighborhoods' determined by accidental contiguity, genealogical isolation, and ethical encounter" ("Kant with Sade, Lacan with Levinas").[12] For Reinhard, treating texts as neighbors "entails creating anamorphic disturbances in the network of perspectival genealogies and intertextual relations. That is, before texts can be compared, one text must be articulated as the uncanny neighbor of the other; this is an assumption of critical obligation, indebtedness, secondariness that has nothing to do with influence, Zeitgeist, or cultural context" (Ibid., 796). Departing from philological tradition, which argues for textual relation based on shared etymology, tropes, aesthetic tastes, and historical trajectories, Reinhard proposes in their stead a theory of "traumatic proximity": "How [he asks] can we re-approach the traumatic proximity of a text, before or beyond comparison and contextualization? Asymmetrical substitution implies that there is no original common ground for textual comparison, but only the trauma of originary nonrelationship, of a gap between the theory and practice of reading that is only retroactively visible" (804). Reinhard's notion of "otherwise than comparison" shifts the problematic from language nomination to the ethics of traumatic proximity.

"Neighboring" describes the traumatic proximity of violence and love, manifest as exploded holes in language or translation gaps. Such spaces of nonrelation can be condemned as signs of profanation, but they are also susceptible to being venerated as signs of sacred incommensurability. These aporias are directly relevant to the problem of how a language names itself because they disrupt predication, the process by which verbal attributes coalesce in a proper name or noun.

The difficult process of depredication, otherwise known as secular criticism, is one of the premier tasks of philology, as conceived by Edward Said in his final writings. In a chapter of *Humanism and Democratic Criticism* devoted to "The Return of Philology," Said wrote:

> Philology is, literally, the love of words, but as a discipline it acquires a quasi-scientific intellectual and spiritual prestige at various periods in all of the major cultural traditions, including the Western and the Arabic-Islamic traditions that have framed my own development.

> Suffice it to recall briefly that in the Islamic tradition, knowledge is premised upon a philological attention to language beginning with the Koran, the uncreated word of God (and indeed the word "Koran" itself means reading), and continuing through the emergence of scientific grammar in Khalil ibn Ahmad and Sibawayh to the rise

of jurisprudence *(fiqh)* and *ijtihad* and *ta'wil,* jurisprudential herme-neutics and interpretation, respectively.[13]

Said makes a sweeping pass through systems of humanistic education based on philology in Arab universities of southern Europe and North Africa in the twelfth century, Judaic tradition in Andalusia, North Africa, the Levant, and Mesopotamia, then on to Vico and Nietzsche. He extols a humanism of reading and interpretation "grounded in the shapes of words as bearers of reality, a reality hidden, misleading, resistant, and difficult. The science of reading, in other words, is paramount for humanistic knowledge" (58).

Just as *Humanism and Democratic Criticism* openly engages Leo Spitzer's philological legacy (Spitzer rather than Auerbach for once!), so too does the 2002 essay "Living in Arabic," which invites being read in tandem with Spitzer's "Learning Turkish." Spitzer with Said plays off the epistemo-logical modalities of "living" and "learning" a language.[14] Where Spitzer fastened on the ontological implications of sequencing in Turkish, and emphasized how the consecutive unfolding ("one by one") of an action mimics the nature of experience, thereby enlivening narration in a uniquely "human and subjective way," Said gleaned significance from the relational gaps of word-by-word analysis. Spitzer was drawn to modes of expression that seemed wreathed in scare-quotes, that somehow marked "what is hap-pening" as things happen. Interrogative enunciations in Turkish such as "He saw me, or did he not?" or "Did he or did he not open the door?" epito-mized for Spitzer a habit of self-questioning that initiated an othering of self within subjectivity. The term *gibi* he suggested, whether attached to verb forms or just thrown out at random, indexed the speaker's loss of convic-tion in his own words. "Words no longer signify a definite event but carry the ambiguity of comparison within them." *Gibi,* then, was interpreted as a part of speech tailored for the philologist, for it called attention to how each word internalizes comparability. Similarly, in his conclusion to "The Return to Philology," Said fixed on the "space of words" as the aporia of comparison. Humanism, he maintained,

> is the means, perhaps the consciousness we have for providing that
> kind of finally antinomian or oppositional analysis between the
> space of words and their various origins and deployments in physical
> and social place, from text to actualized site of either appropriation
> or resistance, to transmission, to reading and interpretation, from
> private to public, from silence to explication and utterance, and
> back again, as we encounter our own silence and mortality—all

of it occurring in the world, on the ground of daily life and history and hopes, and the search for knowledge and justice, and then perhaps also for liberation. (83)

As if anticipating Said's lifelong commitment to a lexicon of exile affording existential humanism, Spitzer delighted in the way in which the grammar of mitigation—the generous sprinkling of equivalent terms for "buts" and "howevers" through Turkish speech—afforded felicitous relief "to the thinking man from the pressures of this difficult life." "In this decreasing voice," Spitzer asserted, "I see our humility. For an instant, the human spirit descends to pessimism to rid itself of numbness, triumphing over difficulty through reason. Thus a small word like 'but,' or 'yet,' though a mere grammatical tool of negation, becomes an emotional manifestation loaded with the weight of life. In these small words, we see humanity deal with adversity." Spitzer traveled down to the micrological stratum of speech particles to observe "life" swimming against the current of "death." Grammatical markers of doubt or negation were cast as valves that released the pressure that builds up in the course of fighting to stay alive, rallying the subject's determination to go on. For Said, these particles comprise a syntax of traumatic incommensurability; they contour the aporias of militant love. Said and Spitzer seem to have entered into stichomythia in their common regard for word spacing as the "program" of life and death, the grammar of grounding and unhoming. Saidian-Spitzerian philology portends the advent of a translational humanism that assumes the disciplinary challenges posed by Turkish and Arabic in their respective circumstances of institutional exile. Turkish and Arabic name, for each of them, a crisis of theo-poetics in secular time.

In his considerations on the status of Arabic language, which one can only speculate might have been the subject of a book-in-the-making, Said experimented with using philology to re-articulate the sacred otherwise. It was as if he were aware of Kenneth Reinhard's conviction that the unconscious—like divine language—comes through in the desire to "re-speak or repunctuate" a language that comes from the outside, bearing "the marks of its strange desires and cruel imperatives."[15] Rather than dodge the issue of how a secular language copes with the mandate of neighboring a sacred tongue, Said took up the problem of "living in Arabic," a task complicated in everyday life by the split between classical (*fus-ha*) and demotic (*'amiya*).[16] Though one of Said's clear intentions in the essay was to reform Arabic so that it could better deal with classical expression in quotidian speech, his greatest concern, it would seem, was to use philology to de-translate the "fundamentalist" attribution of Arabic. To this end, he recalled the term *al-qua'ida* to its philological function (as the word for "grammar," or "base" of language), just as in *Humanism and Democratic Criticism*, he reclaimed *jihad* for secular usage, contextualizing it as commitment to "*isnad*" or hermeneutical community:[17]

> Since in Islam the Koran is the Word of God, it is therefore impossible ever fully to grasp, though it must repeatedly be read. But the fact that it is in language already makes it incumbent on readers first of all to try to understand its literal meaning, with a profound awareness that others before them have attempted the same daunting task. So the presence of others is given as a community of witnesses whose availability to the contemporary reader is retained in the form of a chain, each witness depending to some degree on an earlier one. This system of interdependent readings is called "*isnad*." The common goal is to try to approach the ground of the text, its principle or *usul*, although there must always be a component of personal commitment and extraordinary effort, called "*ijtihad*" in Arabic. (Without a knowledge of Arabic, it is difficult to know that "*ijtihad*" derives from the same root as the now notorious word *jihad*, which does not mainly mean holy war but rather a primarily spiritual exertion on behalf of the truth.) It is not surprising that since the fourteenth century there has been a robust struggle going on about whether *ijtihad* is permissible, to what degree, and within what limits. (68–69)

As this passage affirms, Said was committed to extracting the predicate "terror" from Arabic as the name of a language. But in seeking to secularize the sacred word, Said wandered into the nominalist quandary of how to name languages otherwise. The need to disrupt the deep structural laws by which languages are named after nations, peoples, and God-terms complemented Said's concern to posit a philological humanism no longer hobbled by neo-imperialist jingoism, no longer shy of facing off against the autocracy of theocratic speech-acts, and yet, also no longer able to deny the idea of "life" as an untranslatable singularity, a "cognition of paradise" that assumes tangible guise in Babel or the "afterlife" of translation.[18] Linguistic monotheism (inherent in Derrida's "monolingualism of the other"), Said's paradigm of "Living in Arabic" (the set that excludes itself, the logic of one sacred language constituted as two—*fus-ha* and *'amiya)*, and Spitzer's paradigm of "Learning Turkish" (which activates standing reserves of nontranslation) together push the limits of how language thinks itself, thereby regrounding the prospects for a new comparative literature in the problem of translation.

Notes

1. From *The Translation Zone: A New Comparative Literature* (Princeton: Princeton University Press, 2006), 243–51. Notes are the author's.

2. Giorgio Agamben, *Means without Ends: Notes on Politics,* trans. Vincenzo Binetti and Cesare Casarino (Minneapolis: University of Minnesota Press, 2000).

3. Samuel Weber, "A Touch of Translation: On Walter Benjamin's 'Task of the Translator,'" in *The Ethics of Translation,* eds. Sandra Bermann and Michael Wood (Princeton: Princeton University Press, 2005), 66.

4. "Forcing" in a horticultural sense, as when plants are made to bloom early.

5. Jean-Luc Godard in interview with Manohla Dargis, "Godard's Metaphysics of the Movies," *New York Times,* Nov. 21, 2004, Arts and Leisure, 22.

6. Edouard Glissant, *Poétique de la relation* (Paris: Gallimard, 1990), 88.

7. Jean Bernabé, Patrick Chamoiseau, Raphael Confiant, *Éloge de la créolité.* Edition bilingue français/anglais, trans. M. B. Teleb-Khyar (Paris: Gallimard, 1989), pp. 88–90. Emphasis in italics as appears in the original.

8. Peter Hallward, "Edouard Glissant between the Singular and the Specific," in *The Yale Journal of Criticism* 11:2 (1998), 455.

9. Haun Saussy, *The Great Wall of Discourse and Other Adventures in Cultural China* (Cambridge, Mass.: Harvard East Asian Monographs/Harvard University Press, 2001), 78–79.

10. Jacques Derrida, *Aporias,* trans. Thomas Dutoit (Stanford: Stanford University Press, 1993), 6.

11. The word *négritude* offers a good example of a "prosthesis of origin" since it was coined by Aimé Césaire in Martinique, a place that had no single African language on which to ground it.

12. Kenneth Reinhard, "Kant with Sade, Lacan with Levinas," *Modern Language Notes* 110:4 (1995), 785.

13. Edward Said, *Humanism and Democratic Criticism* (New York: Columbia University Press, 2003), 58.

14. Leo Spitzer, "Learning Turkish," in *Varlik* [Being], Nos. 19, 35, and 37, 1934. Translation by Tülay Atak.

15. "The unconscious is like a text without punctuation written in familiar characters and a foreign language, a sacred or *revealed* text, moreover, in the sense that the discourse it speaks comes from the outside, from the Other, and bears the marks of its strange desires and cruel imperatives. The interpretive work of analysis is not to translate it so much as to *rearticulate* it, to respeak and repunctuate its components: here a stop or blockage separating two morphemes or phonemes is

elided, there an associative connection is severed; or perhaps an isolated and intransigent signifier in the unconscious stream, the pole star of a discursive constellation or 'complex,' is put into significative motion, and another falls out of circulation, as a newly fixed and unspeakable center of gravitation." Kenneth Reinhard, "Lacan and Monotheism: Psychoanalysis and the Traversal of Cultural Fantasy," in *Jouvert* 3:12 (1999), 7. http://social.chass.ncsu.edu /jouvert/v3il2/reinha.htm.

16. On the issue of two Arabic languages in one, see Iman Humaydan Younes, "Thinking *Fussha,* Feeling '*Amiya*: Between Classical and Colloquial Arabic," *Bidoun: Arts and Culture from the Middle East,* 2:1 (2004): 66–67.

17. "In a few years I felt I had no alternative but to commit myself to a re-education in Arabic philology and grammar. (Incidentally, the word for grammar is the plural *qawa'id,* whose singular form is the by now familiar *al-qua'ida,* also the word for a military base, as well as a rule, in the grammatical sense.)" Edward Said, "Living in Arabic," *Raritan* 21:4 (2002), 229.

18. The phrase "cognition of Paradise," close to the concept of "imparadising" that I developed in my chapter on Saidian humanism, was used by Martin Vialon in an unpublished essay on the Arcadian paintings of Traugott Fuchs, another German émigré who made his career in Istanbul under the mentorship of Spitzer and Auerbach. See "The Scars of Exile: Paralipomena concerning the Relationship between History, Literature and Politics—Demonstrated in the Examples of Erich Auerbach, Traugott Fuchs and Their Circle in Istanbul." I am grateful to Martin Vialon for his rich, ongoing research on Auerbach's Istanbul exile, and for his willingness to share work in progress.

BIBLIOGRAPHIES

General • Susan Bassnett, *Comparative Literature: A Critical Introduction*, 1993.
• Sandra Bermann and Michael Wood, eds., *Nation, Language, and the
Ethics of Translation*, 2005. • Charles Bernheimer, ed., *Comparative
Literature in the Age of Multiculturalism*, 1995. • Robert J. Clements,
Comparative Literature as Academic Discipline, 1978. • Dionyz Ďurišin,
Vergleichende Literaturforschung, 1972 • Hugo Dyserinck, *Komparatistik:
Eine Einführung*, 1977. • René Etiemble, *Ouverture(s) sur un comparatisme
planétaire*, 1988. • Manfred Gsteiger, *Littérature nationale et comparatisme*,
1967. • Claudio Guillén, *The Challenge of Comparative Literature*, 1993.
• Margaret Higonnet, *Borderwork: Feminist Engagements with Comparative
Literature*, 1994. • François Jost, *Introduction to Comparative Literature*,
1974. • Earl Miner, *Comparative Poetics*, 1990. • S. S. Prawer, *Comparative
Literature Studies: An Introduction*, 1973. • Haun Saussy, ed., *Comparative
Literature in an Age of Globalization*, 2006. • Manfred Schmeling, *Vergleich-
ende Literaturwissenschaft*, 1981. • Hans-Joachim Schultz and Phillip H.
Rhein, *Comparative Literature: The Early Years*, 1973. • Ulrich Weisstein,
Comparative Literature and Literary Theory, 1973.

Theodor Adorno • Theodor Adorno, *Aesthetic Theory*, 1984. • Theodor Adorno,
The Culture Industry: Selected Essays on Mass Culture, 1991. • Theodor
Adorno, *The Jargon of Authenticity*, 1973. • Theodor Adorno, *Minima
Moralia: Reflections on a Damaged Life* (1951), 1974. • Theodor Adorno,
Negative Dialectics, 1966. • Max Horkheimer and Theodor Adorno,
Dialectic of Enlightenment, 1972. • Nigel Gibson and Andrew Rubin, eds.,
Adorno: A Critical Reader, 2002. • Brian O'Conner, ed., *The Adorno Reader*,
2000. • Theodor Adorno and Walter Benjamin, *Complete Correspondence,
1928–1940*, 1999. • Donald Burke, ed., *Adorno and the Need in Thinking*,
2007. • David Cunningham and Nigel Mapp, eds., *Adorno and Literature*,
2006. • Louis V. DeSalle, *The Dialectic of Ideology in the Thought of Theodor*

W. Adorno, 1984. • Roger Foster, *Adorno: The Recovery of Experience*, 2007.
• Renée Heberle, ed., *Feminist Interpretations of Theodor Adorno*, 2006.
• Tom Huhn, ed., *The Cambridge Companion to Adorno*, 2004. • Simon
Jarvis, ed., *Theodor W. Adorno: Critical Evaluations in Critical Theory*,
2007. • David Jenemann, *Adorno in America*, 2007. • Alistair Morgan,
Adorno's Concept of Life, 2007. • Max Paddison, *Adorno, Modernism and
Mass Culture: Essays on Critical Theory and Music*, 1996.

Emily Apter • Emily Apter, *André Gide and the Codes of Homotextuality*, 1987. • Emily
Apter, *Continental Drift: From National Characters to Virtual Subjects*,
1999. • Emily Apter, *Feminizing the Fetish: Psychoanalysis and Narrative
Obsession in Turn-of-the-Century France*, 1991. • Emily Apter, "'Je ne crois
pas beaucoup à la littérature comparée': Universal Poetics and Postcolonial
Comparatism," in Haun Saussy, ed., *Comparative Literature in an Age of
Globalization*, 2006, 54–62. • Emily Apter, *The Translation Zone: A New
Comparative Literature*, 2006.

Erich Auerbach • Erich Auerbach, *Mimesis: The Representation of Reality in Western
Literature*, 1953. • Erich Auerbach, *Scenes from the Drama of European
Literature*, 1959. • Jan Bremmer, "Erich Auerbach and His Mimesis,"
Poetics Today 20:1 (1999), 3–10. • David Damrosch, "Auerbach in Exile,"
Comparative Literature 47:2 (1995), 97–117. • Geoffrey Green, *Literary
Criticism and the Structures of History: Erich Auerbach and Leo Spitzer*,
1982. • Carl Landauer, "*Mimesis* and Erich Auerbach's Self-Mythologizing,"
German Studies Review 11:1 (1988), 83–96. • Seth Lerer, ed., *Literary
History and the Challenge of Philology: The Legacy of Erich Auerbach*, 1996.
• Edward Said, "Erich Auerbach, Critic of the Earthly World," *boundary 2*
31:2 (2004), 11–34.

Mikhail Bakhtin • Mikhail Bakhtin, *The Dialogic Imagination: Four Essays*, ed.
Michael Holquist, 1981. • Mikhail Bakhtin, *Problems of Dostoevsky's Poetics*,
1973. • Mikhail Bakhtin, *Rabelais and His World*, 1968. • Pam Morris, ed.,
The Bakhtin Reader, 1994. • Craig Brandist, *The Bakhtin Circle: A Philosophical and Historical Introduction*, 2002. • Bracht Branham, ed., *Bakhtin
and the Classics*, 2002. • Katerina Clark and Michael Holquist, *Mikhail
Bakhtin*, 1984. • Frank Farmer, ed., *Landmark Essays on Bakhtin, Rhetoric,
and Writing*, 1998. • Michael Holquist, *Dialogism: Bakhtin and His World*,
1990. • Gary Saul Morson, ed., *Bakhtin: Essays and Dialogues on His Work*,
1986. • Gary Saul Morson and Carol Emerson, *Mikhail Bakhtin: Creation of
a Prosaics*, 1990. • Clive Thomson, ed., *Mikhail Bakhtin and the Epistemology of Discourse*, 1990. • Tzvetan Todorov, *Mikhail Bakhtin: The Dialogical
Principle*, 1984.

Roland Barthes • Roland Barthes, *Critical Essays*, 1972. • Roland Barthes, *The Empire of Signs*, 1982. • Roland Barthes, *The Grain of the Voice*, 1985. • Roland Barthes, *Mythologies*, 1982. • Roland Barthes, *Roland Barthes by Roland Barthes*, 1994. • Susan Sontag, ed., *A Barthes Reader,* 1982. • Norbert-Bertrand Barbe, *Roland Barthes et la théorie esthétique,* 2001. • Carlo Brune, *Roland Barthes: Literatursemiologie und literarisches Schreiben*, 2003. • Jonathan Culler, *Barthes*, 1983. • Jonathan Culler, *Structuralist Poetics*, 1975. • Diana Knight, ed., *Critical Essays on Roland Barthes*, 2000. • Philip Thody and Ann Course, *Introducing Barthes*, 1997. • Annette Lavers, *Roland Barthes, Structuralism and After*, 1982. • Richard Maksey and Eugenio Donato, eds., *The Structuralist Controversy*, 1970. • Jean-Michel Rabaté, ed., *Writing the Image after Roland Barthes*, 1997. • Steven Ungar and Betty McGraw, eds., *Signs in Culture: Roland Barthes Today*, 1989.

Georg Brandes • Georg Brandes, *Aesthetiske Studier,* 1888. • Georg Brandes, *Friedrich Nietzsche,* 1972. • Georg Brandes, *Goethe,* 1922. • Georg Brandes, *Main Currents in Nineteenth Century Literature,* 1901. • Georg Brandes, *Selected Letters,* 1990, ed. W. Glyn Jones. • Klaus Bohnen, ed., *Der Essay als kritischer Spiegel: Georg Brandes und die deutsche Literatur: Eine Aufsatz-Sammlung,* 1980. • Julius Moritzen, *Georg Brandes in Life and Letters,* 1922. • Henning Fenger, *Georg Brandes et la France: La formation de son espirit et ses goûts littéraires,* 1963. • Bertil Nolin, *Georg Brandes,* 1976. • Paul V. Rubow, *Georg Brandes og den Kritiske Tradition i det Nittende Aarhundrede,* 1932. • Henk van der Liet, "Georg Brandes as a Literary Intermediary," *Tijdschrift voor Skandinavistiek* 25:1 (2004), 93–110.

Jean-Marie Carré • Jean-Marie Carré, *Goethe en Angleterre,* 1920. • Jean-Marie Carré, *Voyageurs et écrivains français en Égypte,* 1932. • Marius-François Guyard, *La Littérature comparée. Avant-propos de Jean-Marie Carré,* 1951. • René Etiemble, *Comparaison n'est pas raison,* 1963. • Daniel-Henri Pageaux, "Un Comparatiste à New York: Les carnets inédits de Jean-Marie Carré," *Revue de Littérature Comparée* 1:313 (2005), 75–84. • Henry H. H. Remak, "Comparative Literature at the Crossroads: Diagnosis, Therapy and Prognosis," *Yearbook of Comparative and General Literature* 9 (1960), 1–28.

Pascale Casanova • Pascale Casanova, *The World Republic of Letters,* 2004. • Pascale Casanova, *Samuel Beckett: Anatomy of a Literary Revolution,* 2006. • Christophe Pradeau and Tiphaiine Samoyault, *Où est la littérature mondiale? Textes de Pascale Casanova, Jérôme David, Annie Epelboin,* 2005. • Christopher Prendergast, ed., *Debating World Literature,* 2004. • Ignacio M. Sánchez-Prado, ed., *América Latina en la "literatura mundial,"* 2006.

Ernst Robert Curtius • Ernst Robert Curtius, *Deutscher Geist in Gefahr,* 1932.
• Ernst Robert Curtius, *Essays on European Literature,* 1973. • Ernst Robert
Curtius, *European Literature and the Latin Middle Ages,* 1953. • Walter
Brerschin and Arnold Rothe, eds., *Ernst Robert Curtius: Werk, Wirkung,
Zukunftsperspektiven: Heidelberger Symposion zum hundertsten Guburtstag,*
1989. • William Cain, *The Twentieth-Century Humanist Critics: From
Spitzer to Frye,* 2007. • Hans Helmut Christmann, *Ernst Robert Curtius
und die deutschen Romanisten,* 1987. • Arthur R. Evans, Jr., ed., *On Four
Modern Humanists: Hofmannsthal, Gundolf, Curtius, Kantorowicz,* 1970.
• Karl Thönnisen, *Ethos und Methode: Zur Bestimmung der Metaliteratur
nach Ernst Robert Curtius,* 2001.

Paul de Man • Paul de Man, *Allegories of Reading,* 1979. • Paul de Man, *Blindness
and Insight: Essays in the Rhetoric of Contemporary Criticism,* 1971. • Paul
de Man, *The Resistance to Theory,* 1986. • Paul de Man, *The Rhetoric of
Romanticism,* 1984. • Tom Cohen et al., eds., *Material Events: Paul de Man
and the Afterlife of Theory,* 2001. • Ortwin de Graef, *Titanic Light: Paul de
Man's Post-Romanticism, 1960–1969,* 1995. • Jacques Derrida, *Mémoires:
Pour Paul de Man,* 1988. • Rodolphe Gasché, *Wild Card of Reading: On Paul
de Man,* 1998. • Werner Hamacher et al., eds., *Responses: On Paul de Man's
Wartime Journalism,* 1989. • Luc Herman et al., eds., *(Dis)continuities:
Essays on Paul de Man,* 1989. • David Lehman, *Signs of the Times: Decon-
struction and the Fall of Paul de Man,* 1991. • Martin McQuillan, *Paul de
Man,* 2001. • Christopher Norris, *Paul de Man: Deconstruction and the
Critique of Aesthetic Ideology,* 1988. • Lindsay Waters and Wlad Godzich,
eds., *Reading de Man Reading,* 1989.

Germaine de Staël • Germaine de Staël, *De la littérature* and *De l'Allemagne,* in
Oeuvres, 1820. • Germaine de Staël, *Dix années d'exil,* 1966. • Simone
Balayé, *Madame de Staël: Lumières et liberté,* 1979. • Robert de Luppé, *Idées
littéraires de Madame de Staël et l'héritage des lumières,* 1969. • Machteld
de Poortere, *Philosophical and Literary Ideas of Mme de Staël and of Mme
de Genlis,* 2007. • Sergine Dixon, *Germaine de Staël, Daughter of the En-
lightenment: The Writer and Her Turbulent Era,* 2007. • Maria Fairweather,
Madame de Staël, 2005. • Suzanne Guerlac, "Writing the Nation (Mme de
Staël)," *French Forum* 30:3 (2005), 43–56. • G. E. Gwynne, *Madame de
Staël et la révolution française: Politique, philosophie, littérature,* 1969.

Itamar Even-Zohar • Itamar Even-Zohar, *Papers in Historical Poetics,* 1978. • Itamar
Even-Zohar, ed., "Polysystem Studies," special issue of *Poetics Today* 11:1
(1990). • Itamar Even-Zohar et al., *Avances en teoría de la literatura: Estética
de la recepción, pragmática, teoría empírica y teoría de los polisistemas,* 1994.
• Susan Bassnett, *Translation Studies,* 1991. • Philippe Codde, "Polysystem

Theory Revisited: A New Comparative Introduction," *Poetics Today* 24:1 (2003), 91–126.

Charles Mills Gayley • Charles Mills Gayley, *Classic Myths in English Literature*, 1904. • Charles Mills Gayley, *Guide to the Literature of Aesthetics*, 1890. • Charles Mills Gayley, *Methods and Materials of Literary Criticism*, 1920. • Walter Morris Hart et al., eds., *The Charles Mills Gayley Anniversary Papers* (1922), 1967. • Benjamin Kurtz, *Charles Mills Gayley*, 1943.

Édouard Glissant • Édouard Glissant, *Caribbean Discourse: Selected Essays*, 1989. • Édouard Glissant, *Introduction à une poétique du divers*, 1996. • Suzanne Crosta, *Marronnage créateur: Dynamique textuelle chez Édouard Glissant*, 1991. • J. Michael Dash, *Édouard Glissant*, 1995 • Jean-Louis Joubert, *Édouard Glissant*, 2005. • Natalie Melas, *All the Difference in the World: Postcoloniality and the Ends of Comparison*, 2007. • Daniel Radford, *Édouard Glissant*, 1982. • Barbara J. Webb, *Myth and History in Caribbean Fiction: Alejo Carpentier, Wilson Harris, and Édouard Glissant*, 1992.

J. W. von Goethe and J. P. Eckermann • Johann Peter Eckermann, *Gespräche mit Goethe in den letzten Jahren seines Lebens*, ed. Regine Otto, 1982; trans. John Oxenford as J. W. von Goethe, *Conversations with Eckermann* (1851), 1984. • Johann Wolfgang von Goethe, *Dichtung und Wahrheit aus meinem Leben*, 1949; • Johann Wolfgang von Goethe, *Essays on Art and Literature*, 1986. • Johann Wolfgang von Goethe, *Gesamtausgabe der Werke und Schriften in zweiundzwanzig Bänden*, 1961. •Johann Wolfgang von Goethe, *Poetry and Truth from My Own Life*, 1930. • David Damrosch, *What Is World Literature?* chap. 1, 2003. • Richard Friedenthal, *Goethe, His Life and Times*, 1963. • John Hennig, *Goethe and the English Speaking World*, 1988. • H. H. Houben, *Goethes Eckermann: Die Lebensgeschichte eines bescheidenen Menschen*, 1934. • Georg Lukács, *Goethe and His Age*, 1968. • Hans Naumann, *Aus den Tiefen wächst das Licht: Erdachte Gespräche Goethes mit Eckermann*, 1949. • John Pizer, *The Idea of World Literature*, 2006. • Avital Ronell, *Dictations: On Haunted Writing*, 1993. • Benjamin C. Sax, *Images of Identity: Goethe and the Problem of Self-Conception in the Nineteenth Century*, 1987. • Fritz Strich, *Goethe und die Weltliteratur*, 1946.

Johann Gottfried Herder • Johann Gottfried Herder, *Against Pure Reason: Writings on Religion, Language, and History*, ed. Marcia Bunge, 1992. • Johann Gottfried Herder, *Reflections on the Philosophy of the History of Mankind*, 1968. • Johann Gottfried Herder, *On World History: An Anthology*, ed. Hans Adler et al., 1997. • F. M. Barnard, ed., *Herder on Nationality, Humanity and History*, 2003. • F. M. Bernard, ed., *J. G. Herder on Social and Political Culture*, 1969. • Wulf Koepke, *Johann Gottfried Herder: Language, History,* and the Enlightenment, 1990. • Robert S. Mayo, *Herder and the Beginnings of Comparative Literature*, 1979. • Michael Morton, *Herder and the Poetics of Thought*, 1989. • Robert E. Norton, *Herder's Aesthetics and the European Enlightenment*, 1991.

Barbara Johnson • Barbara Johnson, *The Critical Difference: Essays in the Contemporary Rhetoric of Reading*, 1980. • Barbara Johnson, *The Feminist Difference: Literature, Psychoanalysis, Race and Gender*, 1998. • Barbara Johnson, *The Wake of Deconstruction*, 1994. • Barbara Johnson, *A World of Difference*, 1987. • Susan Gubar, "The Differences Barbara Johnson Makes." *Diacritics* 34:1 (2004), 73–100. • "Difference: Reading with Barbara Johnson," a special issue of *Differences: A Journal of Feminist Cultural Studies*, 17:3 (2006), with contributions by Avital Ronell, Jane Gallop, and others.

Kobayashi Hideo • Kobayashi Hideo, *Literature of the Lost Home: Kobayashi Hideo— Literary Criticism*, ed. Paul Anderer, 1995. • Midori Matsui, "The Implicit Return: Kobayashi Hideo's Failure to Achieve Modernism and the Problems Concerning His Ideological Conversion," in *Literary Intercrossings: East Asia and the West*, 1998. • Hitoshi Oshima, "Kobayashi Hideo, Apologist for the 'Savage Mind,'" *Comparative Literature Studies* 41:4 (2004), 509–19. • Edward Seidensticker, "The Death of Kobayashi Hideo: The End of an Era," *Japan Quarterly* 30:3 (1983), 270–73. • Junko Takamizawa, *My Brother Hideo Kobayashi*, 2001.

Julia Kristeva • Julia Kristeva, *The Crisis of the European Subject*, 2000. • Julia Kristeva, *Desire in Language: A Semiotic Approach to Literature and Art*, 1980. • Julia Kristeva, *The Powers of Horror: An Essay on Abjection*, 1982. • Julia Kristeva, *Revolution in Poetic Language*, 1984. Toril Moi, ed., *The Kristeva Reader*, 1986. • Kelly Oliver, ed., *The Portable Kristeva*, 1997. • Carol Mastrangelo Bové, *Language and Politics in Julia Kristeva: Literature, Art, Therapy* 2006. • John Fletcher and Andrew Benjamin , eds., *Abjection, Melancholia, and Love: The Work of Julia Kristeva*, 1990. • Susan Sellers, ed., *A History of Feminist Literary Criticism*, 2007. • Judith Still, "Continuing Debates about 'French' Feminist Theory," *French Studies* 61:3 (2007), 314–28.

Georg Lukács • Georg Lukács, *Essays on Realism*, 1980. • Georg Lukács, *Goethe and His Age*, 1968. • Georg Lukács, *The Historical Novel*, 1962. • Georg Lukács, *History and Class Consciousness*, 1971. • Georg Lukács, *Soul and Form*, 1974. • Georg Lukács, *Studies in European Realism*, 1950. • Georg Lukács, *Theory of the Novel: A Historico-Philosophical Essay on the Forms of Great Epic Literature* (1917), 1971. • Arpad Kadarkay, ed., *The Lukács Reader*, 1995. • Susan Derwin, *The Ambivalence of Form: Lukács, Freud, and the*

Novel, 1992. • Fariborz Shafai, *The Ontology of Georg Lukács: Studies in Materialist Dialectics*, 1996. • Galin Tikhanov, *The Master and the Slave: Lukács, Bakhtin, and the Ideas of Their Time*, 2000.

Hugo Meltzl • Hugo Meltzl and Samuel Brassai, eds., *Acta Comparationis Litterarum Universarum: Zeitschrift für vergleichende Litteratur*, 1877–88. • Arpad Berczik, "Hugo von Meltzl," *Arbeiten zur deutschen Philologie* 12 (1978), 87–100. • Arpad Berczik, "Weltliteratur, Komparatistik und Übersetzungs-kunst," *Acta Litteraria Academiae Scientiarum Hungaricae* 22 (1980), 119–33. • David Damrosch, "Rebirth of a Discipline," *Comparative Critical Studies* 3:1–2 (2006), 99–112. • Horst Fassel, ed., *Hugo Meltzl und die Anfänge der Komparatistik*, 2005.

Franco Moretti • Franco Moretti, *Atlas of the European Novel, 1800–1900*, 1998. • Franco Moretti, "Conjectures on World Literature," *New Left Review*, 2d ser., Jan.–Feb. 2000, 54–68, reprinted in Christopher Prendergast, ed., *Debating World Literature*, 2004, 148–62. • Franco Moretti, *Graphs, Maps, Trees: Abstract Models for a Literary History*, 2005. • Franco Moretti, *The Modern Epic: The World-System from Goethe to García Márquez*, 1996. • Franco Moretti, *Signs Taken for Wonders: Essays in the Sociology of Literary Forms*, 1988. • Franco Moretti, *The Way of the World: The Bildungsroman in European Culture*, 1987. • Michael Caesar, "Franco Moretti and the World Literature Debate," *Italian Studies* 62:1 (2007), 125–35. • Efraín Kristal, "'Considerando en frío . . .': Una respuesta a Franco Moretti," in Ignacio M. Sánchez-Prado, ed., *América Latina en la "literatura mundial*," 2006, 101–16.

Ngũgĩ wa Thiong'o • Ngũgĩ wa Thiong'o, *Barrel of a Pen: Resistance to Repression in Neo-colonial Kenya*, 1983. • Ngũgĩ wa Thiong'o, *Decolonising the Mind: The Politics of Language in African Literature*, 1986. • Ngũgĩ wa Thiong'o, *Detained: A Writer's Prison Diary*, 1981. • Simon Gikandi and Evan Mwangi, eds., *The Columbia Guide to East African Literature in English Since 1945*, 2007. • G. D. Killam, ed., *Critical Perspectives on Ngũgĩ wa Thiong'o*, 1984. • Peter Nazareth, ed., *Critical Essays on Ngũgĩ wa Thiong'o*, 2000.

Friedrich Nietzsche • Friedrich Nietzsche, *Basic Writings of Nietzsche*, intro. Peter Gay, 2000. • Friedrich Nietzsche, *Beyond Good and Evil*, trans. R. J. Hollingdale, 2003. • Friedrich Nietzsche, *The Birth of Tragedy out of the Spirit of Music*, trans. Shaun Whiteside, 1993. • Friedrich Nietzsche, *Ecce Homo*, trans. Duncan Large, 2007. • Friedrich Nietzsche, *Sämtliche Werke: Kritische Studienausgabe in 15 Bänden*, ed. Giorgio Colli and Mazzino Montinari, 1999. • Sander Gilman et al., eds., *Friedrich Nietzsche on*

Rhetoric and Language, 1989. • Arthur Danto, *Nietzsche as a Philosopher*, 1965. • Sander L. Gilman, *Nietzschean Parody: An Introduction to Reading Nietzsche*, 1976. • Karl Jaspers, *Nietzsche: An Introduction to the Understanding of His Philosophical Activity*, 1965. • Alexander Nehamas, *Nietzsche: Life as Literature*, 1985 • M. S. Silk and J. P. Stern, *Nietzsche on Tragedy*, 1981.

Octavio Paz • Octavio Paz, *El arco y la lira: El poema; La revelación poética; Poesía e historia*, 1956; *The Bow and the Lyre*, trans. Ruth L. C. Simms, 1973. • Octavio Paz, *Convergences: Essays on Art and Literature*, 1987. • Octavio Paz, *Itinerary: An Intellectual Journey*, 1999. • Octavio Paz, *The Labyrinth of Solitude: Life and Thought in Mexico*, 1961. • Frances Chiles, *Octavio Paz, The Mythic Dimension*, 1987. • Ivar Ivask, ed., *Perpetual Present: The Poetry and Prose of Octavio Paz,* 1973. • Monique J. Lemaître, *Octavio Paz, Poesía y poética*, 1976. • Rachel Phillips, *Poetic Modes of Octavio* Paz, 1972. • José Quiroga, *Understanding Octavio Paz,* 1999. • Maya Schärer-Nussberger, *Octavio Paz: Trayectorias y visiones*, 1989. • Leticia Iliana Underwood, *Octavio Paz and the Language of Poetry: A Psycholinguistic Approach*, 1992. • Jason Wilson, *Octavio Paz*, 1986.

Hutcheson Macaulay Posnett • H. M. Posnett, *Comparative Literature* (1886), 1970. • H. M. Posnett, *The Historical Method in Ethics, Jurisprudence, and Political Economy*, 1882. • H. M. Posnett, "The Science of Comparative Literature," in Hans-Joachim Schultz and Phillip Rhein, *Comparative Literature: The Early Years*, 1973, 183–206. • David Damrosch, "Rebirth of a Discipline," *Comparative Critical Studies* 3:1–2 (2006), 99–112. • Michael E. Moriarty, "H. M. Posnett and Two American Comparatists," *Yearbook of Comparative and General Literature* 21 (1972), 15–22. • Elinor Shaffer, "The 'Scientific' Pretensions of Comparative Literature," *Comparative Criticism* 2 (1980), xi–xxi. • K. Saito, "The First Introduction of Posnett's *Comparative Literature* by Shoyo Tsubouchi," *Hikaku Bungaku Nenshi,* October 1965.

Bruce Robbins • Bruce Robbins, *Feeling Global: Internationalism in Distress*, 1999. • Bruce Robbins, *The Servant's Hand: English Fiction from Below*, 1986. • Bruce Robbins, *Upward Mobility and the Common Good: Toward a Literary History of the Welfare State*, 2007. • Bruce Robbins, ed., *The Phantom Public Sphere*, 1993. • Pheng Cheah and Bruce Robbins, eds., *Cosmopolitics: Thinking and Feeling beyond the Nation*, 1998. • K. Anthony Appiah, *Cosmopolitanism: Ethics in a World of Strangers*, 2006.

Edward W. Said • Edward W. Said, *Beginnings: Intention and Method*, 1975. • Edward W. Said, *Culture and Imperialism*, 1994. • Edward W. Said, *Orientalism*,

1978. • Edward W. Said, *Out of Place: A Memoir*, 1999. • Edward W. Said, *The Question of Palestine*, 1979. • Edward W. Said, *Reflections on Exile and Other Essays*, 2000. • Edward W. Said, *The World, the Text, and the Critic*, 1983. • Keith Ansell-Pearson et al., eds., *Cultural Readings of Imperialism: Edward Said and the Gravity of History*, 1997. • Bill Ashcroft and Pal Ahluwalia, *Edward Said*, 2001. • Paul A. Bové, ed., *Edward Said and the Work of the Critic*, 2000. • Roger Bresnahan et al., eds., *Reflections on Orientalism*, 1983. • Ferial J. Ghazoul, ed., *Edward Said and Decolonization*, 2007. • Abdirahman A. Hussein, *Edward Said: Criticism and Society*, 2002. • Mustapha Marrouchi, *Edward Said at the Limits*, 2004. • Silvia Nagy-Zekmi, ed., *Paradoxical Citizenship*, 2006. • Chandreyee Niyogi, ed., *Reorienting Orientalism*, 2006.

Gayatri Chakravorty Spivak • Gayatri C. Spivak, *A Critique of Postcolonial Reason: Toward a History of the Vanishing Present*, 1999. • Gayatri C. Spivak, *Death of a Discipline*, 2003. • Gayatri C. Spivak, *In Other Worlds: Essays in Cultural Politics*, 1987. • Gayatri C. Spivak, *The Post-colonial Critic: Interviews, Strategies, Dialogues*, ed. Sarah Harsym, 1990. • Donna Landry and Gerald MacLean, eds., *The Spivak Reader*, 1996. • Judith Butler and Gayatri C. Spivak, *Who Sings the Nation-State? Language, Politics, Belonging*, 2007. • Terry Eagleton, *Figures of Dissent: Critical Essays on Fish, Spivak, Žižek and Others*, 2005. • Stephen Morton, *Gayatri Spivak: Ethics, Subalternity and the Critique of Postcolonial Reason*, 2007. • Mark Sanders, *Gayatri Chakravorty Spivak: Live Theory*, 2006. • Asha Varadharajan, *Exotic Parodies: Subjectivity in Adorno, Said and Spivak*, 1995.

Lawrence Venuti • Lawrence Venuti, *The Scandals of Translation: Towards an Ethics of Difference*, 1998. • Lawrence Venuti, *The Translator's Invisibility*, 1995. • Lawrence Venuti, "Local Contingencies: Translation and National Identities," in Sandra Bermann and Michael Wood, eds., *Nation, Language, and the Ethics of Translation*, 2005, 177–202. • Lawrence Venuti, ed., *Rethinking Translation: Discourse, Subjectivity, Ideology*, 1992. • Lawrence Venuti, ed., *The Translation Studies Reader*, 2000, rev. ed. 2004.

René Wellek • René Wellek, *The Attack on Literature and Other Essays*, 1982. • René Wellek, *Concepts of Criticism*, 1963. • René Wellek, *Discriminations*, 1970. • René Wellek, *The Literary Theory and Aesthetics of the Prague School*, 1969. • René Wellek and Austin Warren, *Theory of Literature*, 1963. • Martin Bucco, *René Wellek*, 1981. • Michael Holquist, "René Wellek and Enlightenment," *Yearbook of Comparative and General Literature* 44 (1996), 26–31. • William J. Kennedy, "'Interest' in René Wellek," *Yearbook of Comparative and General Literature* 44 (1996), 32–34. • Sarah Lawall, "René Wellek and Modern Literary Criticism," *Comparative Literature* 40:1 (1988), 3–24.

• Vladimír Papousek, "René Wellek and Czech Literary History," *Kosmas: Czechoslovak and Central European Journal* 17:1 (2003), 57–62.

Zhou Xiaoyi and Q. S. Tong • Zhou Xiaoyi and Q. S. Tong, "English Literary Studies and China's Modernity," in *World Englishes* 21:2 (2002), 337–48. • Zhou Xiaoyi and Dan Shen, "Western Literary Theories in China: Reception, Influence and Resistance," *Comparative Critical Studies* 3:1–2 (2006), 139–55. • Zhou Xiaoyi and Q. S. Tong, "Criticism and Society: The Birth of the Modern Critical Subject in China," *boundary 2* 29:1 (2002), 153–76. • Q. S. Tong et al., eds., *Critical Zone 1: A Forum of Chinese and Western Knowledge*, 2004; *Critical Zone 2*, 2006. • Q. S. Tong and Douglas Kerr, eds., *Cross-Cultural Communications: Literature, Language, Ideas*, a special issue of the *Journal of Asian Pacific Communication* 9.1–2 (1999). • John J. Deeney, ed., *Chinese-Western Comparative Literature*, 1980.